THE PICKERING MASTERS

THE JOURNALS OF THOMAS BABINGTON MACAULAY

CONTENTS OF THE EDITION

THE JOURNALS OF THOMAS BABINGTON MACAULAY

VOLUME 4
5 December 1852–31 December 1856

Edited by
William Thomas

LONDON
PICKERING & CHATTO
2008

Published by Pickering & Chatto (Publishers) Limited
21 Bloomsbury Way, London WC1A 2TH

2252 Ridge Road, Brookfield, Vermont 05036-9704, USA

www.pickeringchatto.com

BRITISH LIBRARY CATALOGUING IN PUBLICATION DATA

Macaulay, Thomas Babington Macaulay, Baron, 1800–1859
The journals of Thomas Babington Macaulay. – (The Pickering masters)
1. Macaulay, Thomas Babington Macaulay, Baron, 1800–1859 – Diaries 2. Historians – Great Britain – Diaries
I. Title II. Thomas, William, 1936–
941'.081'092

ISBN–13: 9781851969036

This publication is printed on acid-free paper that conforms to the American National Standard for the Permanence of Paper for Printed Library Materials.

Typeset by Pickering & Chatto (Publishers) Limited
Printed in the United Kingdom at the University Press, Cambridge

CONTENTS

Sunday – December 5 1852

Vile weather. Wrote a little and to Brooks's – sorry for Cornwall Lewis's defeat[1] – sorry too to hear that he has spent a good deal of money to no purpose on his two elections – 8,000£ – and that he will be crippled. Read a foolish book about Russia which I found in the book case in the small parlour. Then by cab to W.T. a pleasant hour and a half there – H. very sensible of the folly of such meetings as that at Sutherland House; – but she justly says that she could hardly avoid it. Home – wrote more – dined alone – finished Br in Ama[2] – Tired of the old lady.

1. Cornewall Lewis had been defeated in the general election in Hertfordshire by protectionist opinion. He was then offered by Lord Fitzwilliam the chance of standing for Peterborough, but on 5 December he lost there too. In both cases he was bottom of the poll.
2. Frances Trollope, *The Barnabys in America: or, The Adventures of the Widow Wedded* (1843).

Monday – December 6

Read Rousseau's Contrat Social while dressing. Great stuff I thought it. At breakfast Lockhart's Life of Scott[1] – wrote – Recognition Act – Then into the city – book good. I am steadily growing rich. To Bloomsbury by omnibus – passed 18 – to Hind's[2] the Surgeon's in Alfred Place about my hands. Then to the Museum – we consulted about half an hour – Ld Seymour[3] – Ld Mahon – Myself – Inglis and Hallam – Goulburn cd not come. He is sitting in judgment on that wretched Beresford.[4] At three we were in Downing Street. We were soon introduced to Ld Derby and Disraeli, and told our story[5] – Ld D chief spokesman – the ministers were civil and promised to consider the matter and to let us hear soon – Walked away with Mahon and Hallam – home – wrote – E to dinner.

1. J. G. Lockhart, *Life of Sir Walter Scott* (1837–8).
2. George William Hind (1801–85), Fellow of the Royal College of Surgeons (1849), was based at 2 Alfred Place.
3. Edward Adolphus Seymour (1804–85), MP for Totnes.
4. William Beresford (1798–1883), Chief Whip and Secretary for War, had managed the election of 1852. He was censured by a Committee of the House for 'reckless indifference to systematic bribery'. See below, entry for 16 December 1852, and *PD*, 16 December 1852.
5. To ask that more space be provided for readers in the British Museum.

Tuesday – December 7

What weather! I was to have gone to W.T., but walking was out of the question, so I staid at home all the morning. In the afternoon I went to the H. of C. and had some talk with Wood and others about the budget. Wood had fallen into an error which happily I set right. To the Club – thirteen – the Bps of Oxford and London, Aberdeen, Senior, Holland, Mure, Sir G. Stainton, Milman, Ld Overstone, Ld Glenelg, Ld Mahon. Pleasant though a little too large or too small a party for good conversation.

Wednesday – December 8

Letter from Ld Monteagle. He is at Hayleybury. Empson in great danger – almost given over. Weather still bad – To the H. of C. – a motion of Evans's[1] which I only half liked – away without voting. To W.T. Thence with H to the Albany. Glad to see George who has done very well indeed at Harrow. Walked in the afternoon – fine sunshine – after a long interval: but while walking I felt a vile cold coming on. Home – to dine with Van der Weyer. Influenza seems common. Hibbert was kept away by it. The party tolerable. A Frenchman or Fleming said that the word pudeur was modern and could not be found in the writers of Louis the XIV's age. I floored him with the Provincial Letters.[2]

1. Sir George de Lacy Evans moved the second reading of the Parliamentary Elections Bill.
2. Blaise Pascal, *Lettres Provinciales* (1656–7).

Thursday – December 9

A cold in all the forms, a bad night. I staid at home till the afternoon partly in the hope of hearing from Monteagle again and then walked to W.T. The morning had been fine, but before I got to the house rain came on. I dined there and had much pleasant chat, but was poorly. H gave me some sal volatile to take home. I swallowed a spoonful in warm water before I went to bed.

Friday – December 10

A tolerable night – that is to say, for an invalid. Still rain – rain – rain. Staid at home all day. Nothing from Ld Monteagle though he had promised to write again very shortly. Nothing to Longman to whom he had made the same promise. In great things or small he is still the same person, always promising so much more than he performs that his performance seems less than another man's even when it is really greater. I am extremely sorry for Empson. He is an excellent, true-hearted generous man, and has been a kind friend to me through many years. But we have seen so little of each other lately that I shall not miss him as I should once have done. Longman spoke to me about the Review. I recommended Cornewall Lewis; and Longman was quite of my opinion. I was surprised and rather pleased to hear that my articles are the mainstay of the Travellers' Library. The sale of them far exceeds the sale of the other works published in that form; and, but for them there wd be a loss instead of a profit in the enterprise. I worked a good deal today, and am in better spirits about my book than for some days past: but my cold is oppressive. Letter at last from Ld M. Poor E alive and that is all. He has been through this stormy scene cheerful, courageous, affectionate, and pious too after his fashion. Longman came later with news that all was over. He had scarcely gone when Ld J's Memoirs of Moore[1] were brought me, a present from the publishers. I read them with great zest. The preface pretty well done – Moore's Memoirs of himself not much. The letters a little heavy – but the Diary most interesting. He makes a charming figure – I suspect that he wrote a little for the public eye. Had he been as frank as poor Pepys who trusted to his shorthand we might have found some very odd disclosures. Much amused by the figure which that bore of bores, Joy,[2] makes. Ellis to dinner. I was very temperate, but went to bed much oppressed by cold in spite of a mustard plaister.

1. Lord John Russell's *Journals and Correspondence of Thomas Moore*, 8 vols (1853–6).
2. Henry Hall Joy, KC (1786–1840), was a barrister.

Saturday – December 11

Bad night; but better in the morning. Less catarrh, less cough, but still oppression of the chest. Finished T.M.'s Diary – H and B came to see me – we chatted half-an hour and they took away the 1st Vol of TM. I had this morning two lines from Monteagle to say that poor E was gone. After finishing TM went to work on the history – pretty well. Read Ignoramus[1] – that is to say as much as is readable. Then Sir W.S.[2] – A mustard poultice. Letter from Walpole. I am not to have the cross[3] – Tant mieux.

1. Perhaps the comedy of this title written in Latin by George Ruggle (1575–1662).
2. Lockhart, *Life of Sir Walter Scott* (cf. above, entry for 6 December 1852)
3. The Prussian Order of Merit. See TBM's letter to Ellis, *LM*, vol. 5, p. 307.

Sunday – December 12

Bad night – vile day. After breakfast wrote a good many letters – one to Humboldt[1] among the rest – did something to the history. Senior called – Sir W.S. – dined on a little boiled mutton and turnip with very weak wine and water – better towards evening. T called in the afternoon and sate half an hour. His personal feelings towards Graham and Disraeli very naturally warp his judgment as to their qualifications for the public service. Mustard poultice again.

1. Friedrich Heinrich Alexander von Humboldt (1769–1859), naturalist, Chancellor of the Prussian Order of Merit.

Monday – December 13

Another bad day. But I had had a good night and felt much easier – Staid at home reading and writing. Longman called to talk about Lewis and the E.R. Ld Monteagle had recommended Stephen,[1] I suspect only in order to get the E.R. out of the hands of the Whigs. For it is impossible that Ld M should not know that Stephen, with great abilities and virtues, is not of the stuff of which editors ought to be made. He is in truth nearly as unfit for such an office as myself; – and if he had it would in less [than] half a year either throw it up or hang himself. H called and sate an hour – a very pleasant hour to me. Milman came while she was here and was very kind and agreeable. Senior has sent me two MSS about his Irish travels and conversations[2] – an odd habit of his to play Boswell to every body that he sees. But his journals are amusing; and I should be ungrateful to blame him. He gives some strange stories told him by agents about their perils and escapes, their habit of riding armed with bodyguards and so forth. A little romance, I suspect, cooked for the taste of the Englishman. There is also a ridiculous story which he seems to believe about an old Irishwoman who pretended to be mesmerized and took in the Archbishop and his family with great skill. Sir W.S. I am a little better. Paired for the night.

1. Sir James Stephen (1789–1859). TBM had recommended him for the Regius Chair of Modern History at Cambridge, and was plainly irritated that he had found the duties uncongenial. He resigned in 1853.
2. Presumably those printed in *Journals, Conversations and Essays Relating to Ireland*, 2 vols (1868).

Tuesday – December 14

Better, but still poorly. Longman came to say that he had seen Lewis who takes a few days to consider. While he was here B and G came. B and her Mamma have an order for the H of C tonight, and wished to arrange with me, about returning. I went down to Brooks's and there found that a division was not expected – Made arrangements for pairing. Went to W.T., told them that most likely I should not be in the H[ouse] this evening – Home – wrote pretty well as I have done for some days – dined – Tony Bar – Finished Sir W.S's Life – poor poor fellow. Read some of Peter's Letters.[1]

1. *Peter's Letters to his Kinsfolk* (1819). Ostensibly by Peter Morris, it was actually by J. G. Lockhart.

Wednesday – December 15

Not very well. The dregs of the Influenza run off slowly. Wrote a little – to W.T. chatted a little – walked across the park – fine when I started, rain before I got to Grosvenor Gate. What weather – home – wrote again – Charles called. I read some ballads and miscellanées of 1690 etc. – and found everywhere confirmation of the view which I now take of that part of our history and which I believe to be quite new. At dinner finished T.B. – The earlier part not without liveliness – the latter unmixedly execrable. Anastasius.[1]

1. The novel by Thomas Hope (*c.* 1770–1831), published in 1819.

Thursday – December 16

Anastasius. Strange how little that book now interests and amuses me. After breakfast wrote letters and history – finished turning over Anastasius – Ld Glenelg called – only, I think, to abuse a bad novel that he has got from a circulating library called the Game of Brag.[1] At four to the H. of C. presented two petitions against the budget. Goulburn brought up the Report on Beresford[2] – a strong censure – yet it might justly have been stronger. Home – Dined – Thackeray Pendennis. At ½ after ten the Carriage to the House – staid till near 4 – generally in the library or the division lobby reading – Heard a little of Disraeli – clever but inconclusive and most impertinent and unhandsome, a little of Gladstone gravely and severely bitter – At last the division.[3] Immense crowd. Immense shout as Hayter[4] took the right hand – still louder shout when the numbers were read – 305 to 286 – In the midst of the shouting I stole away and got to my carriage. Home just at 4 – much exhausted – Wm still up.

1. David Owen Madden, *The Game of Brag; or The Batterary Boys* (1853).
2. Beresford was accused of being party to a system of bribery practised in Derby during the late election; *PD*, 3rd ser., cxxiii, 1569–70.
3. Disraeli spoke several times on this the fourth night of the adjourned debate on his budget. TBM seems to have heard part of his reply to his critics; ibid., 1634–66. Gladstone followed; 1666–93. The division is at 1693–7.
4. William Goodenough Hayter (1792–1878) was Joint Secretary to the Treasury and MP for Wells. He was knighted in 1858.

Friday – December 17

Did not feel much worse for yesterday's exertion till I went out. Then found myself very, very weak; and felt as I used to do at Clifton. To Brooks's – laughed with Waddington and Ryan[1] – to Ellis's – to W.T. Amused by learning that H.T. and G were in the H. of C. yesterday. They all saw me there. Dear B could not go, having a cold. Home – wrote a little – The history of the Session of 1690[2] is taking a tolerable form. – At dinner Pendennis. I like it amazingly.

1. Probably Horatio Waddington (1799–1867) and Sir Edward Ryan, who were elected to Brooks's in 1849. Waddington was Permanent Under-Secretary for the Home Department.
2. *HE*, ch. 15. It is not clear whether TBM means the session that began on 10 January 1690 or that of the new Parliament, which began on 20 March, both described in this chapter.

Saturday – December 18

All the bustle which attends a ministerial crisis. After breakfast to the State Paper Office. There I found calm in the midst of the storm. Walpole who is going out and Ld John who is coming in as quiet as any two country gentlemen met to talk over parish business and as friendly. Ld Mahon and Hallam and Dundas were there. The matters under discussion not very important. To Brooks's: but learned little. Indeed nothing can be known for some days. Ld Lansdowne and Ld Aberdeen have been sent for to Osborne. Ld L, I am afraid, will hardly be able to go. Home – wrote nothing. I never can work in these times of crisis. Dined and read Πεν [Pendennis] I was not well enough to dine with Goulburn.

Sunday – December 19

Brooks's – Athenaeum – W.T. animated talk with T and H about Disraeli – T is inclined to like him because he has made some reforms at the Treasury on T's suggestion, and this is very well. But T, with his usual vehemence of nature, is a little too much inclined to depreciate Wood, by comparison. I gave him some good advice, very earnestly and kindly; and he promised to take it. H's sarcasms were at one moment so keen that poor G cried. But then papa and mamma kissed and made it up most affectionately. Home – Ellis to dinner – oysters – turkey – snipes.

Monday – December 20

An eventful day. After breakfast at the Athenaeum I met Senior who told me that he had been at my chambers to beg me to go to Lansdowne House – that Ld L wished to see me before half after 12. I went. I found him and Ld John closeted together. Ld John read us a letter wh he had received from the Queen – very good, like all her letters that I have seen. She told him that she saw hopes of making a strong and durable govt, at once conservative and reforming – that she had asked Ld Aberdeen to form such a govt – that great exertions and sacrifices wd be necessary, and that she relied on the patriotism of Ld J not to refuse his valuable aid. They asked me what I thought. I said that I could improve the Queen's letter neither in substance nor in language, that she had expressed my sentiments to a tittle. Then Ld J said that of course he should try to help Ld A – but how? There were 2 ways.[1] He might take the lead of the Commons with the foreign office or he might refuse office and support from the back benches. I adjured him not to think of this last course; and I argued and expostulated during a quarter of an hour, with, I thought, a great flow of thoughts and words. I was encouraged by Ld L who nodded, smiled, and rubbed his hands at everything that I said. When I had done Ld L said that I had expressed perfectly his opinion and that of Clarendon. I learned that Ld J had yesterday made up his mind to take the Seals of Secretary, and that domestic advice – in plain words Ly J – had shaken him. He was afraid of being thought to lower himself by serving in a second post after having filled the first. I combated this notion as strongly as I could. I reminded him that the D of Wn had taken the foreign office[2] after having been at the Treasury; and I quoted his own Perth speech on the D[3] – "You said, Ld J, that we could not all win battles of Waterloo but that we might all imitate the old man's patriotism, sense of duty, indifference to selfish interests and vanities when the public welfare was concerned: and now is the time for you to make a sacrifice. Your past services and your name give us a right to expect it." Ld J went away evidently much impressed by what had been said and promising to consult others. When he was gone Ld L told me that I had come just as opportunely as Blucher did at Waterloo. He told me also what affected me and struck me exceedingly – that, in the last resort, he would himself, in spite of the danger to his health and the destruction of his comfort, take the Treasury if in no other way Ld J cd be induced to lead the Commons. But this he keeps wisely secret for the present. At four I went down to the H. Found Ld J there. He took me into the back room and told me that he had seen Clarendon and others whose opinion agreed with mine, and that his present inclination was to lead the H. of C. but without any office; – a great instance of disinterestedness and such as no man is bound to give: I am not sure that it will not be the best course. At ½ past 4 Disraeli[4] announced the resignation and apologised for his ungentlemanlike expressions of Thursday night. The apology was handsomely received by Ld J, Wood and Graham. Then we hurried to the Lds where Ld Derby made a most unhandsome attack on Ld A in his absence.[5] The D of Newcastle on the spur of the moment answered readily and well – Going away I met T H and B and G going into St Stephen's Hall. They had been in the H of Ld. H and B took me home in the carriage. I told them how things stood and what my share in them had been. On reaching my chambers I found the Longmans at the door. C Lewis has accepted. I am glad of it. Dinner – Pendennis. This vile Influenza hangs about me still. I must get out of town.

1. In fact Aberdeen had on the 19th met Russell and formed the impression that he had been willing to take the Foreign Office with the leadership of the Commons. He went to

Osborne on the 19th on that assumption (M. E. Chamberlain, *Lord Aberdeen* (London, 1983), pp. 44–5).

2. In Peel's first ministry, 1834–5.
3. It was in fact given at Stirling, on Russell's receiving the freedom of the burgh. The speech is in *MC*, 23 September 1852, p. 8e. Wellington had died on 14 September.
4. *PD*, 3rd ser., cxxiii, 1709–10. Among other things, Disraeli had referred to Graham 'whom I will not say I greatly respect but rather whom I greatly regard'. See Robert Blake, *Disraeli* (London, 1966), pp. 344–7.
5. *PD*, 3rd ser., cxxiii, 1698–1705. TBM's description of the speech is not borne out by this version. Derby had said that his government had been overthrown by a combination of Whigs, Radicals and Irish, and that he hoped Aberdeen would be treated with more forbearance. Newcastle denied that there had been any concerted combination of the parties, Derby did not attack, and Newcastle did not defend Aberdeen.

Tuesday – December 21

Not in a mood for work. Walked. Met Ryan at Brooks's – to W.T. – chat with H and B – home – a fine day; but my chest oppressed and my breathing difficult – Pen – To Ellis's to dinner though I had better have staid at home.

Wednesday – December 22

Did little in the way of writing – Into the city. By the way saw E. and told him what passed at Lne H. on Monday. To Birchin Lane – kept long inquiring into some blunder made it seems by the broker about my London Dock Stock – bought 500 more 3 1/4s – I am at this moment worth 40,000£ realised, besides some hundreds at my bankers', my furniture, books, etc. and copyrights worth, on a moderate calculation some thousands. What wealth this would have seemed to me twenty years ago. To dine at W.T. Dearest B had had a tooth taken out and had suffered much. I felt for her. George went to the play. I had an agreeable evening of chat. H promised to come to breakfast tomorrow.

Thursday – December 23

Breakfast party – Ld Glenelg, Milman, Senior, Lefevre, Sir R. Inglis – H – very agreeable indeed. She tells me that she thinks my breakfasts the pleasantest parties in London. Walked – Went down to the H. Nothing. No new writs – Disraeli moved an adjournment till 2 tomorrow. I dined at home and finished Pendennis – very clever and powerful book.

Friday – December 24

Delighted to find that Palmerston will join. Alchemist – a remarkable play but not what I once thought it – wrote – Cs and Mt [?Mh] and Anne. Went to Brooks's, nothing known, but strong reports about Cranworth.[1] To the H. of C.

No new writ moved but I learned that Molesworth[2] goes into the cabinet and was glad to learn it. Home. Wrote a little more – dined alone – Red Gauntlet – blue pill.

1. Robert Monsey Rolfe (1790–1868), Baron Cranworth, became Lord Chancellor.
2. He became First Commissioner of Works.

Saturday – December 25

Christmas – it again finds me prosperous and what is better, happy. My family circle unbroken, my fame not eclipsed: the year has brought to me nothing but successes and distinctions. My health is pretty well restored. On the whole I may well be contented and thankful. I never saw London so full at this season. Nor was it, I suppose, ever so full since 1783. Finished the Alchemist – looked over Catiline.[1] Turned over Sallust's story of the conspiracy[2] – liked nothing in it so much as Julius Caesar's incomparable speech. By the bye I do not know that anybody has observed that his allusion to the Rhodians was evidently intended as an *argumentum ad hominem* against Cato whose ancestor the Censor spoke remarkably well for clemency to the Rhodians. – The speech is in Aulus Gellius.[3] To Brooks's – saw Clarendon. I fear that there will be some discontent in our ranks at the large share got by the Peelites. I myself think that we ought to have had either the Lord Lieutenant or the Secretary for Ireland.[4] And I shall think it a great error if Canning shall be pushed up to the exclusion of Clanricarde.[5] How glad I am that I so positively announced at Edinburgh my resolution never again to hold office. Otherwise people might fancy that I was disappointed. Clarendon is much pleased at Lewis's new position.[6] Walked across the parks to W.T. Walked with them all in Kensington Gardens – gave Christmas boxes to the servants – pleasant afternoon passed in gay affectionate chat. An absurd book by Sir Digby Neave[7] afforded us much matter for laughter. The dinner as usual sent by me. The cod and oysters, turkey and ham all excellent. Then came the snapdragon and salt.[8] And by that time dear little Alice had been quite as much excited as her singularly delicate frame will bear. Home by a cab.

1. Ben Jonson, *Catiline his Conspiracy* (1610).
2. The Bellum Catalinae (42 BC).
3. In the *Noctes Atticae* ('Attic Nights'), a miscellany of reading, extracts and compositions published *c.* AD 180.
4. In the Cabinet Peelites and Whigs were equal, with seven places each. TBM seems to be referring to offices outside the Cabinet. The Lord Lieutenancy went to Lord St Germans, and the Chief Secretaryship to Sir John Young, both Peelites.
5. The Marquis of Clanricarde was disappointed at being left out of the Aberdeen Coalition, but Viscount Canning, to his chagrin, was offered only the office of Postmaster General, a post previously held by Clanricarde. See J. B. Conacher, *The Aberdeen Coali-*

tion, 1852–1855: A Study in Mid-Nineteenth-Century Party Politics (London, 1968), p. 30 and n. 2.

6. As editor of *ER*. He held the position until February 1855.
7. Sir Richard Digby Neave (1793–1868), *Four Days in Connemara* (1852). Neave was Charles Trevelyan's cousin.
8. Snapdragon was an old Christmas game of snatching raisins from flaming brandy. I do not know how salt came into it.

Sunday – December 26

Pope's Works – Martinus Scriblerus[1] – what stuff. Yet it gave Sterne a hint which has produced a wonderful effect. To W.T. – pleasant chat there – home – Gurney Married.[2] I had promised to send both parts to dearest B.

1 *Martinus Scriblerus*, mainly written by John Arbuthnot, came out in 1741 in the second volume of Pope's prose works and provided the plan for *Tristram Shandy* (1759). See A. H. Cash, *Laurence Sterne: The Early & Middle Years* (London, 1975), pp. 198–9.

2 By Theodore Hook (1839).

Monday – December 27

Read some anti-Moravian tracts. A precious sect! Went at two to the H. of C. A few writs moved – surprised that Wood's was not among them, followed him out of the house and spoke to him very kindly. He was somewhat excited and seemed to think that he had been ill used. They had offered him the Vice-Chancellorship, but not, it seems, in a very gracious way.[1] I am sorry for this. Ld John, I am afraid, has not looked as he should have done after the interests of his friends or consulted their dignity. He was quite right to be disinterested himself: but that disinterestedness entitled him to press the claims of others more strongly than he has done. There is a disposition to murmur among our people. My business however is to allay their discontent, though I cannot help thinking it reasonable. Home – dined alone – read T.H's Love and Pride[2] – remembered buying this book on the top of the Neilgherry Hills in 1834, and reading it for the first time in the palanquin on the road along the table land and afterwards through the great jungle of Mysore. Moravians.

1. Sir Charles Wood was appointed President of the Board of Control. For the formation of the government, see Conacher, *Aberdeen Coalition*.
2. By Theodore Hook (1833).

Tuesday – December 28

Packed. Off for Brighton – found a good sitting room ready for me at the Norfolk – bedroom, less pleasant, but tolerable. To Temple House – walked with

F – her affection and S's are very pleasing to me – gave F the Lansdowne Shakspeare – read Les Deux Diane.[1]

1. By Alexandre Dumas (*père*) (1841–7). TBM mentions it in a letter to Margaret written on that journey (*LM*, vol. 3, p. 81).

Wednesday – Thursday – Friday – Saturday – [29 December–1 January 1853]

All much the same – walked with F twice a day, sate a little in the morning with her and S – sent them grapes and oysters – strolled about the beach till driven in by rain and wind – wrote something – history of parliamentary corruption, at dinner and afterwards Les Deux Diane, S. Happy, Pk. Heard from Wood. Ld A's[1] explanations have appeased him. Met Hayter on the beach. He is, I see, a malecontent though very well provided for himself.[2]

1. Lord Aberdeen, who had succeeded Lord John Russell as Prime Minister on 19 December.
2. William Goodenough Hayter was patronage secretary to the Treasury, 1850–8.

[Macaulay thought he had been elected for Edinburgh 'unpledged', that is, without political conditions and independent. At first he thought he could combine writing the *History* with his parliamentary duties, but in the course of 1853 he found the latter were too much for him. In February and March he began chapters for the fourth volume. He also completed an essay on Atterbury for the *Encyclopaedia Britannica*. In March he joined the Commons Committee on Indian affairs, appointed to recommend changes in the East India Company's charter, now due for renewal. But the last week of March was spent on a trip to Paris with the Trevelyans and his sister Frances. In May he agreed to accept an honorary DCL from Oxford, and early in June he made the ceremony the excuse for another family excursion, this time including the Ellis girls. He also made two major speeches: one on 1 June, which destroyed Lord Hotham's bill for excluding judges from sitting in the House of Commons, and the other on 30 June, on the India Bill. Both occasions exhausted him, but speaking to a rapt chamber reminded him of his oratorical prime, so that when a journalist called Vizetelly published a two-volume edition of his *Speeches* without consulting him, he tried to have the edition withdrawn and then decided to discredit it with an edition of his own. For a month from 12 July he took a house at Tunbridge Wells, where he wrote out a 'correct' version of those speeches he thought his best. Once more he attended Parliament, on 19 July, to speak for the Repeal of the Edinburgh Annuity Tax. The attempt failed, but he felt he had done his duty to his constituents, and returned to Kent and his speeches. He never spoke in the Commons again. On 20 August Parliament was prorogued, and in the event it would not meet until a short session from 12 to 23 December. In the autumn the 'Eastern Crisis' was deepening. While the Aberdeen government was trying in vain to avoid going to war with Russia on behalf of the Turks, Macaulay and Ellis went on tour, from 26 August until 19 September, through northern France to Cologne, then down the Rhine into Switzerland, taking in Basle, Berne and Geneva, and returning via Lyons and Paris. There were three more country weekends. In December, while Macaulay was at Brighton seeing his older sisters, news came that the Russians had sunk the Turkish fleet at Sinope. The *Speeches* was published early in December, perhaps as an unintended valediction to his parliamentary career. On the last day of the year he wrote, 'My health is failing. My life will not, I think, be long'.]

Sunday – January 2

F took me to Trinity Chapel to hear a famous preacher named Robertson.[1] He preached with considerable eloquence and ingenuity.

1. Revd Frederick William Robinson (1816–53), who became incumbent of Trinity Chapel, Brighton, in 1847.

Monday – January 3

A farewell visit to T.H. – a last walk with F – paid my bill, a high one, and off to town. The Edinburgh people have asked me for 50£ to register their votes. They are strangely wanting in spirit. My Leeds friends would have been ashamed to owe the franchise to any man's liberality. I sent the money however – wrote letters – at dinner – Pottleton Leg[1] – The Moravian tracts.

1. Albert Smith, *The Pottleton Legacy* (1849).

Tuesday – January 4

Moraviana – Wrote – to W.T, all well – went with H to the Haymarket Theatre and secured a private box for Friday. I promise myself much pleasure from seeing dear little Alice at her first play. Dined at home Ποτ – Wilkes's correspondence[1] – trash. Bills coming in fast.

1. Perhaps the edition by John Almon (1805).

Wednesday – January 5

Wrote – To the City – Longman has not yet paid in the 500£. I must take care or I shall overdraw my account. To Janson's in Basinghall Street[1] – settled to lend 400£ on mortgage at 4 ½– not a bad hit. Home – wrote – Ellis to dinner – Cold plagued me – Ipec.

1. Brown, Janson & Co. were bankers. Thomas Cobyn Janson (1809–63) was a partner.

Thursday – January 6

Much better – Read the Avis aux Refugiés[1] at breakfast – bills – bills – and rain – rain – to the Athenaeum – looked over books and tracts and reviews – nothing of great interest. Amused to see myself praised in that quarrelsome Donaldson's Verronianus.[2] Wrote – dined alone – Ποτ – Churchill's[3] Poems. Looked over Delphine.[4] Read it I could not – Wraxall's account of Ld North's fall.[5]

1. Perhaps *Avis Important aux Réfuges sur leur Prochaine Retour en France* (1690).
2. J. W. Donaldson, *Veronianus. A Critical and Historical Introduction to the Ethnography of Ancient Italy* ... (1st edn 1844; 2nd edn 1852). The postscript of the preface quoted *Lays of Ancient Rome.* Donaldson was a distinguished classical scholar and a prolific controversialist.
3. Charles Churchill (1731–64).
4. By Madame de Stäel (1802).
5. Perhaps *Historical Memoirs of My Own Time ... 1772–84* (1815), by Sir Nathaniel Wraxall (1751–1831).

Friday – January 7

Rain in torrents – bills in heaps – they are welcome if only Longman is punctual. To the city and found that he had paid in the 500£ – back. Wrote – To W.T. at four – the weather clearing – dined there and to the Haymarket Theatre with them all. A play by Tom Taylor – Masks and Faces[1] – not much in it, but some droll and some pathetic affects. To me, however Alice was the sight. She was interested, astonished and affected in the highest degree. Then came the pantomime; but I soon stole away. It was near ten when I got home much knocked up.

1. Written in collaboration with Charles Reade: first produced at the Baywater Theatre, 20 November 1852; published 1854.

Saturday – January 8

Fine day – Wraxall – To B.M. Inglis, Goulburn, Hamilton, the Bp of L., Long sitting – Read Mason's trash about Rousseau[1] and Wilson's Life of Cavendish.[2] Then with Goulburn to Gladstone's Committee. He has lost today, but had at

1 a majority of 36.[3] To Brooks's – met Moncrieff[4] there, fresh from Edinburgh. Home – wrote – dined alone. Ποτ – Wraxall.

1. Unidentified.
2. G. Wilson, *The Life ... of Henry Cavendish* (1851).
3. Gladstone had to seek re-election as Member for Oxford University after his appointment as Chancellor of the Exchequer in Aberdeen's government. His re-election was approved and Gladstone was returned by 1,022 votes to 898 when the fifteen days' polling ended on 20 January.
4. James Moncrieff (1811–95) was Lord Advocate, later Baron Moncrieff of Tullibole. He was MP for Leith Boroughs.

Sunday – January 9

Still fine – Wraxall. Wrote a little. To Brooks's – Gladstone gaining. The D. of Wellington Master of the Horse. He has written a very good letter to the Q: saying that his father, if he had lived, would have supported her present ministers. Ld De Mauley. We had a long and amusing chat about old Cavendish the philosopher who was Ld De M's relation and who indeed left near 150,000£ to old Ld Besborough.[1] To W.T. – pleasant except that a Miss Julia Trevelyan,[2] an old Puseyite woman in spectacles, was there. Charles came and his boy[3] whom I tipped – and Macleod. I walked away with Macleod. We met Mahon and his two boys.[4] With them I walked to the Albany – wrote – then Wraxall – Ποτ – The Senator.[5]

1. Lord de Mauley was the grandson of the second Earl of Bessborough, whose wife was the daughter of the third Duke of Devonshire and a cousin of Henry Cavendish. According to the *DNB*, Henry Cavendish (1731–1810) left a fortune of £1,175,000.
2. Julia Trevelyan (1798–1894) was sister of Sir Walter Calverley Trevelyan, sixth Bart. She remained a spinster.
3. Charles Macaulay had two sons, Thomas (b. 1842) and Charles (b. 1849).
4. Arthur Philip Stanhope (1838–1905) became sixth Earl, and Edward Stanhope (1840–93), later a barrister and MP.
5. Perhaps *The Senator, or Clarendon's Parliamentary Chronicle*, printed in London from 1790 to 1802.

Monday – January 10

Senator – wrote in the morning. To Brooks's – dawdled long chatting with Ld Monteagle and Ld De Mauley – to Cawthorn's paid my subscription – paid my lawyer's bill – wrote – Ποτ – Senator.

Tuesday – January 11

Fine morning – To the Temple – sate an hour with Dundas – looked in on Ellis – home – wrote a little – H, B, G and A to lunch.Very happy we were – When they went away I wrote pretty steadily – Ποτ – Sen – Rain.

Wednesday – January 12

Rain still – what a year this has been – drought at one time – deluge at another. Looked over Burke's Appeal from the New to the Old Whigs[1] – wrote – at home all day. In the evening to Ellis's to dinner.

---

1. By Edmund Burke (1791).

Thursday – January 13

Breakfast party. Strange mistake. I thought that I met Sir J. Boileau at the Athenaeum the other day and asked him. It was his brother the Major.[1] Very odd and even vexatious. It would have been nothing but that H who likes much to breakfast here was of the party. They had not met since 1832 when he was dying of love for her, and she was very cruel. I was quite taken by surprise when Antipholus[2] of Madras came instead of Antipholus of Norfolk. I however behaved with perfect self command. So did H. What must he have thought? I do not much care. Macleod was of the party.[3] He had been at Calcutta when the poor Major was paying court in vain, and was extremely astonished. Ld Mahon, Hallam and Dundas of course saw nothing to wonder at. The party not unpleasant after all. A fine day. I walked – wrote – to Inglis's in the evening with H and T, a birthday party. Hallam gave our host's health – stupid business after all, but an excellent fellow. Quarterly Review today.

---

1. Charles Lestock Boileau (1800–89), Major in the Rifle Brigade. He was three times married.
2. See *Comedy of Errors*.
3. Presumably Sir John Macleod (1792–1881).

Friday – January 14

Fine day – Went into city – all right – chat with Thornton – home – wrote – Ellis dined with me.

Saturday – January 15

Chequered day. Wrote a good deal – then to Brooks's etc – to Wood at the Bd of C – W.T. sate with B some time – then Hanson[1] called. Amused by the Quarterly Review. Croker furious against Disraeli[2] – mere spite because D showed him up in Coningsby. They are well matched – two of the greatest scamps living – scandals to literature – scandals to politics – never so well employed as when abusing and exposing each other. Dined at W.T. Uneasy about George – He has got his remove, but is very poorly. He swallowed a marble some days ago; and it disagrees with him apparently.

1. Perhaps Richard Davies Hanson (1805–76), who was then drafting the constitution of Australia. He was knighted in 1869.
2. *QR*, 92 (December 1852), pp. 236–74. Croker denied that he had ever read *Coningsby*, where the character of Rigby was undoubtedly meant to portray him. Disraeli, however, was making an attack on Peel, then thought to be in close consultation with Croker. When Disraeli and Croker met socially, the latter was affable (W. F. Moneypenny and G. E. Buckle, *The Life of Benjamin Disraeli*, 6 vols (London, 1929), vol. 1, p. 624). TBM says he began *Coningsby* on 30 November (see below, entry for 30 November 1853).

Sunday – January 16

Fine morning – Brooks's – walked across the parks – W.T. George came home. Not much the matter with him. I talked with T about Indian politics. We do not quite agree. Home – wrote – Senator at dinner – Ποτ.

Monday – January 17

Wrote – to W.T, to see how G went on – much better – went with dear B to the Albany – Lent her Faust – Read her some thing about the Churchills and Ps Anne – took her home. Parliamentary debates – Ποτ.

Tuesday – January 18

Had to be at the Museum at 1. To Downing Street at 2 – Ld Aberdeen and Gladstone. Told them over again the story which we had told to their predecessors on the 6th of Decr[1] – Gladstone told me that the poll had closed[2] at Oxford! But this afterwards turned out to be a mistake. Wrote – dined alone – Dieu dispose[3] – Parliamentary debates – Burke.

1. See above, entry for 6 December 1852.
2. See above, entry for 8 January, n. 3.
3. By Alexander Dumas (*père*) (1850–1).

Wednesday – January 19

Writing – reading – I forget particulars – Dieu dispose and a good deal of Burke.

Thursday – January 20

Not so well as usual – At home most of the day. In the evening H and T called to take me to the Deanery of St Paul's. Pleasant party – Hallam, The Hollands, the Cardwells, Milman's three boys[1] all silent as the grave – Mrs Drummond. We took Hallam back to Piccadilly. H. very clever and pleasant.

1. William Henry (1825–1908) became a clergyman; Arthur (1829–1913) became a barrister and registrar of London University. Archibald John Scott (1834–1902) became Clerk of the House of Commons.

Friday – January 21

Wrote – to W.T. H brought me back to the Albany. Ellis to dinner, in great glee. He made a capital speech this morning in Achilli and Newman.[1] Dined together pleasantly.

1. This was a legal dispute over a new trial. It was refused on technical grounds, on 26 January.

Saturday – January 22

A breakfast party. Hallam, Milman, Mahon, Inglis – Goulburn for the first time. We were very gay and social. I have now finished reading again most of Burke's works. Admirable. The greatest man since Milton. We went to the Museum – a day lost there. In the evening D.D.

Sunday – January 23

Wrote – Brooks's – chat with Ld de Mauley – I always find him pleasant – W.T. Got from T a copy of my education minute of 1835.[1] Pleased to see it again after eighteen years. It made a great revolution. Wrote – Will Marshall called[2] – immensely improved by years. His son an intelligent boy from Rugby. At dinner D.D.

1. The background to the minute, urging the Supreme Council to use money allocated to various institutions of higher learning for instruction in English rather than Sanskrit, Persian or Arabic, is given in Clive, ch. 22. The minute itself is given in *Selected Writings: Thomas Babington Macaulay*, ed. J. Clive and T. Pinney (Chicago, IL, 1972), pp. 235–57.
2. William Marshall (1796–1872), MP for Carlisle and East Cumberland. His son was Walter James Marshall (1837–99).

Monday – January 24

Staid at home all the morning waiting for Bright, who came at ½ past 1. He told me that I was very much better since he saw me last – very much – and so I feel myself. Odd that since the wind shifted to N and E my cough has left me and my respiration has become easier. To W.T. Walked in the park with my dearest B. We talked about Charlemagne – Venice – etc. Home – I have begun to work on my 2nd vol. By the bye I hear that the success of the French Translation – a trumpery translation too – at Paris has been immense. Pretty well for such a bulky work to have been in four years translated into French – into Dutch – twice into Italian – twice into German – and above a hundred thousand copies circulated in America. Will it last? And how will the continuation succeed? I feel low sometimes, and hopeful at other times. We shall see. In the afternoon a man came to beg me to give my name to a bubble started by an M.P. – Mr Greene[1] – who finds money, and a charlatan chartist – Benyowski who finds humbug – I cut the matter short. At dinner D.D. Afterwards poor Theobald Wolfe Tone.[2]

1. Perhaps Thomas Greene (1794–1872), MP for Lancashire.
2. Perhaps Theobald Wolfe Tone, *Memoirs ... Written by Himself* (1826).

Tuesday – January 25

Theobald Wolfe Tone. A fine fellow in spite of his savage senseless spite to England. A crazy lying puppyish book by the Comte de Marcellus.[1] Wrote and read a good deal – Ellis to dinner.

1. Marie-Louis Jean André Charles de Martin du Tyrac, Comte de Marcellus (1795–1865). TBM may mean his *Politique de la Restauration en 1822 et 1823, Correspondence Intime de M, Le Vicomte de Chateaubriand* (Paris, 1853).

Wednesday – January 26

Finished poor Theobald. Wrote – walked – Paul and G – To dinner in Bedford Place – Carter, son, I think of my old acquaintance Bonham[1] – Miss Seward.[2]

1. Perhaps John Bonham Carter (1817–84), MP for Winchester, 1847–74, son of John Carter (1788–1838), MP for Portsmouth, who added Bonham to his name in 1829. He had been a fellow of Trinity College Cambridge.
2. TBM's copy of the *Letters of Anna Seward* (1811) is in Wallington. Some of the flavour of his annotations can be had from Trevelyan, vol. 2, appendix 4.

Thursday – January 27

Wrote and read – walk. In the evening to W.T. to dinner – An Indian party and consequently stupid. All such rendezvous are dull – Lowe, Mangles, Sir Erskine

Perry,[1] Sir Edward Ryan, Halliday[2] – no ladies but H and B. Perry extremely disagreeable, Lowe clever. Talked about Marcellus – To be sure Lady Clanricarde will box his ears for him, if ever she meets him. Much talk about India.

1. Thomas Erskine Perry (1806–82) was the second son of James Perry, proprietor of the *Morning Chronicle*. He was made Chief Justice of Bombay in 1847 but resigned in 1852.
2. Frederic James Halliday (1806–1901) was an East India Company administrator. He was to become a member of the Supreme Council of India late this year. He was later Governor of Bengal and knighted in 1860.

Friday – January 28

Miss Seward – wrote – Sancroft and Tillotson[1] – City – looked at my book – home – Broderip sent for his ballads and broadsides.[2] He had a good right to do so for I have had them long. Wrote again. Dined with Lady Coltman[3] – the Chancellor[4] – his wife – Monteagle – Hallam – Milman and Mrs M – pretty well.

1. In *HE*, ch. 14, TBM contrasts the leading non-jurors with the latitudinarians, and gives a portrait of Tillotson, but he describes Sancroft's last years after his deportation in *HE*, ch. 17, *CW*, vol. 3, pp. 159–71 and 397–400.
2. He had borrowed them in 1849 (*LM*, vol. 5, p. 32 and n.).
3. Anna Duckworth (1792–1873) married Thomas Coltman (d. 1849), Justice of the Common Pleas. She lived at 8 Hyde Park Gardens.
4. Cranworth.

Saturday – January 29

To Bowood – Ld and Ly Granville in the same train. At Bowood found Caita, Lacaita[1] or some such name, a Neapolitan exile. Ld and Lady Mahon, and her brother Kerrison, M.P. for Eye with his wife. We all got on very well and sate late.

1. (Sir) John Philip Lacaita (1813–95), who came to London in 1852. He became Professor of Italian at Queen's College, London, naturalized as a British subject in 1853 and was made KCMG in 1859.

Sunday – January 30

Dull day – read and chatted – turned over some books about Atterbury. French M.S. verses – Life of Dr Perceval[1] – of Schiller – of Klopstock. Chapel. Sermon from a Mr Jacob.[2] He gave us for a text – Give unto Caesar, etc. – I expected a touch on the martyrdom,[3] but there was none. Dinner and evening pleasant.

1. Perhaps the *Memoirs of Dr. Thomas Percival, by his Son* (1807).

2. Perhaps William Bonnar Jacob, Headmaster of Calne School, or James John Jacob, Chaplain of Salisbury Infirmary.
3. 30 January was the anniversary of the execution of Charles I.

Monday – January 31

Fine day – a little frosty. Ld L proposed a walk and we went up to the hill where the old moat and the yew tree are. The way lay through a perfect Slough of Despond. I, like Pliable, should have turned back, but Lady Mahon's courage shamed me; so on I went. After lunch I went to walk alone in the pleasure ground, but was pestered by a most sociable cur who would not be got rid of. I went into a plantation railed off with gates at each end, and shut the brute out: but he perfectly understood my tactics – curse his intelligence – and waited for me at the other gate. After vainly trying to escape him in this way I shut him in and staid outside myself. When I walked away he saw that he had been outgeneralled by human reason, and set up the most ludicrous howl that I ever heard in my life. He continued to yelp half an hour – nay all night for anything that I know to the contrary. To my room – read Cooper's absurd book about England.[1] The fellow was a perfect monomaniac. He could see nothing here except hatred of America. I have hardly ever seen such crazy ill humour. Sorry to find that the Mahons *and* Granvilles go early tomorrow. I had not ordered my fly till two. I like the Neapolitan much. He is a man of really great acquirements, and speaks English wonderfully well.

1. James Fenimore Cooper, *England with Sketches of Society in the Metropolis* (1837).

Tuesday – February 1

Very fine, but frosty and foggy – our party small – after breakfast walked with Ld L to the park gate and back. Then lunch – then off. They were kind as usual and the children – Ld Shelburne's – are very promising indeed. Journey home through a thick fog – so thick as to be dangerous – read Dieu dispose. We reached Paddington at six. I never but once before saw London so dark. However by the help of links etc. we got home in an hour and a half. The crush and darkness at the end of Park Lane were quite appalling. Dined – finished D.D. – and to bed pretty well.

Wednesday – February 2

A fine day. Trevelyan found me at breakfast and we chatted. I wrote some letters of business. To the Temple – did not find E – looked into Peek's coffee house[1] after a long interval and read magazines – to W.T. H not quite well – all the rest as well as possible – chatted happily for an hour and a half walked home. The walk and the state of the atmosphere affected my chest grievously. I have seldom suffered more in that way. I wrote however and read – Much interested by a strange book called Dying Testimonies[2] which Burton has sent me from Edinburgh. At dinner Mrs Gore's Dean's Daughter.[3] I had begun it at Bowood. I have had a comical correspondence with Mrs G. I forgot to say that I had a letter from Guizot this morning. He has proposed me for the Institute and seems to think my election certain. This is really an honor. To bed – mustard poultice and Ipecacuanha.

1. Peek Brothers were tea and coffee merchants with premises at 4 St Mary-at-Hill and 31 Love Lane, Eastcheap.
2. Perhaps *The Dying Speeches of Several Excellent Persons Who Suffered for their Zeal against Popery, and Arbitrary Government (namely Stephen Colledg, Lord William Russell, Algernon Sidney, Colonel Rumbald, Alice Lisle, & others)* (1689).
3. *The Dean's Daughter, or, The Days we Live In* (1853).

Thursday – February 3

Much better, but a very dull day. I scarcely stirred out. A Mr Maitland[1] called from Spottiswoode and Robertson's about the Annuity Tax Bill – a sensible man. I see pretty well the nature of the point in dispute. Macleod also called and we talked long. I wrote pretty well. At dinner the Dean's Daughter – Miss Seward.

1. John Maitland (*c.* 1793–1865) was senior partner in the firm of Spottiswoode, Robertson and Maitland, parliamentary agents, 27 Great George Street, Westminster. The Annuity Tax was a levy to support the parish ministers in Edinburgh. It was resented by the citizens, particularly because the legal profession, mostly members of the Established Church, were exempted from paying it. See TBM's description of it, *LM*, vol. 6, p. 293.

Friday – February 4

I find that exercise in the open air speedily affects my chest disagreeably. I went to W.T. at lunch time. Dear B was at her French class – I sate an hour with H and Alice. Went with H to take up Lydia Price. Chat about Dundee. Home wrote – read – at dinner Dean's Daughter. Seward's Life of Darwin[1] – what detestable stuff.

1. Anna Seward, *Memoirs of the Life of D. Darwin* (1804).

Saturday – February 5

Walked, but not much – met Stafford.[1] He does not at all like being out of place. Wrote – read absurd Covenanting Tracts – Northcote's life of Reynolds[2] – E to dinner.

1. Augustus Stafford had been Secretary of the Admiralty March–December 1852.

2. James Northcote, *The Life of Sir Joshua Reynolds*, 2 vols (1818).

Sunday – February 6

Reynolds – W.T. Walked with T to Kent House[1] – called at Hallam's. Good account of Mrs C and her twins[2] – glad of it from my soul – met the D. of Argyle and took a turn with him in Belgrave Square. Home – wrote – finished hastily the Dean's Daughter. Began My Novel[3] – pretty good.

1. The town house of Sir George Cornewall Lewis.
2. Hallam's daughter Julia married Captain Cator in 1852. The twins, Julia Maria and Eleanor Louisa, lived until 1924 and 1933 respectively.
3. E. Bulwer-Lytton, *My Novel; or Varieties of English Life by Pisistratus Caxton*, 4 vols (1853).

Monday – February 7

Dear B came to ask me to walk with her. I wrote some time – then went to W.T. We walked across the parks to the British Gallery. Modern pictures – a wretched collection – some tolerable animals and landscapes. The historical pieces execrable. A Macbeth very bad. A Daniel with the Lions, still worse.[1] I took B back in a fly – walked home – at dinner My Novel.

1. The British Institution had an exhibition of the work of some distinguished painters and sculptors this year. TBM particularly disliked painters Henry Courtney Selous (1802–90) (*Macbeth* (no. 259)) and Henry Barraud (1811–74) (*Daniel Delivered from the Lions* (no. 517)).

Tuesday – February 8

An odd day. First came my decoration from the King of Prussia, then the official communication of my election at the Institute of France. I spent much of the morning in writing letters of acknowledgment. Then wrote something – To dinner at Ellis's – dearest B had spent the day there. Gave her my badge of the Order of Merit to take to her mother.

Wednesday – [February 9]

Fine – EW – wrote a little – walked. It is odd how much I suffer from walking. It affects me much more than the cold air. To W.T. H brought me back. Bulwer has sent me his Novel. I like it better than almost anything that he has done. But there is a good deal of it. E to dinner.

Thursday – [February 10]

Cold and dull weather. Vexed to think that parliament is about to recommence work. Wrote. Went down to Westminster I found the new official men crowded together under the gallery. I walked up with Ld John, at his request, then took my seat in the bench behind the ministers with George Grey and Goulburn. Nothing very particular. Ld J's announcement that the Reform Bill is to be put off till next Session[1] was better received than I had expected. Home to dinner – My N.

1. *PD*, 3rd ser., cxxiv, 22.

Friday – February 11

Cold and dull again. Wrote – walked down to the House and back. Very little doing. I saved Moncrieff from a great mistake. He was sitting in the House with his hat on and just going to make a speech, without having been sworn in since his re-election.[1] He might have forfeited half his fortune in ten minutes. Home – Duke of Buckingham's Memoirs of G III.[2] The letters curious. The Duke's part detestable. His ignorance gross beyond belief. His grandfather the first Marquis was a great rogue[3] and as dirty a fellow as ever lived. What in this foolish book is called punctilious sense of honor was in truth only an insatiable greediness for titles. My Novel.

1. James Moncrieff, presumably upon his re-election as MP after his appointment as Lord Advocate.
2. Duke of Buckingham, *Memoirs of the Court and Cabinets of George the Third* (1853).
3. George Nugent-Temple Grenville, first Marquis of Buckingham (1753–1813).

Saturday – February 12

Snow. Museum – wrote a good many notes and letters there and after coming home. A little of the history – Limerick. To W.T. to dinner. I am tolerably well today in spite of the cold: but walking affects me much. Pleasant evening – except that I am vexed by finding T bent on being a witness before the East Indian Committee. Very bad, I think, in his position.

Sunday – February 13

I staid at home the whole day – a dull comfortless day – wrote much, and read – very comfortable and cheerful. T called – talked again about the E.I. Committee, but did not agree. I finished *My Novel* – One of B's best – D. of B. again.

Monday – February 14

Bad weather. I do not know that I should have gone out if Wood had not sent for me to talk about India. To Chatham Place – found him on his back with lumbago. Wish he had been so when he made that unlucky speech at Halifax.[1] Clarendon came. We talked some time. Then I went to the House – presented petitions, D'I's question[2] – Ld J's answer. They will not make much of it. Home – wrote – Ledbury[3] – Bisset on Sacheverell.[4]

1. In a speech in the by-election made necessary by his appointment as President of the Board of Control, Wood had made injudicious criticisms of Napoleon III that prompted Disraeli to ask whether the government had abandoned the policy of friendly relations towards France. The matter was raised in both Houses of Parliament on 14 February and again in the Commons on 18 February.
2. *PD*, 3rd ser., cxxiv, 83–5.
3. Albert Smith, *The Adventures of Mr. Ledbury* (1844).
4. William Bisset was the author of *The Modern Fanatick* (1710–14) and of *Remarks on Dr Sach—'s Sermon* (1709) attacking Sacheverell.

Tuesday – February 15

Still very cold – staid at home all day – wrote well – read – pamphlets on Burnet – very interesting – Ledb.

Wednesday – February 16

To breakfast H, Ld Glenelg, Milman, Denison. Hallam should have come but one of the little twins is dying[1] – Alas! Not that the loss in itself is much – but he has now only one stake; and he has been so often unfortunate. Our party pleasant. Fine day – walked about an hour. Wrote a little. L[imeric]k finished for the present[2] – Life of a strange crazy atheist Burridge,[3] and other pamphlets. Inglis called – E to dinner.

1. See above, entry for 6 February 1853.
2. The Siege of Limerick, *HE*, ch. 16, *CW*, vol. 3, pp. 319–28.
3. Perhaps Richard Burridge, *Religio Libertini: or, The Faith of a Converted Atheist* (1712).

Tuesday – February 17

Wrote a good deal. To Ld Aberdeen with Tufnell about the Annuity Tax.[1] We agreed very well – wrote to the Ld Provost who is at York. Glad to get home again – a miserable day – snowy, frosty, gloomy – wrote on – read two pamphlets of Sullivan's about India[2] – ill conditioned, angry, fellow – read Dunton's absurd attack[3] on Kennet's absurd funeral eulogium on the 1st Duke of Devonshire. At dinner Ledb.

1. See *LM*, vol. 5, p. 310 and n. 3.
2. By Sir Richard J. Sullivan (1752–1806) or Sir Edward Robert Sullivan (1826–99).
3. John Dunton, *The Hazard of Death-Bed Repentance* ...(1708), in answer to White Kennet's *A Sermon Preach'd at the Funeral of William, Duke of Devonshire* (1707). Dunton (1659–1733) was a bookseller and Satirist.

Friday – February 18

Glorious day, though cold. Walked to the British Museum – found Ld Braybrooke[1] with Holmes. Made notes from the Dutch dispatches about the Close of the Irish War – did not find much but what I have written is confirmed – to W.T. – B not there – chatted an hour with H and A. Home – rummaged books to find out something about Ld Coningsby.[2] To the House – but turned back by the way: I feel that I must take care of myself. Home – bad cough. The pills gave me a good night however – Ledb – Pamphlets and tracts – Dialogue of Durfey with Smith and Johnson etc[3] Flood's Life.[4]

1. Richard Griffin (1783–1858), third Baron.
2. Thomas Coningsby (*c.* 1656–1729), one of the three Lord Justices of Ireland, first Earl of Coningsby and MP for Leominster, 1679–1716.
3. *Wit for Money: or Poet Stutter. A Dialogue between Smith, Johnson, and Poet Stutter* ... (1691), perhaps by Thomas Brown. 'Stutter' was Durfey.
4. Warden Flood, *Memoirs of Henry Flood* (1838).

Saturday – February 19

To breakfast with Mahon. He is suffering from cough etc. Met Ingersoll and Miss Wilcox[1] – a nice looking girl, as I had heard. Hallam, to my great joy, the twins well – Cornwall Lewis, Carlisle – pleasant party. Mahon lent me some sheets of an account written by Ld Chesterfield[2] of the amours of George I and George II, very clever and piquant but grossly indecent. I am afraid that, if M. publishes, he will bring a hornet's nest about his ears. Walked to the R.I. looked at the Acts of Parliament and Journals – home – wrote. An amazingly absurd petition from a man called John Chapman in Fifeshire. His prayer is that parliament will buy him some books which he wants to possess, and will fix the minimum rate of interest at 7 ½ per cent, 5 to the lender and 2 ½ to the broker. The fellow must be cracked. At d[inne]r Ledb – Flood.

1. James Reed Ingersoll (1786–1868), a lawyer and Whig Congressman, was US ambassador to Britain, accompanied formally by his unmarried niece, Mary Waln Wilcox (b. 1828), later Mrs Alexander Dallas Campbell. Carlisle's record of this breakfast includes Mrs Ingersoll (Carlisle, J19/8/30, f. 50).

2. Philip Dormer Stanhope, fourth Earl of Chesterfield (1694–1773), the writer of the famous letters to his son.

Sunday – February 20

Fine cold day. My chest poorly. Went to W.T. however and made it worse. E sent in the morning very kindly inviting himself to dinner – had some difficulty in laying in provision for him – treated him with oysters, turkey and a wild duck – could eat very little myself – mustard plaister. Bad night.

Monday – February 21

Determined to stay at home resolutely. The weather very trying. Read and wrote all day. Reid on the Human Mind.[1] Ledb. Young's conspiracy.[2] Another mustard poultice, and a very stinging one – a better night.

1. Thomas Reid, *An Inquiry into the Human Mind* (1764).
2. *HE*, ch. 18, *CW*, vol. 3, pp. 554–62.

Tuesday – February 22

Another day of confinement – a breakfast party wh sate till ½ after 1. Hallam, Ld Carlisle,[1] C. Lewis, Ld Glenelg. H and B called – H to dine here tomorrow. The time passed pleasantly enough in reading and writing. I once little thought how well I could bear such imprisonment. Ledb. Carleton. Letter from the Ld Provost.[2]

1. Carlisle records the topics discussed: 'We had his old classification of the six first poets from Macaulay. Great praise and much quotation from the Oedipus Tyrannus. Hallam thinks the scene of the gradual discovery the most tragic conceivable.' They also talk about Lucan, suicide and monogamy among Greeks and Jews, times of meals in antiquity, when 'London' first appears in 'grave verse'. 'We censured Ld. John's assigning the supremacy of lyric poetry to Moore. We agreed ... that panegyric had been laid too thickly upon Peel since his death. He had stifled his convictions for a long time which enabled him at last to be of immense service to his country by sacrificing himself' (Carlisle, J19/8/30, ff. 53–4).
2. Of Edinburgh: Duncan McLaren.

Wednesday – February 23

T called while I was at breakfast and took something – I sate reading and writing all day. I sent for Bright who prescribed calomel etc. The Ld Advocate[1] called. At 6 H – we had a pleasant dinner together, though I ate but little.

1. James Moncrieff.

Thursday – February 24

Strongly affected by Bright's pills – better certainly. Bright called again – so did the Ld Advocate. He found me writing to the Ld Provost. After he was gone I finished the letter, and summoned Maclaren up to town – I do not know whether I have judged wise. But, shut up as I am, it is as well that Maclaren should be here. Read and wrote – still on Young – Hervey's Meditations – Theron and Aspasia[1] – what stuff! Odd that so fair a Greek scholar as he seems to have been should have had so un-Greek a taste. Mothers and D[aughte]rs[2] at d[inne]r – some appetite.

1. James Hervey (1714–58), *Meditations among the Tombs* (1746) and *Theron and Aspasia* (1745).
2. By Mrs Catherine Gore (1831).

Friday – [February 25]

Hervey – Trevelyan to breakfast – a second breakfast – with my dear little Alice – read and wrote all day as before. E.R. – article on Beattie excellent.[1] Sitting down to a leg of mutton at 7, with M and D, in came E – glad to see him – sent the mutton to the fire – ordered a wild duck to be roasted for the 2nd course – pleasant evening.

1. Perhaps a review of Beattie's *Life of Thomas Campbell*; but I find no such article in the *Edinburgh* about this date.

Saturday – [February 26]

E. R. – Read and wrote till 12 – then H, F and B came to lunch – read to them W's visit to the Hague – the villainy of Marlborough – the surrender of Limerick – the Treason Bill – Oates.[1] They seemed most interested and were so, I believe. The truth is that my book will be the best on the subject in almost all respects and particularly in style and art of colouring: but it will be immeasurably below what I wish it to be. They went at ½ after two – W. Marshall called – how he has improved since our younger days. Hallam called while M. was with me. When they were gone wrote again – at dinner H. Lorrequer.[2] In the evening Garrick Correspondence.[3]

1. In *HE*, chs 17 and 18.
2. Charles Lever, *Harry Lorrequer* (1837).
3. *The Private Correspondence of David Garrick*, ed. James Boaden (1831).

Sunday – February 27

Fine day – but staid at home – read more than I wrote – began the 1st siege of Namur – cleared away and catalogued a great many pamphlets. H.L. Garrick – Miss Edgeworth's Ennui.[1]

1. In *Tales of Fashionable Life* (1809).

Monday – February 28

Ennui – Maitland called[1] – went out for the first time since the 20th. Fine but cold. To W.T. I have been vexed by a Yankee trick. Some N.Y. bookseller[2] has printed everything in Hansard that has my name to it and calls the farrago Macaulay's Speeches. After all what does it matter? Chatted two hours at W.T. – home – meant to write but Ld Glenelg called – Marshall – put pamphlets to rights. That is now nearly done: and I shall go to work comfortably tomorrow – Lorrequer. By the bye I lent Ld Glenelg Moore's Poems.

1. Presumably the parliamentary agent; see above, entry for 3 February 1853, n. 1.
2. J. S. Redfield; cf. *LM*, vol. 5, p. 339n.

Tuesday – March 1

Very bad day – snow – staid at home – did not write, but read and planned. Baba looked in for a minute – dear child – I sent for the old courier who went with Ellis and me to France – dissatisfied with what I have written – out of spirits – HL. Miss Edgeworth's Ennui – very good.

Wednesday [March 2]

Staid at home again – read and planned but wrote little or nothing. Cator called – then the Duke of Argyle about India – wrote something about Atterbury. I must work regularly at that job.[1] H.L. Miss Edgeworth – Manoeuvring – The Absentee[2] – nothing can be better than Ld Colambre's incognito. It is the best thing of the kind since the Odyssey. Winter's Life – by Jay.[3]

1. It was to be the essay on Francis Atterbury for Black's *Encyclopaedia Britannica*; *CW*, vol. 7, pp. 283–96.
2. In *Tales of Fashionable Life* (1809).
3. Perhaps William Jay, *Memoirs of… the Rev. Cornelius Winter* (1808).

Friday [Thursday – March 3][1]

Fine, though cold – forced to go into the City to sell out stock – my accounts in a good state. Came home and found H and B waiting for me. They sate with me half an hour. The courier called, and I agreed with him. Cameron called. I wrote – completed my account of Young's conspiracy or nearly so. I try to get as fast as I can over what is dull, and I dwell as long as I can on what can be made picturesque and dramatic – I believe this to be the most instructive, as well as the most popular way of writing history. Wrote – Mrs Gore's Preferment[2] – Berkeley's Minute Philosopher[3] – Hydr – a very slight tendency to giddiness for a moment.

---

1. TBM originally wrote 'Friday'. The correction is George Trevelyan's.
2. Mrs Catherine Gore, *Preferment: or, My Uncle the Earl*, 3 vols (1840).
3. George Berkeley, *Alciphron, or the Minute Philosopher* (1732).

Friday – March 4

Berkeley – wrote a few letters – then went out – fine day. West wind. Walked an hour or so – R.I. journals – Acts of Pt. – met Hibbert – home – wrote – Nat. debt[1] – Atterbury – At dinner Preferment – Berkeley.

---

1. *HE*, ch. 19, *CW*, vol. 3, pp. 611–21.

Saturday – March 5

Breakfasted a quarter of an hour earlier than usual. Berkeley. The Ld Provost,[1] Maitland, Tufnell came. Cowan came unasked. Then the Ld Advocate. We discussed the Annuity Tax question – I am afraid that we shall find great difficulty. The Provost and I were perfectly civil. Milman came, to my sorrow, to say that he cannot breakfast here on Monday. Then came Adolphus and sate an hour. I wrote on the national debt. Charles and Mr Janson about the mortgage. I am but half satisfied with myself for the change which I have made. But after all it is only 400£. At dinner Preferment – finished Berkeley's Minute Philosopher. Burton Anatomy of Melancholy.[2]

---

1. Cf. *LM*, vol. 5, p. 319 and n. 5.
2. Richard Burton, *The Anatomy of Melancholy* (1621).

Sunday – March 6

Burton – To Brooks's – to W.T. – found Price and his wife there – asked them to breakfast tomorrow – walked home – pretty well. Wrote National Debt – Preferment at dinner – Burton – Strutt called.

Monday – March 7

Breakfast party – H – Price and Lydia – Ld Carlisle[1] – the Ld Advocate – Hallam and Cator – very pleasant. The ladies particularly agreeable. I staid at home after they were gone and wrote. Dr Holland called. Finished Preferment at dinner. Received today the 2nd vol of the Translation of my History from France – It seems to have made a great sensation. Several journals came with it – all pretty favourable.

1. In his Journal, Carlisle noted: 'Ly T. is very pleasing, and Macaulay always makes it pleasant. He talked with his usual very absolute incredulity on Phrenology, Clairvoyance, etc., and not for the first time in my experience told us of Mrs. Veal's ghost' (Carlisle, J19/8/30, f. 60).

Tuesday – March 8

After breakfast Trevelyan called with Macleod of Macleod. I wrote and read – sent some corrections to my French translator. Macleod came – we talked about the national debt. He seemed to like what I had written; and I like it myself. Then Mahon. He and Macleod together for some time. Mahon left me some trifles of Ld Chesterfield – not as good as the specimen of the memoirs which he left me some time ago. Wrote and read – could not go out. At dinner Larpent's journal[1] – poor work – all the plums picked out by the papers already and not many of them. Hume's dialogue on Natural Religion.[2]

1. Francis Seymour Larpent (1776–1845), *Private Journal*, ed. Sir George Larpent (1853).
2. David Hume, *Dialogues Concerning Natural Religion* (1779).

Wednesday – March 9

Hume – wrote a little – letter from Μακφ.[1] To Brooks's – to W.T. pleasant hour there – walked home – delicious day – but I – how changed. Yet I keep my faculties and my affections and my temper – and I really am very happy, whatever Philo and Demea[2] may say – home – wrote. Longman called – I was to have dined with him today. At dinner Ormond[3] – corrected proofs of my paper on the Comic Dramatists[4] – Burton.

1. MacFarlane.
2. Philo and Demea are speakers in Hume's Dialogues.
3. Either Maria Edgeworth's *Ormond* (1817) or Sophia Lee, *Ormond, or, the Debauchee* (1810).
4. Originally published in *ER*, 72 (January 1841).

Thursday – March 10

Wrote a little. Walked to the Treasury – saw the boxes of law papers – then to W.T. and back. I hope that this matter of the national debt is getting right. What with that and Atterbury I work very fairly now. By the bye an impudent vagabond named Ashworth has sent me a quantity of M.S.S. in verse enough to make out two volumes and begs me to read them, to pronounce judgment on them, and if they are good to find a publisher for them and to arrange the terms. A fool – I sent them back with a note to say that I was too busy. At dinner Ormond – Burton.

Friday – March 11

Fine still. To the City. Saw Longman – gave him the proofs of the paper on the Comic Dramatists – walked home – quantum mutatus[1] – except in mind and heart – wrote very well, I thought – sent a line to ask Macleod to call tomorrow. Ld Glenelg came and we chatted about India. I am afraid that my friends will be in a scrape. At dinner Elphinstone[2] – then Burton.

1. *Quantum mutatus ab illo Hectore* (Latin): 'How terribly changed from the Hector / Who came back from bombarding the Greek navy with fire ...' (Virgil, *Aeneid* 2.274; C. Day Lewis's translation (London, 1954), p. 39).
2. By Alfred Butler (1841).

Saturday – March 12

Fine – wrote – walked to Athenaeum – home – wrote – Macleod – sate two hours. I am pleased with what I have written on the funding system. Trevelyan looked in at ½ after six. At dinner Elphinstone – finished Burton – Johnson's Adventurers.[1] An amazingly clever fellow Burton – but he tires me to death.

1. Essays written, twice weekly, by Samuel Johnson for a periodical the *Adventurer*, from 3 March 1753 to 2 March 1754.

Sunday – March 13

Johnson's Adventurers – wrote something about Atterbury – not quite right – must take Hydr – walked to Brooks's – there I found Hobhouse and Ld De Mauley. All seem to be agreed that our friends are in a scrape – to W.T. Sate an hour with H and A before T and B came. I am anxious about G. I am afraid that he will be bullied when he goes into a Master's house, and that his sensitive nature will suffer. My own recollections make me more apprehensive than his mother is; and I do not chuse to frighten her – home – delicious weather – wrote Mohun[1] – began to write on the first siege of Namur.[2] At dinner Elphinstone.

1. Charles, Lord Mohun (1675–1712); *HE*, ch. 19, *CW*, vol. 3, pp. 604–6.
2. By the French. *HE*, ch. 19., *CW*, vol. 3, pp. 574–5.

Monday – March 14

Wet – nevertheless I went to the Athenaeum to look at Racine's account of the Siege of Namur[1] – very poor – he had none of the qualities of a historian. I got Atterbury's Correspondence[2] from the London Library, and wrote hard – finished Namur – got on with Atterbury. H called. The courier came for orders and at dinner and afterwards David Copperfield. I like it better than the first time – but it is far inferior to Pickwick and even to O.T. and N.N. – nay, inferior I think to MC – better to be sure than Dombey.

1. *Relation du Siège de Namur* (1692), used in *HE*, ch. 19, *CW*, vol. 3, p. 575.
2. *The Miscellaneous Works of Bishop Atterbury*, ed. J. Nicholls, 5 vols (1789–98); or J. H. Glover, *The Stuart Papers I: Letters of Francis Atterbury to the Chevalier de St. George* (1847).

Tuesday – March 15

Very fine. Wrote a little – then Renton came[1] about medical legislation – the old story – they are all together by the ears – never was there such a set of quarrelsome unreasonable fellows. It is the Glasgow faculty that now refuses to concur. To W.T. walked with dearest B – the first time after a long interval. We talked of the different proportions of the Latin and AngloSaxon element in different English styles – then of foreign languages – the proportions of Latin in French and Italian – excellent girl, and intelligent as excellent. Home – wrote and read. At dinner DC.

1. Dr Robert Renton (*c.* 1794–1884), an Edinburgh doctor; he came to discuss a bill for the licensing of doctors.

Wednesday – March 16

Fine morning – bad afternoon. Went into the City and got French gold. In the afternoon Moncrieff called about the Annuity Tax, and Grey about India. To dinner, after a long interval, at W.T. Gladstone, Ld Glenelg, Goulburn; Wilson of the Œconomist, the Prices, Lefevre and his wife, Mrs Drummond, Senior and his daughter – Sir S. Northcote[1] – not unpleasant. Much laughing about Mrs Becher Stowe and what we were to give her. I referred the ladies to Goldsmith's poems for what I should give. Nobody but H and Lydia understood me. But some of them have since been thumbing Goldsmith to make out the riddle.[2] I brought Ld Glenelg to the Albany.

1. Sir Stafford Northcote (1818–87) was cooperating with Trevelyan in their joint report on the civil service.

2. Sir George Otto Trevelyan decided to reveal the solution to the riddle in his biography of Macaulay. It is in Goldsmith's poem 'The Gift: to Iris, in Bow-Street, Covent Garden'.

I'll give thee something yet unpaid,
Not less sincere, than civil;
I'll give thee – Ah! Too charming maid;
I'll give thee – to the Devil.

An odd comparison, since Iris, addressed in the first stanza as 'Dear mercenary beauty', was a streetwalker.

Thursday – March 17

A vile day – meant to have gone to the India Committee, but could not venture out. H. called. Worked – chiefly Atterbury – at dinner D.C. finished it. Pretty well.

Friday – March 18

Cold – but went to the Athenaeum and to the London Library – got Glover's Vol. of Stuart correspondence.[1] Atterbury. Letter from Hawes about Arthur Ellis – sent it to his father. Renton again about medical legislation. At dinner Ni jamais ni toujours.[2] More's Divine Dialogues.[3]

1. John Hulbert Glover, *The Stuart Papers* (1847).
2. By Charles-Paul de Kock (1836).
3. Henry More, *Divine Dialogues* (1668).

Saturday – March 19

The Courier came – very satisfactory report – to W.T., and home. My chief work till I go to France will be the finishing of this article on Atterbury. Divine Dialogues – Social Religion[1] – NJNT.

1. Matthias Maurice, *Social Religion Exemplify'd* (1759).

Sunday – March 20

Wrote – Att[erbur]y – to Brooks's – to W.T. – home – met Macleod and walked with him talking about India. Atterbury – Social Religion – N.J.N.T.

Monday – March 20 [21]

Bad weather – Got on with Atterbury all the morning. Finished it. I mean to start for France tomorrow afternoon – Ly Mn OB and OF[1] Will Huntington.

1. Lady (Sydney) Morgan, *The O'Briens and the O'Flahertys* (1827).

Tuesday – March 22

Not very inviting day – went to the R.I. met the Bp of Exeter[1] in Albemarle Street. He was amazingly, overpoweringly civil. The courier came. Off to the Station having sent my Atterbury to Black. An M.P. named, as I found, Dodd of Maidstone,[2] was at London Bridge and forced me into the carriage in which his wife and sister were. The wife – rather good looking and speaking French capitally – but a great fool and chatterbox – "Are you really the great Mr Macaulay?" I disclaimed all right to the appellation. In ten minutes more "But are you really, etc – –?" Glad to get to Folkestone – tolerable dinner – read Guzman d'Alfarache. Slept ill – cold – heavy fall of snow – bad omens – however the water is smooth enough which is a matter of more importance particularly to the ladies.

1. Henry Phillpotts.
2. George Dodd (1790–1864) was MP for Maidstone. In April his election was declared void after a petition. He married Georgina Saunders (*c.* 1820–65). I can find no record of a sister, but a sister-in-law, Emma Eliza Saunders (b. *c.* 1827) is registered by the 1851 census as living at Dodd's London home, 9 Grosvenor Place, SW.

Wednesday – March 23

Breakfast before nine. To the Station. They soon came – a dreary cold day as ever I saw. We went instantly on board. The snow was falling so I was forced to remain till almost the end of the voyage in the cabin below among basins the sight of which was enough to disturb my stomach. I fixed my eyes and thoughts on Guzman and thus got on without any qualm. The French coast was almost as white with snow as ours. Boulogne. Hotel des Bains. Poor George's delight at finding himself in France was quite comical. I gave him an eighty franc piece – 10 naps to each of the ladies to please themselves – we walked out – to the old town – but were soon driven in by snow. I read them some of Roderic Random to their great delight. The ribaldry is easily separated from what is good. We dined well, and set off soon after five for Paris – a tedious journey in the dark – but we were very merry – reached the end of our journey at half after ten – got all six into a Cittadine[1] and were at the Hotel de Wagram soon after eleven – found tea bread butter and eggs ready – the tea bad – the rest good – really nice rooms excellently distributed. Glad to get to bed and slept sound. The night was clear and the view of the gardens of the Tuilleries and the quay on the other side of the Seine by lamplight was very striking.

1. Hackney coach.

Thursday – March 24

After breakfast we sallied out and took a long walk along the quays – to Notre Dame – by the Hotel de ville – to the Palais Royal then along the Rue Vivienne and back by the Rue Richelieu to the Hotel. Lunched on bread, butter and vin ordinaire. In the afternoon came a very good carriage and pair which I had ordered the Courier to hire for the week. We drove to Longchamps. The weather was so cold that the snow was not what it usually is. We crossed the Emperor and Empress but I could hardly see them and did not see much to admire in their equipage. Home – read RR – dined comfortably – RR.

Friday – March 25

The ladies to Church – I to Galignani's and walked about a good deal. I was much struck by St Eustache. In the afternoon they went to see Churches and I staid at home. Dinner as before and RR.

Saturday – March 26

After a little shopping we went to Versailles and walked about the immense palace. I have been there often, and all of us except George once at least. I saw now, however for the first time the private apartments. Very mean, I thought, ill situated and ill arranged. Lunched at the neighbouring Restaurant's [*sic*] and back. Trevelyan dined at the Embassy. We had a pleasant evening over RR.

Sunday – March 26 [27]

The ladies to the English Church. I went to Notre Dame – immense crowd. In the afternoon I took a walk with H about the Boulevards and through several galleries while the rest went to the Pere la Chaise. After dinner we read Hall's excellent Review of Zeal without Innovation[1] and were all delighted with both the style and substance.

1. Robert Hall's memoir of James Bean's *Zeal Without Innovation* in the *Eclectic Review*, reprinted in his *Works*, ed. O. Gregory, 6 vols (London, 1832), vol. 4, pp. 46–125.

Monday – March 27 [28]

After breakfast to the Invalides – An old soldier of Wagram and Borodino showed us about to dear George's infinite delight. The pictures are viler daubs than those at Versailles, and that is a bold word. From the Invalides to the Hotel de Cluny but found it closed – to the Chapelle Sainte – a wonderful bijou, but too much a bijou. Home. I called on Guizot – found him in a small but comfortable house, buried among books, professing to have done with politics and to live entirely with the English minds of the seventeenth century. Of the present man he talked with contempt and dislike. We were right to strengthen our defences – C'est un cerveau malade. None of the qualities of a good ruler – l'esprit – but merely l'esprit d'un conspirateur – desperately debauched and likely to ruin his constitution. We dined at the Trois Frères. I had ordered a very handsome entertainment, and it was excellent. We took a turn about the Palais Royal by lamplight, and then went home.

Tuesday – [March 29]

Our last day here. I have kept such strict incognito that though T has dined and breakfasted at the embassy, they are not aware that I am at Paris. The ladies shopped in the morning. Then we went to the Luxembourg – and the Chamber of Peers – now the Senate House – a poor affair – then drove to the Palais Royale which interested them all greatly as it has interested everybody to whom I have shown it – then home by the boulevards. Dumont to dinner. A good dinner. He rather bored us at last, though he is an excellent fellow; but, having to rise tomorrow before daybreak, I was glad to see him depart.

Wednesday – March 30

Dressed by candlelight – breakfasted and off to the Station – We reached Boulogne soon after one and went to the harbour immediately. The day fine the water smooth. By the bye in the train from Paris we travelled to Abbeville with the Principal of the Abbeville College – a very good natured man apparently – a man of sense and learning.[1] He took to George much, and was greatly interested with the account which G gave him in his broken French of Harrow. Our passage very pleasant. I was on deck the whole time – not quite two hours. There was one drawback – Thornton and his wretched woman were there.[2] I of course shook hands with her: but H and B kept out of sight. Very painful, old times remembered. At Folkestone we dined and read a little of RR – then off to town – got in at half after ten. At the Albany I found many letters, but none of importance. The Memoirs of Bohun the Licenser[3] which I looked through before I went to bed.

---

1. He was Joseph Ferdinand Farochon (1803–72), and he was Principal of the College from 1850 until 1853, when he became an inspector of schools in Algeria.
2. Henry Thornton and his second wife, Emily Dealtry, sister of his deceased wife Harriet. See E. M. Forster, *Marianne Thornton* (London, 1956).
3. S. Wilton Rix (ed.), *Diary and Autobiography of Edmund Bohun Esq.* (1853). Bohun (1645–99) was Licenser of the Press.

Thursday – March 31

Settled with the Courier. To the Temple. E not come back – to W.T. All well. Home. At dinner Reine Margot[1] – wrote a letter to make H an April fool – how Mrs Beecher Stowe had come to my Chambers and invited herself to lunch tomorrow – how she had brought with her a parson – a man of colour – the Rev. Caesar Ugbark and his wife – etc etc – Sent it to the Post.

1. By Alexandre Dumas (*père*) (1845).

Friday – April 1

To W.T. To my great vexation H had not received the letter. Miserable state of the post office arrangements. However, we laughed over my attempt and my failure. Home – wrote – parliamentary reform Place Bill etc. At dinner R.M.

Saturday – April 2

To the Temple – saw E – tried to see Thom at the H. of L. but failed – wrote a little – R.M.

Sunday – April 3

Wrote – W.T. took H to Lincoln's Inn Chapel to hear a Mr Maurice[1] – was disappointed and so was she. He preached about the absurdity of deferring baptism to the end of life. The error about the nature of post-baptismal sin he seemed to think the prevailing heresy of our time. He said much of Constantine's case – I could not help thinking of Walter Shandy. "Also abstain – that is as much as thou canst – from coots, didappers and waterhens".[2] The Duchess of Sutherland the Duke of Argyle were there. By the bye my letter about Mrs Stowe took in several people – Trevelyan, Lydia Price and Selina among the rest. H went her way and I mine – wrote a little – R.M.

1. (John) Frederick Denison Maurice (1805–72) was Chaplain of Lincoln's Inn, 1846–60, and until 1853 Professor of English Literature and History at King's College London. Presumably the Emperor Constantine illustrated the prevailing heresy of adult baptism.
2. Laurence Sterne, *Tristram Shandy* (1760–7), vol. 8, ch. 34: 'Carefully abstain – that is, as much as thou canst, from peacocks, cranes, coots, didappers and water-hens –.'

Monday – April 4

Wrote – To the House of Lords – could not find Thom – to the Commons – went to the Speaker. The Ld Advocate unable to go – got a most clear and precise account of our position respecting the Annuity Tax Bill and sent it to the Ld Provost. Then to the India Committee. We examined Clerk of Umballa[1] as we used to call him – a very able man. To the House. Ld John on education,[2] nothing great, but sensible and good. Home – E to dinner – pleasant.

1. Sir George Russell Clark (1801–89), Lt-Governor of NW provinces and of Bengal, and Governor of Bombay. He retired in 1847.
2. *PD*, 3rd ser., cxxv, 522–50.

Tuesday – April 5

A bad day. I remained at home reading and writing. In the evening to dinner in Bedford Place. Walter has done very well. Glad of it.

Wednesday – April 6

To W.T. sate some time and walked with H and B to two or three places – walked home – fine day – read and wrote – E to dinner read him what I had written on the national debt. Glad to find him pleased.

Thursday – April 7

To the H of Ls – found Thom at last and made my extracts. In his room were French[1] and another Irish blackguard and jobber abusing Trevelyan. I spoke pretty coolly and resolutely to them. To the India Committee. Sir E. Perry[2] – an ass and a coxcomb. I cross examined pretty smartly. Never was there a more complete smash. Home – wrote a little – the 3rd and 4th vols of Tom Moore's Life came in. I read most of them this evening – At dinner La Dame de Monsoreau.[3] A prince born today.

1. Fitzstephen French (1801–73), MP for Roscommon, 1832–73. Cf. *LM*, vol. 5, p. 324 and n.
2. Perry wanted to see the East India Company abolished. Cf. *LM*, vol. 5, p. 325 and n., and above, entry for 27 January 1853.
3. By Alexandre Dumas (*père*) (1846)

Friday – April 8

Finished the Life of Moore – to breakfast with C Wood. Grey there. We discussed Indian affairs during some hours. I like the scheme on the whole, though it has faults. Home in a heavy shower which prevented me from going to the Palace to set down my name. Sent Moore to H. Wrote and read – At dinner D de M.

Saturday – April 9

To the palace to put down my name.[1] To the British Museum – Long sitting there. Home – wrote and read – at dinner D de M. Letter from Simpson.[2]

1. After the birth of Queen Victoria's son Leopold, Duke of Albany, on 7 April.
2. Probably James Simpson (1781–1853), an Edinburgh advocate and writer on educational issues.

Sunday – April 10

To W.T. sate with H, B, A, and G some time. Walked away with H – met T. left H at Mrs T's. Home wrote and read – at dinner finished D de M. Wrote a letter to Simpson – sharp enough.

Monday – April 11

Soon after breakfast to the H. of L. made extracts from the Place Bill and The Triennial Bill of 1692/3 – to the Library of the H. of C. to consult the Journals. Then to the India Committee. Perry again – a most absurd coxcomb – Gambier[1] – little to say. Struck more than ever today by the detestable badness of the frescoes from the English poets. Horsley's from Milton[2] is beyond belief vile and mean – and so noble a subject – perhaps the finest in poetry – all forms of beauty, human, male and female, Angelic – Diabolical – the very background so fine. Home – Macleod called – to W.T. dined there pleasantly – read them some of R.R.[3]

1. Sir Edward John Gambier (1794–1879), Puisne Judge at Madras, and Chief of Justice, 1842–9.
2. *Satan Surprised at the Ear of Eve.* John Calcott Horsley (1817–1903) was a Royal Academician.
3. Possibly *Roderick Random.*

Tuesday – April 12

To breakfast at Hallam's – Ingersoll, Ld Granville, his son-in-law Acton,[1] Cator, Senior. Not unpleasant. Then to E's in the Temple – then home – wrote and read. At dinner began 45.[2] Letter to F about Gladstone's financial plan.[3] Amusing to see the fright of all the ladies who have anything in the funds – and without the slightest reason for alarm.

1. John Emmerich Edward Acton (1834–1902), eighth Bart and first Baron Acton. Sir Ferdinand Acton, his father, had died in 1832, and his widow married in 1840 the second Earl Granville. Acton was therefore Granville's stepson.
2. By Alexandre Dumas (*père*) (1848).
3. *LM*, vol. 5, pp. 326–7.

Wednesday – April 13

Party to breakfast – Hallam, Dundas, Senior, Cator, Goulburn, Lefevre, Grey was detained by the Taunton Committee[1] – very agreeable. Wrote a little. Off to Downing Street to join a deputation[2] which waited on Ld Aberdeen about the Advocates' Library. Back and wrote again. E to dinner.

1. This was George Grey, and the Committee concerned the incidence of bribery at the election at Taunton. See *PD*, 3rd ser., cxxv, 1348.
2. The Faculty of Advocates had asked for an annual grant of £500 for its library. It was refused, but the request advanced the process of recognition of the Library's public function. *The Times* of 14 April gave the name of the members of the delegation (p. 5a).

Thursday – April 14

Soon after breakfast to the H of C. wrote there about the Scotch Tests. To the India Committee. Cameron did well. Then was called Lewin, and the most hideous and repulsive looking of human beings came forward.[1] I went away – at dinner 45.

1. Perhaps Malcolm Lewin (1800–69), Judge of the Sudder Court in Madras and writer on Indian affairs.

Friday – April 15

Found that there would be no debate at present about the Scotch Tests. Wrote and read – to W.T. felt rheumatic – home – paired for the new debate. Moncrieff called. The Annuity Tax business smashed. I think the government will not bring in the bill, and I do not expect any good unless it is brought in by goverment. Ascanio[1] at dinner.

1. By Alexandre Dumas (*père*) (1843).

Saturday – April 16

After breakfast to Inglis's. He read me what he has prepared for a report about the Speaker's functions. To the B.M. Hinckes.[1] I examined him about the principles on which the Ninevite Inscriptions have been deciphered. The whole seems to me to be mere charlatanism. There is no point de départ at all. I could hardly refrain from laughing out. Then to W.T. – was told of a picture in Bond Street very like B. Went in the carriage with H and B to Bond Street – saw the picture – a likeness, but not striking. Walked back to W.T. with B – dear excellent child. We talked about Warburton – Pope – Bolingbroke – Waller. Home read and wrote – then to E's. At his door took leave of the page who has been with me five years and is now going to Lord Foley's.[2] Pleasant enough – Home with the new page.

---

1. Edward Hinckes (1792–1866) was a graduate of Trinity College Dublin, and became Rector of Killileagh in Co. Down. He played a very important part, at the same time as Rawlinson, in the decipherment of cuneiform.
2. Thomas Henry Foley (1808–69), fourth Baron Foley. The page was William Catchpole (b. 1836).

Sunday – April 17

Wrote a little. Brooks's. W.T. after a walk in Kensington Gardens – Harrison,[1] Thornton's old butler came to shake hands and take leave. T is coming to live in Connaught Terrace while preparations are making at Battersea Rise. Walked home – wrote T Bill – Read about Cagliostro – at dinner Ascanio.

---

1. Frederick Harrison (b. *c.* 1786) had evidently become a victim of the Dealtry scandal. See Forster, *Marianne Thornton*, p.188.

Monday – April 18

After breakfast came Maitland – then Hastings about the Medical Bill[1] – then I went to the City – then to the Indian Committee. Lewin – a wretch – I never saw such an exhibition of spite and absurdity – Leith – a good fellow.[2] To the House – Gladstone very good indeed.[3] Home to dinner with E.

---

1. Sir Charles Hastings (1794–1866), founder of the BMA.
2. John Farley Leith (1808–87), Advocate of the Supreme Court in Calcutta 1840–9. Professor of Law at Haileybury.
3. *PD*, 3rd ser., cxxv, 1350–423. This was Gladstone's budget statement.

Tuesday – April 19

I like G's plan amazingly. After breakfast came a Mr Turner[1] to talk about the law of copyright. I went to W.T. walked with dear B – long and pleasant chat with H. The day went very fast. In the evening some of RR. Parr's Dedication of Tracts.

---

1. Perhaps Alfred Turner (1797–1864), a London solicitor, of 32 Red Lion Square, member of a family firm that specialised in literary copyright law. He advised Murray and Longmans. He was Secretary to the Association for the Protection of Literature established in 1843. See J. J. Barnes, *Authors, Publishers and Politicians* (London, Routledge & Kegan Paul, 1974), esp. ch. 6.

Wednesday – April 20

Wrote a little after breakfast – to the House to present petitions. Walked – Temple. Left a note – wrote to F about Oxford. Home – wrote a little but not amiss. Turned over the Foundling Hospital of Wit.[1] My respiration again affected after a long interval, but not much. At dinner Amaury[2] – soon gave in and read Sayings and Doings.[3]

1. Samuel Silence (pseud.), *The Foundling Hospital for Wit* (1743–9).
2. By Alexandre Dumas (*père*) (1844).
3. The collection title for nine novels written from 1826 to 1829 by Theodore Hook.

Thursday – April 21

Breakfast with Milnes – Senior – Murray was there – India Committee – Leith – good, but a little too voluble and discursive. Wrote a little – Sayings and Doings.

Friday – April 22

Writing and reading – British Museum – Bohun – Blount – Walker etc.[1] A new light struck me about Bohun's affair. S and D Φεδ.

1. *HE*, ch. 19, *CW*, vol. 3, pp. 633–44. Edmund Bohun was Licenser of the Press (see above, entry for 30 March 1853, n. 3). Charles Blount (1654–93) was a deist and an advocate of the liberty of the press, who sought to discredit Bohun by persuading him to license a book that led the Commons to call for his dismissal. Walker was presumably 'the honest old clergyman' who wrote a book claiming that John Gauden, not King Charles I, was the author of *Ikon Basilike* (*CW*, vol. 3, p. 634).

Saturday – April 23

Temple – saw E – W.T. walked with B – Mrs Rose *and* Mrs Price[1] to dinner – pleasant.

1. Lydia Babington Rose (1789–1880), Macaulay's cousin; her daughter was Mrs Price (1812–91).

Sunday – April 24

Bad day – hardly stirred out. T called – wrote and read. In the evening it was a little finer. I went to Lord Lansdowne's to a small dinner. Nobody but the family, Rutherfurd, and Ld and Lady H.[1] We had a pleasant evening. Poor R has suffered much but is better. We talked – after the ladies had left us

– about that strange jointure which George IV had made of his daughter and Leopold.[2]

1. Perhaps Lord and Lady Holland or else Hardwicke. See below, entry for 29 April 1853.
2. George IV's daughter Charlotte Augusta married Leopold of Saxe-Coburg, but died in childbirth in 1817.

Monday – April 25

To breakfast with Hallam. The Bp of Oxford, Milnes, the Duke of Argyle, Mahon, Inglis. Did not go to the India Committee today – bought tickets for myself and B to Thomas's lectures.[1] To the Museum to look again at this Bohun affair. Home and worked. E to dinner.

1. Alexander Thomas, an exiled Professor of the University of Paris, who lectured on the age of Louis XIV.

Tuesday – April 26

Lost the morning in sitting to Partridge – to W.T. took B to Thomas's lecture – very good it was – walked back with her – home – S and D. Wesley's journal.

Wednesday – April 27

Breakfast party – the people whom I met on Monday with Denison. Talk about electricity and the rotatory motion of tables under electrical influence. I was very incredulous. We tried the experiment on my table; and there certainly was a rotatory motion, but probably impressed by the Bishop, though he declared that he was not quite certain whether he had pushed or not. We tried again – then after we had given it up, he certainly pushed and caused a rotatory motion exactly similar to what we had seen before. The experiment therefore failed. At the same time I would not confidently say in this case, as I say in cases of clairvoyance that there must be deceptions. I know too little of electricity to judge.[1] Walked to the House of Commons and sate there a short time – out of sorts and out of tone – Φεδ– wrote a little. S and D. – Wesley.

1. There is another account of this experiment in the Duke of Argyll's *Autobiography and Memoirs*, 2 vols (London, 1906), vol. 1, pp. 405–7.

Thursday – April 28

After breakfast called on Rutherfurd – home and wrote letters etc. – to the India Committee – long and idle discussion. Everybody complained of the waste of time and went on wasting it. At dinner CO'M by Lever.[1] Wesley. A book came from Ld John. Memoirs of Fox[2]. I fell to – much interested. Yet I wish Ld J would not do what, situated as he is, it is impossible for him to do well.

1. *Charles O'Malley* (1840).
2. *Memoirs and Correspondence of Charles James Fox*, ed. Lord John Russell, 2 vols (1853).

Friday – April 29

Bad day. That fellow Ward[1] called – always crazy and now impertinent – not the painter – a vagabond who went mad about the Museum. I was forced to turn him out of the room. Finished Fox's memoirs – wrote – licensing. H called at 3 – we went to the National Gallery. The Exhibition very good indeed. Capital Landseers – one excellent Stanfield[2] – a very good Roberts. Ward good.[3] But I was struck by one obvious fault in the picture of Montrose's execution – a fault perhaps inseparable from such subjects. Montrose was a meanlooking man; and Ward thought it necessary to follow the likenesses and perhaps this was right. But all the other figures are imaginary, and each is, in its own way, striking. The consequence is that the central figure – the important figure – is not only mean in itself but made meaner by contrast. Now in pictures where all the figures are imaginary this will not occur, nor will it often occur in pictures where all the figures are real. There is one of the latter class by Ward in this very exhibition – Josephine signing the instrument of divorce. There all is as it should be. There was much Pre-Raphaelite trash – and one picture by Millais[4] which was an improvement on his old manner – another – Lovers in a Hollow Tree, bad beyond description. We met the Mahons – the Milmans – Ld Lansdowne – Ld Hardwicke.[5] Very bad cold raw weather. My chest was much affected. However after dinner C.O'M. I went down to the House and found that there was no chance of a division till Monday. So I went home and to bed.

1. Unidentified.
2. Perhaps *'The Victory' Coming in to Gibraltar with the Body of Nelson*, which was in this exhibition.
3. Edward Matthew Ward (1816–79). The two pictures referred to by TBM were *The Executioner Tying Wishart's Book Around the Neck of Montrose, at his Execution on 21 May 1650*, the first of a series of eight for the Houses of Parliament, and *Josephine Signing the Act of her Divorce at the Tuileries on 16 December 1809.*
4. *The Order of Release*, perhaps, which Lord Carlisle thought 'full of the highest merits of paintings and expression, and barely any Pre-Raphaellism [*sic*]' (Carlisle, J19/8/31, f. 10).
5. Charles Philip Yorke, fourth Earl of Hardwicke (1799–1873).

Saturday – April 30

Fine weather and warm – walked long – to W.T. Then to Regent Street in the carriage with H and B. Home – wrote – Wesley. E to dinner.

Sunday – May 1

To B[rooks] – to W.T. – home and prepared for the debate – the Judges' Exclusion Bill[1] – very satisfactorily I thought. At dinner – Lever's Charles O'Malley.

1. See below, entries for 4 May, 31 May and 1 June 1853.

Monday – May 2

Breakfast at the Bp of Oxford's – pleasant enough – thought a good deal about Ld H's Bill. After dinner C.O'[M]. Went to the House – heard D'I – and Ld J – neither was very good – triumphant division.[1] Glad to have been there. Home – at near 3 in the morning much exhausted and scant of breath.

1. Disraeli was speaking on the fourth night of the long debate on the budget. *PD*, 3rd ser., cxxvi, 963–93. Russell followed, 993–1004. The division is at col. 1004.

Tuesday – May 3

To breakfast, though not in great force, with the Mahons – pleasant but was forced to leave them early in order to sit to Grant. Denison took me to Grant's, and I met H there. G is a coxcomb but may be a very good painter, and is so, though not first rate.[1] With H to W.T. It was bad weather and I was knocked up by my late sitting in the H. of C. so I did not go to Thomas's – Home and passed a quiet evening. CO'M – Huntington.

1. Francis Grant (1803–78) was knighted in 1866, the year he was elected President of the Royal Academy. Perhaps 'coxcomb' was TBM's reaction to Grant's well-known aristocratic charm. The portrait is now in Trinity College, Cambridge, and is reproduced in Volume 1, p. xlvi.

Wednesday – May 4

Soon after breakfast to the H. Ld H's bill[1] did not come on. But I was glad to have an opportunity of voting against an absurd bill of Halford's[2] for restraining contracts between labourers and their employers. Drummond there. His wonderfully droll speech of yesterday is the universal topic.[3] Nothing could be cleverer. His attack on Rich was cruel, but yet deserved. Odd how soon a notion that I was to speak spread through the House. I was told that many came down to hear me. I am sorry for it – Home – heard from Oxford, and wrote to secure apartments. 15 Gns. for the rooms. I am quite content. Dinner – CO'M.

1. Lord Hotham's bill for excluding judges from the House of Commons. See below, entries for 31 May and 1 June 1853.
2. Sir Henry Halford, second Bart (1798–1868), was Conservative MP for South Leicestershire, 1852–7.

3. In the debate on bribery in the Chatham election of 1852, Henry Drummond made a racy and down-to-earth speech pouring scorn on those who thought that the use of influence could and should be eliminated, and made a scathing reference to the motion by Rich concerning the Government of India Bill. See *PD*, 3rd ser., cxxvi, 1069–74.

Thursday – May [5]

Thought a good deal about the ballot – visit from a French man about Lamartine's schemes – then changed my mind and resolved not to say anything on the subject this year at any rate, though I have much to say. Walked long – wrote a little – at dinner CO'M – finished.

Friday – May [6]

Not very pleasant day – deputation of Cork Cutters – wrote and read – H. called for me – to Thomas's lecture – Very good – to W.T. Happy evening – finished reading Roderick Random to them – Home.

Saturday – May [7]

To the Museum. Then to Stafford House – with H and B – stupid crowd – beautiful rooms – the superb Duchess most gracious to me.[1] Mrs Stow an ugly commonplace woman, but deserves great praise for not quite losing her head – her husband a charlatan – her brother a bore. The husband, before I came, had made an oration – poor creature! It was pouring with rain. I was glad however to give H and B the pleasure of walking through that magnificent house. Home – wrote – read half the βατραχοι[2] – struck by some metrical observations. To E's – dined and chatted pleasantly. Guzman D'Alfarache.

1. This was the Duchess of Sutherland's reception for Harriet Beecher Stowe. Her husband was Calvin Ellis Stowe (1802–86), who married her in 1836. Her son was Henry Ward Beecher (1813–87). Lord Shaftesbury made a speech on behalf of the Women of England, and the Duchess presented Mrs Stowe with a gold bracelet in the form of a slave's shackle. Lord Carlisle's account in his journal says the ovation TBM missed was by Mrs Stowe's brother. He gave one possible reason for TBM's unease: 'The Quakers mustered thick' (Carlisle, J19/8/31, ff. 15–16).
2. *The Frogs*.

Sunday – May 8

No fire in my bedroom – the first time for months. And yet a fire was as much wanted as in January – for it was very cold. G.D'A – To Br[ooks] – to W.T. Only Alice for near an hour – sweet child – Then B – Then my brother Charles. As he and I were going away H came. She had been to Clapham to see Mrs Synnot[1] who is very ill. Charles and I walked away talking about pictures – Millais, etc

– ballot etc. Read Theocritus. Wrote – Sir H. Holland called. At dinner La Mare au Diable[2] – Stuff.

1. Probably Henrietta (b. 1808), daughter of Henry Thornton of Clapham, who married Richard Walter Synnot (d. 1841). She died on 11 May, three days after this entry.
2. By George Sand (1846).

Monday – May 9

Breakfast party – Ld and Lady Mahon. Ld and Lady Hatherton. H, Dundas, Ld Glenelg, Hallam, the Bp of Oxford. Pleasant – Vile weather in the morning – then it cleared up and I walked home and wrote – got from Smith's in Soho Square some pamphlets – particularly Mrs Piozzi's correspondence with Conway.[1] Macleod called – read him something. Ellis to dinner – Message from Hayter begging me to go down.[2] Went immediately and would have staid if necessary: but he paired me satisfactorily. Glad to get home.

1. *Love Letters of Mrs Piozzi, Written When she was Eighty to W. A. Conway* (1843).
2. W. G. Hayter was the Liberal Whip.

Tuesday – May 10

Mare au Diable. An impudent letter from a fellow on Prince Edwards' Island begging me to send him all my works with my autograph in each volume – three or four pounds worth. To W.T. and thence to Willis's with H and B. By the way stopped at Fortnum and Mason's and gave H a pâté de foie gras for her banquet tomorrow. Lecture on the mistresses of L XIV especially on Mme de Maintenon. But it was such as B might hear without any impropriety. H called for her. Dined at home – M au D.

Wednesday – May 11

To breakfast at W.T. A great crowd – Ld Glenelg, Hallam, the Prices, the Diceys, the Milmans – to meet Mrs Stowe. I was next the Lioness and found her simple and sensible. We exchanged no compliments – no allusions to each other's writings. It was agreeable to me and I dare say to her that it was so. The party went off well. Home – and wrote. At dinner Fille du Regent.[1] W. Huntington.

1. By Alexandre Dumas (*père*) (1848).

Thursday – May 12

Read and wrote – to W.T. took B to Christie's to see Louis Philippe's Spanish pictures which are on sale there. One or two good Murillos – Velasquez too – a Philip the Second said to be by Titian – if not, it is a good copy. I made acquaintance with Zurbaran[1] a powerful painter though a mannerist and not of the most pleasant sort. There is an Adoration by Velasquez – remarkable in some respects, but not to my taste. Took B home in a cab – walked back – wrote – at dinner F du R.

1. Francisco de Zurbaran (1598–1664), Spanish painter.

Friday – [May 13]

To breakfast at Thomas's Hotel[1] with the Hatherton's – Hallam, D'Azeglio,[2] Miss Fazakerley – not unpleasant – then home – read and wrote. At two Ld Lansdowne called very kindly. Before he went B came to go with me to Thomas's. Ld L says that the Trustees of the National Gallery have bought for a great price the Adoration[3] which I saw yesterday and which did not much take my fancy. To Willis's – good lecture from Thomas on the high monarchical doctrines held by the French of the age of L XIV. H called for B – Home – wrote and read. F du R.

1. In Berkeley Square, West Side.
2. Massimo Taparelli, Marquese d'Azeglio (1798–1866), Prime Minister of Piedmont, 1849–52. He was sharing a studio at this time with the sculptor Marochetti, and selling his own paintings.
3. 2,050 guineas. *Annual Register* (1853), p. 64.

Saturday – May 14

I walked much this morning – then home and wrote – to dinner with Ellis – Hallam – H and T – the Pagets[1] – Cleasby[2] – Ryan – Miss Gayangos. It was not amiss – Hallam very cheerful – Fry on Moravians.[3]

1. The strongly legal flavour to this gathering suggests that these were John Paget the barrister (1811–98) and his wife Elizabeth (*c.* 1813–98), daughter of William Rathbone of Liverpool (1787–1868). Paget was the son of a Leicester banker and he was called to the bar in 1838. At this time he was Secretary to the Lord Chancellor, Cranworth.
2. Probably Anthony Cleasby (1804–79), a Fellow of Trinity, and a barrister, then a Baron of the Exchequer; later knighted.
3. Unidentified. SC, no. 587, is 'Moravians, tracts relating to by Lavington, Russius, and others in one vol.'.

Sunday – May 15

Wrote after breakfast – then to B[rooks] – then across the park to W.T. sate an hour and back – wrote – Swift – Temple etc. at dinner F du R – Moravians.

[Sunday – May 15]

Wrote – B [rooks] – W.T. a short time with H – walked home – wrote and read – finished F du R.

Monday – May 16

After breakfast to Grant's – fine day – the first summer day. A sitting made agreeable by H. She read some papers of the Spectator and we chatted between whiles. Took her home – then walked – Covent Garden – sent home some asparagus and grapes – Home and wrote – E to dinner.

Tuesday – May 17

Wrote and read – Then to W.T. took B first to Christie's where there was a new batch of Spanish pictures – hardly equal to the former – then to Willis's where Thomas lectured well – then to W.T. dined there and read in the evening some of my history. Debt – Parl[iamen]tary reform. They seemed pleased – but H and B agreed that I read my own compositions very ill. Grenville correspondence[1] from Murray Vols 3 and 4.

1. Perhaps *The Grenville Papers*, ed. W. J. Smith (1852–3).

Wednesday – May 18

Grenville Correspondence. Interesting, but a stupid editor. Ward came at eleven. I had a long sitting. I am tired to death of these sittings. He did not go till three; and would not have gone then if I had not sent him away. I walked some time – wrote. At dinner Mrs Armytage[1] – finished Grenville Correspondence.

1. By Catherine Gore (1836).

Thursday – May 19

Another sitting. To Grant's. Dearest B came. She read two or three of Elia's essays. Grant is droll and a coxcomb, but a good painter. Took B to W.T. Then with her and her Mamma to Regent Street – House of Commons – petitions – Home wrote and read – Mrs A – Swift.

Friday – May 20

Went into the city – ordered the first instalment to be paid for my new L & N.W. Stock – home calling by the way in the Temple – wrote – to call on Professor Aytoun[1] – who had called on me. He wished to speak with me on University business. I was very polite, I hope – but I have no great fondness for the Professor who is certainly clever, but I think a great humbug. To Willis's – Excellent lecture from Thomas – the last. Shook hands with him – poor fellow! I wish I could serve him. He thanked me for attending him. I really did so for my own pleasure and profit – Home – wrote – Mrs A – Swift.

1. William Edmonstoun Aytoun (1813–65) was Professor of Rhetoric and Belles Lettres at Edinburgh. He married Jane Emily Wilson, daughter of 'Christopher North', and like his father-in-law wrote regularly for *Blackwoods*. His *Lays of the Scottish Cavaliers* (1849) owed much to Scott's poetry and TBM's *Lays of Ancient Rome*.

Saturday – May 21

After breakfast walked into the city merely for a walk – home – wrote – Macleod called – letter from Thomas – I wish I could be of use to him. Finished Campaign of 1693. Began Smyrna fleet[1] – Swift. Sent for Dumas's Spéronare.[2] A look at it was enough. To dinner with Ld Clarendon – after a long interval. A large party – some foreigners unknown to me – Labouchere and his wife, Lewis, Lady Theresa and Lady T's daughter,[3] Wood and Lady Mary, Charles Greville – in the evening Ld John Ld Lansdowne etc. Ld C complained that he was overworked and seemed sick of office – Lady C the same.[4] He is at it 12 hours a day – the D. of Newcastle 15. Thank heaven that I am not such a slave.

1. *HE*, ch. 20, *CW*, vol. 4, pp. 27–9.
2. By Alexandre Dumas (*père*) (1842).
3. By Thomas Lister (1800–42), Theresa Villiers had a son Thomas (1832–1902) and two daughters, Marie Thérèse (1836–63) and Alice Beatrice (1842–98). TBM must have met the elder sister, who became the wife of Sir William Harcourt.
4. She had been Lady Katherine Barham (d. 1874). She married Clarendon in 1839.

Sunday – May 22

Wrote a little – Smyrna Fleet– B[rooks] – W.T. – then home wrote a little more – but it did not come easy – read debates and pamphlets – on the whole my subject clears before me – at dinner Mrs A.

Monday – May 23

After breakfast to Rogers – the dentist – could not see him. To Grant's painting room – B came and read some of my paper on Addison. Her Mamma called for us. Back to Rogers's – learned that nothing can be done. I must bear the pain which is not very severe – E to dinner.

Tuesday – May 24

To the Museum – collected a little matter there – home and wrote the Smyrna Fleet – tolerable – At dinner Albert.[1]

1. Perhaps Albert Smith; see below, entry for 29 May 1853.

Wednesday – May 25

Ward for my Sins. He sate all day in the room filling it with the smell of paint. At one I went out – came back at four and found him still there. He has made me uglier than a daguerreotype.[1] However he is a clever fellow. When he was gone I wrote something. I am reading Swift – and Albt.

1. This portrait is now in the National Portrait Gallery.

Thursday – [May 26]

To breakfast with Milman. To my vexation Hayward was there – a smart fellow but bad and offensive to the last degree. Hallam – Brewster. I tried to get tickets for the Theatre – but I fear to little purpose. Home – read and wrote – to W.T. to dinner.

Friday – May 27

Burning day – found walking very hard exercicse – read – wrote. To dinner with E – family party – Rain began.

Saturday – May 28

Rain and hail by violent fits. To W.T. – thence to Kensington Gore to see Wilberforce's old house, now turned into a Museum of cabinet work and tapestry. The old rooms interested me altered as they are. The gallery upstairs I remembered well and my game of blind man's buff there near 42 years ago. The garden even better than I recollected it. Home read a good deal in M.S.S. about Harley, Somers etc – E to dinner – forced to have a fire.

Sunday – May 29 –

Weather unsettled – wrote – Hotham – much and to the purpose – B[rooks] – W.T. – In the evening χταδ[1] and Swift.

1. TBM's abbreviation for *Christopher Tadpole*, the novel by Albert Smith.

Monday – May 30

Sitting again. Uncertain weather. H came to Grant's – read Johnson's Life of Swift. I took her home. Then to the Albany – wrote letters and a little Hot[ha]m – now nearly complete – Then Sunderland – at dinner χταδ – Swift.

Tuesday – May 31

Thought of Ld H's bill.[1] Craig called and sate two hours. His account of the state of things at Edinburgh is as good as possible. I went to the R.I. and to Brooks's – then home and thought again over this bill – at dinner χταδ – In the evening the bill. Anxious and apprehensive of complete failure. Yet I must stand the hazard.

1. Beaumont Hotham, third Baron Hotham (1794–1870), MP for East Riding (1841–68). His bill sought to exclude judges from the House of Commons.

Wednesday – June 1

A day of painful anxiety and great success. I thought that I should fail, and, though no failure can now destroy my reputation which rests on other than parliamentary successes, it would have mortified me deeply. I was vexed to find how much expectation had been excited. I was sure that I should not, however well I might speak, satisfy that expectation. However down I went – first we were three hours on an Irish criminal law bill. Then the Judges Exclusion Bill came on – Drummond moved to put off the 3rd reading for six months, and spoke tersely and keenly, but did not anticipate anything at all important that had occurred to me. When he sate down nobody rose. There was a cry of divide. Then I rose. The House filled and was as still as death – a great trial to the nerves of a man returning after an absence of 6 years to an arena where he had once made a great figure. I should have been more discomposed if I had known that my dear H and B were in the gallery. They had got tickets; but kept their intention strictly secret from me, meaning, if I failed, not to let me know that they had witnessed my failure. I spoke with great ease to myself, great applause, and, better than applause, complete success. We beat Lord Hotham by more than a hundred votes,[1] and everybody ascribes the victory to me. I was warmly congratulated by all my friends and acquaintance. In the midst of the first tumult of applause a note was handed to me from B – to say that she and her Mamma were above. I went up to them while Ld H was stammering through a wretched attempt at reply. They were very kind and very happy. To have given them pleasure is to me the best part of this triumph. To be sure I am glad to have stopped a most mischievous course of legislation, and to find that, even for public conflict, my faculties are in full vigour and alertness. I walked towards the Treasury with H and B. We met Trevelyan by the way. He had heard a flattering account of what had passed from my brother Charles and Macleod who were in the gallery. Craig, I hear, was also in the gallery; and his kind heart will be pleased with my success. Home – at dinner χταδ – knocked up.

1. The bill was rejected by 224 votes to 123. Macaulay's speech is printed in *PD*, 3rd ser., cxxvii, 996–1008, and reprinted in his Collected *Speeches* (London, 1854), pp. 521–38; *CW*, vol. 8, pp. 429–42.

Thursday – [June 2]

After a bad night rose with a disagreeable toothache or rather faceache. To breakfast with Mahon – Marochetti[1] – Azeglio. I hear much of my victory of yesterday. In truth I threw Ld H's bill out; and I doubt whether any other man could have done it, at least by such a majority. I wrote a little, but I shall hardly settle to work again till I come back from Oxford. To W.T. – pleasant afternoon there – Fanny and Selina came. We had a cheerful dinner. Charles came in the evening.

1. Baron Carlo Marochetti (1805–67). Italian sculptor. See below, entry for 4 June 1853.

Friday – June 3

After breakfast. Maitland came – The Ld Provost and some Baillies are coming up to bore the Govt about the Annuity Tax. Before Maitland went Fanny came with the two dear girls. I read them the battle of Landen[1] which they applauded – walked with them to Oxford Street – then to Downing Street – saw Ld Aberdeen's private Secretary and begged him to arrange a meeting for tomorrow. Walked to the Temple – saw E – to the H. of C. Wood on India[2] – ['abominably' deleted] long and dull and feeble. He evidently wanted confidence. I could have made all the same points in a third part of the time. I went away at the end of the 2nd hour – dined – and to the Palace. A concert – a great crowd – chatted and strolled about the picture gallery with the Chancellor[3] – met many other friends – saw Romilly – did not go to him – but wondered a little that he did not come to me. Went home after the first Act with a pain in my face, as usual. Glad to be in bed.

1. *HE*, ch. 20, *CW*, vol. 4, pp. 20–7.
2. Sir Charles Wood's speech introducing his Government of India Bill lasted five hours. *PD*, 3rd ser., cxxvii,1092–169.
3. Lord Cranworth.

Saturday – June 4

Read Wood's speech – The plan a great improvement on the present system. Some of Bright's objections are absurd and the rest greatly exaggerated. But I fear that the feebleness of W's speech and the vigour of Bright's[1] will do harm. On the 2nd reading I will see whether I cannot deal with the Manchester Champion. To a meeting at Willis's about Marochetti's Richard Coeur de Lion.[2] Very well managed. Thence to Downing Street where Ld Aberdeen was to receive us at two. I presented the Lord Provost who told his story well. Ld A, as I had forseen, gave them fair words, but referred to Ld J, as manager of the H. of C. We went to the Pay Office to look for Ld J; but he was not there. Moncrieff undertook to see him, and I to write to him. Home – found Macleod and walked with him to W.T. where I was to have walked with B. She had gone out in the carriage, despairing of my coming. Home. My face plagues me: but, as I hear that many people are affected in the same way, I take courage. I wrote to excuse myself from dining with the Bp of London. Dined at home – Ch Ta. Swift's Sermons. Very kind letter from Romilly.

---

1. *PD*, 3rd. ser., cxxvii, 1169–94. Bright criticized Wood for praising the government of India *and* calling for its reform. He recalled TBM's speech on the India bill of 1833, one clause of which declared that it would choose its employees without regard to colour, caste, religion or place of birth. But he said that its record was one of neglecting the masses of India, and spending the revenue on expensive wars and lavish salaries.
2. Baron Carlo Marochetti's model of the statue of Richard I had been shown at the Great Exhibition in 1851; the statue itself was placed in Old Palace Yard in 1860.

Sunday – June 5

Ellis to breakfast at 2 after 10. Walked with him in the Park – to W.T. pleasant hour there – Brooke's – Home – read Burton History of Scotland[1] etc etc. At dinner χταδ. Packing etc.

---

1. John Hill Burton, *History of Scotland from the Revolution to 1748* (1853).

Monday – June 6

Up early – to W.T. to breakfast. Frank and his sisters came.[1] Pleasant party – dear little Alice very amusing. We set off at eleven. Got to Oxford soon after one – found our rooms in the High Street very handsome and comfortable. The ladies lunched; and we sallied out – first to All Souls which interested them much – then to Magdalene [*sic*] which delighted them far more. Marian and Louisa had never seen any college before. Then to New College – the Chapel and the charming garden, looking more charming than ever. Then to St John's College and garden, also very beautiful. Thence to our lodging. Anxious about tickets. We dined at six. While we were at table Chambers the Tutor of Worcester called.[2] H became acquainted with him at the time of William Trevelyan's illness.[3] Nothing could be kinder. From Chambers we got two tickets. A Mr Marriott[4] promised us a third; we have two chances of a fourth. At sunset I took the three girls to Christ Church and walked with them round the Quadrangle. Frank had started for London. Home to tea. I looked into D'I's Henrietta Temple.[5] Poor stuff.

---

1. Frank, Marian and Louisa Ellis, children of T. F. Ellis.
2. Presumably William Chambers (1827–1910), Fellow of Worcester College, 1852–65; Vice-Provost, 1860.
3. Charles Trevelyan's brother (1812–95), who matriculated at Worcester in 1848 (aged thirty-six).
4. Perhaps Charles Marriott (1811–58), Fellow of Oriel, 1853–8; Vicar of St Mary's, 1850–8.
5. Disraeli's *Henrietta Temple* was published in 1837.

Tuesday – June 7

Letter from Wood. He is nervous about his bill and me. Answered him. The two tickets came. All the ladies set off for the Theatre, and I walked to Worcester with Chambers. He is a very intelligent and well read man – with a little of Academic stiffness about his manner particularly with ladies, to whom he is Academically attentive. I liked him much. At Worcester the Doctors present and future were assembling round the Hall door and within the Hall. I shook hands with many acquaintances – friends I can hardly say – for most of them were my political opponents. Then we marched in procession, all in scarlet, to the Schools. There the Doctors in futuro staid while the Doctors in praesenti went into the Convocation. In half an hour we were admitted in single file – Ld Blandford[1] leading the way. The coup d'oeil of the Theatre was very fine. When I entered somebody in the gallery called out "History of England". There came a great tumult of applause and hissing: but the applause greatly predominated. I was pleased with Ld D's reception of his son[2] – "fili mi dilectissime". This was loudly cheered. Phillimore[3] did his part well. The Latinity of the speech with which he presented me was very good. The galleries applauded me much with a very slight mixture of hissing. I saw H and B in one part of the theatre – Marian and Louise in another, *and* was glad to think how well we had managed. After shaking hands with Ld D I took my seat among the Doctors. Nobody was so well received as I, except Ld Stanley and D'I[sraeli]. There was a good deal of hissing at D'I. But the effect was to make the applause more vehement and longer. Then came a dull Latin oration by the public orator[4] – then some Greek Sapphics which, as far as I could follow them, seemed good, some Greek Iambics which were so ill recited – from agitation – that I could hardly catch a word – two tolerable English poems – an

English Essay, read short, and some Latin verse which did not strike me as excellent. After the Convocation I went with the ladies to Worcester. There was a handsome collation in a tent – a horticultural show in four or five other tents, a great crowd, and a delicious mixture of shade and sunshine. Thence I went home to rest myself till it was time to dress for dinner at Worcester. We met in the Library. There was a really handsome banquet in the Hall. I had Phillimore on one side, which was very well – but Warren[5] on the other which was intolerable. After dinner came all sorts of silly spouting. I went away soon after ten, seeing that people were leaving their seats, returned to my lodgings took the ladies to the town hall where there was a ball, and went home to bed. They staid at the ball till past midnight.

---

1. John Winston Spencer Churchill (1822–83), Marquis of Blandford and later seventh Duke of Marlborough.
2. Lord Derby, Chancellor of the University, conferred an honorary LLD on his son, Lord Stanley.
3. Joseph Phillimore (1775–1855), Regius Professor of Civil Law, 1809–55.
4. Richard Michell, BD (1815–77), Vice-Principal of Magdalen Hall and later first Principal of Hertford College.
5. Samuel Warren (1809–77), the author of *Ten Thousand a Year*, who had also received the honorary degree of DCL.

Wednesday – June 8

Another gloriously fine day. We were at breakfast when Chambers called. I was vexed to find that, after I had left the Hall of Worcester, the VC[1] gave my health. It mattered not much to be sure; for others whose healths were given had also left – Ld St L[2] among them. I took the ladies to Oriel where a polite fellow struck by my scarlet gown insisted on being our Cicerone. He did not learn who I was till we had seen everything and were going away. To Christ Ch – showed them the Hall and the Cathedral – then to Christ Ch meadow – then to Merton which charmed them extremely – the old library and the garden especially – then home for a little rest – then to lunch at All Souls in the Hall. I sate next the Dean of Winchester.[3] Then we saw the Library and Chapel. Then to the Radcliffe Library. H sate below. I and the girls went up to the leads and enjoyed the prospect – then to Magdalene taking Queen's by the way. Queen's none of them liked, nor would they admit that, however open to criticism in itself, it adds to the grandeur of the High Street. At Magdalen we were welcomed by the Dean Dr Bloxam[4] who is a great admirer of my book and grateful as a Magdalene man ought to be, for what I have said of the college. We walked about it with him and were admitted into the Chapel by a postern. The service was pleasing, though I had much rather hear the prayers well read than chanted. Home to dress for the dinner at Christ Ch. I was but just in time. They were saying Grace. I got to table between Ld Dynevor[5] and Walpole,[6] and made a very good meal. The hall looked very noble. The party must have been about four hundred – all members of the College except the strangers and the great University Dignitaries. I was amused to see before the Dean[7] a huge cheese cake as it appeared – it turned out to be a marrow pudding. After dinner the speechifying began – but less in quantity and better in quality than the speechifying of yesterday. The Dean uttered only words of form. He seems to be a mere heavy taciturn, sluggish, pedant. Ld Derby and Gladstone spoke well, and received pretty equal applause. What struck me most was the intensity and exclusiveness of Christ Ch feeling which appeared in all that was said. One would have thought that Christ Ch was Oxford. There was no risk of my health being given here, as the Dean strictly confined himself to official toasts. The Chancellor – High Steward,[8] Burgesses etc. Glad to be at our lodgings again – pleasant chat with H and the girls.

---

1. Richard Lynch Cotton, DD (1794–1880), Provost of Worcester College 1839–80; Vice-Chancellor 1852–6.
2. Lord St Leonards: Edward Burtenshaw Sugden (1781–1875), Lord Chancellor, February–December 1852.
3. Thomas Garnier (1776–1873), Dean of Winchester, 1840–72.
4. John Rouse Bloxam (1807–91), Fellow of Magdalen College, 1835–63; he was bursar, librarian and Vice-President, but never Dean. His interest in TBM's *History* was recorded in his collection of documents on *Magdalen College and James II* (1886).
5. George Rice, fourth Baron Divenor (1795–1869).
6. Spencer Walpole, lately Home Secretary, who had been given the degree of DCL.
7. Thomas Gaisford (1779–1855). He had been Dean since 1831.
8. William Courtenay, tenth Earl of Devon (1777–1859). He was High Steward from 1838. The two Burgesses were TBM's friend Sir Robert Inglis and W. E. Gladstone.

Thursday – June 9

Not so fine a day. Indeed some rain fell. Chambers came with his usual indefatigable kindness and gallantry. He had got three tickets for ladies to the Divinity Schools to see the procession – They had no wish to go again to the Theatre. B. insisted on ceding her ticket to Louise, and walked with me through Brazen nose while the others went into the schools. I was taking her home when Chambers overtook us with another ticket. I consigned her to his care and joined the muster of Doctors in the Radcliffe Library. I congratulated Grote and Mure[1] – Grote with special warmth: for he has really, with all his faults of style, done wonders. I also shook hands with Sir E. Lytton. I walked in the procession to the Divinity School – then fell out of file and joined the ladies. Another day of the Theatre would have killed me. I pointed people out to them till the procession had disappeared. Then we went, Chambers always with us, to Wadham. Though the day was but dull the building and garden were charming – then to Trinity, Balliol and St John's – we got into St John's Library which I have never seen since June 1812, but of which I retained some vivid recollections. I recollected particularly the Charles I with the Book of Psalms written in the lines of the face – a thing for a child to notice and remember. Then to the front of Christ Ch and home through Christ Ch. Paid bills – our host tried to extort five pounds extra from me, but failed. Then to the station and to London. It was some time before I could get Marian and Louise into a cab at Paddington. We parted at last. I came home, dined, read χρ ταδ at dinner. To bed very much tired.

1. George Grote and Col. William Mure of Caldwell (1799–1860), MP for Renfrewshire. Mure was a classical scholar, and member of the Club (see *LM*, vol. 5, p. 401n.). TBM had defeated him in the election for the Lord Rectorship of Glasgow.

Friday – June 10

Lounged about all the morning – thought about India – must speak – over Waterloo Bridge – χρ ταδ. To the H. of C – chat with Grey – Glad to find that the ministers are certain to carry their India Bill[1] – Paired for tonight – to W.T. dined there – pleasant.

1. For establishing recruitment by open examination for the Indian Civil Service, and so ending the patronage of the Directors. It also extended the authority of the Governor General and strengthened the legal side of his council.

Saturday – June 11

Delightful day – forced to go to the B.M. – passed some time there – home – fetched up Journal – E to dinner.

Sunday – June 12

Dull day – B[rook]s's – walked long in gardens – to W.T. – pleasant – then to E's. We went to Greenwich together and dined there.

Monday – June 13

To breakfast with the Bp of Oxford, Inglis, Ld and Lady Ashburton, Milman, Milnes, etc – To the Athenaeum – very rainy – read a good while – home and to Grant's – H met me there and read and chatted during the sitting. Well that she did: for Grant would bore me to death. However he paints good portraits. To the H. of C. I must speak on the 2nd reading of the India Bill – ill I fear – but we will see what we can do. Sorry to hear how ill poor Tufnell is: – talked with Clay[1] in the lobby about a scheme of his for taking the votes – home to dinner χρ ταδ – wrote letters in the evening – one to Christison[2] about M.D. degrees which gave me much trouble.

1. Perhaps Sir William Clay (1791–1869), Liberal MP for Tower Hamlets, 1832–57; Secretary of the Board of Control, 1839–41.
2. Robert Christison (1797–1882), medical professor at Edinburgh 1822–77, an expert on poisons; created a baronet, 1871.

Tuesday – June 14

A letter from Tauchnitz enclosing bills for £114.16. These Germans are good customers. After breakfast to the city with my bills – then to W.T. Chatted with H the girls and went with H and A to Hyde Park Corner – thence walked home – looked over the newspapers containing the India debate – poor stuff generally particularly the performances of Young India. To dinner with the Club. Not a very good meeting – Sir G. Staunton, our Doyen, Milman, Pemberton Leigh, Sir H. Holland and Lord Glenelg.

Wednesday – June 15

To breakfast with Milnes – his sister and wife[1] – Ld Stanley, the Duke of Argyle, etc. etc. – home – to W.T. took B to the British Gallery – not a very good exhibition for that Gallery – but some fine things. I was wonderfully lucky in guessing at the artists. I guessed three Ruysdaels, all good – a Hobbema – a Vandevoelde – a Domenichino – a Wouvermans – several Claudes and Cuyps.[2] There was a fresco by Michael, finely drawn no doubt but not much to my taste.[3] I never saw Reynolds to so little advantage. There was a caricature painted by him in Italy, and curious only as having been painted by him.[4] There was a Salvator which I was pleased to see because the thought has occurred to me. An oak struck by lightening – The Augurs looking at it in dismay.[5] Took B home – then to dress for a dinner at the Prices, – pleasant enough. Lydia, the Lewises, The Merivales, Professor Vaughan from Oxford,[6] H and T – dressed for the Queen's ball – I staid late.

1. Milnes's sister, Henrietta Eliza (*c.* 1814–91), married George Edward Arundell, sixth Viscount Galway, who was Conservative MP for East Retford, 1847–76. Milnes married Annabella Hungerford (1814–74), daughter of John, second Lord Crewe.
2. All listed in A. Graves, *A Century of Loan Exhibitions, 1813 to 1912*, 5 vols (London, 1913). There were four pictures by Jacob Ruysdael (1630–82); the Hobbema was *Landscape, Summer*; the Willem van de Velde (1633–1702) was *A Calm*; the Domenichino was *St Cecilia*; there were four by Philip Wouverman (1614–68); three Claude Lorraines, and four Albert Cuyps (1605–91).
3. There were two frescoes by Michelangelo, painted with Sebastiano del Piombo.
4. Reynolds's 'caricature' was of Lord Wicklow, and there were three other portraits.

5. This was lent by Lord Derby.
6. Henry Halford Vaughan (1811–85), Regius Professor of Modern History, 1848–58. A reformer who advocated a strengthened Professoriate that would 'investigate, reflect and write', he mostly did the first two.

Thursday – June 16

Breakfast with Mahon, a prettyish daughter of Lord Chesterfield.[1] Ld Stanley – etc. Walked – thought about the India Bill – not very easy at having to speak, nor readily seeing my way. To the H. of C at four. Keogh's explanation.[2] Ld Naas and Beresford[3] made a mighty poor figure – home to dinner – E came – H fes – Read Crabbe's posthumous poems and life.

1. Lady Evelyn Stanhope (1834–75). She was the only daughter of the sixth Earl of Chesterfield. She married the Earl of Carnarvon in 1861.
2. William Nicholas Keogh (1817–78) was an Irish Roman Catholic Conservative MP for Athlone. His acceptance of office as Solicitor-General for Ireland in Aberdeen's ministry of December 1852 offended the extreme wing of the Irish party and also some Conservatives. It was attacked by Lord Westmeath in the Lords. Keogh's explanatory speech is in *PD*, 3rd ser., cxxviii, 257–74. In Palmerston's ministry of 1855, he became Attorney-General for Ireland.
3. Ibid., 274–285. William Beresford was MP for the Northern Division of Essex.

Friday – June 17

Thought about India. Walked to W.T. – took H to see the British Gallery – then to the New Water Colours – some pretty landscapes, buildings – pieces of still life. The history all bad – to dinner with E – Baron Green[1] was there.

1. Richard Wilson Greene (1792–1861), Baron of the Court of Exchequer of Ireland, 1852–61.

Saturday – June 18

Waterloo day – no Waterloo banquet. He is gone – fine old fellow. Thought much about India and saw my way more clearly – went to Holborn and bought a book – H. Carey's poems[1] – another – Ld Gambier's Trial[2] – walked home. Macleod came at three. We talked two hours and a half about India. I learned something. I think that I shall probably do some good. Read Fletcher – Bonduca[3] – dined alone – χ ταδ.

1. Henry Carey (1687–1743), author of 'Sally in our Alley'. His poems were published in 1713.
2. *Minutes of the Trial of … James Lord Gambier* (1809). This trial was a court martial, demanded by Admiral Gambier himself, to rebut the charge that he was slow and over-

cautious in an action against the French fleet, brought by one of his junior officers, Thomas Cochrane. Gambier was acquitted.

3. Probably by John Fletcher and Francis Beaumont (1614, printed 1647).

Sunday – June 19

Bad weather – Brooks's – W.T. talked with T about India – They liked my line of battle. Home – read – at dinner χ τ. Sleepy in the evening.

Monday – June 20

Up before seven and to work. Not very genially at first. Again after breakfast and was better satisfied. To W.T. to walk with B. Wet and my teeth plaguing me – took her to Westminster Hall and back by cab. Then home myself. E to dinner. Milton Death and Sin Statuette.

Tuesday – June 21

Up again pretty early and worked. Again after breakfast and got on well. T came and gave useful hints – Rain and my teeth plaguing me. I staid at home. Found that the Mining Test Bill is fixed for Friday when I mean to speak on India. On both subjects I cannot speak the same day. Read newspapers of 1771 – strange deposition in the Grosvenor case.[1] At dinner χ ταδ – Dunciad. Letter from Sir F Lewis inclosing the letters which I wrote from Calcutta to Miss Berry whose ex[ecut]or he is. How strange it is to read a letter written by one's self 18 years ago. I was moved to tears by the change, yet I am happier now than I was then.

1. The first Earl Grosvenor sued Prince Henry, Duke of Cumberland, for criminal conversation with his wife Henrietta in 1770. The jury awarded £10,000 damages against the Prince.

Wednesday – June 22

Up at seven – worked. At breakfast P came and then a stupid Glasgow professor – then Simpson hang him! to beg: Then I got to work again – my task is nearly done and in very good time – but how? We shall see. To Grant's through the rain. My teeth better, but still troublesome. Sate – Dear B read some papers from the first volume of the Rambler. The last sitting. Glad to have done with it. To W.T. with B. – home – This speech which I must make and which cannot be good for many reasons, distresses me. CT.

Thursday – June 23

Up early again – thought all the morning about this business. My teeth fortunately are better. The weather very warm. To the House to pair and make arrangements. They promised to adjourn the House for me.[1] Home to dinner – CT.

---

1. So that TBM would speak first in the debate. See below, entry for 24 June 1853, and Trevelyan, vol. 2, p. 271.

Friday – June 24

Looked at the debate – stupid – thought all day over my speech painfully anxious but, as usual, recovered courage as the time drew near. Went down at 5 – found that the debate was not to begin till past six and that Hume had adjourned the House, by some mismanagement of Ld J's. I had to follow him: but though it was the deadest time of the evening when I rose – about 20 minutes to 8. The House was very well filled. I spoke an hour and a half pretty well[1] – others say very well. I did not satisfy myself; but on the whole I succeeded better than I had expected – I was much exhausted though I had by no means exhausted my subject. H and B were again in the gallery without my knowledge, and were again much pleased. How much I love them. Got home, quite knocked up at ½ after 9 – dined – I had eaten nothing since breakfast. Read or tried to read Dumas Guerre des Femmes.[2]

---

1. *PD*, 3rd ser., cxxviii, 739–59. He approved of the reduction in the number of directors, and in the increased powers given to the Governor General. But the main thrust of his speech was in defence of the recruitment of Indian civil servants by competitive examination. To the objection that scholastic brilliance was not essential for a good administrator, he laid down a 'general rule' that 'those men who distinguish themselves most in academical composition when they are young, are the men who, in after life, distinguish themselves most in the competition of the world' (col. 753).
2. By Alexandre Dumas (*père*) (1845).

Saturday – June 25

Bad night. T called while I was in bed. I went to W.T. a little before one. They were much pleased – In the afternoon John Murray sent me the Memoirs of Sir H Lowe[1] just published – three vols – I fell to eagerly. At dinner G des F.

---

1. *History of the Captivity of Napoleon on St. Helena, from the Letters and Journals of ... Sir H. Lowe*. By W. Forsyth (1812–99), Fellow of Trinity College, 1835–42, and editor of the *Annual Register*.

Sunday – June 26

Before breakfast I finished the 3 Vols – There is much skip to be sure; and the editor is an ass. I am ashamed for Trinity College that such a man should be a Fellow. The book makes little change in my opinion. For I did not think ill of Sir

Hudson as most people and I thought worse of OM[1] for sometime back, than most people – Poor Sir H had a cruel fate. I doubt whether in his place the best of men would not have been just as much persecuted and decried. To Brooks's – to W.T. Macleod – Young Bryant[2] – Animated talk about the parliamentary orators of the last generation – walked to the Albany with Macleod. I think of speaking on Tuesday – The Scotch Tests[3] – but I doubt whether I shall be in force. My teeth are plaguing me again.

1. Barry Edward O'Meara (*c.* 1770–1836), author of *Napoleon in Exile* (1822).
2. Perhaps Henry Strickland Bryant (*c.* 1826–1919), a Trinity graduate and the son of Sir Jeremiah Bryant (*c.* 1783–1845).
3. TBM had spoken on this subject in the House of Commons on 9 July 1845. His speech is in *CW*, vol. 8, pp. 334–48. He was now asked to present a petition against parts of the Scottish Universities Bill, which he did on 28 June. Cf. *LM*, vol. 5, p. 325 and n. 2.

Monday – June 27

Up early – Scotch Tests. I do not think that I shall speak. My face is in pain, and the subject is one which I exhausted in 1845 and on which I cannot speak again without repeating myself. Went down to the House and paired. To dine with E tête à tête. Home. Getting into bed I received a note from Hayter to say that he had paired me. I was very unwilling to go out at that hour, and afraid of the night air – but I have a horror of the least suspicion of foul play. So I dressed and went down, settled the matter about the pairs, and came back at near twelve o'clock.

Tuesday – [June 28]

The day wet. My face bad – speaking out of the question – went down however at 12. Found to my great joy that the matter had been settled, and that there wd be no opposition. Home – wrote some of my history after a long interval. Macleod called. At dinner La Guerre des Femmes. Went to sleep soon after nine – This habit grows on me. Read a good deal about Swift – Orrery[1] – What trash! – Deane Swift.[2]

1. Presumably John Boyle, fifth Earl of Orrery, *Remarks on the Life and Writings of Dr. Jonathan Swift* (1752).
2. *An Essay upon the Life ... of Dr. Jonathan Swift* (1755).

Wednesday – [June 29]

D Swift. Examiners of 1710. Wrote a little. To the House at twelve thinking that the Annuity Tax Bill[1] wd come on. Found that I had been misled by a blunder in the votes. Nothing about that unfortunate question can be done without a blunder. Home. To dinner at W.T. after a pleasant walk with B. I tried to help her to learn something about Victor Hugo's life for her French master – but after rummaging the London Library and the Athenaeum we were forced to give it up – pleasant dinner and evening.

1. See below, entry for 19 July 1853.

Thursday – June 30

Swift's letters. Wrote about Anderton's Trial.[1] In the evening to the House – heard Wood[1] – better than his opening speech – part of D'I – poor stuff – went to the library and read Windham's speeches there – back – Ld J replied well. Capital division – It surprised both parties, I imagine. My carriage was waiting. I got home at ½ after 2 much knocked up.

1. *HE*, ch. 20, *CW*, vol. 4, pp. 30–3.
2. He was speaking on the second reading of the Government of India Bill. *PD*, 3rd ser., cxxviii, 1019–32. Perhaps TBM did not hear all of Disraeli's speech (1032–64), in which he was attacked (1052).

Friday – July 1

Bad night. Swift's letters. Wrote – Anderton – To W.T. at lunchtime – Dumas G des Femmes – Tooth not quite well.

Saturday – July 2

Good night. Tooth better. After breakfast to the Ld Advocate's office[1] – he was not there – to Fenton's Hotel[2] – caught him just getting into a cab – talked about a poor fellow whom Mrs Empson[3] wishes to provide for, and about the Annuity Tax. As to the Tax, I see that nothing will or can be done. To Ellis – sate and walked with him an hour – Home – wrote – Sunderland. I am pestered for subscriptions. Paid ten guineas today for Marochetti's statue – willingly – I like the work *and* I like the artist – five pounds to a Free Church School at Edinburgh unwillingly. Was asked to give a second subscription for Campbell's statue – not a farthing. He was a poor creature who wrote perhaps a hundred good and ten thousand middling or bad lines. The public does not care for him; and for that reason his booby biographer[4] calls on me to subscribe again. I will read the 3 vols of the stupidest of all lives first. To dinner with Adolphus – Pollock – Wightman[5] – Ellis. Some thing that I ate or drank disagreed with me. I had a bad night with indigestion.

1. James Moncrieff.
2. 63 St James's Street. Francis Henry Fenton was its proprietor.
3. Charlotte Wilkes Empson (*c.* 1815–97).

4. William Beattie, *Life and Letters of Thomas Campbell ...* (1849).
5. Perhaps Sir William Wightman (1784–1863), judge of the Queen's Bench since 1841.

Sunday – [July 3]

Not very well – to B[rooks]'s – to W.T. – Sir C Wood called at lunch time – long chat about Indian affairs – to Brooks's to meet the Ld Advocate who never came – walked over Westminster Bridge and got into a Greenwich stage – dined at the Trafalgar. I could not now walk as I used to do. Read G des F. Back by railway. Swift's letters.

Monday – [July 4]

After breakfast to St George's to see Miss Gore married.[1] Great crowd. But nobody seemed to care much about the matter – It was the noosing of a young – or rather ci-devant young – flirt to an old rake. The whole service was read without mercy. I never heard some parts of it before. I was glad to get away. Called at Vernon Smith's, and chatted with him about Indian affairs. Got Haydon's Memoirs.[2] Strange disagreeable book – one long record of impotent effort and of misery, pitiable though richly deserved. Dined alone – G des F. To the H. of C. talked with Wood and Drummond and home. I do not think that we shall hear much more of the Annuity Tax.

1. Mrs Catherine Gore's daughter Cecilia Anne Mary (1826–79) married Lord Edward Thynne (1807–84).
2. T. Taylor (ed.), *Life of B. R. Haydon From His Autobiography and Journals* (1853); cf. *LM*, vol. 5, p. 340 and n. 1.

Tuesday – July 5

To breakfast with Hallam – The Mahons, Milnes. I thought and so did Lady M that H was nervous and restless. But his daughter seemed cheerful; and her children are well. To W.T. walked with B. read Haydon – to dine with Ld Rosse.[1] The stupidest of all parties. Most of the people I did not know and there was not one person that I cared to meet. My tooth troublesome.

1. He was President of the Royal Society from 1848 to 1854. His Countess was a pioneer photographer.

Wednesday – July 6

On returning yesterday evening I found a letter from that vagabond Vizetelly[1] who has had the impudence to advertise an edition of my speeches by Special License. I have answered him as he deserves. A listless day. Finished H's disagreeable Book. To Holland House – much against the grain. I shall not be able to work till I get away from town – if then. Wrote to Longman desiring him to call tomorrow afternoon to consult about Vizetelly. Dined at Strutt's – small and not unpleasant party – Lady Cranworth,[2] the Prices, C. Howard.

1. Henry Vizetelly (1820–94), wood-engraver, journalist and publisher.
2. Laura Carr (*c*. 1808–68), daughter of Thomas W. Carr.

Thursday – [July 7]

To breakfast with Mahon – she looks remarkably well – The Argyles, Lady Evelyn Stanhope, Ld H Vane and Reeve. Home just in time for H B and A who came to lunch. They were very happy and I very happy to have them with me. To the National Gallery. Turner's Building of Carthage[1] is really a noble painting – equal to any Claude that I ever saw. Home – Longman. I shall publish my speeches in one Volume – The correcting etc will take some time but I do not know that I should have given that time to my history. I can retouch a speech as well in the country as in town. The history is quite a different matter. Dined and finished the Champagne which was opened for H and B – G d F. Finished Examiners of 1711 and 1712.

1. *Dido Building Carthage; or the Rise of the Carthaginian Empire*, exhibited at the Royal Academy in 1815; bequeathed by Turner to hang next to the two Claudes in the National Gallery. Turner had died in 1851.

Friday – July 8

Up early and off to Tunbridge Wells – took the Arabian Nights with me – unread for many years. The interest which they now excite is languid compared with what it was when I was a boy – languid compared with that of a novel which is a picture of human life – but still I read them with pleasure. A good breakfast at the Calverley Hotel – then househunting – chose well I think[1] – but the rent high – the situation excellent – back at 20 minutes after 1 – left William to complete the arrangements. Glorious weather. My tooth easier – yet I must see Rogers before I leave town. At dinner [illeg.] Russell. In the evening to the H. of C – India Committee – very dull – voted with the Govt. – Hollow – Saw that the opposition had no chance and went away.

1. He rented 1 Wellington Place.

Saturday – July 9

Arabian Nights – finished. Trevelyan came while I was at breakfast and read me a good deal of his evidence on Indian finance. His ability and vigour are great but I feel many doubts. To the wine merchant's and ordered a supply for my expedition – to Cawthorn's – to the City – drew 120£ – to Longman's. Our advertisement was a few hours too late. Vizetelly had got many copies subscribed for by the trade yesterday morning. The fellow, it seems, hanged himself not long ago, and was cut down. I suppose that he is ruined, and is catching at this twig. Bought in the Arcade a novel of Soulié's and another of Paul Féval's – a large supply of wine has just come in. At dinner Russell – after dinner walked to W.T. and chatted with them.

Sunday – July 10

After breakfast wrote letters – Brooks's – W.T. Macleod called. To call on Craig at the Vivians'.[1] He not at home. To Hallam. Chat about the inscription on Ld L's bust. To Brooks's – found Craig – vexed to find that this Annuity Tax will probably cut up my holiday. Home – dined at Holland House – superb place to be sure. It strikes me more generally than in old times – but the Library less – much less. The pictures are gone. The gloom is gone – The room looks less vast and antique than formerly.[2] Nothing could exceed the civility and kindness of both my Ld and Lady – Osborne and his wife,[3] Lady Davy, an Italian Countess and three or four people whom I did not know. I got on pretty well, but was glad to escape.

1. Craig's wife was Elizabeth Sarah Vivian (*c.* 1818–95), daughter of John Henry Vivian (1785–1855), MP for Swansea, 1833–55. The Vivians were ironmasters, and they lived at 101 Eaton Street.
2. For the redecoration of Holland House by Henry, fourth Lord Holland, see Lord Ilchester, *Chronicles of Holland House* (London, 1937), ch. 14.
3. Perhaps Ralph Bernal Osborne (1808–82), then Secretary to the Admiralty and MP for Middlesex, 1852–7. He married Catherine Isabella Osborne (*c.* 1819–80), and by royal licence added her name to his.

Monday – [July 11]

To breakfast with the Lewises – pleasant party – Hallam, Senior, Ld H. Vane, Elliot,[1] C Wood and Lady Mary – walked away with Hallam – home – made arrangements. Dined – read Swift. To the House – found that the ministers were certain to have everything their own way. Home and to bed.

1. Probably T. F. Elliot of the Colonial Office; see Volume 3, entry for 23 August 1852.

Tuesday – July 12

Up early – went out at eight leaving the servants ready to depart. Walked to Holborn – κρεμ– to the Athenaeum – breakfasted – a crust hurt my loose tooth severely and the pain did not quite leave me all day – read some time in the rooms above – Burke's correspondence – to W.T. saw them, chatted, and took leave. At ½ after 4 started from London Bridge – at The Calverley Hotel soon after 7. Dined there – read on the journey and at dinner Féval's Forêt Noire[1] – poor stuff. Then to my house – found everything ready and soon went to bed.

1. Paul Féval, *La Forêt Noire* (1852).

Wednesday – July 13

Breakfast at 9 – fine day, but not brilliant. Went to the Pantiles and The Grove. I had not seen the Grove since 1828 and I can hardly say that I had seen the Pantiles since. Sate in Nash's reading room[1] in the old well remembered corner looking out at the heath. Amused by seeing among the books the Self Tormentor 1789 – Sally More's novel[2] – unseen since 1816. Home and looked into the Annuity Tax question. I can make a good case I think, in plain language and concisely. Walked on the heath, finished La Forêt Noire. Read Plato's Phaedrus – wonderful irony, eloquence, ingenuity, fancy – what a state of morals – what a distortion of the imagination. Home at six – the weather seems likely to be wet. At dinner and afterwards the Veau d'Or – Electric Telegraph – alarmed – afraid of some mischief to H, B or A or G – only a message from Maitland that the Annuity Tax does not come on tomorrow. Baillie Douglas[3] called at nine to tell me the same. He has run down to the Wells for a single night.

1. In the Parade. Robert Nash (1807–80) was an actuary. He owned, besides a libary, a stamp-distribution business, a savings bank, an assembly and a billiard room.
2. Sarah (Sally) More (1743–1817), *The Self-Tormentor*, 3 vols (1789). It was published anonymously. She was a sister of Hannah More.
3. Francis Brown Douglas (1814–85), Advocate and Lord Provost of Edinburgh, 1859–62.

Thursday – July 14

Heaps of letters – wrote eight or nine answers. Then to my speeches – the speech of July 5 1831[1] – wrote vigorously during several hours. I could not go out; for the rain was falling by pailfulls and the wind blowing a hurricane. I wrote with great spirit or it seemed to me; remade a speech very like the real one in language, and in substance exactly the real one – very different from the wretched report in Hansard. I had half performed my task at five. I read some of Plato. At dinner Frédéric Soulié – Le Veau d'Or.[2] After dinner as it did not absolutely rain I strolled out for half an hour but was driven in.

1. *PD*, 3rd ser., iv, 773–83 (5 July 1831).
2. 1853.

Friday – July 15

The day fine but gusty and frequently overcast. I walked more and wrote less than yesterday. Read on the heath Plato's Lysis and most of the Protagoras. Socrates's childish quibbling provokes me. Surely Protagoras's reasoning is the better and more manly. I am much more convinced that the merit of Plato lies in his talent for narrative and description, in his rhetoric, in his humour and in his exquisite Greek. The introductions of the Phaedrus, the Lysis and the Protagoras are all three first rate. The Protagoras best. The imitations of the style of Prodicus and Hippias are very amusing, and, I dare say, like. As to Socrates, I do not wonder that they poisoned him. A pest of a fellow – his delight in humbling every body else, his mock humility, his quakerlike patience more provoking than any insolence, would have driven me mad. At dinner Soulié – Walked on the heath after dinner. Fine but cold and windy. The sky had a stormy look.

Saturday – July 16

The sky kept its word. Wind and rain. After breakfast I finished the speech of July 5, 1831, and began to rewrite the speech on the Metropolitan Members. A letter from Lady Anne Maria Donkin who is here.[1] Tant pis. However I must be civil – I must say nothing about Vizetelly hanging himself in casa de un dannato[2]. It cleared up a little at one. I went to the reading room. Walked home – finished The Protagoras – Went out again to call on Lady A.M.D. Found her and sate with her half-an-hour – then walked and read Plato or rather some sophist who tried to imitate Plato. The Laches is evidently spurious, and I think, the Charmides. The Euthyphron is more likely to be genuine though not one of Plato's best. At home read Lucian's Dream and Prometheus. At dinner Soulié. Had a fire in the evening. The weather very bad.

1. 1786–1855. She was the widow of Sir Rufane Donkin (1773–1841). TBM met her in 1832; see *LM*, vol. 2, p. 153, n. 2.
2. (Italian): 'in the condition of a damned man', but TBM's handwriting is hard to read.

Sunday – July 17

A much finer day – still windy however and with occasional showers. To church in the well remembered old building. It was, I imagine, the same which was built in Charles II's days and which the Tantivies[1] wished to dedicate to St Charles the Martyr. A bad sermon as usual. Walked long about the grove and heath – read a good deal of the Gorgias – my favourite dialogue or nearly so since my college days. Odd that such trumpery fallacies should have imposed on such powerful minds. Home and wrote out most of the speech of July 1831. Read some of Lucian's Nigrinus. At dinner Soulié. Walked for an hour or more. A fine evening.

1. Nickname given to High Churchmen and Tories in the reigns of Charles II and James II.

Monday – July 18

A doubtful looking day – The sun contending with the clouds. Studied the Edinburgh Annuity Tax question. I will try to make a Lysias like speech[1] on it. Read some of the Gorgias – finished the Nigrinus. Wrote a good deal of the speech on the Metropolitan Districts.[2] At dinner Soulié. Went out in the evening for a short time.

1. See Trevelyan, vol. 2, pp. 279n. Lysias was a forensic orator of the fourth century BC. TBM presumably meant to destroy 'the voluntaries'.
2. On 28 February 1832, *PD*, 3rd ser., x, 926–33; repr. in *CW*, vol. 8, pp. 79–85.

Tuesday – July 19

Up early – to the Station and to town. Drove instantly to the H. of C. Found the Ld Provost, Baillie Morrison and Maitland[1] in the lobby – short talk with them. A ridiculous mistake in the votes. Some fool has given an absurd notice about yachting, and my name has been put to it. At twelve business began – The Ld Advocate opened the matter. Then Smith M.P. for Stockport[2] I think made a furious voluntary speech against the Edinburgh clergy and proposed to read the bill again that day three months. A Mr Hadfield[3] seconded him and made an absurd speech against establishments without any H's. Then I spoke, without any preparation as to language, but with perfect fluency, and with considerable effect. I smashed Smith completely. I was heartily glad to have got it over. I have now done the handsome thing by my constituents.[4] The Ld Provost and the Baillie were loud in commendation. I have my doubts of his Lp's sincerity. It soon became clear that we should not be able to divide before four, so that the day would be lost. I was surprised at the excessive malignity and unreasonableness of the voluntaries. I have no particular love for establishments and priests. But the rancour of these men disgusts me. At the moment at which the clock struck 4 The Speaker rose; I ran to Palace Yard, got a cab and drove to the station. There I found dear H already in a carriage. We had a pleasant journey to Tunbridge Wells – The weather very fine. She liked the house and situation. We dined together cheerfully – then walked to the Pantiles and back and chatted till ten.

1. Duncan MacLaren was Lord Provost. Adam Morrison (*c.* 1801–75) and John Maitland.
2. John Benjamin Smith (1794–1879). He represented Stockport from 1852 to 1874. He had been the first Chairman of the Anti-Corn Law League, and as a Unitarian he was against any sort of Church establishment.

3. George Hadfield (1787–1879), MP for Sheffield, 1852–74, a Manchester solicitor and also a founder member of the Anti-Corn Law League.
4. *PD*, 3rd ser., cxxix, 451–60. This was Macaulay's last speech in the House of Commons. The House was counted out.

Wednesday – July 20

A fine day happily, and in all respects a pleasant one. After breakfast we walked down to the Pantiles – then to the parsonage to call on Pearson[1] – then home, – had much laughing by the way about the True Briton, a periodical edited, it seems by Miss Pearson. H lunched. Then an open carriage came and we drove to Frant – back by a pleasant road – saw the back of Lord Abergavenny's castle[2] – striking. Home. I wrote and she read. Then she worked and I read to her some of Beloe's Sexagenarian.[3] Pleasant dinner – and then a pleasant walk.

---

1. John Norman Pearson (1787–1865), Vicar of Holy Trinity, Tunbridge Wells, from 1839 to 1853; Miss Pearson is presumably his daughter.
2. Eridge Castle, designed in the 1820s by George Ledwell Taylor for the second Earl of Abergavenny (1755–1843); it was demolished in 1938–9, and replaced by an austere Georgian-style house designed by John Denman.
3. William Beloe, *The Sexagenarian* (1817).

Thursday – July 21

Another fine day spent like the last – After breakfast a walk to the Pantiles and to the Grove. H does not like, or affects not to like the Grove. Home. She lunched – The carriage again. Southborough – Bidborough – pleasant drive. Home – read and wrote. Mrs P called[1] – I read some of my history to H – dinner and a very agreeable walk on the heath.

---

1. Harriette Pearson, née Puller (1790–1870), was sister of Sir Christopher Puller, Chief Justice of Bengal.

Friday – July 22

Rain and mist. Very bad day. After breakfast we chatted some time. Then I took her down to the Station and saw her off. Home and sate down to work – The speech against Repeal in Feby, 1833.[1] Letter today from my landlord's agent. Referred him to the bank. I shall always pay my rent there. Read Lucian Timon. At dinner Soulié. Very cold – forced to have a fire.

---

1. The speech on the Repeal of the Union with Ireland (6 February 1833). *PD*, 3rd ser., xv, 250–64.

Saturday – July 23

Beautiful day after a vile day. Letter from H. T summoned to Enmore by electric telegraph. The end probably approaching.[1] Wrote much and well – Repeal – went to the Pantiles – then walked to Broom Hill to leave a card on Alderman Salomons[2] who had left one on me. A handsome seat, though a little Cockneyish – a very pretty walk. Home. By the way finished the Veau d'Or – Stuff, but amusing. To the station at six – E came. We had a very pleasant dinner and chat in the evening.

---

1. Charles Trevelyan's mother lived in Enmore, near Bridgwater. She died on 15 February 1854.
2. David Salomon (1797–1873). An alderman of the City of London, he was elected MP for Greenwich in 1857 but was disqualified because he would not take the oath. He was to become in 1855 the first Jewish Lord Mayor and was made a baronet in 1869. He owned the Broom Hill estate; his house was designed by Decimus Burton.

Sunday – July 24

Fine day. Meant to go to Church but we did not. We walked to Renthal Common – saw the Toad Rock and many other Rocks – the Pantiles – dull on a Sunday – The Grove. E lunched – Then we went in an open carriage to Frant and back by the same road that Hannah took me. The sky was overcast during our drive and some rain fell. Home. I read Lucian, and E corrected proofs. Dinner. Very cold – I had a fire in the drawing room and ordered the dessert to be put there. We had a long evening by the fireside.

Monday – July 25

Breakfast early on E's account. The fly too late, as before. I was very angry. However he just saved his distance. I wrote hard – finished the Repeal Speech and was pretty well satisfied. Transcribed the whole of the Metropolitan Borough Speech. In the course of the day I looked into Nash's and dawdled over some books. At dinner began Sue's Thérese Dunoyer.[1] Walked in the evening. A most beautiful evening. The effect of the distant town from the Pantiles was charming.

---

1. Eugene Sue, *Thérèse Dunoyer* (1842).

Tuesday – July 26

Another day of hard work. It was vile weather so there was no temptation to go out. I had many letters to answer first. By the bye I find that the Edinburgh people are much pleased with my speech on the Annuity Tax. I wrote the whole of the Jew speech of April 1833[1] and liked it better than I expected. I wrote to Alice who had sent me an amusing account of her playgoing. At dinner Sue's TD. Sate after dinner in the drawing room by a fire.

1. *PD*, 2nd ser., xxiii, 1308–14; repr. in *CW*, vol. 8, pp. 100–10.

Wednesday – July 27

Better weather – worked and read the Euthydemus on the heath. I find that my Edinburgh speeches will require less correction than my parliamentary speeches. In the evening TD. Pearson sent me today Aristotle's Politics. I found what I wanted.

Thursday – July 28

Another good day. Wrote – not with much heart – for it was that unfortunate speech on Buller's motion in 1840[1] – one of the few unlucky things in a lucky life. I cannot conceive why it failed. It is far superior to many of my speeches which have succeeded. But as old Demosthenes said the power of oratory is as much in the ear as in the tongue. How odd the fate of plays is – Why was the Double Dealer damned? Why the Way of the World?[2] Why the Britannicus? Why Athalie?[3] Walked, called on Pearson and returned his book – read the Theaetetus – liked it better than formerly – The frame of the dialogue is first rate. Back and wrote out most of the Repeal Speech. Dined and read T.D. Walked again for an hour in the evening.

1. 29 January 1840, *PD*, 3rd ser., li, 815; *CW*, vol. 8, pp. 160–78. For its failure, there is a partial explanation in Trevelyan, vol. 2, pp. 23–5.
2. Both by Congreve, they were written in 1694 and 1700.
3. By Racine, 1669 and 1691.

Friday – July 29

Fine day again. Wrote some of that unlucky speech. Letter from Longman – More than 1300£ besides the 500£ and the profits of the Traveller's Library which have not been computed. I am really a rich man. Walked – Theaetetus – I like it better and better. Wandered through a pleasant woody path and to my surprise came out close to the Jew's mansion. Heard from poor Hannah. She has been one of the sufferers by the cab strike. I would make no concession to these fellows – none. I intend to stick to the 6d henceforth.[1] Finished writing out my Irish Repeal Speech. Dined – walked in the evening – finished T D – stuff – began Eugenie Grandet[2] for the third or fourth time. I do not know why I never could get on with it.

1. On 27 July the cabmen had struck for higher fares, and the cab proprietors removed their cabs from the public stands. Many hired vehicles took up the demand. The proprietors

then appealed to the Home Office to amend the Hackney Carriages Act to allow them to raise their fares, and this was agreed to.

2. By Honoré de Balzac (1833).

Saturday – July 30

After breakfast wrote that unfortunate speech and liked it much. – I made great progress – then walked – to the library – read a trashy pamphlet about Miss Gunning and Lord Lorne[1] – then read the Theaetetus on the heath. Very fine things in it, mixed no doubt with much Trash. Home – wrote out the greater part of the Jew speech – fair. At dinner Eugénie Grandet – walked in the evening.

1. Unidentified. The Marquis of Lorne, fifth Duke of Argyll (1723–1806), married Susannah Gunning, a celebrated beauty.

Sunday – July 31

Fine – after breakfast walked and went to Church. Sate in the free sittings and was very comfortable. John Pearson preached well as to substance and style, but his manner is very unfortunate – his utterance a monstrous sing song. He is short sighted, and holds up his MS with one hand to his eyes while he gesticulates with the other. Thought about those lines which I began long ago – the fairy and made some new verses – not amiss – read some more of the the Theaetetus a wonderful mixture of what is excellent and what is worthless. Home – finished writing the speech on Confidence[1] – and finished writing out the Jew Speech. At dinner Eugénie Grandet – a powerful book, but unpleasing. Walked pleasantly in the evening.

1. The speech of 29 January 1840 on Buller's motion of no confidence in Melbourne's ministry.

Monday – August 1

A very fine day – the finest since I came hither. A letter from George – Answered him. A good boy. Walked to the Pantiles and looked at the papers – then walked on the heath and through the same wood where I rambled on Friday, – finished the Theaetetus and began the Menon. Home – wrote some of the China Speech[1] and began to transcribe the Confidence Speech but had little heart for the work, I do not know why – So I went out again and read the Menon – At dinner Eugénie – Clever. Walked in the evening.

1. 7 April 1840, *PD*, 3rd ser., liii, 704–20; repr. in *CW*, vol. 8, pp. 179–94.

Tuesday – August 2

East wind for the first time since I came here – Fine though not bright – Finished EG – a clever though unpleasant book. Wrote – China – walked – reading room – heath – finished the Menon and read the Euthydemus again. Home – finished writing the China speech – I like it much. Begun the Apology. At dinner Balzac – Vie de Province.[1] Walked in the evening – came back and finished the Apology – looked through the Crito – They are fine in parts. But the story about the Oracle – the divine monitor – the dream about ἤματι κεν τριτατω[2] etc are absurd. I imagine that with all his skill in logomachy, he was a strange fanciful superstitious old fellow. Extreme credulity has often gone with extreme logical subtlety. Witness some of the schoolmen. Witness John Wesley. I do not much wonder at the violence of the hatred which Socrates had provoked. He had, evidently, a thorough spiteful enjoyment in making men look small, and particularly men who had a great mean name for wisdom. He really seems to me to have dealt with Protagoras much as Euthydemus dealt with himself. His command of temper too was more provoking than noisy triumph and insolence would have been. There was a meek malignity about him which gave wounds such as must have smarted long. I should not have condemned him. But I should have cut him, if I had been one of his contemporaries.

1. *Scènes de La Vie de Province*, one of the sections of *La Comédie Humaine* by Honoré de Balzac.
2. 'On the third day', in *Crito* 44, a–b. Socrates talks of his dream and how he knows he will die on the day after the arrival on the morrow of a ship from Delos. A woman appears in his dream and quotes the *Iliad* (9.363), which begins with this phrase.

Wednesday – August 3

After breakfast wrote Copyright No 2. Walked to the Library – then on the heath – read the Phaedrus with admiration and contempt mingled. What writing! and what reasoning! On the whole the theory of the αρμονια[1] is what I lean to but que-sais-je? The close is wonderfully fine. It is impossible not to be struck by the humanity of the Athenians in inflicting the punishment of death, at least on fellow citizens. The easiest mode of dissolution seems to have been selected. The convict was allowed the greatest liberty of intercourse with his family and friends – unwatched intercourse too; and the gaolers seem to have behaved with much tenderness. Home and finished the Copyright speech[2] – but it will require much rearranging etc in transcribing. Transcribed a little of the Confidence Speech.[3] That is not pleasant work to me. Read some of the Hippias Major while attending to my hands. It is clever. But it must be grossly unfair. Hippias was a puppy I believe. But Plato makes him a mere noodle. We may be sure that a sophist who in that age made more money than any two sophists – who beat Protagoras and Gorgias in popularity was at any rate a clever plausible fellow. At dinner Balzac – walked – Fine day.

1. Harmonia.
2. 5 February 1841, *PD*, 3rd ser., lvi, 344–57; *CW*, vol. 8, pp. 195.
3. Of 29 January 1840.

Thursday – August 4

Worked hard at Copyright No 2[1] – and succeeded pretty well – transcribed it all. Read the first Book of Plato's Republic on the heath – began the Chartist Speech.[2] At dinner Balzac – walked in the evening. A very quiet uniform life.

1. 6 April 1842, *PD* 3rd ser., lxi, 1363–71; *CW*, vol. 8, pp. 209–16.
2. 3 May 1842, *PD*, 3rd ser., lxiii, 43–52; *CW*, vol. 8, pp. 219–27.

Friday – August 5

Worked at the Chartist speech and made great progress. Read the 2nd book of Plato, Republic and some of the third. At dinner Balzac.

Saturday – August 6

Little to relate – finished the Chartist Speech – began the Somnauth Speech[1] – finished the 3rd book of the Republic and began the fourth – began Sue's Mysteres de Paris [*sic*] and read it at dinner. A fool named Wood[2] who lives at Ramsgate has sent me a ranting Sociolist [*sic*] and Chartist essay begging that I will get it published and telling me that he applies to me because I am the Incarnation of his principles. I will send him an answer that he shall remember the longest day that he lives. Walked on the heath till past nine – Dr Twiss here.

1. 'On the Gates of Somnauth', 9 March 1843, *PD*, 3rd ser., lxvii, 612–28; *CW*, vol. 8, pp. 228–44.
2. Perhaps John Stephen Wood (*c.* 1824–80), a master butcher, who is the only Wood in the Poll Book for East Kent in 1852.

Sunday – August 7

Not devoutly disposed .Walked through the wood and about the Renthall common and the heath reading Sue. Went on with the Somnauth Speech– a very good one, I think. I cannot help expecting that my volume will have some success. At all events it will, I really think, deserve success. At the worst it will smash Vizetelly. Plato on the heath in the afternoon. At dinner Sue. Walked in the evening.

Monday – [August 8]

Still glorious weather – Somnauth – liked it much – walked a good deal and read Sue. He has quite put poor Plato's nose out of joint. Walked in the evening.

Tuesday – [August 9]

Another glorious day, and not too hot, though bright – William went to town early – Letter from μακφ – Somnauth – walked long on the heath and read Sue. Came in and finished Somnauth. The day ended as usual. A most extraordinary and romantic trial about the Ashton property near Bristol.[1] Many people in such cases are interested for the claimant. The case is quite different with me. I am always for the man in possession. A letter today from Black's son[2] in Chili – An intelligent fellow. My tooth a little and but a little troublesome.

---

1. See *LM*, vol. 5, p. 349, n. 6.
2. Presumably the elder of Adam Black's two sons, Francis Black (1831–92); or else William (1836–98).

Wednesday – August 10

Still fine. Began to write out the Chartist speech. I see that the Appropriation Act is brought in. This Ashton trial is the queerest that I ever read or heard of. It beats Warren's Ten Thousand a Year. The Library and the heath – Sue [at] dinner and walk as usual.

Thursday – August 11

One day just like another. The Irish speech of 1844.[1] The heath – Sue – dinner – walk.

---

1. 'The State of Ireland', 19 February 1844, *PD*, 3rd ser., lxxii, 1169–94; *CW*, vol. 8, pp. 245–69.

Friday – August 12

Again.

Saturday – August 13

Again – Finished the Irish speech – Finished N de P and began Les Memoires d'un Medecin.[1]

---

1. Alexander Dumas (*père*), *Notaire de Paris; Memoirs d'un Médecin* (1846–8).

Sunday – August 14

Began and indeed finished the Dis[sente]rs Chapel Sp[eec]h[1] – walked to Southborough and back by the Jew's House and the woody lane. Mem d'un M. Yesterday and today the 5th Bk of Plato's Republic – dinner etc. as usual.

1. 6 June 1844, *PD*, 3rd ser., lxxv, 338–51; repr. in *CW*, vol. 8, pp. 270–83.

Monday – August 15

Strange weather of late – The only August that I remember like March – cloudy – windy – dry – bleak. I have seen wet Augusts that were cold and hot Augusts that were dry – but cold and dry together is strange. I finished today writing out the Confidence Speech. I think it one of my best – But Dis aliter[1] – I read some of Mem d'un M on the heath – stuff – But it amuses me. Dined and walked as usual.

1. *Dis aliter visum* (Latin): 'The gods see it differently'.

Tuesday – August 16

Change of wind and weather – Rainy and very chill. I staid at home all day and wrote – first letters – one in answer to Ellis who is at Liverpool – then the China Speech[1] – wrote it out – Dumas – fire in the evening.

1. 7 April 1840 on the war with China, *PD*, 3rd ser., liii, 704–20.

Wednesday – August 17

Fine again though with an occasional shower. Wrote out part of the Somnauth. Speech – walked and read M. d'un M. – walk in evening.

Thursday – August 18

My last day here. Finished writing out the Somnauth Speech – walked and read – called at Lady Murchison's who yesterday sent me an oration of Sir Roderic, on the Pearsons – packed – walked dined walked again – not very sorry to go.

Friday – August 19

Early breakfast – to station. In London before eleven. To the Athenaeum – found Senior there breakfasting – long chat – looked at the magazines etc – to the House – presented a petition – off to the King's Cross Station – met T there – to Hatfield in half-an-hour. H and the children on the platform – a happy and affectionate meeting – T and the children played on the lawn at trap ball[1] and shot at a target. H and I sate and talked – a pleasant house inside, and a pretty little pleasure ground. I find that it was the house of my old schoolfellow Ben Peile[2] – a poor sneaking snivelling milksop he was as a boy – always doing wrong and always the first to peach – but he seems to have turned out a decent man. There are many such changes. Pleasant dinner and evening – Miss Raymond, A's governess is of the party with a foot which has been hurt and confines her to the house. I had rather have been in a family party – not that I have any fault to find with Miss R, who seems a very good governess.

---

1. Also known as 'knur and spell'; it involved a wooden ball ejected from a box or trap, and struck with a stick topped with a six-inch pommel.
2. This is presumably the Benjamin Peile (b. 1798) who came up to Trinity in 1817. He became Curate for Bishop Hatfield, Hertfordshire, but died in 1842. His son, Arthur Lewis Babington Peile (1830–1915), held the same living from 1853 to 1859. He later became Vicar of Holy Trinity, Ventnor, Isle of Wight.

Saturday – August 20

Pleasant day – pleasant breakfast – pleasant chat – read a speech – two to H and B. Then we went – all but G – to Hatfield It is a noble house much beyond my expectation. The grand parts I could not wish otherwise. The bedrooms and dressing rooms want comfort. The pictures are almost without exception, execrable as works of art, though two or three are valuable historically. The lady who acted as Cicerone was grossly ignorant: She showed us two boxes which she assured us were Queen Elizabeth's tea caddies, and told us that a picture of Mary Queen of Scots was painted the evening before the execution at Fotheringay though Aet 36 1573[1] was legible twenty feet off on the canvass. In the afternoon read more speeches. They read well and H and B seem to like them much. In the evening T came. We walked about the grounds at Hatfield and had fine views of the house. I repeated the ballad of Alice Brand[2] to dear little A who was charmed with it beyond measure. Home and a pleasant dinner and evening.

---

1. She was born in 1542 and executed in 1587, hence she was thirty-one in 1573.
2. From the fourth canto of Sir Walter Scott's *Lady of the Lake.*

Sunday – August 21

Up early for breakfast – fine day – Hatfield Church rather handsome in spite of pewing and patching – delightful chimes – middling sermon. In the afternoon we sate and talked under the trees very pleasantly. After dinner repeated hymns. I very gravely gave them Herrick's fine Litany.[1] In the evening I read them my favourite passages from Paradise Regained. I have had little time here to read; but I have read or rather glanced over some religious biographies, and a book of

Dr Cardwell's on the Anglican Liturgy[2] – I must look at him again; not that he knows half so much about the Comprehension Scheme of 1689 as I.

1. Robert Herrick, 'His Litany with the Holy Spirit in Noble Numbers' (1647).
2. Edward Cardwell (1787–1861), *The Two Books of Common Prayer, Set Forth in the Reign of King Edward VI, Compared* (1838). Cardwell was Principal of St Alban Hall, Oxford, and a considerable Church historian.

Monday – August 22

Another happy day. I love them all dearly. It was fine. I read them some more speeches with great success. We walked in Ld S's woods[1] – very noble indeed. I think that I have scarcely ever seen finer or more picturesque oaks, elms and ash trees – the fern luxuriant – the deer and rabbits enlivened the while. We were very joyous and affectionate. The dinner and evening were again pleasant.

1. Lord Salisbury's. He was James Brownlow William Cecil (1791–1868), second Marquis of Salisbury.

Tuesday – August 23

Forced to go against my will. We chatted from breakfast till the time of separation. Off at 12 for town – found my table at the Albany heaped with papers pamphlets etc. – cleared off business pretty well, ordered a new portmanteau. Wolmar not to be got – a certain George Franz of Cologne came[1] – kind letters from Ld Lansdowne. I may possibly meet him in Switzerland – walked – wrote the Irish speech – dined – Finished M d'un M.

1. I have not traced this man. TBM praised him and his work as a courier highly in a letter to Hannah. *LM*, vol. 5, p. 352.

Wednesday – August 24

After breakfast Professor Smyth of Edinburgh came about the observatory[1] – to the city – drew 250£ – difficulty about finding a good way of carrying the money – spent a good many shillings to little purpose. I must cure myself of this bad habit of buying things without sufficient consideration. I have got two money bags and a travelling cap, none of which I shall probably use. I gave the other day thirty shillings for a knife which turned out a mere incumbrance. Home – wrote. E to dinner. Settled our plans. We start at Friday afternoon.

1. Charles Piazzi Smyth (1819–1900), Astronomer-Royal for Scotland, 1845–88.

Thursday – August 25

Sent some books to the Treasury for H. The Courier came with the passports – sent him to E at the Temple – wrote – walked – bought κρεμ – Hair cut – packed – nearly finished that Irish speech – a very long one and though I say it, not a bad one. I have been reading Tone – poor fellow! I took him up to verify a reference in speech and could not help going on. Cockton's Steward[1] – What trash – at dinner – Tone and an odd book by Amyas Griffiths.[2]

1. Henry Cockton, *The Steward* (1850).
2. Author of several tracts between 1787 and 1788.

Friday – August 26

Amyas Griffiths and Tone before breakfast. After breakfast finished writing out the Irish Speech – all my arrangements complete. Off in the afternoon. The journal of my tour will be in a small book.[1] Letter from Ld L accepting very kindly my dedication.[2]

1. Volume 7 of his journal, 26 August to 17 September 1853.
2. Of TBM's *Speeches* (1854).

Friday – August 26

Having finished writing out the speech on Irish affairs – 1844 – went out – with Carlton in my pocket – overtaken by rain – got into a cab – to Ellis's – parted with my [illeg.] by the way – E not come home – read some of Desmerais[1] poor stuff. E came and in coming into the room broke his head against the glass door of his bookcase. We soon set off for the London Bridge Station – Franz – a capital fellow – had arranged everything. We reached Dover soon after seven. The wind high by fits starts, rain failing, the sea white with foam and promising rough weather. We could not get a room to sit in – dined in the Coffee room[2] – a place which I remembered well. I dined there when I landed from the continent in the beginning of 1839 – on the day of the meeting of parliament or thereabouts. Stupid it is to dine with a friend in a coffee room. Alone one can read. Tête à tête you can talk. But with overhearers you cannot try anything but platitudes. To bed in two great rooms, one within the other, mine the outer, large and handsomely furnished but vilely lighted.

1. Perhaps a work by Desmerets de Saint-Sorlin (1596–1676), dramatist and poet.
2. Sutton's, at 61, Swangate Street.

Saturday – August 27

Stormy and rainy. Some doubt whether it would be possible for the steamer to take passengers on board. But at last we got in. The wind, though there was too much of it, was in our favour, and we had a rapid run. I was well, as usual, But the other passengers were generally in a bad way – The women squalled [*sic*] and laughed hysterically. E was not himself for some hours. Landed at Calais before two and walked about the town, much like Dieppe, I thought. Off at 3 – Fine afternoon. Got to Ghent at half after seven, dined late, and to bed. Much amused by a Sir John Kynaston[1] who travelled with us, a regular John Bull – a Sir Anthony Absolute growling in a blunt good-natured testy sort of way at everything, weather, inns, carriages, but specially at a lout of a courier who was a mere incumbrance. Sir John envied me Franz and not without reason.

1. Sir John Roger Kynaston (1797–1866). Educated at Rugby and Christ Church, he succeeded as third Bart in 1839. Sir Anthony Absolute is a character in Sheridan's *The Rivals*.

Sunday – August 28

I did not sleep well. I rarely do when I dine largely just before going to bed. At about two got up and looked at the Place. Beautiful in the moonlight and as still as death. A fine morning – breakfasted and off. A long day's journey. We had for company a Russian employé with his English wife and three odious brats, who fought, kissed, ate, teased each other and us, littered the carriage with their toys, sweetmeats, pieces of paper and ends of string, and made me long for a Massacre of the Innocents. Liege looked beautiful, and so did the country between Liege and Herbesthal. We got to Cologne at a little after six. Franz had arranged everything; and we found a carriage from the Hotel de Bellevue waiting for us at the station. We went through the town over the bridge to our inn. The crowd of idlers and starers immense especially on the bridge. Some people looked so hard into the carriage that I was fool enough to think that my coming had been notified and that some of my German readers had assembled to stare at me. Thank Heaven I kept my coxcombry to myself; and I soon found that the curiosity which I had observed was merely the ordinary curiosity of Sunday idlers. We were shown into a very handsome sitting room overlooking the river. Between our windows and the bank was a sort of tea garden where people of a class much superior to those who frequent the teagardens of London came to drink to chat and to hear music. The tables were shaded by horse chestnuts and by trellice work. The band very good. We dined luxuriously, and I tasted for the first time the trout of the Rhine and the Asmanhauser Hock[1] – very pleasant light drink. In the evening E wrote to his family; and I sauntered about the balcony. Nothing can be conceived more beautiful than the evening; The lights of the city, the reflection of those lights on the Rhine, the crowd of happy people on the bridge – To bed. I had always heard of the shortness of German beds and though not very tall, I could hardly find room in mine. I slept however very well.

1. Assmannhauser.

Monday – August 29

Wrote to H. Breakfast. Then to the city across the bridge – bought a pair of spectacles from a celebrated optician. I had broken one glass of mine in the railway carriage. I left him the broken pair to mend. To the Cathedral. Vast and, even in its unfinished state, most magnificent. Yet I was a little disappointed. My expectation had been raised too high and perhaps nothing could quite have satisfied me. However it is a Gothic Church of the very first class, and will be finer than it is. But it will never be equal to St Ouen, I think hardly to York Minster. We lounged about the town till the rain forced us to take a hackney coach. Drove to St Peter's Church to see a Rubens[1]. The painting was of course powerful; the subject loathsome – The Saint crucified with his head downwards. How frightfully superstition distorts and deforms art. The rain heavier and heavier. To Bonn by railway. We lost little by the bad weather: for the country was as flat as Lincolnshire. A good inn and good dinner.

1. Rubens's *Crucifixion of St. Peter* was painted for St Peter's Church, where the painter's father was buried. It was completed between 1638 and 1640.

Tuesday – August 30

A glorious day after the rain. We breakfasted and embarked on the Rhine in high spirits. Our voyage lasted from half after eight in the morning till near eight in the evening. The first part disappointed me. But when we had passed Coblentz and Ehrenbreitstein the scenery became exquisitely beautiful. Woods, crags, ruined castles, neat white towns clustering round churches, terraces of vineyards. I was charmed. I have gone down the Rhone and both down and up the Loire, and both are fine rivers; but neither is at all comparable to the Rhine. We reached Mayence as the lamps were lighting – good dinner – first rate Rhenish wine – slept well.

Wednesday – August 31

After breakfast we lounged about Mayence, saw the Cathedral, the front detestable, other views rather fine. Off by railway to Frankfort. To the Museum – saw several chefs d'oeuvre, as they are considered of modern German art – all, to my thinking, very poor – a Daniel in the den of Lions[1] which it is a shame to exhibit. I did not even like the John Huss[2] – still less Overbeck's trashy allegory[3]. One of Stanfield's landscapes or of Landseer's hunting pieces is worth all the mystic daubs of all the Germans. To Goethe's house[4] – found it with some difficulty – greatly interested; not that he is one of my first favourites; but the earlier books of his life of himself have a great charm for me; and the old house plays a great part in the narrative. The house of Wilhelm Meister's father too is evidently this house at Frankfort. To the bridge – the Cathedral. E gets on with German infinitely better than I. The Cathedral has little to recommend it but vast size and historical recollections. The lanthorn is however striking. To the Judengasse. Most striking – to the Cemetery to see some bas reliefs by Thorwaldsen[5]. I did not much admire them. The figures were graceful enough. But nothing could be colder or more insipid, I might add more absurd than the allegorical designs. I very seldom like sculptures which go beyond a single figure. If there is a group it ought to be very simple, and to represent real and not allegorical persons – least of all real and allegorical persons mixed, like these works of Thorwaldsen. To Heidelberg by railway – the road beautiful, the Bergstrasse not much unlike the banks of the Rhine in character – got to Heidelberg soon after dark. Not very well lodged or entertained, the town very full, and we were forced to go to the second inn. Our Asmanhauser fell off, and E had no carpet to his bedroom which vexed me much. He picked up today a German translation of my Lays[6] – some very happy lines, others very bad. The translator I apprehend is not much of a scholar, though an ingenious man.

1. By Alfred Rethel (1816–59), exhibited 1838. Rethel was a student of Johann Gottfried Schadow (1764–1850) and was also influenced by Lessing.
2. *Huss before the Council of Constance* by Carl Friedrich Lessing (1808–80).
3. Johann Friedrich Overbeck (1789–1869) was a founder of the *Lukasbund*, who came to be called the Nazarenes. The allegory TBM saw was *The Triumph of Religion in the Arts* (1840).
4. Grosse Hirschgraben 23, where Goethe spent the first seventeen years of his life.
5. In 1824 Thorwaldsen created a monument to Philip Bethmann-Hollweg in this cemetery. It is now in the Liebieghaus Gallery in Frankfurt.
6. *Macaulays Gedichte: Lieder des alten Rom. Ivry. Die Armada. Übersetzt von J.S., herausgegeben und mit einem Vorworte begleitet von F. Buelau* (Leipzig, 1853).

Thursday – September 1

Another very fine day. We staid at Heidelberg that our linen might be washed. Soon after nine we set off in a carriage with two strong horses for the Konigstuhl, thence to the Castle – thence to the Wolfsburg and fishponds. The excursion occupied near 6 hours and was delightful. I hardly know so beautiful a scene or so fine a view. Wrote to Baba[1]. Tomorrow I hope to hear that they are all well. In the afternoon walked with E to the castle, wandered about the terraces – beautiful. The Neckar bright with the western sun, the ruins wonderfully affecting and grand. Then back to our trout and Rhenish wine. The courier – an excellent one – brought his account – very reasonable. To bed tired and happy.

1. *LM*, vol. 5, p. 351.

Friday – September 2

The morning not so fine. However we walked on the right bank of the Neckar some time. Then off by rail for Strasburg. A vixen Englishwoman and her cool, sneering, apathetic husband were in the carriage. Her irritability and pouting and his dry imperturbable manner were very diverting. He reminded me of Miss Austen's Mr Bennet[1] [illeg.] of ND. in old times. At Strasburg we were very well lodged, and set out for the P.O. No letters, at which I was not a little vexed. To the Cathedral. The steeple at a distance is not pleasing to the eye. It even reminded me of the ugliest of all objects, the huge iron excrescence at Rouen. But as we approached, the tower of Strasburg became more and more beautiful, and when at last we got a good view of it, I thought it the most exquisite *morceau* of Gothic architecture that I ever saw. We went in. The interior is grand, but has faults. The side aisles are too broad for their height – even the central aisle would be better if it were narrower. The end of the vista is wretched. Nevertheless it is a Church of the first rank. The steeple entitles it to be placed above the Cathedral of Cologne. But I have yet seen nothing equal to St Ouen at Rouen.

To the battlements, lounged there a little, to the Lutheran Church to see Saxe's tomb[2]. Pigalle seems to me to have been a feebler Roubiliac – there is the same sort of fancy, the same sort of manual skill; but Roubiliac had more ingenuity and spirit. The taste of both in groupes was detestable. The man who showed the monument wanted to introduce us to some well preserved corpses; but I had no taste for such nauseous exhibitions. We dined pretty well.

1. In *Pride and Prejudice*.
2. Maurice, Comte de Saxe (1696–1750), was the natural son of Augustus II of Saxony, who made him a count. He fought in his youth under Prince Eugene, but served as a Marshal of France under Louis XV. The sculptor Jean Baptiste Pigalle (1714–85) completed the monument in St Thomas's church in 1777.

Saturday – September 3

Off by rail to Basle. A pleasant journey with the Vosges hills on our right, a succession of pretty little towns round their steeples – At Basle we were busied some time in making arrangements with a voiturin – we walked about – saw the Cathedral. I was much interested by the grave of Erasmus,[1] a pleasing venerable cloister, the ramparts interesting. The Rhine a noble river, though so far from the sea. How it rushed and raved under our windows. A letter from H – all well – Thank God.

---

1. Desiderius Erasmus (*c.* 1467–1536), the great humanist scholar and friend of Sir Thomas More.

Sunday – September 4

Off as the clock struck 8 – a glorious day and a delightful journey. I have never seen nature in so grand and at the same so lovely an aspect as during our passage through the valley of the Birs. I shall never forget it. We lunched on hard boiled eggs and a bottle of Hermitage at Bellerive and got to Malleray at six – a most pleasant, though by no means a fine inn – had a very tolerable dinner, excellent trout and fair claret. Slept sound.

Tuesday – September 5

The luck begins to turn against us. The morning rather dull looking. However there was no rain and we had a pleasant journey through the Jura to Bienne, except that we could not see the Alps. We went on to Berne through a dull country, in vain trying to catch a glimpse of the eternal snow. Lunched at Aarberg. Reached Berne before 5. A most interesting old city. I had expected nothing and was agreeably disappointed. I have seldom seen a more picturesque place. It is in every way greatly superior to Basle. Walked to the Cathedral, under the arcades of the High Street, and on the terraces, trying in vain to see the Alps. This is a set off against much good fortune. Dined comfortably by a wood fire; for it was very cold.

Tuesday – September 6

Rain. So much the better; for now the clouds may empty themselves; and we may see something of the Alps. Wrote to H. Walked up and down the High Street while E was writing a letter. Market day. Immense crowd – Most interesting old town. Meanwhile Franz got our passports visa-ed for France. He found Wolmar here. Wolmar it seems has been travelling since May with some English ladies. He came to us, very goodnaturedly engaged to secure us accommodations at Vevay. At 12 or thereabouts we started with a return voiturin whom Franz had got for 20 francs less than I must have paid for a voiturin at first hand. We had a wet miserable journey to Fribourg. Fribourg is a finely situated town with two remarkable bridges. But the rain was so heavy that I did not venture to walk about it; and the view from my window though fine, was much less fine than it would have been if the sun had been out. E walked a little – I read Venetia[1]. We had a fire and a pretty good dinner, but very indifferent wine.

1. By Benjamin Disraeli (1837).

Wednesday – September 7

The weather still bad – a wretched journey from Fribourg to Vevay. We waited at a place called Bulle, the most stupid, dreary, and detestable spot on earth, to my thinking. The inn, a very mean one was crowded with parties of travellers and with all the riff-raff of the town. Whether the rain outside or the company within were the more odious I hardly know. Glad to get away. At Vevay we could only get two bedrooms. The house was overflowing with English, Yankees, French and Germans. However thanks to Franz we got a tolerable dinner in one of the bedrooms. The view of the lake and of the mountains, bad as the weather was, struck us much. It was grand though very gloomy. The lake roared and tossed "fluctibus et strepitu marino"[1]; and Franz augured a very rough voyage for tomorrow.

1. *fluctibus et fremiter adsurgens Benace marino* (Latin): '[Lake] Benacus that tosses and growls like a little ocean' (Virgil, *Georgics* 2.160; C. Day Lewis's translation, p. 40).

Thursday – September 8

The weather better – the wind gone down – but still there was not a gleam of sunshine. We breakfasted in a room below. I looked over such newspapers as I could find – a stray number of Galignani – another of The Débats another of the Sunday Times – another of The Evening Mail. I saw that there had been a dreadful accident on The Great Northern Railway, to the very train by which T goes to Hatfield daily after his work. But as his name was not mentioned in the list of sufferers I felt at ease – The Ld Mayor,[1] Sir James Duke,[2] Ld Enfield,[3] The Bp of Lincoln,[4] have all been hurt. Mrs Norton,[5] I find, has been writing a long letter in answer to her husband. E and I went up to St Martin's Church, to see Ludlow's monument with a detestable Latin inscription[6]. The Church pleasantly situated among trees and vineyards. Then looked at his house. At twelve off by voiture to Lausanne. Lodged tolerably well at the Hotel de Gibbon. Uncertain weather, a little sun and much drizzling rain. We walked however round the old town, most picturesque old place. We went into the Cathedral, a fine Church, quite equal to our Cathedrals of the third rank, to Worcester Cathedral for example. To our inn – good dinner and wine. The sky clearing. The stars coming out.

1. This was Thomas Challis (1795–1874), who was MP for Finsbury, 1852–57.
2. Sir James Duke, Bart (1792–1873), was MP for the City of London, 1849–65.

3. George Stevens Byng (1806–86) was Viscount Enfield, but sat in the Lords as Baron Strafford in 1853. He became Earl of Strafford on his father's death in 1860.
4. John Jackson (1811–85), Bishop of Lincoln, 1853–69, then translated to London.
5. This was the last battle in Caroline Norton's campaign for the right of a separated or divorced woman to keep her own property. The letters in *The Times*, starting on 20 August, were provoked by the case of *Thrupp* vs *Norton*, in which her husband had laid claim to all her property and was upheld by the court on a technicality.
6. Edmund Ludlow (1616 or 1617–92), republican and regicide, spent his last years in Vevay. The inscription is in C. H. Firth (ed.), *Memoirs of Edmund Ludlow*, 2 vols (1894), vol. 2, appendix 8, p. 514. TBM used this experience in his portrait of Ludlow in *HE*, ch. 15, *CW*, vol. 3, p. 201.

Friday – September 9

A beautiful morning. Rose at four, wrapped myself up warm opened the window and passed three hours at it. The daybreak on the Alps was glorious – Mont Blanc full in my eye. The lake which yesterday and the day before had a sullen, though grand aspect, now seemed beautiful with more than the beauty of Killarney. The low country, the vineyards, the meadows, the gardens, the woods, the little white towns and villas presented the most charming of all contrasts to the crags and snow. The gilding of the mountain tops, the flashing of the snow was beyond description lovely. After breakfast we walked down to the port and embarked for Geneva. A beautiful day, a delightful voyage, as far as prospects and weather went. I found several old acquaintances on board – the Merivales,[1] Judge Talfourd. In little more than two hours we landed, and found comfortable rooms at the Hotel des Bergues. Our windows commanded a full view of Mont Blanc in all his glory. We got our letters. T had a narrow escape – Thank God – He had to look after Sir James Duke and the Ld Mayor who seemed to be very grateful for his attention to them. We walked to the junction of the Rhone and the Arve. My old friend the Rhone is what he is down at Port St Esprit, the bluest, brightest, swiftest, most joyous of rivers. Took a long walk in the ramparts – most interesting. Home – wrote letters – to dinner to bed early. I had been up ever since four.

---

1. There were two Merivale brothers: Herman (1806–74), who went from Harrow to Oriel College, Oxford, and was a political economist and civil servant, who succeeded James Stephen as Permanent Under-Secretary to the Colonial Office; and Charles (1808–93), who was also at Harrow, but went from there to Trinity College, Cambridge, became Dean of Ely, and was a historian of Rome. It seems more likely that TBM met the older brother, who was more an old acquaintance than the Dean. Mrs Herman Merivale had been Caroline Penelope Robinson. She died in 1881.

Saturday – September 10

Up again at 4 to see the sun rise. The outline of Mont Blanc the neighbouring range was perfectly distinct and sharp against the saffron sky. I sate at the window till past six, then went to bed again, and slept a little more. At breakfast a note from Mrs Drummond[1] who is in the hotel. Called and found her with her daughters – two of them – growing into very fine young women. Ld Lansdowne arrived last night at the Hotel on the other side of the water – went to him. A short and most friendly chat. With his usual kindness he asked me to let him go with E and myself to Ferney. I accepted the proposal with great pleasure. We have settled to start for Lyons tomorrow. At ½ after 12 the carriage came and we set out for Ferney. The road was most interesting. The views of Mont Blanc and the Savoy Alps sublime. At last we came to an avenue of one great length which brought us to a mean looking stone Church, not much unlike a country Church, in the highlands of Scotland. This was the building on which was once inscribed "Deo erexit Voltaire" But the inscription has long been removed. Opposite had once stood the theatre where Mme Denis,[2] the ugliest of human beings, used to act Andromaque[3] and Zaire[4]. The Chateau was close by – not by any means a large or fine house, but such as a Genevan merchant of 1500£ or 2,000£ a year might be supposed to have. The salon was small, the cabinet where Voltaire used to write smaller, and both looked, not towards Mont Blanc of which he might have had a noble view, but towards a terrace and a grove of trees. Perhaps he wished to spare his eyes. He used to complain that the snow hurt them. The rooms were not long ago hung with the pictures which he had placed there: but now scarcely anything except the walls and floor remains as in his time. The gardens are less changed. There was a long close woven arcade – berceau they call it – of a sort of elm. Here he used to walk in hot or rainy weather. There was a kind of wilderness which might have been in an English pleasure ground. The trees grew well and with a pleasing irregularity. One tree planted by himself was pointed out, a tall elm. I was glad to have seen a place about which I had read so much and dreamed so much, – a place which was, eighty years ago, regarded with the deepest interest all over Europe, and visited by pilgrims of the highest rank and greatest genius. I suppose that no private house ever received such a number of illustrious guests during the same time as were entertained in Ferney between 1768 and 1778. I thought of Marmontel and his ambre chevalier, of la Harpe and his quarrel with the Patriarch,[5] of Mme de Genlis, of the Stallion,[6] of the Fornicateur,[7] and of all the tattle which fills Grimm's Correspondence. Ld L was much pleased. E less so. He is no Voltairian, nor am I exactly. But I take a great interest in the literary history of the last century. Back to Geneva. E and I walked about the town. Marcet met us[8] and introduced himself. He made us very kind offers of hospitality. We went at ½ past 5 to dine with Ld L at the Ecu, a quiet comfortable dinner and pleasant chat till 8 o'clock. Home, drank some

Seltzer Water. E to bed early. I sate up a little longer reading Venetia. The fellow has plundered me impudently[9]. Bad weather.

1. Maria Drummond had three daughters: Mary Elizabeth (1837–*c*. 1901), who became Mrs Kay; Emily (1835–1930); and Fanny Eleanor (1840–71). TBM presumably met the two elder.
2. Voltaire's niece and later mistress, Marie Elisabeth Denis (1724–71). She married Nicolas Denis, conseiller du roi and commissaire des guerres, who died in 1744.
3. The heroine of Racine's tragedy (1667).
4. Voltaire's tragedy, produced in 1732.
5. Jean-Francois de La Harpe (1739–1803), poet and playwright, who admired Voltaire but after the Revolution turned against the philosophers. He was charged by Voltaire with having stolen some of his manuscripts and expelled from Ferney in 1768.
6. The French word for this, *l'etalon*, points to Jacques Marie Bertrand d'Étallonde (b. 1749), who was accused with Jean-François Lefebre, Chevalier de la Barre, of showing disrespect for Christian symbols and practice. La Barre was executed, and Voltaire used his example to pour scorn on the Church, but d'Étallonde escaped and became for a time a soldier of Frederick the Great.
7. He was Robert Covelle, a clockmaker and citizen, whom the Genevan Consitory found guilty of fornication and summoned to kneel before it and confess. He refused. He appears in Voltaire's *La Guerre Civile de Genève*.
8. Probably François Marcet (1803–83), the physicist and eldest son of Alexande Marcet (1770–1822) and his wife Jane. Like the Rogets and Romillys, they were equally at home in Geneva and London.
9. In the novel Disraeli quotes, with as much acknowledgement as an anonymous article could have, Macaulay's paragraph beginning 'We know no spectacle so ridiculous as the British public in one of its periodical fits of morality', from the essay on Byron (*CHE*, vol. 1, pp. 315–16). See *Venetia*, bk IV, ch. 18.

Sunday – September 11

Settled accounts again with Franz. – We have got hither for 64£ – not much, all things considered – Packing. At 11 or thereabouts off in a calèche with three horses by post for Lyons. The road from the time that we entered the pass of the Jura was very interesting and even beautiful. At Bellegarde while our baggage was rummaged by the custom house officers we saw the Valserin and what, if the weather had been dry, would have been the Porte Du Rhone – then on to Nantice. There we were forced to rough it. We dined indifferently in a bedroom. I had to wash in a pie-dish and our other accommodations were much of a piece with these specimens. The only salon was occupied by my old friend Sir George Napier and his wife[1]. They wished to see us and we had some chat. We met last in France as inmates of the same hotel, five years ago almost to a day, he travelling with his wife and I with Ellis. He talked freely about his brother who is just dead[2] – a brave and able man, no doubt, with all his faults. He seemed much softened by the approach of death, and begged his brother William[3] to abstain from saying anything harsh about the people with whom they had been quarrelling.

---

1. Sir George Thomas Napier (1794–1855) was a Peninsula War veteran. He lost his right arm at Cuidad Rodrigo in January 1812. He later became Governor of the Cape of Good Hope, from 1837 to 1843. His second wife was Frances Dorothea Williams-Freeman, née Blencowe. She died in 1881.
2. Sir Charles James Napier (1782–1853). He was the Conqueror of Sind. He died on 29 August.
3. Sir William Francis Patrick Napier (1785–1860) was also a Peninsula veteran. His *History of the War in the Peninsula and in the South of France* was published in six volumes from 1828 to 1840. He developed strongly radical political views, and was a combative writer.

Monday – September 12

A very fine day. I had slept well. We breakfasted and set out early – a very fine country as far as Cerdon. I never saw a nobler road than that by which we descended from the top of The Jura to the plain. After that the country was rather tame. The rain had been heavy for the waters were out. We got to Lyons soon after five, a noble city – finer than it seemed to me fifteen years ago. The improvement has extended to the inns. I was stunk to death and frozen to death here in January 1839. But we are now as well lodged as if we were at Cheltenham or Brighton. At the door of our inn – L'Univers – I found Charles Howard. Denison called in the evening. A good dinner – fair Cote Rotie – first rate Hermitage. We had walked to the confluence and back.

Tuesday – September 13

A good night. A fine morning. Wrote to my dear Baba. Then set out with E to roam about the town and did so from about half after ten to half after six – a fine day – very warm for the time of year – much like an English July. We went along the Rhone almost to the extremity of the town, up the stream, then to the Hotel de Ville – to the Museum – a strange and interesting sight. The building a great convent, still bearing numerous marks of its old character, but now an exchange, a gallery of sculpture, a gallery of painting, a Library, etc. In the old Chapel or refectory, I hardly know which, was a crowd of buyers and sellers bawling at the top of their voices among images of saints and under an immense picture of the Last Supper. The cloisters were lined with monuments mostly Pagan, a few Christian, found in the neighbourhood of Lyons. Some of the inscriptions were pleasing and interesting, some most absurd. The grammar and spelling frequently execrable. I noted, as I had noted at Rome, the extreme meanness and rudeness of the Christian monuments as compared with those of the Pagans The explanation is obvious. The famous speech of Claudius[1] is the great curiosity of the Museum. But the wisdom of the authorities has placed the brass so high that it cannot be read so that I must trust to books for the words. The pictures were, with scarcely an exception, abominable. We took a fiacre and were driven up an immense ascent to the eminence which overlooks the city – The view was really very noble. Mont Blanc might be faintly discerned. But the real sight was the city – the vicinity – the course of the two great rivers. There was a sham fight going on within view but I did not care much for it. The whole city swarms with soldiers and bristles with fortifications. We then went to the Cathedral – a fine old Church – home quite tired and hungry – dined and to bed.

1. The speech was on bronze tablets, and it recommended that Gauls be admitted to the Senate. Claudius was born in Lyons (Lugdunum) in 10 BC. He died AD 54.

Wednesday – September 14

Up pretty early – and off by the 9 o'clock boat for Chalons – a fine day. The steamer the vilest I ever saw – The longest narrowest, beastliest, and the beastliest set of passengers – However we got through the day pretty well, and at sunset landed at Chalons. How well I remembered that place and the miserable day which I passed there near fifteen years ago. I was then very unhappy. Now I am as happy as any man can easily be – at least a man of near 53. We had a good dinner and tolerable wine – not quite so good as we might have expected for the best prices and in the heart of Burgundy. To bed early, having to rise early.

Thursday – September 15

Up soon after 4 – breakfast – left Chalons by train for Paris at 6 – and reached Paris at 4 in the afternoon – Franz had written to the Hotel de Bristol: but it was overflowing; and we were sent to the Hotel de Chatham – a second rate house: but it will do for two days. To The Frères Provençaux, got a capital dinner and home to bed at ten.

Friday – September 16

A good night – But this vile entresol is so dark, that, by the most brilliant sunlight one must sit at the window to read or write. A letter from H – God bless her – All well – wrote to her[1] – Much vexed that letters addressed to me both at Strasburg and Geneva have miscarried, particularly one from dear little Alice. Went with E to St Eustache – a noble Church. I cannot make out the secret of the effect which it produces on me. The union of Gothic and Palladian generally so offensive is here in the highest degree grand and pleasing. In truth the front which is purely Palladian is the only thing that I dislike. To the Louvre, staid there till the shutting up. To the Garden of The Thuilleries – walked there – to the Place de Concorde – then by the Boulevards to Galignani's and thence to the Frères Provençaux where we found a good dinner and matchless Burgundy. After a stroll in the Palais Royal home to bed. We are now in much better apartments

1. *LM*, vol. 5, p. 353.

Saturday – September 17

Yesterday I began, and this morning in bed I finished a book on the last naval war by a French Officer named De La Gravière.[1] It seems to me, both fairly and sensibly written. After breakfast wrote to dear little Alice. Began Ariosto's Cassaria[2] – a strange jumble of times and manners – walked with E to St Sulpice, to the Chapelle Sainte, to Notre Dame. Then he went home to rest himself, and I walked on. Went for him at five. The Boulevards – Passage des Panoramas – Ealynam's – dinner at Frères Provençaux.

1. J. P. E. J. de La Gravière, *Guerres maritimes sous la République et l'Empire ...* (1847).
2. *Cassaria* (1508).

Sunday – September 18

Off early for Amiens by rail. Breakfasted in the refreshment room at Amiens on a cold veal pie and wine. Then to the Cathedral. I had not seen it since 1840 – It has been much improved especially by the removal of a detestable screen utterly at variance with the general style of the building. A noble Church. I should like the interior better on the whole than that of any Gothic Cathedral were it not for the nakedness of the windows. The nave is finer than that of York, of Cologne, or of Strasburg. St Ouen still retains its superiority in my opinion. But St Ouen is not a Cathedral. From Amiens proceeded by the afternoon train to Boulogne, found the town busied with preparations for an Imperial visit. Trellice work, garlands, festoons, arches everywhere, boats practising on the water for a boatrace etc. Could not find room at The Hotel des Bains. Taken in at The Hotel Meurice – tolerably comfortable, and the people very civil. Went across the water to find E's old house – then to the Haute Ville and sauntered about the ramparts – a favourite walk of mine. To the Hotel to dinner. Not equal to the Frères certainly, but tolerable.

Monday – September 19

Walked again round the ramparts of the Haute Ville. Then on board, and had a most pleasant, quiet, sunny voyage to Folkestone. The water was as smooth as that of Lake Leman on Friday week. From Folkstone to London by express train. I have read two of Ariosto's Comedies on this journey home – The Cassaria and the Suppositi[1]. From the Suppositi much in the Taming of the Shrew has been borrowed – Whether by Shakspeare or by some earlier writer whose work S retouched is a question. The comedies of Ariosto are formed on the model of the Latin translations from the plays of Menander and Diphilus. Plautus seems to have been more in Ariosto's eye than Terence and I was surprised to find the versification trimeter iambic. They have no great merit. Dramatic writing was not A's forte, but vigorous lively narrative. At the station parted from E, and went home. All well – satisfactory letters – one from F – one from dearest B – bales of letters from correspondents for whom I cared less – dined – read a book by Charles Bernard – le Noeud Gordien[2] – The first tale is entitled La Femme de Quarante Ans. Cleverish, but not as good as some other pieces by him. After dinner wrote a good many letters.

1. *I Suppositi* (1509).
2. Published in 1838.

Tuesday – September 20

In bed went on with the Noeud Gordien – found that I had read some of the tales before. It was at the Burlington Hotel in January 1847. After breakfast finished clearing off my arrears of correspondence, then walked an hour or two, came back and set to work on my speeches. So ends this journal of my travels – very pleasant travels they were. I had good health, generally good weather, a good friend and a good servant.

Tuesday – September 20

Ellis to dinner – a quiet pleasant evening. Franz came – I settled with him. An excellent servant.

Wednesday – September 21

Not very well. The Port and Sherry do not agree with me after the light wines. I walked into the City – saw the Longmans, and made some arrangements – back – bought by the way D'Israeli's Coningsby and Philipps's Memoirs of Curran[1] – wrote – Maynooth[2] – Dissenter's Chapel Bill. At dinner Collier de la Reine.[3] In the evening Philipps – execrable scribbler.

1. Charles Philips, *Recollections of Curran* (1818).
2. 14 April 1845, *PD*, 3rd ser., lxxix, 646–58; repr. in *CW*, vol. 8, pp. 303–15.
3. By Alexandre Dumas (*père*) (1849–50).

Thursday – September 22

Finished Philipps trash in bed. I do not like the look of the Cholera at all. After Breakfast Spottiswoode's foreman came. I talked with him about my book and promised to have something ready for him tomorrow. Walked – to the Board of Health saw Tom Taylor and Charles who seems an excellent public servant.[1] Athenaeum journals etc – home and wrote Dissenters' Chapels Bill etc – Interrupted by Mr Pettegrew[2] an antiquary who had written to me about cards – At dinner Collier etc in the evening – but was a little drowsy.

1. Charles Macaulay was Secretary to the Board of Health, 1850–4; Tom Taylor was, in addition to his writing for *Punch*, Under-Secretary for the same period and succeeded as Secretary in 1854 when Charles Macaulay moved to the Board of Audit.
2. Thomas Joseph Pettegrew (1791–1865), surgeon, historian and biographer.

Friday – September 23

In bed Lady Mary Wortley Montague – or rather her descendant's[1] excellent reminiscences, full of spirit and sense. After breakfast to New Street Square. Gave seven speeches to be printed. To Birchin Lane – All right – Home – finished DCB[2] or nearly so. At dinner Collier de la Reine – Sleepy again in the evening.

1. Perhaps Lord Wharncliffe, whose three-volume *Letters and Works of Lady M. W. Montagu* appeared in 1837. He was her grandson.
2. Dissenters' Chapel Bill.

Saturday – September 24

Finished D.C. Bill. I have now 21 speeches completed. I have nine more to write and 4 ready written – to the R.I. – Then to the Temple. By rail and coach to Bromley. Walked with the girls to Widmore – a shower and a little thunder. Sate half an hour with the good old ladies[1] then took a long walk with E to Chiselhurst Common and through the grounds of Sundridge[2] – Dinner – Fesc ικμ.

1. These were the Misses Telford, cousins of Ellis's wife Susan, and sisters of Henry Telford, who was partner of the elder John Ruskin. They are described affectionately in his son's *Praeterita*, paras. 27–8. They were Sarah (*c.* 1781–1861), Mary Anne (1783–1869) and Susannah (*c.* 1787–1862).
2. Sundridge Park at Bromley was the seat of Samuel Scott (1807–69).

Sunday – September 25

Day stormy and rainy. Regular equinoctial weather. To Church however and heard a very bad sermon. In the afternoon it cleared up. The wind was still high: but the sun was bright. E and I had a long walk to Hayes – Hayes Common

– along Holwood. Came home soon after 6 – I read a book of Bristed's on Cambridge.[1] The book contains much that is good, though the writer is an offensive fellow. Dined at ½ after 9 – to bed very sleepy.

1. C. A. Bristed, *Five Years in an English University* (1852).

Monday – September 26

Good night. After breakfast off by coach. Captain Cator joined us. I find that Hallam was in Hayes Church when E and I passed it in our walk yesterday. From London Bridge walked with E to the Temple – thence home – found a letter from B – wrote to her and S – wrote a little – Maynooth – walked – came back and wrote again. Tomorrow will finish the speech, I hope – at dinner Collier de la Reine. After dinner drowsy. Today I bought a new pair of spectacles, a little, and but a little, stronger.

Tuesday – September 27

While dressing read the report of Miss Wagner's case[1] by Adolphus and Ellis – interesting. After breakfast wrote a little Maynooth – then walked – home wrote more – the famous peroration. How white poor Peel looked while I was speaking. I remember the effect of the words "There you sit" – Collier de La Reine. Letter from my Dutch translator. He is startled by the severity of some of my speeches and no wonder. He knows nothing of the conflicts of parties.

1. Johanna Wagner, née Jackmann (1826–94) was a German soprano and the adopted daughter of the composer. She was contracted in 1852 to sing at Her Majesty's Theatre, but broke her contract with Lumley, its manager, in order to sing for two months at Covent Garden at the invitation of Frederick Gye (1809–78). Lumley sued Gye for £30,000 in damages. The jury in the Queen's Bench found effectively for the defendant, and Lumley was ruined.

Wednesday – September 28

Proofs of the first sheet of my volume – corrected them; and sent them back. Walked long – crossed Hungerford Bridge – home and wrote fair the greater part of the Maynooth Speech. A letter from De Morgan about Newton and Mrs Barton[1] – Answered him – E to dinner – Fes – H – la.

1. Hannah Barton, Sir Isaac Newton's stepsister. For the letter to De Morgan, see *LM*, vol. 5, pp. 355–7.

Thursday – September 29

Rainy day. Staid at home – lighted a fire – wrote to Selina and Hannah – finished transcribing the Maynooth Speech. More proofs – Corrected them. Began the University Tests Speech[1] – Dined alone – C de la R.

1. 9 July 1845, *PD*, 3rd ser., lxxxii, 227–42; repr. in *CW*, vol. 8, pp. 334–8.

Friday – September 30

To the city. At the Longmans – got my account. Excellent – 2047£ to be paid in at Christmas. To the Museum to look for a speech which I made at Edinburgh[1] in the beginning of 1840. Found it in the Morning Chronicle – One of the attendants got me a transcriber. I then went to the Temple. Walked with Ellis to the Houses of Parliament – home – wrote. At dinner Ange Pitou.

1. Presumably that to the Edinburgh Electors on 21 January 1840. TBM refers to it below (entry for 5 October) as of February 1840, but that might be because the *MC* printed it late.

Saturday – October 1

Wrote – a good deal employed now on proofs etc – to the British Museum – the speech not quite transcribed yet – Home – wrote etc – Ange Pitou.

Sunday – October 2

Brooks's – Walked in the Park. Home and wrote – this speech gets on slowly. I am much interrupted by proofs.

Monday – October 3

Passed part of the morning at the R.I. in getting the China speech right. To the Museum and got the Edinburgh Speech. Proofs – Wrote – Vexed to find how slowly this University speech gets on. Dined with E. Walked home – fine night.

Tuesday – October 4

Bad day – staid at home – corrected proofs, and finished after much labour the University Speech – had several letters to write at dinner A.P. A box of grapes came in the evening. I was puzzled at first; but I soon felt sure that they were from Widmore.

Wednesday – October 5

Bad day again. However I sallied out and by help of an omnibus got to New Street Square and gave the printers some more manuscript. To the Temple. Then home by cab. Determined not to print the Edinburgh Speech of February 1840. Worked on the Corn Law Speech of December 1845[1] and got on much to my satisfaction. Not quite well – but nothing to speak of. At dinner Comtesse de Charny.[2]

1. On 2 December 1845, given in Edinburgh; repr. in *CW*, vol. 8, pp. 349–59.
2. By Alexandre Dumas (*père*) (1852).

Thursday – October 6

Letter from dear little Alice – answered her. Walked a little. At R.I. met Barlow.[1] Ld Campbell called in the afternoon – very kind. I finished the corn law speech and like it much. Then Comtesse de Charny. This morning I ordered dinner at the Clarendon for a small party tomorrow. A folly – I do not know why I committed it. But n'importe.

1. Revd John Barlow, Secretary to the Royal Institution, 1842–62.

Friday – October 7

Corrected some more proofs. Walked into the City – back by Omnibus to Tottenham Court Road – Saw [illeg.] and was [illeg.] – but [illeg.] . Wrote a little of the Factory Speech[1] and a few words of the Phil Inst Speech[2] – read C de Cy – looked at Aristophanes. To dinner at Clarendon – Panizzi, Holmes, Ellis. A good dinner, and not an unpleasant party, except that honest H took a little too much and became more voluble than intelligible.

1. On the Ten Hours Bill, 22 May 1846. *PD*, 3rd ser., lxxxvi, 1028–44; *CW*, vol. 8, pp. 360–76.
2. 4 November 1846, 'On the Literature of Britain', delivered at the opening of the Edinburgh Philosophical Institution; *CW*, vol. 8, pp. 377–84.

Saturday – October 8

To the Museum – Long stupid sitting. Wrote letters. Worked at the Factory Speech, but did little. I like the speech amazingly. I rather think that it is my very best. But I do not get on fast with the corrections. Ctse de Charny. A violent thunder storm in the afternoon.

Sunday – October 9

Quite a summer day after the storm of yesterday. I went to Brooks's – then walked in the park – felt a little uneasiness of the head – as I used to do in the spring – the effect perhaps of the change of weather. Went by steamer to Chelsea and walked home. Charles called – talked about Cholera – wrote, but not much. Ctse de Charny – finished it.

Monday – October 10

Still fine. Proofs etc. – wrote. Into the city – saw my book – all right – called on Ld Campbell – home and wrote again. I am copying out fair the Factory Speech. I am very partial to it. Read some of Paul Féval's Parvenus[1] – E to dinner – sate late.

1. Paul Féval, *Les Parvenus* (1853).

Tuesday – October 11

Vexed to hear by a letter from H that an American blackguard has published in the N.Y. Tribune a story about my having destroyed my faculties with opium.[1] And yet of all calumnies the least pernicious is one so flagrantly false that nobody who knows me will give it a moment's attention. Walked – called on Hallam – missed him. He called at the same time here and missed me. Vexatious. Wrote with spirit and success. Read some of the new No. of the E.R. – A very good paper on the Newspaper stamp by Russell.[2] A very clever paper which will make a great deal of noise on Church parties – evidently by Stephen.[3] Ariosto's Lena[4] – Féval's Parvenus.

1. TBM hotly rejected it; see *LM*, vol. 5, pp. 360–1.
2. *ER*, 98 (October 1843), pp. 488–578. Alexander Russell (1814–76) was originally a printer who became a journalist; he edited the *Kilmarnock Chronicle* and finally the *Scotsman*.
3. It was actually by W. J. Conybeare; see *ER*, 98 (October 1843), pp. 273–342.
4. Lodovico Ariosto, *La Lena* (1537).

Wednesday – October 12

Rainy day. Sate quiet and worked. Speech on Factories. Very good I think, Hallam called – pleasant chat. In the evening to dine with E.

Thursday – October 13

Letter from H about George. To the Temple in consequence – E not there sate long and read the Crito and half the Apology again. Thought of them much as I did when I read them at Tunbridge Wells two months ago – to the Athenaeum. Home and finished the Factories Speech – my best I think, finished the Parvenus – Stuff – Dressed and went to Stratheden House[1] – small party but not unpleasant – Lewis – Lady Theresa and Panizzi. Read some of King's Memoirs.[2] Today wrote to dearest B whose birthday is tomorrow.

1. The London residence of Lord Campbell and his wife, Lady Stratheden.
2. Perhaps the *Political and Literary Anecdotes of His Own Time* (1818) of William King (1685–1763), principal of St Mary's Hall, Oxford.

Friday – October 14

To the Temple again – lines on the French Grenadiers – corrected the Edinburgh Speech of May 1839.[1] It would have been easier to rewrite it. Plagued with this absurd opium lie. A Letter from America enclosing a queer article in an Albany paper and containing good advice. I was rather glad of the opportunity of contradicting the impudent slander. I dare say that the contradiction will soon be published. Dr King – note his eulogy on Burnett s disinterestedness. Dined at home – Bleak House – Better than I thought it.

1. 29 May 1839, separately printed; repr. in *CW*, vol. 8, pp. 143–59.

Saturday – October 15

Letter from dearest B. Good, affectionate child – God bless her. Correcting the first Edinburgh speech – tedious work. Then went to Brooks's – laughed over the opium story with Ryan and Tufnell – to the Athenaeum – looked at the Quarterly – not much in it. Home – began the Speech against which Professor Forbes wrote a silly book[1] – got on pretty well – at dinner and in the evening Bleak House. It has plenty of faults; but it is better than Dombey or Copperfield.

1. The speech delivered 4 November 1846 on the opening of the Edinburgh Philosophical Institution provoked Professor James David Forbes (1809–68) to write *The Dangers of Superficial Knowledge* (1849). Reprinted in *CW*, vol. 8, pp. 377–84.

Sunday – October 16

Very bad day – wrote the rest of the Philosophical Institute Speech. It is open to the carping of disingenuous critics: but it is lively and contains much truth. Finished Bleak House – much moved by it. But it is a most exaggerated picture of life and manners. Then began Dombey and Son.

Monday – October 17

Began the Speech on Education and the Speech at Edinburgh in 1847.[1] Went to the Athenaeum – looked at the Quarterly. Not much – To Charles at the Board of Health – Walked – Dombey – dined at ½ after 6 – to W.T. – delighted to see them so well and happy.

1. 19 April 1847: *PD*, 3rd ser., xci, 1006–26; repr. in *CW*, vol. 8, pp. 385–405. 27 July 1847: repr. in the *Scotsman* for 28 July 1847 not reprinted in *CW.*

Tuesday – October 18

Nothing from the printers. Went to New Square to complain – Then home by a devious route – bought some French novels secondhand in the Strand. Wrote some more of the Edn Speech – To dinner at W.T. – Pleasant evening.

Wednesday – October 19

Some more proofs at last – corrected them. Then the Education Speech. Longman called. Vexed by his telling me that some traveller of his House had told him a year ago that I took too much wine. These things are more galling to me than they ought to be. This more than the opium for I do drink wine; and I take no opium. Went on writing – looked over two or three Vols of Ben Jonson – Gifford's malice is really laughable.[1] Dombey – To dine with E – Adolphus – Atherton[2] – pleasant enough. I puzzled them with pingues oves – deductum carmen. I am sure that I am right

1. William Gifford, editor of the *Quarterly Review*, published an edition of the works of Ben Jonson with a biographical memoir in 1816.
2. Perhaps (Sir) William Atherton (1806–64), MP for Durham, QC; solicitor and Attorney General.

Thursday – October 20

Resolved not to publish the Edinburgh Speech of 1847.[1] Corrected proofs. To the R.I. and wrote the prefatory notices of seven speeches – sent four off to the printer. To W.T. walked with my dear B to the Pantheon to see Haydon's Lazarus[2] – wretched, we both agreed; but more than kept in countenance by the ridiculous daubs round it – took her home talking about Roman Britain. Dear child – she is reading Gibbon. Excellent sense she has. Home – E to dinner – fes.

1. On 27 July 1847. The speech is in the *Scotsman* for 28 July 1847.
2. 'The Raising of Lazarus', finished 1822.

Friday – October 21

Wrote to Palmerston in favour of Stodart who wants to be Solicitor to the Post Office[1] at Edinburgh – corrected proofs – went on with the Education speech, walked to Westminster looked at the opening where the new Street is to be in which perhaps I may end my days[2] – to Hungerford Bridge – home – vile day – wrote a little more – next week, I hope will finish this job, except indeed the correcting of the press. I shall then take to the history again. Dombie [*sic*] and Son. Dr Holland called. Sir H, I should say.

1. John Riddle Stodart (*c.* 1793–1871), WS. He was not successful, even though he was one of TBM's supporters.
2. Macaulay is presumably referring to Victoria Street, begun at this time; and was perhaps thinking that he might occupy one of the flats in the first block to be built in London by Henry Ashton (1801–72).

Saturday – October 22

To breakfast with Sir H and Lady Holland – pleasant – then home and revised proofs. Wrote a little – to W.T. Dear B has a cold – took a short walk with her in the Park. The Conybeares were at W.T.[1] Clever fellow he has turned out. Home and wrote – the Education Speech is finished, or nearly so in the rough copy. Finished Dombey – At dinner began M[artin] C[huzzlewit].

1. Conybeare's wife was Eliza Rose, daughter of the Vicar of Rothley.

Sunday – October 23

M.C. – after breakfast corrected proof – The Chartist speech – Then to Brooks's – Ld De Mauley – Across the Park and through Kensington Gardens to W.T. H and B poorly and had not been to Church – sate there two hours. Conybeare lunched with them – Home – Corrected the Edinburgh speech of last November.[1] I now see land ahead at no great distance. Read over a good deal of my first Chapter of Wm III[2] – pretty well satisfied. It may be made very good – At dinner and afterwards M.C.

1. Of 2 November 1852, to the Electors of Edinburgh; repr. *CW*, vol. 8, pp. 414–28.
2. *HE*, ch. 13.

Monday – October 24

Letter from the Chester and Holyhead about the renewal of my 3,000£ loan. After breakfast and reading the rest of my 1st Chap of W III went into the City to talk with my bankers and the broker. Determined to ask 5 per cent for 3 years or to be paid off – to Longman's – to E's – to the Athenaeum – read the last 4 vols of Lord Castlereagh's papers.[1] Nothing of much value – But as to him – he was not si diable qu'il était noir. Going home, met Labouchere – walked and chatted. By the bye at the Athenaeum I met Lewis and Bowring and had some chat with them – Bowring I cannot bear. Home at last – wrote out some of the Education Speech – I bought today the pamphlet on the Exorbitant Grants of Wm The Third and Roberton on καν the name has a historical interest – At dinner and afterwards MC.

1. Robert Stewart (1769–1822), Viscount Castlereagh. His papers were edited by his brother Charles in twelve volumes, 1848–53.

Tuesday – October 25

I am fifty three years old today – It is pleasant to think that the last year has been prosperous and, better than prosperous, happy. My health improved – my fortune easy – my family everything that I could wish. At W.T. nothing but affection for me and for each other. Corrected proofs – to the R.I to look at Journals etc and to write prefaces – home and wrote some more of the Education Speech. It is not bad: but it drags. Charles paid in the quarter's interest on the mortgage – To W.T. to dinner – Very happy.

Wednesday – October 26

Corrected proofs – wrote more of the Education Speech – then went out – walked some time – Athenaeum – Alexandre Dumas's Memoirs[1] – stuff – bought some books on the other side of Westminster Bridge – while walking read Sir Herbert Taylor's account of the death of the Duke of York.[2] Odd that I should not have read it at the time. I remember Cobbett's allusions to it – Mightily absurd – Yet those accounts of lingering deaths have a mournful interest as one grows older. Home wrote more – M.C. – Letter from F 128 pounds to pay for her and S. Thank heaven, it is the last.

1. Alexandre Dumas (*père*), *Mes Mémoires*, 2 vols (1852–5).
2. Sir Herbert Taylor, *A Memoir of the Last Seven Months of the Life of his Late Royal Highness the Duke of York* (1827). Frederick Augustus, Duke of York and Albany, was born in 1763.

Thursday – October 27

Corrected proofs – to the R.I. – Prefaces – Wrote Education Speech – to Bedford Square to call on Inglis who has lost his sister.[1] To W.T. Baba not quite well and heavy rain – sate with her an hour. Home by cab – wrote – read pamphlets – Ralph, I imagine, in answer to the Duchess of Marlborough.[2] Curious book by a crazy quaker dedicated to Queen Anne – finished M.C – at dinner NN – More pamphlets – NN.

1. Mary Louisa Inglis had died aged sixty-four on 20 October at 7, Bedford Square, London.
2. Perhaps James Ralph, *The Other Side of the Quakers* (1742), confuting R. N. Hookes, *Account of the Conduct of the Duchess of Marlborough*. The Duchess published her Memoirs in 1742.

Friday – October 28

Correcting proofs – then to R.I. – Then to Brooks's – Met Rutherford – Long talk – most pleasant and satisfactory – discussed reform etc – Walked – home – wrote – finished Education Speech at last – a twelve days business or nearly so – and why I cannot conceive. I like it much. Only one more left to be written. Read a French book of Travels in England. D'Inverness à Brighton[1] – At dinner N.N.

1. Pierre Trabaud, *D'Inverness à Brighton* (London, 1853).

Saturday – October 29

Not quite the thing – My eyes and head do not bear much work. Otherwise pretty well. Corrected proofs. To the R.I. To W.T. showed them a letter of a great fool who wants me to tell him What is Truth. He has sent, he says, the same query to many people, and has got a collection of most curious and interesting answers. Home – wrote some of the Master of the Rolls Speech[1] – the last that I have to write, heaven be praised. A letter from the Hoggs[2] – answered it. Read the crazy Restoration of Israel by Rabbi Crooll, and Scott's absurd answer to it.[3] A well matched pair. Trevelyan called. The danger of war seems to be over. At dinner NN – In the evening corrected proofs.

1. See above, entry for 1 June 1853; in *CW*, vol. 8, pp. 429–42.
2. Perhaps Sir James Weir Hogg (1790–1876), MP for Honiton, a Chairman of the East India Company. He married Mary Claudina Swinton (*c.* 1805–74).
3. Joseph Crool, *The Restoration of Israel ... and an Answer by Thomas Scott* (1814).

Sunday – October 30

Wrote a little – to Brooks's – Lord De Mauley – Talked about a mighty foolish letter of Fitzroy's to the Presbytery of Edinburgh[1] – to W.T. pleasant hour and a half there – Home – wrote more – and well – read some of the 12th Chapter of my History. At dinner N.N. – finished it – Began Little Pedlington.[2]

1. Perhaps Henry Fitzroy (1807–59), Under-Secretary for the Home Department, 1852–55.

2. John Poole, *Little Pedlington and the Pedlingtonians* (1839).

Monday – October 31

Went on with my last speech – and satisfactorily. Read some of the History – at dinner finished LP.

Tuesday – November 1

Finished the speech – Thank heaven – to the H of C and ordered a copy of my Black Act Minute.[1] To W.T. – walked with dearest B to Regent Street and back. Alice had a little guest – a daughter of James Cropper[2] – the two girls with their dolls were diverting beyond measure. I forgot to mention that in the morning I went into the City to my bankers and ordered the purchase of 2,000£ worth of L & N.W. and L. & S.W. – good investments I think, at present prices – very near 5 per cent. I shall be paid off by the C and H. E to dinner. He was plagued with sciatica. I was uneasy about him.

---

1. For the 'Black Act' of 1836, see Clive, pp. 333–41. There were in fact three minutes, and they are given in C. D. Dharker, *Lord Macaulay's Legislative Minutes* (1946), pp. 168–97.
2. James Cropper (1823–1900) was nephew of Edward Cropper, TBM's brother-in-law. He had two daughters, Frances Anne (1847–1933) and Mary Wakefield (*c.* 1849–1943).

Wednesday – November 2

Examining my history all day. much pleased with the whole – I think it less taking than the first part. But compared with anything that has ever yet been written about W III's reign, it stands high. In the evening a book of the Marquis de Foudras[1] – Caprice d'une grande Dame.

---

1. By Théodore Louis Auguste, Marquis de Foudras (1840).

Thursday – November 3

To the Temple to see how E was going on. Franz was there. Much better – to the H. of Lords to get a sight of the place bills of 1692/3 and 1693/4. Thom very kind; but cannot have them ready for me till tomorrow. Home after lounging at the Athenaeum. Wrote some of my History after a long interval. Commercial legislation of 1693/4. At dinner Dickens O.T.

Friday – November 4

After breakfast correcting sheets. Ld Glenelg called. To the H. of L. – While waiting in the Library for Thom looked over the works of Drummond of Hawthornden[1] – not much in them. Process against the Templars[2]. Curious – I should like to study it. Found the bill which I wanted to see. The place bill of 1693/4. Home – wrote more – to W.T. took a short walk with H and B – a walk shortened by the East wind which is becoming very cold. To W.T. chatted – dined there – pleasant – Home, corrected sheets till bedtime.

1. William Drummond (1585–1649). He wrote poetry and a *History of Scotland*.
2. Perhaps J. Michelet, *Procès des Templiers*, 2 vols (Paris, 1841–51). It was part of a series, 'Collection de documents inédits sur l'histoire de France'.

Saturday – November 5

Guy Faux in all his glory – more so than usual, I think. Wrote a little – then to the City – gave to my bankers orders about the Chester and Holyhead bonds – bought the Dublin University Magazine to see what was said about Sarsfield,[1] but found little that was new to me. Home – wrote pretty well – India & India Company – every subject has a striking and interesting side if people could find it out. At dinner O.T. In the evening corrected proofs.

1. The *Dublin University Magazine* for November 1853 (pp. 509–32) contained a biographical article on Patrick Sarsfield, Earl of Lucan (d. 1693).

Sunday – November 6

Wrote a little – to Brooks's – then walked in the Park and Kensington Gardens. To W.T. – pleasant hour or two there – Read Mr Medhurst's account of the system of Chinese examination.[1] Walked along the New Road – Home by an omnibus from Baker Street. Wrote again; but I must go to the Museum before I can make much more progress with this EIC matter. Finished OT. Began the Old Curiosity Shop.

1. Walter Henry Medhurst (1756–1857), Chinese Missionary. His book *China: Its State and Prospects, with Especial Reference to the Spread of the Gospel; Containing Allusions to the Antiquity, Extent, Population, Civilisation, Literature, and Religion of the Chinese*, published London (1838), contains a section on Chinese examinations (pp. 144–51).

Monday – November 7

After breakfast to the R.I. Wrote prefatory notices to the three last speeches. To the B.M. Passed some hours there over Indian pamphlets of the 17th Century – into the City – left a card on Milman – bought some books near the Museum.

Home – wrote E.I.C.[1] E to dinner at ½ after 7 – In the evening corrected proofs and sent to the printer the last copy.

1. *HE*, ch. 18, *CW*, vol. 3, pp. 467–81.

Tuesday – November 8

Lang – wrote a little – Museum – found much that was curious. To W.T. walked with B to Albany – amused her with my new dressing gown. How she laughed. Then we walked to Soho Square I bought some books at Russell's – took her home in a cab – back – wrote a little of the preface.[1] Looked at my newly purchased books – At dinner and afterwards finished the Old Curiosity Shop.

1. To his *Speeches* (1854).

Wednesday – November 9

Corrected proofs – wrote some of the preface. Macleod called – long talk about metaphysics. In the afternoon H B and A called – took them to Westminster Hall and walked about the Houses – H and A went on to Clapham. I walked with B to W.T. – met Ld Lansdowne in the Green Park. He very kind as usual – pleasant walk and talk – We met Sir James Stephen at Hyde Park Corner. I love him and owe much to him. Yet he is not in a pleasant state of mind, I hardly know how. Home. At dinner Ten Thousand a Year. Carlisle's Freemasonry.[1] By the bye among my purchases of yesterday was an exquisitely absurd Life of that stupid, worthless, drunken, dirty beast Tom Paine by a Mr Clio Rickman.[2] There is not a line in Tom that any sixth rate radical and infidel might not write who would stoop to write it.

1. Richard Carlile, *Manual of Freemasonry* (1845).
2. Thomas 'Clio' Rickman (1761–1834), *The Life of Thomas Paine ...* (London, 1819). He was a Quaker.

Thursday – November 10

Corrected proofs – began preface – some of the history. Into the City and saw Thornton. I think of buying more railway stock – bought a painting of a female figure something like St Seb[astia]n or E [illeg.] – dined at home. 10,000£ a year.

Friday – November 11

Walked – preface etc – dined with Ellis.

Saturday – November 12

Museum – thence home to give a lunch to the W.T. party – Vexed that G was not there. Very pleasant – then wrote – dined alone – 10,000.

Sunday – November 13

Wrote preface – Brooks's – W.T. – T gave me a paper on the organization of the public offices. Very good, – by himself and Northcote.[1] Saw Hankey[2] and talked with him about the Bank. Home and wrote – at dinner 10,000.

1. The paper of Sir Charles Trevelyan and Sir Stafford Northcote on *The Organisation of the Permanent Civil Service* (1853).
2. Thomas Hankey (1805–93), director of the Bank of England.

Monday – November 14

Wrote to good purpose both E.I.C. and preface. Hallam called – a pleasant hour with him. To dine at W.T. – very pleasant – but I felt painfully the approach of the cold weather.

Tuesday – November 15

A thick fog – forced to light my fire and to dress by candle light. I sent excuses to Wood on whom I was to have called and to the Milmans with whom I was to have dined. Wrote a good deal – both preface and history. At three Wood called – long and interesting talk about both the Law Commission and the Competition. I promised to see both Macleod and Ellis, and to get answers from them both by the time that he returns from Windsor.[1] T. called. I told him what had passed. At dinner 10,000.

1. Wood had appointed a law commission for India; Ellis and Macleod were members. Also under consideration were proposals for competitive entry to the Indian Civil Service. Cf. R. J. Moore, *Sir Charles Wood's Indian Policy* (Manchester, 1966), esp. chs 4 and 5.

Wednesday – November 16

Fine day. Corrected proofs. H and B called – went back with them to W.T. H disturbed by an idle report about T and Madras. They will never offer it to him; and if they did, it would be madness in him to go.[1] To Macleod's. He not at home. Left a note. To B. M. looked at newspapers of 1844 – Home – wrote – Macleod came – settled the whole with him as easily as possible and not without some diplomatic skill. E to dinner. Settled also with him.

1. Trevelyan was offered and accepted the Governorship of Madras in 1859.

Thursday – November 17

After breakfast finished the preface, put it in my pocket went into the city – signed the necessary papers for my S.W. Stock. To the printing office and gave my preface to the managing man. Then home – wrote to Wood. Today a Mr Somers got 5£ from me[1] for a free library in Marylebone. Mrs Holland wrote to ask me to write a sketch of the state of the Church at the time when her father became a clergyman. Declined for many reasons. Sydney[2] had many excellent qualities: but it was not as a priest that he shone; and I will not prostitute my pen. Sent a good many sheets to Franz at the Hague.[3] Wrote – India – at dinner half ashamed – Val V.[4]

1. Possibly Judah George Somers (1810–79), a wholesale stationer and publisher living in Bury Street, St Mary Axe.
2. Smith. His daughter Saba (1802–66) married Dr Henry Holland in 1834. Since her husband's knighthood, she was Lady Holland. She published her own Life of her father in 1855.
3. Emilius Franz, Dutch translator of *HE*.
4. Henry Cockton, *Life and Adventures of Valentine Vox the Ventriloquist* (1840).

Friday – November 18

Chest unpleasant – after breakfast to Ld Lansdown's. Meeting about poor Mackintosh's monument[1] – Walked away with Mahon – to R.I. looked again at Times – altered my preface for the better. In the afternoon suffered a good deal. Wrote something but was unstrung. Read Mathew's Life.[2] In the evening had a mustard poultice and took some rhubarb and Ipecacuanha.

1. William Theed (1804–91) executed a bust of Sir James Mackintosh, which was installed in Westminster Abbey in 1857. See Volume 3, entry for 22 May 1852.
2. Perhaps *Memoirs of Charles Matthews* (1839).

Saturday – November 19

Better. It was fit that I should be so, as I had a breakfast party. Dearest H – The Dean and Mrs M – Dundas, Sir C Wood, Hallam and Macleod – very pleasant – sate till one – Tauchnitz – civil and friendly. He ought to be; for he has, I believe, made much by me; but he has done so quite fairly, and by taking a risk which I should not have taken. I went out but only for a short time. Easier today and wrote more – Mathews – VV – stuff.

Sunday – November 20

A miserable day. Staid at home – wrote, but not very much – looked into Apuleius – read Aulus Gellius, pretty nearly through, that is to say as such books ought to be read, skipping a good deal. My old Indian notes were of use to me – I found one very amusing one. T called – I showed him part of what I had written about the EIC – he liked it. E to dinner – Soirées de Neuilly.[1]

1. H. A. Cavé and A. Dittmer, *Les Soirées de Neuilly: Esquisses Dramatiques et Historiques* (Brussels, 1827).

Monday – November 21

Soirees at breakfast. Note from Thornton. He had bought me 1400£ of Midland & Gt Wn Ireland. I shall have an income this year much larger than that of last year, and, as far as I can foresee, a smaller expenditure. To R.I. to examine the journals about the E.I.C. To W.T. – Back with H and B in the carriage to Fortnum & Mason's – got H some Curaçao[1] and Maraschino.[2] Home – not well – Percy Effingham[3] – Stuff.

1. An orange liqueur, named after the Caribbean island.
2. A liqueur distilled from the *marasca* cherry, grown in Dalmatia.
3. By Henry Cockton (1853).

Tuesday – November 22

Dreadfully foggy day – staid at home – but no great heart for writing – my respiration dreadfully oppressed. H and B called – Ld Lansdowne – Sir H. Holland – E to dinner. He went home through a tremendous fog – I had a blister.

Wednesday – [November 23]

Worse than yesterday. Trevelyan and Baba came at breakfast time. The blister had done nothing: so I sent for Bright. He pronounced my general health much improved and gave me a prescription. I wrote and read all day – Ate and drank little and went early to bed. Julian[1] – GSG.

1. *George St. George Julian, the Prince*, by Cockton.

Thursday – November 24

Better certainly, but still poorly. Wrote to F to take rooms for me at Brighton – At home all day reading and writing – H and A called with Miss R, A's governess. In the evening E very kindly came to dinner. Cradock's Memoirs.

Friday – November 25

Better weather. I am much the same as yesterday. Cradock – wrote – finished E.I.C. now for the Bank of England – Longman – He assents – eagerly indeed

– to my proposition of ¾. I am content. No doubt I could drive a harder bargain. Bright came. Approved of Brighton – forbade me to dine out today. Vexed on H's account. B came to beg me to go. Very sorry to refuse. But my own sensations confirmed Bright's opinion. Letter from F. She has done excellently. Read a good deal – Cradock. At dinner Julian – Cradock again. Not yet well.

Saturday – November 26

Better – At breakfast H, B and T. Pleasant half hour with them – packed – read Napier's article on the Life of Sir John Moore[1] – looked into Seymour's History of London[2] – etc. Glad to have done with the E.I.C.. When I settle here again I shall soon dispatch the Bank – then the military events of 1694 – Then the reform of the coinage – then the negotiation. All this, I hope, by Easter. Then the narrative will be connected from beginning to end. It will require, to be sure, immense correction, insertion, etc. But I think that a year of hard work will do the whole. Then I am a free man and probably a rich man. Soon after one off for Brighton. Bad weather – got to Brighton – soon after four – F had secured for me excellent lodgings in Regency Square – fronting the sea – first floor – warm and comfortable – wrote letters, dined alone, read Julian – Bunyan – F and S called, kind, and sate an hour in the evening.

1. Sir William Napier reviewed James Carrick Moore's *Life of Sir John Moore* in the *Edinburgh Review* for April 1834, vol. 59, pp. 1–29. James Moore was Sir John's brother.
2. Perhaps Robert Seymour, *A Survey of the Cities of London and Westminster* (1734). This was the work of John Mottley (1692–1740), who used the pseudonym Robert Seymour in what was an edition of Stow.

Sunday – November 27

Bad weather – staid at home and wrote a good deal of my article on Bunyan for Black.[1] F called. Fully and not unpleasantly employed all day. In the evening Julian.

1. One of the biographies written by Macaulay for the *Encyclopaedia Britannica*, at the request of Adam Black.

Monday – November 28

Still dull weather – went out however with F – to the fruiterer's to order dessert – to the fishmonger's and sent them a barrel of oysters – to the bookseller's and bought a novel about Derry by Charlotte Elizabeth.[1] The woman is or was a fool. But there might have been some reference to some authority which had excaped me. Home – wrote – read Derry. F and S to dinner – pleasant evening. Looked at Derry and found it utter trash.

1. Charlotte Elizabeth (pseudonym of C. E. Phelan, afterwards Tonna), *Derry, a Tale of the Revolution* (1833).

Tuesday – November 29

Rain – at home all day writing and reading – dined alone – S and F have an oyster party. Tulipe Noire.[1]

1. By Alexandre Dumas (*père*) (1850).

Wednesday – November 30

Dull day – but a little better than yesterday – short walk with F – reading and writing hard. In the evening began Coningsby – S and F dine out.

Thursday – December 1

Fine day at last – very fine – took a pleasant walk with F – bought a ridiculous Puseyite version of the Pilgrim's Progress.[1] Sent S and F some more oysters and a good supply of game. Then home and worked hard. I have all but finished this article for Black. S and F to dinner – read them the paper in the evening and some bits of the Holy War which they didn't seem to know and liked much.

1. Presumably the edition by John Mason Neale, published in 1853, included in Macaulay's sale catalogue and probably also the work referred to scathingly in his article on Bunyan, *CW*, vol. 7, pp. 297–309.

Friday – [December 2]

Fine day again. Finished my article on Bunyan or nearly so. Walk with F – met E Cropper[1] to my surprise – to Temple House – took leave of S and F. I am much pleased to see them so comfortable. They are very kind and much more grateful than I at all deserve. Bills paid – off to the station and to town. Read Coningsby occasionally by the way. The satire is often clever. The philosophical parts utterly worthless in matter and manner. Whatever is not trifle or truism is blunder; and the affected sententiousness with which so many foolish things are said is most disgusting. He is a thorough mountebank. Examined papers and letters – answered some – E to dinner.

1. Edward Cropper, now married to his third wife, Henry Macaulay's widow, Margaret.

Saturday – December 3

A fool named Macknight[1] called – I never saw so loathsome a compound of ass and jackanape; – smirking, confident, perfectly at ease, and disposed to honor me with his friendship. He had been treating with Bentley about publishing a book, thought Bentley's terms hard, and came to ask my advice. The terms are such as Mr M'Knight's betters, I for one, have often willingly taken. I told him that they seemed fair. But he would not be got rid of. He told me that his book was a Life of Disraeli[2] – well matched – coxcomb and charlatans both. But I do not think that MK, though he quite equals the Jew in impudence equals him in ability. The fellow wanted me to revise his sheets. I gave him a firm cold refusal: but he did not seem to be dashed. When he was gone W. Longman came. We held a council against Vizetelly; and I suggested a scheme which W.L. approved highly and which, I really think, will answer. Then to R.I. to look at Magazines etc. Then by cab to W.T. pleasant two hours.[3] Dear B not quite well. A[lice] delightful. H brought me home. Read Roger North's Lives of DN and JN.[4] At dinner C[oningsb]y, after dinner Ld Hervey. Took hydr.

1. Thomas McKnight (1829–99), journalist and biographer.
2. T. Macknight, *The Rt. Hon. B. Disraeli* (1854).
3. Vizetelly had threatened legal action; see *LM*, vol. 5, pp. 370 and n., 371. Perhaps the scheme included the *Examiner* article below, entry for 11 December 1853.
4. Roger North, *Lives of the Norths* (his brothers Francis, Dudley and John), appeared in 1742–4.

Sunday – December 4

Vile day – Thick fog – staid at home – wrote – Bank – looked over a good deal. Very well satisfied on the whole. The book will do, I think. T called in the afternoon – Ld H[ervey]. At dinner Cy.

Monday – December 5

Dull day – Off for the G.W. Station. Too early by an hour in consequence of a blunder in Bradshaw's Railway Guide. To W.T. and sate with H – Off at last – bought at the Station a No. of Thackeray's Novel[1] and Carlton's Squanders[2] – Read Thackeray and finished Disraeli's Coningsby. Mrs Milman[3] in the carriage, going to her eldest son who has broken his arm. I felt much for her. At Chippenham a carriage waiting for me as I had ordered – broke my spectacles. Happily at Bowood I found Senior who had two pair, and lent me one. Lady Theresa her husband and her daughter made, with the family, a very pleasant party. There were also two artists Philipps and Watts[4] – clever men. I suffered much from my cough and was forced to leave the table during the dessert. In the evening I was better: but at night I got no rest.

1. Presumably *The Newcomes*, published serially 1853–55.
2. William Carlton, *The Squanders of Castle Squander* (1852).
3. See *LM*, vol. 5, pp. 368–9 for a fuller account.
4. Henry Wyndham Phillipps (1820–68) and George Frederick Watts (1817–1904).

Tuesday – December 6

Staid at home all day – the artists gone – pleasant chat with the ladies. In the afternoon read Calamy's Memoirs[1] which I must consult again. Looked at the memoirs of Joseph Buonaparte[2] – read a good deal of Plumer Ward's Diary[3] – better in the evening than yesterday. But the night as bad as the last – Resolved to go home tomorrow. Senior gone.

1. Edmund Calamy (1671–1732), *An Historical Account of my own Life by Edmund Calamy*, ed. J. T. Rutt (1829).
2. *Mémoires et Correspondence ... du Roi Joseph*, ed. P. E. A. Du Casse (1853).
3. *Memoirs of the Political and Literary Life of Robert Plumer Ward*, ed. E. Phipps (1850).

Wednesday – December 7

Dull day – passed the morning very pleasantly in chat with the ladies and Lewis. I have looked over another volume of poor Ld Holland's Reminiscences.[1] Very ill written, but they contain some curious information and interesting judgments on character. After lunch off for Chippenham. Thence by express to town – Read Carlton's Sq[uanders] during the journey and at dinner. In the evening Ld Hervey.

1. Perhaps Lord Holland's *Memoirs of the Whig Party*, 2 vols (1852–4), edited by his son.

Thursday – December 8

Foggy day – In spite of the weather I went to E's and to W.T. – G is at home for his holidays. He has done very well – Home – much oppressed by phlegm. Looked into historical matters. Read a good deal of the State Poems[1] – Ld H – Letter from M[illeg.][2]. By the bye Ballis [?] has reason to cry [two words illeg.] – E to dinner – Hydr.

1. *State Poems ... From the Time of O. Cromwell to ... 1697.*
2. Perhaps 'McFarlane'.

Friday – December 9

The weather bad. However I went out to the City on business. I find that the Gt M[idland] & W[ester]n I[relan]d is going to pay me off – 5,000£ and it is necessary to think about investments. I was sorry that T was not at the Bank. Home, and wrote – Sir J Knight and the Dutch.[1] At dinner Carlton – poor stuff. Letter from the Cambridge Union asking for my speeches.

1. *HE*, ch. 20, *CW*, vol. 4, pp. 82–3.

Saturday – December 10

Cold, but clear. To the R.I. – to the Museum – looked over the Dutch Despatches – then to the Board. Odd scene. Inglis and one of the Socy of Antiquaries had written a very cool letter to himself and the rest of us as Trustees. We were exclaiming against the impertinence of the letter, when he told us that it was his own. Happily he is an excellently constituted man; and his good humour carried it well off. Home and wrote – Adolphus called – At dinner Jacob πιστ[1] Ld H[ervey].

1. Frederick Marryat, *Jacob Faithful*; πιστικός = faithful.

Sunday – December 11

Vile day – However to Brooks's – The Examiner civil to me about the speeches[1] – The Advertiser very eulogistic – The Spectator snapping and snarling as usual – Qu'importe? To W.T. Found H not very well – Mangles called and my brother Charles. I settled that G and B should dine with me on Tuesday. Home in a cab and wrote. At dinner Jacob then Mrs Inchbald's Memoirs[2] – a stupid existence and a stupid Book – Bubb Dodington.[3]

1. *Examiner*, 2393 (10 December 1853), p. 788: a full account of Vizetelly's dishonesty and a warm appreciation of TBM's career.
2. *Memoirs of Mrs. Inchbald*, ed. J. Boaden (1833).
3. Perhaps *Diary of the Late George Bubb Dodington*, ed. H. P. Wyndham (1784).

Monday – December 12

Staid at home all day – a vile day – wrote a great deal – Sir JK etc – E to dinner – He could not stay long – finished Dodington.

Tuesday – December 13

Still vile fog and East wind – Letter from Tauchnitz with contract – Sir J Hawkins.[1] Then wrote – Eleventh Chapter – got on well. In the evening George and Baba dined with me; very pleasant they were.

1. Perhaps TBM was reading his *Life of Samuel Johnson* (1787). See below, entry for 18 December 1853.

Wednesday – December 14

At home all day – the Eleventh Chapter – annotating – correcting adding, omitting, etc. Much pleased – Hallam called – told me that Vizetelly has been attacking me in the Standard – sent out for it. Nothing. H left me a droll jeu d'esprit enough – Mr Verdant Green[1] – laughed over it heartily – Plumer Ward's Diary.

1. Edward Bradley (pseud. Cuthbert Bede) (1827–89), *The Adventures of Mr. Verdant Green, an Oxford Freshman* (1853).

Thursday – December 15

The old story – Chap XI – at home all day – got on much to my satisfaction. Finished Mr V.G. – Ld Malmesbury's Diary.[1]

1. *Diaries and Correspondence of... Earl of Malmesbury* (1844).

Friday – December 16

Palmerston's resignation![1] Another day of work – Chap XII I am really in high spirits about my book. H to dinner. Read her Bunyan.[2] Very pleasant dinner and chat in the evening. I am most happy in my family thank God.

1. He resigned in protest at the radicalism of Russell's proposals for parliamentary reform, but by Christmas he had come to regret his impulsiveness (or the way his bluff had been called) and was persuaded to return. See J. B. Conacher, *The Aberdeen Coalition* (1968), ch. ix.
2. His short biography for the *Encyclopaedia Britannica*.

Saturday – December 17

Again the same, except that I stole out for half an hour to the R.I. – consulted journals and Statute Book, and looked at the papers. I see that I am blamed for abusing Vizetelly. Perhaps I stooped too much in naming him. Got on very well with my Scotch narrative. Still in good spirits. The 2nd part will, I think, take nearly, if not quite, as much as the first. At dinner Peter Simple. Finished Ld Malmesbury. Two more vols of Tom Moore[1] – I am mentioned but with the greatest civility.

1. Vols 5 and 6.

Sunday – December 18

Finished Tom Moore – put it in my pocket for H – to Brooks's – Saw Stevenson[1] – N Macdonald,[2] Lord de Mauley – chat – awkward business this of Palmerston – doubt about Ld L. I am surprised to find how strong the sentiment of moderate and sensible men seems to be against Ld Aberdeen's foreign policy. To W.T.

pleasant hour and a half there. Much amused by Alice's mixed love and fear of her dog, which seems to be a general favourite. – Home – Went through Toleration Act and Comprehension Bill.[3] In a few days Chap XII will be ready for the press. At dinner P.S. Then Hawkins's Life of Johnson.

1. Perhaps Augustus Keppel Stephenson (1827–1904), at this time Recorder of Bedford. He seems to be the only member of Brooks's Club of this name at this time.
2. Norman Macdonald, Controller of the Lord Chamberlain's Department, 1852–7; son of Sir John McDonald, Adjutant General.
3. *HE*, ch. 11, *CW*, vol. 2, pp. 461–75.

Monday – [December 19]

Work all day – E to dinner – Very happy and comfortable.

Tuesday – [December 20]

Another day of work and solitude. I enjoy this invalid life extremely. Kind letter from Shelburne.

Wednesday – December 21

St Thomas's. To the City to see Thornton. Had ten words with him and made my arrangements: back wrote – not well – coughed much, Hydr.

Thursday – [December 22]

Another day of work – Better – H and T to dinner – very agreeable.

Friday – [December 23]

Again shut up working – E to dinner – Letter from Ld Lansdowne.

Saturday – December 24

Today we keep Christmas. Worked all the morning. In the afternoon to W.T. A happy afternoon and evening. The pleasure which I take in their society and I think, their affection for me increases. In spite of my gradually sinking health, this has been a happy year. I went and returned in my Brougham.

Sunday – December 25

Work – to W.T. in a cab and sate an hour or two very pleasantly – back and worked again – read over my journal of the latter part of 1850 – At dinner finished PS.[2]

1. *Peter Simple*, by Frederick Marryat.

Monday – December 26

I am alone – T, H, B, G, A, E – all out of town for some days. I have plenty to do and my spirits are excellent. I staid at home writing and reading. Scotch affairs. I like Scotch parliamentary business less than any other part of my task. However it must be done. The weather cold. It affected my respiration in spite of closed windows and blazing fire – At dinner LM Coct[1] – In the evening Life of Ld Eldon.[2] Hydr.

1. Henry Cockton, *The Love Match* (1845).
2. H. Twiss, *Public and Private Life of Lord Chancellor Eldon* (1844).

Tuesday – December 27

Very cold – At home all day – 10£ to Μακφ – wrote and read – Scotch parlt of 1689.[1] Unsatisfactory: but it must be done – Austin called.[2] I had not seen him for years. He looks much better. We had a long and very pleasant talk. No man is more agreeable; and I cannot help liking him. I wish that he were less penurious. At dinner LM. Then Ld Eldon.

1. *HE*, ch. 13, *CW*, vol. 3, pp. 1–101.
2. John Austin: his brother Charles was not penurious.

Wednesday – December 28

Still frost. Again staid at home – In the afternoon the snow came down rather heavily. Letter from dear B. Wrote and read. Scotch parlt still. I wish it were over. Sir H Holland called – talked long. War seems coming at last – LM – Ld Eldon. Another impudent begging circular letter from Buckingham[1] – Impudent fool! An odd incident in the evening υπν.

1. James Silk Buckingham (1786–1855).

Thursday – December 29

I went to the Athenaeum in spite of frost, and made some useful extracts. I went home and worked. In the afternoon my breath was painfully affected, and I was rather low. I fought on however. L.M. Finished Twiss Life of Eldon – Boswell – I have not read the Life of Johnson now these many years. Hydr.

Friday – December 30

Better. Dear B and G called soon after breakfast – Promised to dine at W.T. though with some misgivings, which increased as the day grew worse and worse. A furious snow storm – I read and wrote. The Dean of St Paul's called and sate half an hour. At four to W.T. in my carriage wrapped up, and handkerchief at mouth. Very pleasant evening. Not worse for it I think.

Saturday –[December 31]

Letter from E – very cold – staid at home all day – finished the Scotch parlt of 1689 – began upon Chap XVI and Schomberg. On the whole I am working to good purpose. E to dinner. So ends the year. Happily on the whole. My health is failing. My life will not, I think, be long. But I have clear faculties warm affections, abundant sources of pleasure.

[A severe winter played havoc with Macaulay's health. Frosts and fog made him cough painfully when he went out, and he even considered, in May, moving to chambers elsewhere. He cut down on social engagements and used his seclusion to read for the *History*. Much of 1854, however, was taken up with the Irish and Scottish parts of the *History*, which belong to volume 3, and much of volume 4 still lay ahead. He also worked vigorously and decisively on the Committee that planned the form of examination for the Indian Civil Service, Trevelyan's and Northcote's plan for competitive examining forming the model. The Committee's Report, which ended the system by which recruits to the civil service in India were admitted to Haileybury at sixteen, was written by Macaulay himself, and the unusual frequency of Jowett's name in the Journal indicates that at least one Oxford figure grasped its importance for the ancient universities. With the Report's publication at the end of November, Macaulay's political obligations were over. Although he attended Parliament occasionally, and kept up his work as a Trustee of the British Museum, it is clear that the *History* came to absorb him to the exclusion of all society but that of his friend Ellis and his sister Hannah and her children. The spring tour with them was a trip to York, Castle Howard and Durham in April. In the summer the Trevelyans rented a house at Esher. Macaulay took another at nearby Thames Ditton, from 5 July to 30 September, so as to see them regularly. The break from the air of central London did him good. He had energy enough in September to take ten days with Ellis in France, touring round Paris and working in the archives. In October he spent a week in Oxford libraries before taking Hannah and Margaret on a visit to John Macaulay in Aldingham. The Journal entries from November onwards are more and more perfunctory, always a sign with Macaulay that he was in the throes of composition. War in the Crimea is only occasionally mentioned.]

Sunday – January 1 1854

This will I hope be a year of industry. I began pretty well. Chap XIV will require a good deal of work. I toiled on it some hours and now and then felt dispirited. But we must be resolute and work doggedly as Johnson said. Read some of his life with great delight – LM at dinner.

Monday – January 2

Worked in solitude. Very cold. In the evening dear B and G to dinner – had a very pleasant chat with them.

Tuesday – January 3

Still at home, – frost, – snow – worked on Schomberg's campaign – LM Finished Johnson's Life. Looked at Edgeworth's Life – dull.[1]

1. *Memoirs of Richard Lovell Edgworth, Esq., begun by himself and concluded by his daughter Maria Edgeworth*, 2 vols (1820).

Wednesday – January 4

Heavy fall of snow. I do not know that I have seen the streets of London in such a state since January 1814 – forty years ago. I remained at home and made myself as warm and comfortable as I could – Schomberg – Bourienne. At dinner LM.

Thursday – January 5

The wind west – milder weather, but very dreary and the streets deep in snow. I staid by my fire – meditated on new arrangement of my history. Arrangement and transition are arts which I value much, but which I do not flatter myself that I have attained. However something may be done. Read a good deal of what I have written – Tolerable – LM Mordaunt – Edward[1] – Hydr.

1. Novels by John Moore (1729–1802): *Edward* (1796) and *Mordaunt* (1800).

Friday – January 6

West wind – milder – however not weather in which to venture out. At breakfast Edward.[1] T called – H cannot come – I am glad of it: for the weather is trying. To work on Chap XIV. Letter from H with Memoirs of Bp Bathurst.[2] Sent her 10£ for the party of Tuesday next. Queer letter from a Johnian named Bushby[3] about Butler's Analogy. Lost a great deal of time in answering him – Sylv Son[4] – Edward.

1. By John Moore (1796).

2. Henry Bathurst, *Memoirs of the late Dr Henry Bathurst, Lord Bishop of Norwich* ... (1837).
3. Edward Bushby (1793–1877), Fellow of St John's College, Cambridge and Vicar of Impington. Said by Venn to have published an edition of the *Analogy*, but none appears in BL Catalogue.
4. Henry Cockton, *Sylvester Sound, the Somnambulist* (1849).

Saturday – January 7

A thaw. Did not stir out. Wrote and read much. I begin to think it certain that, nothing unforeseen preventing, I shall be able to go to press in the Autumn – E to dinner.

Sunday – January 8

Beautiful weather. I wrote a little, and after a week of close imprisonment went to Brooks's. Stephenson[1] chatted – turned over Magazines. To W.T. sate there two or three hours. Macleod came, my brother Charles, a Mr Philip Bouverie[2] – back by Omnibus – wrote on. Read the last No. of the Newcomes at dinner – tracts and pamphlets afterwards.

1. Perhaps Sir Augustus Frederick William Keppel Stephenson (1827–1904).
2. Perhaps Philip Pleydell Bouverie (1788–1872), whose daughter Maria was the bride of Charles Trevelyan's brother William.

Monday – January 9

Bad day again though not very cold – staid at home and worked. Much pleased with Chap XV. I like it now quite as well as Chap XIII or better. The Third Volume will certainly do. There is more doubt about the fourth. Read lampoons etc. New no. of the E.R. At dinner Sylv S. Miss Seward's absurd Life of Darwin.[1] I read it often as a mere study of bad writing and a warning from everything which at all resembles her faults. Thirlwall. Schliermacher.[2]

1. Anna Seward, *Memoirs of the Life of Dr Darwin* ... (1804).
2. Connop Thirlwall, *A Critical Essay on the Gospel of St Luke, by Dr F. Schleiermacher; with an Introduction by the Translator* ... (1825).

Tuesday – January 10

Lewis's WI.[1] After breakfast wrote a little, then to W.T. by cab, as I shall be unable to go in the evening, chatted a while, and back. Wrote hard and well. Scotch affairs in 1690. At dinner Sylv – Thirlwall – Schliermacher – nothing satisfactory.

1. Matthew Gregory (Monk) Lewis, *Journal of a West Indian Proprietor* ... (1834).

Wednesday – January 11

Lewis – Wrote – then to W.T. – glad to find that all went off excellently yesterday. Home – wrote – Thornton called. I ordered a thousand more of L & S.W. I have determined against Canadian bonds; and he seems to think me in the right. At dinner Lever J.H.[1] Then Squibs of 1820. Then Lewis.

1. Charles Lever, *Jack Hinton the Guardsman* (1843).

Thursday – January 12

Lewis – After breakfast wrote vigorously. Still Scotch affairs. By the bye yesterday a Mr Walker left here a curious MS by an Irish officer in James's army,[1] almost illegible and a queer mixture of bad Latin and bad French with English; began on the legal establishment of Presbyterianism. H to dinner. Very pleasant.

1. Probably 'A Light to the Blind', first published by Sir John T. Gilbert as *A Jacobite Narrative* (1892) and reprinted by Professor J. G. Simms as *A Jacobite Narrative of the War in Ireland 1682–91* (Shannon, 1971). Gilbert thought the author was Nicholas Plunket (*c.* 1629–1718), a brother of the Earl of Fingall. Recent scholarship suggests it was by Col. Nicholas Talbot of Drogheda: see *ODNB*, s.v. 'Nicholas Plunket'. Macaulay was the first to use the manuscript in *HE*, ch. 12, *CW*, vol. 2, pp. 513–14.

Friday – January 13

Wrote and read, chiefly about the Presbyterian Establishment. At dinner J.H. Life of Polwhele.[1]

1. Part 1 of the volumes of reminiscences of Richard Polwhele (1760–1838).

Saturday – January 14

No R.I.– To the Museum – long stupid sitting; but I amused myself with reading Southwell's memoranda[1] – curious M.S.S. – fate of a dog. I read also a life of Judson the Missionary.[2] A noble M.S. of the fourteenth century on agriculture with most curious paintings illustrative of the common life of that age. Home and wrote – E to dinner he came early – Fes.

1. Sir Robert Southwell (1635–1702) was a diplomat who had been English envoy in Portugal, 1665–8. TBM may have been reading his manuscript 'Reflections on the Irish Rebellion', Add. MSS 2112g.
2. Perhaps *A Memoir of the Life and Labours of the Rev. A. Judson* (1853).

Sunday – January 15

Wrote – Then by cab to W.T. Sate there two hours. Then home again and wrote – This subject interests me much and may, I think, be made interesting to others. J.H. Pamphlets on Presbyterianism. Wilkie's Memoirs.[1]

1. Perhaps Alan Cunningham, *Biography of Sir David Wilkie* (1843).

Monday – January 16

After breakfast to the City. It was mild. My affairs are at last all in order. I have invested the 5000£ from the Gt S.W. r[ailroa]d, the 3000£ from the Chester and Holyhead, and 1600£ or 1700£ from Longman and have added about eighty pounds a year to my income. Pretty well. A good balance too. Home and wrote hard. At dinner J.H. Wilkie.

Tuesday – January 17

A queer letter from a Yankee Girl[1] – in her teens, she says – enough to turn a young man's head. Walked some time. Home and wrote – finished the rough copy of my account of the Establishment of the Presbyterian Church[2] – finished the Life of Wilkie – tedious and ill written. Queer letter from a Glasgow [illeg. ?padre] who fancies himself a poet, and writes sonnets in lines of all lengths from eight syllables to twelve. Dear B to dinner – very pleasant; but I thought her poorly. She has just been reading Dryden's Æneid and judges of it very justly.

1. *LM*, vol 5, p. 378n.
2. *HE*, ch. 13, *CW*, vol. 3, pp. 1–36.

Wednesday – January 18

A mild moist day – walked then wrote long and with success. The account of the Presbyterian Establishment is nearly finished. To W.T. forgot that there was to be a party and did not dress. It mattered little – GGB had not dressed. His wife, Mrs Rose and Lady Parker were there – pleasant enough – But the old times can never return. I was sorry to see him so poorly. Dearest B ill with a face ache.

Thursday – January 19

A bad night. But not amiss in the morning. Wrote – then walked. Dearest B has the mumps – then worked – E to dinner.

Friday – January 20

Fine day. To W.T. B. much better. Doubtful whether she has the mumps. I do not think that she has. She has difficulty about eating and requires support. Sent her a quart of turtle from the Queen's purveyors. Home – wrote – finished this Scotch matter. Astley Cooper's Life[1] – At dinner J.H.

1. B. B. Cooper, *The Life of Sir Astley Cooper ...* (1843).

Saturday – January 21

Party to breakfast – H, Milman and Mrs M. Hallam, Dundas, Ld Glenelg, Inglis, D. of Argyle. Very pleasant; and I think they all found it so. Then walked. Then home and read my XVIth Chapter. I shall go to work on it tomorrow – looked over the 17th also. C.O'My[1] – Memoirs of Sir Astley Cooper and his body snatchers. What a set.

1. C.-J. Lever, *Charles O'Malley* (1841).

Sunday – January 22

Beautiful day. New idea about 1691. Excellent, I think – and true. It solves everything. Finished Sir Astley – wrote to Emilius Frank at the Hague. To W.T. Saw my dear B. She looked very poorly – I am uneasy about her cough. Home – wrote and read C.O'M – at dinner Forsyth's Sir Hudson Lowe.[1]

1. William Forsyth, *History of the Captivity of Napoleon at St Helena, from the Letters and Journals of the late Lieut. Gen. Sir H. Lowe ...* (1853).

Monday – January 23

After breakfast hunted by a begging Lieutenant or ex lieut. cashiered by Court Martial. Walked long – bought Lathbury's history of Convocation[1] – a stupid contemptible book. I wish I had my money again. Sent to W.T. good report – wrote about Marlborough – looked again over Chap XI which will soon, I think, be quite ready for transcription. Forsyth – C.O'M.

1. Thomas Lathbury, *A History of the Convocation of the Church of England ...* (1842).

Tuesday – January 24

Letter from a Leipzig bookseller shuffling about the 30£ and writing for a promise of the proof sheets of the history. I settled the matter by at once giving up the 30£ and by declining to promise anything as to the history. The begging Lieut again – got rid of him as well as I could. After breakfast to the Athenaeum looking at Journals Statutes – Then to W.T. dearest B a great deal better. Alice very amusing, sorting and reading again all the letters that she ever received in her life – Home through heavy rain in a cab – wrote Marlborough. Chap XI. Chap XVI nearly finished[1] – that is for this stage of finishing. Northcote's Life of Reynolds.[2] C.O'M.

1. It is hard to see which passage TBM refers to. Marlborough does not figure in ch. 11, the first chapter of vol. 3. Marlborough's avarice is briefly described in ch. 14. In ch. 15 the Churchills' power over Princess Anne is described at length. Ch. 16 deals with the Irish campaign in 1690 and Marlborough's capture of Cork and Kinsale.
2. James Northcote, *Life of Sir Joshua Reynolds ...* (1818).

Wednesday – January 25

The begging Lieut. William gave him a sovereign. After breakfast wrote corrected. Then to W.T. Dearest B better and better. Went with H and A in the carriage. They set me down at Mahon's. Chat with My Lord and Lady. He walked away with me. Wrote and corrected again. Lewis called. Then Trevelyan – C.O'M. Finished Northcote – Reynolds' Discourses.[1]

1. Sir Joshua Reynolds's *Discourses Delivered to Students at the Royal Academy* (1769–90).

Thursday – January 26

Warmed by a visit from T. who told me that H. had a very bad sore throat, but nothing dangerous. I was not quite at ease. I went to W.T. and had a pretty good account. Sent again in the evening. E dined with me but staid a very short time. I went on writing and correcting. Reynolds.

Friday – January 27

Another visit from T. All going on well. The City – everything satisfactory – W.T. saw dear B. again and Alice – then home – wrote and corrected. C.O'M – Parriana.[1]

1. E. H. Barker, *Parriana; or, Notices of the Rev. Samuel Parr ...* (1796).

Saturday – January 28

T. with better news still of H. Good public news also. The plan for appointing public servants by competition[1] is to be adopted on a large scale and mentioned in the Q's speech. I went to the Athenaeum and looked at the journals. Home

– wrote and corrected. To Ellis's to dinner. I was sorry to find his leg tied up. A rheumatism fixed in the knee joint I believe.

1. See above, entry for 13 November 1853. This was one of the principal recommendations of the Report of Sir Stafford Northcote and Sir Charles Trevelyan.

Sunday – January 29

The severest shook that I have had since Jany 1835[1]. A note from B to say that H has scarlet fever. B. too exposed. I was quite overset – could eat nothing – could do nothing but weep for half-an-hour. They begged me – she for her sake not to go. But I could not stay away. I went – saw B and T. greatly relieved. It means that the crisis is over, and that the worst was passed before the nature of the disease was known. Still I am anxious. Home in far better spirits – wrote and corrected. In the afternoon to Hallam's to inquire about him. He too is ill; and I should be greatly concerned but that W.T. puts everything else out of my head. Much distressed by learning that Hallam has had a paralytic seizure. Mrs Cator was in Wilton Crescent attending on him. I saw him on his sofa, and was much affected. His speech and faculties are entire. But he has lost partially at least the use of an arm and leg. He tried to bear up, but was evidently low. We talked about the Q.R. etc. – I staid eight or ten minutes only. He is, by Holland's orders, to see two or three friends a day – one at a time – and none for a long time – Home – dined – much knocked up by mental uneasiness – Headache. C.O'M. Dr Parr.

1. When he heard the news of his sister Margaret's death.

Monday – January 30

Better. After breakfast to W.T. B. out in the carriage – H going on well. Museum – bought books – Kettlewell's Life,[1] etc. – Home and wrote – Chap XVII – Russell – La Hogue[2] – C.O'M. Kettlewell.

1. Perhaps George Hicks, *Memoirs of the Life of J. Kettlewell ...* (1796).
2. *HE*, ch. 18, *CW*, vol. 3, pp. 547–53.

Tuesday – January 31

Fine day – went to W.T. saw dear B – delighted to find that H is going on very well, but weak and wants support. I sent them some game and some first-rate Hock. In the afternoon B returned my call. Glad to find that H liked the Hock – B took me to Brooks's. I was pleased to find that the Queen and Prince Albert were not ill received. The late attacks on Prince Albert[1] have been infamous and absurd to the last degree. Nothing so shameful since the Warming Pan story. I am ashamed for my country. However the reaction has begun – B took me to Wilton Crescent. I inquired after Hallam but did not go in as I found Milman at the door. Better was the answer. Then to Westminster Hall – a little rheumatic. The usual scene at the beginning of a Session – much shaking of hands. I had been uneasy about the Convocation. But a short answer given by Ld John to a rigmarole question put by Packington settled that matter satisfactorily.[2] I staid to hear the mover – well enough – the seconder – detestable – Baillie[3] – disowned by all his own people – Blacket,[4] he was too much for me; and I went home to dinner – C.O'M, Parr.

1. See Conacher, *Aberdeen Coalition*, pp. 269–70.
2. Sir John Pakington asked whether Convocation would be prorogued by the Crown, if it were not prorogued in the usual way by the Archbishop, after the single day to which its meetings were then confined. Lord John Russell replied that it would be so prorogued if necessary. *PD*, 3rd ser., cxxx, 108–10.
3. H. J. Baillie, MP for Inverness. Ibid., 125–32.
4. John Fenwick Burgoyne Blackett (1821–56), MP for Newcastle upon Tyne. Ibid., 132–5.

Wednesday – February 1

Breakfast party – two missing who should have been there, Hannah and Hallam – Mahon and Lady M, Lewis and Lady T, Ellis, Dundas, Glenelg, Goulburn. Pretty well – Wrote a little – then to R.I. – Magazines – Review of my speeches in Blackwood.[1] Not favourable – but not malignant. I am afraid that the volume is a failure, though not a shameful or ludicrous failure. We must do better. Then to Brooks's. Then by the Green Park to Hallam's. Palgrave with him.[2] Saw Cator and Mrs C and came away. Poor fellow! I feel for him extremely. To W.T. – saw B. all well – I begin to be nervous about her, now that her mother is safe. Alas alas that I should have staked so much on what may be so easily lost. Yet I would not have it otherwise. Home – wrote more – Luxemburg – Steinkirk – now for Grandval[3] – I must positively get over that business tomorrow. It has long hung in hand. I do not know why I dislike it. To dinner with Ellis. Pleasant enough.

1. Vol. 75 (February 1854). It was by W. E. Aytoun.
2. Sir Francis Palgrave (1788–1861), lawyer and medieval historian. He was the first Deputy Keeper of the Public Records, and a member of the circle of antiquarians who met in Murray's at 50 Albemarle Street.
3. *HE*, ch. 19, *CW*, vol. 3, pp. 577–87.

Thursday – February 2

Looked over the papers about Turkey and Russia. Going out met T – delighted to learn that dearest H is now quite convalescent. Charles came and his boy

Tommy. I tipped Tommy. Long talk with T about the projected examination. I am afraid that he will pay the examiners too high and turn the whole thing into a job. I am anxious on this head. If the thing succeeds it will be of immense benefit to the country. I wrote about Young's villainy.[1] B called – took me to Lne House and left me. Saw Ld L. – Glad I was to see him so well. Excellent old fellow – I love him dearly. Talk about Russia and Turkey etc – I walked a little – left a card with Ld Stanley who called on me yesterday, and then went home and wrote an introduction to my Irish narrative in Chap XII – Parr – C.O'M – Monthly Reviews.

1. *HE*, ch. 18, *CW*, vol. 3, pp. 554–62.

Friday – February 3

A desperately thick fog. Forced to dress and breakfast by candle light. Determined to stay at home all day, and did so. But the fog found its way to my lungs. I had great difficulty in breathing and a violent cough. I went through the Irish part of Chap XII and was pretty well satisfied. Ate little and drank less. Put on a mustard poultice and took hydr. Read Monthly Reviews a novel of Carleton called Red Hall.[1]

1. William Carleton, *The Red Hall, or The Baronet's Daughter* (republished as *Black Baronet*, 1852).

Saturday – [February 4]

A fine clear day. Wind turning South. I meant to work hard: but a parcel came to me from poor Empson's executors containing my letters to him and Jeffrey – some as far back as 1825. I could do nothing but read them till I had finished them all. They interested me very deeply, sometimes painfully. Had to leave them however twice though I said that I could do nothing till I had finished them – first to go to Lne House and talk about Mackintosh's Monument – 2ndly to go out in the carriage with my dear B who called in the afternoon. H as well as possible in the circumstances. At Lne House met Ld John. We were most friendly. Letter from Thornton – By the bye my South & Wns are greatly risen in value. I shall have 40£ year more than I counted upon. And it is needful that I should: for today my servants represented that their board wages would not do with the present prices. I have added half a guinea a week among the three – more than they asked. Got to work towards five o'clock. E to dinner. Excellent Hock. Letters from F and Alice. Monthly Reviews.

Sunday – February 5

To W.T. Dearest B poorly and in bed. I was much depressed, though not as I was last Sunday. I do not now anticipate anything very serious. Home – Holland called – talked about scarlet fever. etc. He gives a good account of Hallam. At dinner Carleton's book – extravagant and feeble compared to his good works. M.R.

Monday – February 6

T called – to W.T. – B poorly but better than yesterday. Her Mamma going on well – Worked hard at altering and arrangement of the 1st 3 Chapters – What labour it is to make a tolerable book; and how little readers know how much trouble the ordering of the parts has cost the writer. Saw Hallam – much better. To the H. of C. Nothing of interest – looked at the Irish Statutes and Journals – Home – at dinner Carleton – M.R.

Tuesday – February 7

To W.T. H going on well – B I think has caught it. Walked a little – worked much – Carleton – M.R.

Wednesday – February 8

The same story – W.T. – walk – work – Carleton – M.R.

Thursday – February 9

Did not go to W.T. The weather very bad – wrote – good news and a letter from dearest H – most kind. Sir C. Wood called. I rated him about Redington.[1] He threw the blame on Ld John who, I must say, acts very ill in matters of that sort. We talked about India. I mentioned Macleod for the direction. But I saw that it would not do. Glad to hear an excellent account of Ellis's goings on. Worked. In the afternoon it was fine, and I went out, but found the air cold – E to dinner.

1. Probably Sir Thomas Redington, Secretary of the Board of Control, 1852–6. He had been Under-Secretary of State for Ireland at the time of the famine and worked with Sir Charles Wood and Charles Trevelyan. I do not know what TBM is referring to on this occasion.

Friday – February 10

To breakfast with Ld Mahon. D and Ds of Argyle – Ld Stanley, George Grey, Bp of Oxford – pleasant. Ld S remarkably civil to me and even empressé. To the Athenaeum – vexed not to see Macleod's name among the successful candidates. I am afraid he has been blackballed. No man will like it less. To the City – Nothing can go on better than my money matters – an increasing income and a great balance. I shall invest 500£ more before Easter. Home. Dearest B now is declared to have the scarlet fever, but very slightly. I sent them my Catalogue of books to choose from. I must pass a fortnight, I am afraid, without seeing either of the two persons whom I love most in the world. Worked in the history. To dinner in Bedford Place.

Saturday – February 11

To breakfast with Milnes. Lord Stanley again, Bp of Oxford again, Stirling,[1] D and Ds of Argyle again, and a Yankee who turned out to be General Webb Editor of The New York Courier[2] I think. I should not have been so civil to him if I had known who he was. Pleasant enough. To the Museum. Then home; suffered for my imprudence in going out on so cold a day – forced to put on a strong mustard poultice which flayed my chest but relieved me. Hydr – Monthly Review – Carleton.

1. Sir William Stirling (later Stirling-Maxwell) was a Trinity graduate, a collector and connoisseur of paintings, a founder of the Philobiblion Society, and at this time MP for Perthshire.
2. James Watson Webb (1802–84), editor and publisher of the *Morning Courier and New-York Enquirer*.

Sunday – February 12

Excused myself to Ld Lne. Staid at home all day – looked out books for H from a list which she had drawn up, and sent them to her by the boy in a cab. Wrote and read – at dinner – Carleton – M.R.

Monday – [February 13]

At home all day writing and reading. Sent as usual to W.T. – All right. Today Ld J is to bring in his new Reform Bill. I had meant to go down, but did not venture. How different a world from that which was convulsed by the first Reform Bill. How different a day this from the 1st of March 1831[1] an epoch in my life as well as in that of the nation. – Lever's HA[2] – M.R.

1. When the first Reform Bill was introduced by Russell, in the House of Commons.
2. Samuel Lever (1797–1868), *Handy Andy* (1842).

Tuesday – February 14

Breakfast party. Ld Lne – Ld Stanley, Ld Mahon, Dundas, Stirling, Milman, Milnes – Very pleasant I thought. Staid at home reading and writing. All right at

W.T. But poor old Mrs T[1] is very ill at Enmore and T is gone down. HA – MR – Letter from Fanny in the evening – Dear little Alice wants her books.

1. Harriet Trevelyan (née Neave) had been a widow since 1827.

Wednesday – February 15

Sent off Alice's books. Wrote and read. Cold weather – Letter from W.T. – Mrs T. dead. I am sorry. Yet what can one wish for in such a case? Macleod called – a little out of sorts – H.A. – M.R.

Thursday – February 16

Line from B to say that she hoped to be able to call. I staid at home and did nothing. Unprofitable day. I tried to work, but had a feeling of impotence and despondency to which I am subject, but which I have not had now for some time. B did not come after all – Dear child she has caught cold again – I am anxious – H.A. M.R.

Friday – February 17

After breakfast to W.T. Weather milder – Wind West. Saw dear B. much pulled down. At the door just shook hands with T going to his office. He too looks ill. The death of the good old lady has tried them all. Yet never was there a quieter or a happier death. She went off in sleep. Utinam![1] – Home – Sent 20£ to S and F. I thought that these high prices might finish them. Sate about doggedly to work and got on very tolerably. State of England at the time of Wm's return[2] from the Continent in 1692 – HA – M.R.

1. (Latin): 'If only ...'.
2. *HE*, ch. 19, *CW*, vol. 3, pp. 591–5.

Saturday – February 18

Snow. Staid at home. Good accounts from W.T. Worked on – tolerably. Looked over Tom Brown's works[1] and picked up some hints etc. Reform Bill – thought about the provision for the benefit of minorities,[2] and liked it much. Letter from F – very grateful and affectionate. E to dinner.

1. Thomas Brown (1663–1704). Macaulay quoted from his *Amusements, Serious and Comical* in *HE*, ch. 11, *CW*, vol. 2, p. 475n.
2. Russell's bill of 1854 was the first to consider giving the vote to qualifications rather than property, what would be called 'fancy franchises'.

Sunday – February 19

At home all day – Still good news – more work – Charles called in the afternoon – H.A. – M.R.

Monday – February 20

Sent to W.T. – Note from B. They are just starting. I shall be anxious till I hear how they get over the journey – wrote on and corrected – finished HA. Monk Lewis's Life[1] – Very odd fellow. One of the best of men if he had not had a trick of writing profane and indecent books. Excellent son – excellent master – and in most trying circumstances, for he was the son of a vile brace of parents and the master of a stupid ungrateful gang of negroes. I made notes today from the Journals at the Athenaeum.

1. *Life and Correspondence of Matthew Gregory ('Monk') Lewis* (1839).

Tuesday – February 21

To B.M. – Dutch Despatches. Milman came and went to work opposite me – Then came the Duke of Aumale,[1] to whom I was more respectful than I should have been if his father had been on the throne. Going away I found Dundas showing the M.S.S. to a bevy of women. Mrs Strutt among them and a good-looking Miss West[2] with whom I fancied that David was philandering. I staid with them and did the honors of the Alexandrian M.S. Miss showed herself an Hellenist, and displayed her skill in distinguishing Θ from O. I did not find much today that will be of use – I worked, and read. Sorry that I could not go to E's. But I suffered even for this short exposure in the morning. Good news from Brighton.[3] Cl Review – Smollett's blackguardly abuse of Grainger and puffing of himself[4] – Odious fellow. Began the Daltons.[5]

1. Henri, Duc d'Aumale (1822–97), was the fifth son of King Louis Philippe.
2. Perhaps one of the two daughers of Frederick Richard West, MP for Denbigh, 1847–57. They were Georgiana (1831–1915), later Mrs Peacock, and Florence (1833–1906).
3. Conveyed by TBM's sister Selina, concerning Hannah and her daughters, who had gone there to convalesce. Cf. *LM*, vol. 6, pp. 382–3.
4. The *Critical Review*, established in 1756 in rivalry to the *Monthly Review*, was edited by Smollett from 1756 to 1759. He had attacked James Grainger's edition of Tibullus in the *Critical Review* in 1759 and 1760. Grainger (*c.* 1721–66) was a contributor to the *Monthly*, a physician and poet.
5. By Charles James Lever (1852).

Wednesday – February 22

Went on working. The wind, W. Took a longer walk than I have taken this long time. Bought history of the King of the Swindlers[1] – no date but about 1784, a strange periodical work of 1710, and Mrs Gore's Manners of the Day[2] – came back with my pockets stuffed. Worked away. Still the Session of 1692/3. At dinner the Daltons – read my new purchases – Gentleman's Magazine – 1791 – Letter from B – satisfactory. Present from Dr Vaughan of Harrow – a Lecture on Cicero.[3] Wrote very civilly in acknowledgment of the gift and of a very handsome mention which he has made of me. But I defended my opinion of Cicero, which, I am quite certain, is wellfounded.

---

1. *Life of Major Semple Lisle, the King of the Swindlers* (SC, p. 263).
2. Catherine Gore, *Women as They Are; on the Manners of the Day* (1830).
3. C. J. Vaughan, *Passage from the Life of Cicero. A Lecture* (1854), p. 7. 'When the great Reviewer, in girding himself for his celebrated onslaught upon Lord Bacon, throws a passing dart at the character of Cicero as an eloquent and accomplished trimmer', "whose soul was under the dominion of a girlish vanity and a craven fear", he seems to me to have discarded, for the moment, the reverence for true greatness which is by no means incompatible with the keenest critical acumen.'

Thursday – February 23

Letter from a Quaker at Sudbury enclosing three letters from my father to me written when I was fourteen. They interested me extremely. Odd that they are all admonitory and rather severe. My Quaker's father, it seems, lived at Buntingford, and got these with other waste paper from the servants at Aspenden Hall. I wrote most civilly to my honest Quaker.[1] Few of his sect would have behaved so well to me. Worked away – Land Tax. The day fine and I had a petition to present. So I walked out. To Hallam's. He was out taking an airing. To the H. of C. looked over Acts and returns apropos of the Land Tax. Very sorry to hear that poor Tufnell is laid up again. Presented my petition.[2] Pleasant chat on the benches for half an hour. Glad to hear that the Reform Bill will not be debated on the 13th. Home – wrote a little – E to dinner.

---

1. Buntingford, Hertfordshire, was in the parish of Aspenden, near Aspenden Hall, where Preston moved his school in 1814. The only Quakers living in Buntingford in 1814 and in Sudbury in 1854 were the family of James Wright, grocer (b. 1775). His son, also James Wright (1810–85), was born in Buntingford, but was living in Market Hill, Sudbury, in 1854, along with several relatives, and working as a master painter. It looks from the records as if he was TBM's honest Quaker.
2. On behalf of the Scottish National Education Association.

Friday – February 24

Ld Glenelg called to talk about The Eastern question – Longman with a letter from the wretched Robert Montgomery,[1] begging hard to be taken out of the pillory. Never, with my consent. He is the meanest as well as the silliest scribbler of my time, and that his books sell among a certain class is a reason for keeping my protest on record. Besides he has calumniated me in print; and I will not seem to be bullied into a concession. I wrote – Land tax – walked. At five or thereabouts E called. He read my paper on Atterbury[2] – He could not stay to dinner – Daltons – Civil answer from Vaughan. E ill. Longman writes that they must print 5000 more of the Essays.

1. Robert Montgomery (1807–55) was a writer, poet and clergyman in London. The 'pillory' was a reprint of TBM's review of Montgomery's *Poems* in *ER*, April 1830.
2. For the *Encyclopaedia Britannica*.

Saturday – February 25

Trevelyan called while I was dressing and staid while I breakfasted. Talked much about his mother, the war, the Civil Service Plan, etc etc. He is going down to Brighton today. Line from E inviting himself to dinner. Tant mieux – walked – very fine day and I took a longer ramble than I have taken for a long time. Home and wrote. Finished the English parliamentary history of 1692/3.[1] Irish and Scotch work remains to be done and is not at all to my taste. Macleod called. My hair cut; GM – Bye the bye this morning I picked up some Mormonite works in Jewin Street[2] – Stupid they are to be so absurd. I really cannot read them. They could not be duller if they were orthodox. E to dinner. He goes to Sessions and Circuit next week.

1. *HB*, ch. 19.
2. Eli B. Kelsey at no. 35 was the only bookseller in the street in 1854 (*London Directory*).

Sunday – February 26

Fine day, though wind North – Walked with much enjoyment. Brooks's, nothing. Home – read, but wrote nothing. GM[1] – Daltons. CZM called – I hope that he may get the Secretaryship to the Audit Board.[2]

1. *Gentleman's Magazine*.
2. He did. See below, entry for 3 March 1854, and *LM*, vol. 5, p. 387, prompting the mock complaint: 'All my brothers and brothers in law are now comfortably quartered on the public, and I alone remain without a halfpenny of the Queen's money.'

Monday – February 27

Another fine day. I worked all the morning at Trenchard – Lunt – Lancashire trials[1] – very well pleased. Snow called – gave him a Mercuriale[2] – shall give him another if I have an opportunity. He talked of privateering. Why not of going on the highway or housebreaking? M de Bonnechose called. He had sent me his book – Les Quatre conquêtes.[3] I liked it much. We talked together an hour or so in French. I thought that I got on tolerably. I walked out when he was gone – to Brooks's. Strong feeling that the Reform Bill ought to be put off. I agree – But I will not vote against Ld J in his extremity. G.M. – Daltons.

1. *HE*, ch. 20, *CW*, vol. 4, pp. 106–11.
2. A rebuke.
3. F. P. E. Boisnormand de Bonnechose, *Les Quatre Conquêtes de l'Angleterre* ... (1852). Cf. *LM*, vol. 5, p. 384 and n.

Tuesday – February 28

A fine day and a happy one. To Brighton. Found good room at The Norfolk, ordered dinner. To Temple House, for if I had gone first to Bedford Square S and F wd not have let me in. Found S poorly, F well, Alice looking like a little angel. Then to Bedford Square. How happy I was to see H and B again, and well everything considered. We sate and talked, then walked a little on the esplanade and met S in a carriage F and A walking. The quarantine is not quite strict in the open air. Then H B and I got into a fly, had an airing to the extremity of the East Cliff and back. I sate with them till it was time for me to go to dinner. After dinner I came back and sate as long as it was proper to do. For dear H is still not strong. Back to the Norfolk. Daltons.

Wednesday – March 1

Up to breakfast in Bedford Square at nine. At half past ten came an open carriage and pair in which I took H and B to Rottingdean. Delightful drive – delightful day. I was very happy. I sate with them when we returned till it was time to look after my bill. Away by the half past three train – At the station bought a new No. of The Newcomes[1] and a book called Queachey.[2] Read the Newcomes by the way and thought it very good. At home by six. Found Parriana, the 2nd vol which I had never seen before, but have picked up at Brown's in Old Street[3] – much amused. At dinner – Daltons.

1. By Thackeray.
2. Elizabeth Wetherell (pseudonym of Susan Warren), *Queachy* (1852).
3. William Brown, 130 Old Street, St Luke's.

Thursday – March 2

Letters to answer – then city – affairs thriving – ordered the purchase of 500£ 3¼ Stock. To B.M. Mrs Strutt and a German female companion were in Holmes's room looking over the Bedford Missal. Made some notes about the Lancashire Trials from the Dutch Dispatches. Home – wrote on – well enough. Parriana – Daltons.

Friday – March 3

Staid at home all day. In the morning there was a fog which made it necessary for me to use a candle to dress. It affected my breath, and made me cough much. I finished the Lancashire business and began on Brest. Note from Charles. He has got the place. Thank God. Yet I was sad and desponding all day. I thought that my book would be a failure, that I had written myself out, that my reputation would go down in my lifetime and that I should be left, like Hayley and other such men,[1] among people who would wonder why I had ever been thought much of. These clouds will pass away, no doubt. Read a good deal of Charles Lesley.[2] Odious fellow. Daltons – In the evening – Hydr.

---

1. William Hayley (1745–1820) was a man of independent means, who failed as a dramatist and turned to poetry. He refused the offer of the laureateship, however.
2. Charles Leslie (1650–1722), non-juror and Jacobite polemicist.

Saturday – March 4

To work again and got on. Brest and Dieppe etc. – I shall soon finish the summer and autumn of 1694. Then to the Session of 1693/4. When that is done the narrative will be approaching completeness. Sir George Hayter[1]called. I was very civil. But what can I do? He wants the public to give 5000 Gns for his picture of the H. of C. – How can I be of use in such a matter? The Irish Chapter.[2] I went to Brooks's. Everybody open mouthed against Shelley's speech of last night,[3] open mouthed too, I am sorry to say, against T's plans about the Civil Service. He has been too sanguine. The pear is not ripe. I always thought so. The time will come – but it is not come yet. I am afraid that he will be much mortified G. M. Daltons.

---

1. Sir George Hayter (1792–1871) was a portrait painter. His *Morning of the Address in the First Meeting of the Reformed House of Commons* is now in the National Portrait Gallery. It was finished in 1848.
2. *HE*, ch. 16.
3. Sir John Shelley protested against the decision announced by Lord John Russell that a reform bill would be postponed and was interpreted as suggesting that the government's plans for reform had been insincere (*PD,* 3rd ser., cxxxi, 283).

Sunday – [March 5]

Cold day. Staid at home – wrote about the Fleet in the Mediterranean 1694.[1] [Five lines obliterated]. But he will get through his difficulties which he feels less than I should in his place, less indeed than I feel them for him. I was nervous about him and out of spirits the whole evening – G.M. – Dns – finished.

1. *HE*, ch. 20, *CW*, vol. 4, pp. 105–6.

Monday – March 6

A fog worthy of Christmas. I staid at home – looked at the Scotch Chapter.[1] I like it less than the Irish. But it is not bad and may be made very good. Read about the Session of 1693/4. I do not yet see my way through the maze of faction at that time. The truth is that I am building without sufficient materials. Sir Roderic Murchison called. In the evening I was plagued with cough and oppression of the chest. Mustard poultice – Began a new novel of Mrs Gore's.[2] Hydr.

1. *HE*, ch. 11.
2. Catherine Gore published *Progress and Prejudice* in 1854. It was advertised in *The Times* on 17 March as 'now ready in all the Libraries, in 3 vols.'.

Tuesday – March 7

Gladstone's budget. Much what was expected. But I do not admire his financial principles. However he is a good and an able man. I hurt my loose tooth two days ago; and it still plagues me. As early as my Hydr would let me to W.T. Delighted to see them again. H convinced that there is no reason for uneasiness about T. Home and worked – read – Mrs G's new book.

Wednesday – March 8

Wrote in the morning – Then to W.T. pleasant afternoon and evening. T told the history of the Cabal against him. All right.

Thursday – March 9

To breakfast with Milnes – Stupid. I knew nobody but Lowe and the Ld Advocate. Walked away with the Ld Adv. – Talked about his Education Bill and Ld J's Reform Bill. We agreed perfectly. In the afternoon worked chiefly on Scotland – Chap XIII. Mrs G – GM.

Friday – March 10

Wrote in the morning. Chap XIII – to W.T. met George and Sarah Anne[1] there. Sad to see him so poorly Alas! Alas! But it is not my fault. Mrs Merivale[2] called.

Laughed a good deal about her projected expedition to Portsmouth. I went out with H and B in the carriage. Arthur O'Leary[3] – GM.

1. George Gisborne Babington and his wife.
2. Judith Mary Sophia Frere (1817–1906), daughter of George Frere, barrister. She married the Revd Charles Merivale (1808–93) in 1850.
3. By Charles Lever (1844).

Saturday – March 11

Wrote a little but well. To BM staid there late to settle about The Gualterio papers[1] – Walked away with Dundas and Ld Seymour. Ld S left us in Piccadilly. D and I walked together to Knightsbridge and back. Very pleasant he was. Home – too late to work – letters etc – AO'L – GM – I see my way now to making this thirteenth chapter very good unless I am mistaken. C Buxton sent me a zoological lecture.[2] Sent him back a critique on it.

1. The family papers of the Marquis Filippo Antonio Gualterio, extracts from which were sent to TBM by James Montgomery Stuart, who subsequently initiated their sale to the British Museum for £1,200. They included the official papers of Cardinal Filippo Antonio Gualterio, Papal Nuncio at the Court of Louis XIV in the early eighteenth century and a correspondent of many prominent Jacobites, and those of his nephew Cardinal Luigi Gualterio. See James Montgomery Stuart, *Reminiscences and Essays* (London, 1884), pp. 15–18.
2. Charles Buxton's *Lectures on the Theory of Construction of Birds* were published in 1854.

Sunday – March 12

Worked. To W.T. T not at home. H and B very pleasant – C – walked away – beautiful day. Met Ld E Howard[1] – then Edward Ellice. Unlucky business this at the Reform Club.[2] Ellice talks good sense about the Reform Bill. Home – wrote – read AO – That is not Arthur O'Leary but Mrs Gore's AO[3] – GM.

1. Edward George Howard (1818–83), MP for Arundel, 1852–68; later first Baron Glossop.
2. On 7 March Palmerston presided over a farewell dinner at the Reform Club for Admiral Sir Charles Napier, who was appointed to command the Baltic fleet. Speeches were made by Palmerston, Graham (First Lord of the Admiralty) and Molesworth, among others, that were resented by some as being unnecessarily lighthearted and bellicose, taking it for granted that war would be declared against Russia (the ultimatum was still unanswered), and suggesting to some that the Napier appointment was made on political rather than professional grounds. The occasion provoked a storm in the House of Commons on 13 March; see entry below.
3. Perhaps *Cecil: Adventures of a Coxcomb* (1841), at least I can find no work of Mrs Gore that seems more plausible.

Monday – March 13

Staid at home and worked all the morning. This Scotch business is done at last, and pretty well. In the afternoon B called. Walked with her across the park – bought a stuffed bird for Cora[1] and laughed to see how the poor brute was surprised and amused – then to the H. of C. questioning about the Reform Club dinner. Bright disagreeable but in the right and powerful. Palmerston lost his temper and good manners and disgusted me, and, I dare say, others. Graham was rather shabby on the other hand. Molesworth, who indeed had less to excuse, was spirited and said nothing improper.[2] Home – dined – AO GM.

1. A Mexican spaniel of Margaret's. Trevelyan, vol. 2, pp. 332.
2. For the Reform Club episode, see Conacher, *Aberdeen Coalition*, pp. 280–1. Among other remarks that gave offence was Palmerston's reference to Bright (who had objected to the frivolous tone of the Reform Club speeches) as 'the Honorable and Reverend Member'. TBM did not stay for the cleverest speech of the debate, by Disraeli. *PD*, 3rd ser., cxxxi, 674–88. Cf. *LM*, vol. 5, p. 390.

Tuesday – March 14

To the Museum. Looked at John Dunton's tracts[1] in the Grenville Room. Found only one to my purpose – Life of Tyrconnel. Must look at it again. Home – worked – Chap XIV. This will be tough work – But I shall get it into form at last – I see that there is a notice on the votes of the H. of C which may produce something that will be of use to me. AO – GM – Guizot's Life of Cromwell[2] in an English Translation. Curious and interesting. Civil answer from C Brooke,[3] answered him.

1. John Dunton (1659–1777), bookseller, author, publisher and satirist.
2. F. P. G. Guizot, *History of Oliver Cromwell and the English Commonwealth* ... (English translation by A. R. Scoble (1854)).
3. Perhaps Sir Charles Anthony Johnson-Brooke (1829–1917), a naval officer who became Rajah of Sarawak.

Wednesday – March 15

Wrote. A Deputation of Scotch Dissenters about the Education Bill, very moderate and sensible. To W.T. saw dear little A again and was glad to see her. Their Mamma is in Bedfordshire and is going to Enmore. Walked home with B. The carriage came for her and took her back – dear good child. Soon came another Deputation on the Education question. Adam Black Dr Guthrie[1] etc. I like Guthrie amazingly. We agreed perfectly. Worked. I really think that I shall get this tangled skein into good order. To dinner after a long long interval at V. Smith's.[2] I have not dressed for a party there, I do not know how many weeks or rather months. Tried on my levee dress at the same time. The party not unpleasant. Ld L – The Speaker and Mrs L[3] – Horseman[4] – young Holland[5] and his wife.

1. Dr Thomas Guthrie (1803–73).
2. Robert Vernon Smith, later Baron Lyveden. He lived at 20 Saville Row.
3. Charles Shaw Lefevre (1794–1888) married Emma Laura Whitbread (1798–1857).
4. Presumably Edward Horsman (1807–76). He was MP for Stroud, 1853–68, and for Liskeard, 1869–76; Chief Secretary for Ireland, 1855–7.
5. Henry Thurstan Holland (1825–1914) married Elizabeth Margaret Hibbert (*c.* 1834–55), daughter of Nathanial Hibbert. His second wife was Margaret Trevelyan (Baba).

Thursday – March 16

Got on with Chap XIV walked. Soho Bazaar for the first time after many years. Picked up the Memoirs of that vagabond Theodore Hook.[1] Queachy at dinner.

1. Perhaps R. H. D. Barham, *The Life and Remains of Theodore Hook* (1849).

Friday – March 17

Party to breakfast – Ld Mahon, Ld Stanley – Howard – Dundas – Goulburn. Pleasant – then to Brooks's – then to W.T. George there with his bad foot – quite laid up. Home – wrote – Qy. T Hook.

Saturday – March 18

Worked. B and A came to borrow a book for George. Lent them Harte's G.A.[1] – I do not at all like Ld J's Oxford Bill.[2] I hope that it is better than it looks in the report of the Times. Macleod called. Qy – finished it – poor work.

1. Perhaps Walter Harte, *History of… Gustavus Adolphus* (1759).
2. For its provisions, see M. G. Brock and M. C. Curthoys, *The History of the University of Oxford*, 8 vols (Oxford, 1984–2000), vol. 6, p. 332.

Sunday – March 19

Worked. To W.T. by cab – bad day. Found them anxious about George. Adkins and Hawkins[1] consulted, and pronounced the case less serious than had been apprehended; but he must be quiet some weeks – talked with him about his studies, with T about Indian appointments etc. C came. They expect H on Wednesday. Home – wrote – at dinner Shirley – finished Hook.

1. Alfred Atkyns (*c.* 1813–81) was at 6 James Terrace, New North Road, a surgeon and in general practice. There were two brothers Hawkins, Francis (1794–1877), of 18 Bolton Street, Physician in Ordinary to the Royal Household, and Caesar Henry (1798–1884), of 26 Grosvenor Street, a surgeon at St George's Hospital, Kensington.

Monday – March 20

To breakfast at Mahon's – D of Argyle, Ld Caernarvon[1], George Grey and my lady. We got on pleasantly. Then home and took a cabfull of books to W.T. for George. Scapula[2] – Ainsworth[3] – Lucian – Quintus Curtius. Home – had to write several letters – to Guizot – Thanks for his book, really a very remarkable book – to Dumont on a new crazy theory about Junius. When shall I see the last of these theories? To Charpentier, a bookseller at Paris to thank him for a copy of a new translation of my history by M. Emile Montégut.[4] Ld Glenelg called. At last I got to work and wrote little but satisfactorily. I am in Chap XX. At dinner Shirley[5] – then GM 1756. Ld J's bill a little better than I thought.

1. Henry Howard Molyneux Herbert (1831–90), fourth Earl. He succeeed to the title in 1849. His son, the fifth Earl, was an Egyptologist.
2. Joannes Scapula, *Lexicon Graeco-Latinum* ... (various editions).
3. Perhaps Robert Ainsworth's *Thesaurus Linguae Latinae* (first published in 1736).
4. Jean Baptiste Joseph Emile Montégut (1825–95); translation published in 1854.
5. By Charlotte Brontë (1849).

Tuesday – March 21

Got to work in pretty good time today. Chap XV. Bad day. Did not go to the Club. Shirley – but tired to death of it. Ld Lansdowne called, and was very pleasant. GM.

Wednesday – March 22

Chap XV – Dressed for leveé. Thin entree. The Queen and Prince most gracious. I sent away my carriage, and Ld Marcus Hill[1] took me home. To work again. At dinner Mid E.[2] In the evening several of Swift's tracts.

1. Lord Arthur Marcus Cecil Hill (later Lord Sandys), 1798–1863. He had been Comptroller and Treasurer of the Household.
2. F. Marryat, *Mr Midshipman Easy* (1836).

Thursday – March 23

Cold – N.E. – Breakfast with Inglis. To W.T. however to see H after her absence – Glad to see her. They are all well now except G, whose malady is not alarming. Home and wrote. In the evening, unwillingly, to dine with Wood – The party dull – I knew nobody except the D and Duchess of Bedford and Ld Lne – I had however some tolerably pleasant chat with the Duke and Lady Mary[1] near whom I sate. But my chest plagued me. There was a large assembly in the evening; but I stole away early. Invitation from the Queen for Monday – Very civil.

1. Lady Mary Wood, née Grey (1807–84). She was the fifth daughter of Lord Grey, the Prime Minister.

Friday – March 24

At breakfast looked again at Mr Verdant Green. After breakfast wrote – then to W.T. found dear B. with a very bad cold, which settles all our plans of visiting the crystal palace tomorrow. Gave her twenty guineas to equip herself for the drawing room. Chatted some time and home. Wrote to C Black in Chile.[1] Black the father called with a younger son. I dined at home – VG – Milman. A very able and learned book,[2] with faults of course.

1. Charles Bertram Black (1821–1906) was Adam Black's eldest son. See *LM*, vol. 5, p. 294n. There were three other sons: James Tait (b. 1836), Francis (*c.* 1831–92) and Adam William (1836–98).
2. H. H. Milman, *History of Latin Christianity* ... (1854–5).

Saturday – March 25

Worked to good purpose – R.I. – walked – VG – P Keen[1] – Milman.

1. *Percival Keene* by Frederick Marryatt (1842).

Sunday – March 26

Worked – good spirits – to W.T. pleasant two hours there – But bad account of John's eldest boy.[1] His eldest girl about to be married, I hope.[2] Back and worked – P.K. Milman.

1. Henry George Macaulay (1837–69). He gave the family considerable anxiety, to judge from the fragments gathered by Professor Pinney; see *LM*, vol. 6, p. 93n. He left no will when he died, and his effects were valued at £150.
2. John's eldest daughter was Selina Jane (1835–1913). She married the Revd William Henry Fell (1830–69) in 1855. He was curate of St John's, Lancaster. Selina Fell 'went over to Rome'.

Monday – March 27

Dundas to breakfast. Van de W, Rutherford and Glenelg all failed me. Pleasant however. To the Bd of Controul. Met there Ld Ashburton, Jowett, Lefevre[1] and Melville.[2] They are to breakfast with me and fall to work on Wednesday Week. Walked away with Lefevre – to Athenaeum looked at reviews – journals etc – to the H. of C. to present petitions but was prevented by the press of private business. Had some talk with G Grey. We quite agreed, as to the Universities[3] and also as to the Reform Bill. He has seen Ld and Lady J – as I thought Ly J is the impracticable person – wretched adviser. I spoke to Ld J about announcing the Cambridge plan before the Oxford plan is debated: but he seemed very unwilling. The message – a solemn scene.[4] Home – found a M.S. which Sir R Inglis has procured for me from Joshua Watson[5] – the Eccl Commission. I was interdicted from transcribing: so I made only a few memoranda of dates to correct my narrative by, which is easily done. To dinner at the palace. The Archbp of Y and Mrs M,[6] Ld and Lady John, The Duke of Newcastle,[7] The Marquess Cholmondeley,[8] Several Brigadiers, Colonel Grey,[9] a Baron Hunker.[10] A dull evening as usual at the palace. The Q and P very gracious to me. I hope that I and the Archbp between us prevailed on Ld J to give up the abominable clause about the residence of Fellows.[11] Grey was sensible and amusing, I thought.

1. Sir John George Shaw-Lefevre.
2. The Committee for examining proposals to appoint the Indian Civil Service by competitive examination. See below, entry for 5 April 1854. The Revd Henry Melville (1798–1871) was Principal of Haileybury College, 1843–57.
3. Lord John Russell had secured the appointment of a Royal Commission in Oxford and Cambridge in 1850. In December 1853 Lord Palmerston had written to the Chancellors of the Universities setting out the principles on which the government thought reform desirable and asking for proposals. Russell introduced a bill in the Commons on 17 March for reform at Oxford that was passed in August. The Cambridge Bill was not passed until 1856. See A. I. Tillyard, *A History of University Reform* (Cambridge, *c.* 1905, 1913); D. A. Winstanley, *Early Victorian Cambridge* (Cambridge, 1940), W. R. Ward, *Victorian Oxford* (London, 1965).
4. The Queen's message reporting the breakdown of negotations with Russia and the government's determination to help Turkey against Russian demands. The next day war was declared.
5. Joshua Watson (1771–1855) had been leader of the 'Hackney Phalanx' and proponent of an Ecclesiastical Commission to reform the Church's revenues and administration. TBM may have been revising the passage on the Ecclesiastical Commission in *HE*, ch. 14, *CW*, vol. 3, pp. 172–7, so it may be that the manuscript he had been lent was Williams's Diary, used in that chapter, and printed this year. Williams was Bishop of Chichester.
6. Thomas Musgrave (1788–1860). His wife was Catherine Cavendish (*c.* 1805–63), daughter of Richard Cavendish, second Lord Waterpark.
7. Henry Pelham Pelham-Clinton (1811–64), fifth Duke, Secretary at War, 1854–5.
8. George Horatio Cholmondeley (1792–1870), second Marquess, was Joint Hereditary Great Chamberlain of England.
9. Hon. Charles Grey (1804–70) was Private Secretary to the Prince Consort. He became a Major General in June this year.
10. Unidentified.
11. TBM was referring to the clause in the Oxford University Bill that required Fellows to reside. He had already protested to its framer, Gladstone (*LM*, vol. 5, p. 391). He

thought it would prevent any able man from starting a career elsewhere, as his own Fellowship of Trinity had allowed him to do, or would force him to abandon one. .

Tuesday – March 28

Not a good night – In the morning. T called. I wrote to Wood explaining some of my difficulties about Hayleybury.[1] By the bye a few days ago a mad German named Lipke[2] left two pamphlets here in French. Nothing so absurd was ever written. He says that he has found out how to square the circle, and that he has discovered that money is only a commodity like other commodities, the effect of which discovery must be that all interest of money all profit or fixed and circulating capital must cease, that labour will be all in all, that there will be a complete social revolution etc etc etc. I had forgotten his nonsense. But yesterday afternoon I received a strange crazy letter from him the most important part of which was that he threatened to murder all the Bunsens, except *une bonne brin de fille*. I hardly knew what to do. But as there is always a bare possibility that a maniac may be mischievous, I thought it best to send the letter to Bunsen. Today I received Bunsen's acknowledgments. He has taken precautions. I went to W.T. passed two hours there pleasantly, though my dear B. is at Culverton – Home – wrote. R.I. transcribed from Acts of the Council of Ephesus.[3] At dinner novel by Chamier Perils of Beauty[4] – trash. In the evening very sleepy – I did not sleep much last night.

1. The India Act of 1853, piloted through Parliament by Sir Charles Wood, recommended that recruitment to the civil service in India should be, as at home, by open competitive examination. Until then, applicants like Charles Trevelyan had had to secure the nomination of one of the Directors of the East India Company, which then led to study at its college at Haileybury. They entered at sixteen or seventeen. Competitive entry open to all university graduates would end this. In effect, TBM's Committee (see above, entry for 27 March 1854) had to decide the fate of Haileybury.
2. I have not found the dates of Wilhelm Lipke, but the titles of his pamphlets are given in *LM*, vol. 5, p. 386n.
3. He quotes them in *HE*, ch. 14, *CW*, vol. 3, pp. 175.
4. Frederick Chamier, *The Perils of Beauty* (1843).

Wednesday – March 29

At breakfast looked at L'Almanach des Gourmands.[1] Wrote. To the House – presented petitions. Walked long – beautiful day – Home and worked – I get on well. At dinner finished Chamier's trash – Fanny Butler's book about America.[2] By the bye today I bought Josephine,[3] for twopence – a memorial of my childhood.

1. Published in Paris, 4 vols (1803–6).
2. F. A. Butler, née Kemble, *Journal of a Residence in America* (1835).
3. *Josephine or, Early Trials*, by Catherine Grace Godwin (1837).

Thursday – March 30

Fanny Butler's Book – eccentric – affected – full of bad taste – but not without spirit and ability. Worked a little – then to the Temple. E came – Mrs Marny – to W.T. G going on well. That Mrs H.T. always hateful, is now more hateful than ever.[1] Walked a little with H. home by the New Road – worked again. Chap XVI is drawing towards a close. I have only to touch up the part about Scotland – To dine with Labouchere. Ld Lne, Ld John, George Grey, Mahon, Lewis and Lady Theresa.

1. Emilia Anne Greig (1814–94) was the wife of Henry Willoughby Trevelyan (1803–76), Charles Trevelyan's brother.

Friday – March 31

Wrote – read – walked – E to dinner.

Saturday – April 1

W.T. went in the carriage with H and G – worked – At dinner the Dodds.[1]

1. Perhaps *The Dodd Family Abroad*, by Charles James Lever (1853–4).

Sunday – April 2

Worked – walked Waterloo Bridge and to W.T. – dear B at home. All well – walked away with G and A – met T. With him across the Park. Home worked – GM – Dodds.

Monday – April 3

Worked till H and B called to take me to the Railway Station at London Bridge – thence to the Crystal Palace. We got out too soon and had to take a fly to the building. Noble sight – beautiful things within – Greek, Italian, Gothic, Moorish, Assyrian, Egyptian – But I fear that it can never remunerate the Company and that it will soon shut up. I admire much the taste and splendour which appear almost everywhere. We walked down to the nearest Station and returned. I lost my stick – not a great loss, and yet, as Pepys says, it troubled me. A stick is one of those inanimate things to which one becomes attached; and this had been a good friend to me. Home – worked – to dine with Ld Lne – Ld Caernarvon and his sister and mother[1] – Lady Valletort[2] – Layard – Lord Somers.

1. Lady Eveline Alicia Juliana Herbert (1834–1906). She married in 1855 the Earl of Portsmouth. Her mother, the Dowager Countess, was Henrietta-Anna Howard (1804–76). She had entertained TBM in Rome in 1838.

2. Caroline Augusta Fielding (1808–81) had married Ernest Augustus Edgcumbe, third Earl of Mount Edgcumbe (1797–1861) in 1831, when he was Viscount Valletort. TBM may have referred to her by her earlier title.

Tuesday – April 4

To the City – found that the Irish Midland[1] had been doing business à l'Irlandaise, that is to say blunderingly and fraudulently. Home – worked. To dine with the Club – much concerned to hear from Dundas that Holmes of the Museum was dead.[2] He was a very good courteous intelligent friendly person. I sincerely regret him. The Bishop of Ln, Milman, Dundas, Mahon, Whewell. Staunton and Leake Mutes. We had some good talk. I went down to the House to vote for the Ld Advocate's Education Bill: but I found that it would not come on. Irish notices stopped the way – I had an hour's talk with Gladstone about the Oxford Bill, and made, I hope, some impression on him. Then home, and to bed – I worked hard today on Penn.

1. The Midland Great Western Railway of Ireland was then in dispute with some of its contractors, the case being in the Irish Court of Common Pleas.
2. He died on 1 April at his home in Highgate.

Wednesday – April 5

The Committee on the Civil Service of India breakfasted with me.[1] We set to work and made great progress. Ld Ashburton is really a great bore and very unwise. Jowett and Lefevre are excellent men. We sate till ½ past two. We determined to meet again on Monday at one, and I wrote to ask Ryan to join us. Then to work – finished Chap XVI. I shall I hope finish XVII before Easter – Then the transcribing may begin. To W.T. pleasant dinner and evening.

1. See R. J. Moore, 'The Abolition of Patronage in the Indian Civil Service and the Closure of Haileybury College', *Historical Journal*, 7:2 (1964) pp. 246–57.

Thursday – April 6

A very fine warm day – I went to work on Chap XVII – walked – met Van de Weyer at Hallam's door. Pleased to find Hallam much better – home – slight cold from checked perspiration I think. Read poems on Sacheverell[1] etc. Two French books came for me. Poor Bellot's Journals,[2] full of interest – a noble creature as ever lived – Pichot's History of Charles V[3] – to be read when I have leisure. To dinner with E.

1. *Poems for and against Sacheverell.* TBM's Library Sale Catalogue lists various items in the volume (SC, no. 731).

2. Joseph René Bellot, *Journal d'un voyage aux mers polaries, exécuté à la recherche de Sir John Franklin* ... (1854).
3. Amedée Pichot, *Charles Quint, Chronique de sa vie intérieuse, et de sa vie politique* ... (1854).

Friday – April 7

Worked – walked to W.T. pleasant chat – home – worked and read satires etc E to dinner.

Saturday – April 8

To breakfast with Milman – fine day – left off my great coat. Whewell, Milnes – Caitor[1] or some such name. Dundas. Walked away with Dundas. B.M. settled about the Gualterio papers.[2] Deo Gratias. I have been bored to death about them. I read during the sitting a most extraordinary French work – Le Livre d'Or – a crazy book about some fanatic who has visions and revelations and about the imposter who calls himself L XVII. I also amused myself with making out a Lapponian New Testament by the help of a Norwegian Dictionary. With time I could learn a good deal of the two languages in this way. Walked away with Dundas – Home – wrote and read – dined at home alone – the first time since Sunday – The Dodds – Warburton's Tracts[3] – very amusing article on the Mormons in the E.R.[4]

---

1. Unidentified.
2. See above, entry for 11 March 1854.
3. Perhaps *Warbutonian Controversy: Tracts in Controversy with the Author of the Divine Legation of Moses ... 1738–68*, SC, no. 906.
4. 'Mormonism' was by W. J. Conybeare, *ER*, 99 (April 1854), pp. 319–83. It reviewed fourteen works on the subject.

Sunday – April 9

Fine day – as all the days are now – Warburton – G.M. 1746 worked at XVII – to W.T. [Twelve lines obliterated] Home – worked on XVII – not satisfactorily. I have come to one of the most difficult parts of my task. At dinner the Dodds – Warburton.

Monday – April 10

Vile East Wind – very cold after much warmth. I felt my chest oppressed throughout the day and coughed much, though I staid at home. I worked in the morning, though not to much purpose – At one our Committee assembled; and Ryan joined us. We got on well. I staid at home and dined alone. The Dodds – Warburton – Law – Wrote several letters. Corrected proofs of Bunyan.

Tuesday – April 11

Breakfast party – H, Milman Mrs M, Van de Weyer, Goulburn, Rutherford. It was very pleasant; and both the ladies thought it so, which was the great thing. When the rest were gone H staid and G and B called for her at 1. I prevailed on them to stay lunch. We had out the reliques of the breakfast – cold fowl, tongue and potted char which with the help of a pint of Champagne did very well. They went at a little before three. I walked down to the House anxious to hear what Ld J was to say. I met Horseman who frightened me.[1] Yet I could not believe that what he predicted would happen. Then we met Grey who said that all was right. I had two words with C. Wood about our Committee. Then into the House. Ld J did his part very well.[2] He was at the close much overcome. The sympathy of the House was strongly expressed; and his agitation was the best plea that he could have set up. I came away after hearing him, satisfied that all must go well. Met Merivale and talked with him about the Oxford Bill. Home – dined – Dodds – G.M. – 1748 – 1749.

1. Presumably Edward Horsman, misspelled as before, 15 March.
2. Russell had been obliged, to avoid the break-up of the Ministry, to withdraw his bill for parliamentary reform. *PD*, 3rd ser., cxxxii, 836–44

Wednesday – April 12

To the City to get money for our expedition.[1] To W.T. – found that T could not go. Did no serious work – E to dinner.

1. To York and Durham.

Thursday – April 13

To the King's Cross Station. Journey pleasant, except that my chest was painfully affected by the motion, the talking and the East Wind. I was sorry for T's absence. We were very well lodged and fed at the Station Hotel, an excellent house, if the attendance had been better. We all, except H walked to the Cathedral yard and returned by the Ferry, then had a comfortable dinner and chatted all the evening.

Friday – April 14

The whole party, myself excepted who could not stand the cold went to the Cathedral. In the afternoon we took a carriage and pair and drove to Castle Howard. I saw it near 28 years ago with Sydney[1] – he is dead; and I am in parte alt 'uom da quel ch era.[2] I remembered little except the hall, the gallery and the Three Maries. The last I admired more than ever. The building I liked less than formerly. Even the terrace front seemed less vast and imposing than it used to be. But we did not see it from a sufficiently great distance and Vanbrugh's effects always require distance. Some excellent Reynoldses, and one very good Jackson.[3] I did not think that Jackson could have painted such a picture – a portrait of Northcote. Back to our Inn – dinner.

1. Sydney Smith.
2. 'I am rather a different man from the one I was'. TBM is quoting, or perhaps deliberately misquoting, Petrarch, Sonnet 1, line 4, in which the poet looks back on his love for Laura: *quand'era in parte altr'uom de quel ch'i sono.*
3. Perhaps the portrait of James Northcote, RA (1746–1831), by John Jackson, RA (1778–1831), said by *DNB* to have been presented to the National Gallery.

Saturday – April 15

Up early to Durham – a miserable town and a miserable walk from the Railway Station to the Cathedral. The Cathedral I have not visited since 1833. My impression of it proved quite correct. A striking specimen of rude barbarian power with little art and no grace. There is something Egyptian about it – Back by the Express train – some plague about tickets. However I paid. When I see that people are not trying to cheat me I would always rather pay than quarrel – Home – dinner as before.

Sunday – April 16

Many Easter Sundays have passed since I could venture into a Cathedral. I walked on the battlements while they were at Church, walked with them again to the Cathedral in the afternoon, just looked into the Chapter House, fine and finely repaired and decorated, and went home. Read to H and the rest some of Jay's Life of Winter.[1] We passed the evening pleasantly over it, and agreed that Jay was a good writer – a much better indeed than Winter who never could frame a paragraph of decent English.

1. William Jay, *Memoirs of the Life and Character of ... C. Winter ...* (1808).

Monday – April 17

Back to town. My chest has plagued me much during the whole trip. Found my table covered with letters – a Life of Jay left here – very odd coincidence. Wrote till dinner – Dodds – wrote again – G.M. – Hydr.

Tuesday – April 18

Writing letters all the morning. The Oxford Bill greatly improved. Did not stir out – Wrote – but not much – Marlborough – Looked over Wood's education dispatch. Excellent – Dodds – G.M. – Journal to Stella.

Wednesday – April 19

Coming into my room found dearest B – chatted with her pleasantly – went out. Quarterly Review on the Reform Bill[1] – contemptible trash. Croker's dotage is the most stupid and spiteful that I ever hear of. Poor old creature – κρεμ 7 – Home and wrote pretty well – at dinner finished Dodds – G.M. – Stella.

1. *QR*, 94 (March 1854), pp. 558–605.

Thursday – April 20

Worked a little – then to W.T. found Alice, Cora, G and B all, in one way, or other, poorly. I was myself wretched – much as when I went to Clifton last July year except that my pulse was regular. In the afternoon my loose tooth began to plague me – a sign that rain is coming, I suspect; and sure enough the rain did come though not in great quantities. We shall soon have more. E to dinner – The first asparagus. He showed me some exercises of Walter's. The Greek bad – though not worse than might be expected – The Latin Prose of great promise – The Latin elegiacs positively good.

Friday – April 21

Vexatious toothache. Can neither eat nor talk – Ate with difficulty two eggs for breakfast. Staid at home all day and got on well with the Aghrim Campaign.[1] Sir H. Holland called – I talked, though not very articulately. Dined on turtle soup and asparagus – Tom Jones – G M. – Stella.

1. *HE*, ch. 17, *CW*, vol. 3, pp. 437–40.

Saturday – April 22

Still toothache. Breakfasted on eggs and coffee – staid at home all day. H, B and G called and passed a pleasant hour here. Dined, on scotch broth, asparagus, and jelly, very tolerably. Wrote and read, and got pretty well through the day. J.S.

Sunday – April 23

The toothache better. Staid at home. T called. I read and wrote very comfortably and dined, still on things which required little or no use of the teeth – Scotch broth. sweetbread, asparagus, and jelly.

Monday – April 24

The toothache gone or nearly so. Cold day – East wind which has probably taken away one complaint and is very likely to bring another. Immediately after breakfast letter from Adolphus. Mrs A wishes H to present her. I went to W.T. and H consented very kindly, though the office is not much to her taste. Home – E had called – I suppose about the same business. Read and wrote. To dinner, much against my will, with Sir G Philips[1] – Lady P laid up. The party very dull. But for Dundas I should have gone to sleep – Ld Campbell and Ly Stratheden. Ly Murray[2] – her brother in law – Ld and Ly Duncan[3] and some people whom I did not know.

1. Sir George Richard Philips, second Bart (1789–1883), MP. He married Sarah Georgiana Cavendish (*c.* 1791–1874), daughter of Richard, the second Lord Waterpark. Her sister was Archbishop Musgrave's wife, Catherine.
2. She was Mary Rigby (*c.* 1789–1862), who married J. A. Murray in 1826. Her brother-in-law was William Murray of Henderland (*c.* 1774–1854).
3. Adam Duncan, Viscount Duncan (1812–67), was MP for Forfarshire. He later became Earl of Camperdown. His wife was Juliana Philips (1821–98), Sir G. Philips's daughter.

Tuesday – April 25

Still N.E. wind – and as cold as Xtmas. Longman to tell me that he has got me a good Amanuensis on pretty high terms: but I am content. Read and wrote. He left the proofsheets of some philosophical dialogues which Sir B Brodie is bringing out[1] – La La – but some good things. Macleod called. Cameron does not seem to manage well on the Law Commission.[2] To dine with Sir R. Murchison – Mrs Malcolm[3] – I remembered her as Miss Georgiana Vernon in 1828 a handsome girl then, a handsome woman still – Sir F Lewis and Lady L. – Dundas. I sate between Mrs M and Lady L and got on pretty well.

1. *Psychological Inquiries: Essays ... Intended to Illustrate the Mutual Relations of the Physical Organisation and the Mental Faculties*, published anonymously in this year.
2. Charles Henry Cameron, member of the Law Commission in India.
3. She was a daughter of Edward Vernon Harcourt, Archbishop of York. Cf *LM*, vol. 5, p. 397 and n. 4.

Wednesday – [April 26]

Fast day,[1] or rather day of humiliation. While I was dressing Dr R. Renton[2] called – a good fellow, but the visit was not very seasonable and not very short. He staid near two hours, and talked about medical legislation. I gave him a note for Palmerston.[3] Then to St Anne's[4] heard the service and a middling sermon. The Church I well remembered. I had repeatedly gone to it in old times. Thence to W.T. – saw them all – Charles – tomorrow dearest B is to be presented. I am a little anxious about her – home – wrote – Murchison called, and bored me – to dinner with E – all the children there.

1. A fast day in consequence of the declaration of war against Russia (TBM did not fast: *LM*, vol. 5, p. 396, and n).
2. Robert Renton, an Edinburgh doctor.
3. *LM*, vol 5, p. 397.
4. St Anne's church, Dean Street, Soho.

Thursday – [April 27]

Change of weather – much rain – to W.T. to see B in her Court dress. She looked charmingly. Home – It cleared up. Having a petition to present I went to the H. of C. – everybody very friendly and civil – Home – E to dinner.

Friday – [April 28]

Fine day. Finished Tom Jones – a great work though with many blemishes. Wrote. I have now finished the Brest business and Russell's Spanish proceedings.[1] To the private view of the R.A. pictures with H and B. Dined at home alone – 1st time since Sunday – Joseph Andrews.[2]

1. *HE*, ch. 20, *CW*, vol. 4, pp. 104–5. Russell's proceedings were the naval expedition to Barcelona to support the Spanish against the French. TBM's claim that Marlborough warned James II of the impending English attack upon Brest was the kernel of Paget's rebuttal in the *New Examen* (pp. 3–31).
2. By Henry Fielding (1742).

Saturday – [April 29]

Cold and rainy. Staid at home all day – wrote – read. Macleod called. At the Exhibition yesterday I thought my own portrait and Ld J's by Grant[1] excellent – Maclise[2] has a picture after his fashion full of ingenuity and spirit and yet not good as a whole to my thinking; – Ward[3] a very good picture; – I liked Leslie's picture[4] from the Rape of the Lock less than anything that I ever saw of his. There was a large Landseer not much to my taste.[5] The Queen laughing over a deer and fawn just killed – not an amiable expression for a woman. An Eastlake Eastlakish in the highest degree.[6] Execrable Prae-Raphaelitism – some good landscape – but I must go again. At dinner some of Amelia[7] – Dosed in the evening.

1. Sir Francis Grant's portraits of Macaulay and Lord John Russell were nos. 69 and 193 respectively. That of Russell is in the National Portrait Gallery; Algernon Graves, *The Royal Academy of Arts ... Dictionary of Contributors ... 1769–1904*. TBM's portrait was later owned by J. E. Denison.
2. Daniel Maclise, RA, *The Marriage of Richard de Clare, Earl of Pembroke [Strongbow] and Eva*, now in the National Gallery, Dublin.
3. Edward Matthew Lord exhibited (no. 403) *The Last Sleep of Argyle*. Intended for the corridor of the House of Commons, it is based on TBM's passage in *HE*, ch. 5, *CW*, vol. 1, p. 439, describing Argyle's last hours before his execution.
4. Charles Robert Leslie, Bart, exhibited (no. 192) *From 'The Rape of the Lock': Sir Plume demands the restoration of the lock.*
5. Landseer had two pictures, nos 63 and 360. TBM refers to no. 63, *Royal Sport on Hill and Lock: the Queen, the Prince Consort and the Prince of Wales, etc.*
6. The President, Sir Charles Eastlake, exhibited no. 129, *Irene*.
7. By Henry Fielding (1781).

Sunday – April 30

Cold for the eve of May day. Wrote – to W.T. Mr Upsher called.[1] Chatted with them pleasantly. Home and wrote more – Burton Foster – Clarissa – I shall soon dispose of 1695 now.

1. Perhaps Henry Ramey Upcher (1810–97). The family were Norfolk gentry and connected by marriage with the Buxtons.

Monday – May 1

A dull wet May day. My new Amanuensis came with Longman, and went to work. The handwriting good – He seems a very well informed intelligent person. A Balliol man and a barrister – yet not above his work.[1] Longman tells me shocking scandal about Ld Ribblesdale[2] and scandal still more shocking, and I hope, false, about Ruskin.[3] To dinner with E.

1. Patrick Cumin (1823–90) matriculated as a Snell exhibitioner at Balliol in 1841. He was the son of a Glasgow professor of midwifery, William Cumin. He was called to the Bar in 1855.
2. Thomas Lister, third Baron Ribblesdale (1828–76), had in 1853 married Emma Mure, daughter of Colonel Mure of Caldwell. He was a keen racehorse owner. In 1851 he had bought General Peel's racehorses and stud but, with insufficient capital, his debts grew. In that year he sold his Malton estate. Their son, the fourth Baron, and the subject of Sargeant's famous portrait, was born in Fontainebleau in October of this year.
3. Ruskin's wife left him in April 1854; in July she secured the annulment of her marriage and she married Millais a year later.

Tuesday – May 2

Very poorly – giddy – excused myself from breakfasting with the Bp of Oxford and sent for Bright. He tells me that the liver is in fault and gave me strong doses of calomel. A wretched day. H and B called and were very kind. I wish it were over. But I should like to finish these two vols first – Bright again in the evening. I took some broth and two eggs for dinner. I read Clarissa.

Wednesday – May 3

Better – B, H and T and G called – pulled down by Calomel. Ventured out and found myself though weak, able to walk. I went to the Museum, forgetting that it is not open during the 1st week of May. Home – read – but wrote nothing – Corrected Cumin's transcription. To dinner at W.T. sate between H and Lady T – Lady M. Wood,[1] Mrs Strutt, Greenwood,[2] the Hankeys[3] – pleasant enough.

1. The wife of Sir Charles Wood, later Viscount Halifax. I cannot identify 'Lady T', which may be a slip of TBM's pen.
2. Perhaps John Greenwood (1800–71), at the time assistant solicitor to the Treasury.
3. Thomson Hankey (1805–93) was MP for Peterborough. His wife was Apolline Agatha Alexander (*c.* 1808–88).

Thursday – May 4

Read and wrote – pretty well in health. Bright recommended more calomel. I went to W.T. and then with H and B to Mrs Smith's in the New Chambers at Pimlico. I must, I think, live in Chambers; and H and B seem to be of the same mind. They went on to Clapham and set me down at Vauxhall. I walked to Westminster Bridge and came home by Omnibus – wrote and read – dined alone. Strat Def[1] in the evening Philipp's most absurd Recollections of Curran.[2] Calomel.

1. By Mary Meeke.
2. Perhaps Charles Philipps, *Curran and Some of his Contemporaries* (1818).

Friday – May 5

Funeral of my neighbour – poor Ld Anglesey.[1] Worked. Newmarket etc. R.I. to W.T. walked with H and B across Hyde Park and The Green Park to Pall Mall. Sent them home through the rain by a cab. Home myself – worked a little more. E to dinner – pleasant – more Calomel.

1. Anglesey died on 28 April at Uxbridge House, Old Burlington Street. He was buried on 6 May in the family vault in Lichfield Cathedral.

Saturday – May 6

Not very well – probably affected by the remedies rather than by the disease. The weather too is disagreeable – squally, chilly, rainy. By the bye I was much vexed yesterday to find that T is plagued by two or three of his companions at the Treasury. He will soon I hope be rid of that blackguard Wilson.[1] I wrote a little, and read. At one was the meeting of our Committee. I ought to have mentioned that yesterday Macleod called and gave me some new lights as to that matter. I walked; but did not feel well. R.I. – A poor woman, the wife of a man of letters named Cole,[2] wrote to beg for help. I sent her 5£ and received a warm letter of thanks. To dinner with Ld Granville. There were Ld and Ly J and Ld Lansdowne – a very pleasant small party.

1. James Wilson (see Volume 3, entry for 10 November 1852, n. 4).
2. Not identified.

Sunday – May 7

A bad night – my old Clifton symptoms – I want tonics; and Bright, in relieving my liver has weakened me much. Better after breakfast – corrected and annotated Chap XI – to W.T. glad to find that T is more agreeably situated – Home – wrote – read old tracts – dined alone – *Σπατ ησσ*.

Monday – May 8

At 3 to Stafford House with dear B. Lecture on Dante from La Caita. Some interesting things. I followed him easily when he spoke slow, but, when he warmed, he outran me. Dearest B much interested. In the evening to the palace – Music – I staid in the picture gallery and chatted with Ld Grey, Sir H. Bulwer, Ld Canning, etc etc.

Tuesday – May 9

To breakfast with the Bp of Oxford – Gladstone – Inglis – etc – dined at home – Strat Def.

Wednesday – May 10

Steady work. Nothing particular.

Thursday – May 11

Breakfast at Gladstone's – La Caita. Sate long at the Athenaeum. Walked with Baba – saw the French pictures in Pall Mall[1] – Admired the death of Guise and

The Rimini lovers – not much besides. To dinner with Romilly I was most unfortunately seated and found the party dull.

1. Ernest Gambard (1814–1902) had set up a business, Gambard and Junin, importing foreign prints, which was at 120–4 Pall Mall. He collected and exhibited paintings. *The Death of Guise* (no. 39) was by Paul Delaroche (1797–1856), the leading French historical painter. By the Rimini Lovers TBM must mean no. 126, by Ary Scheffer (1795–1858): *Francesca da Rimini*, with its motto from Dante's Inferno, 'Amor condusse noi ad una morte'. This exhibition was the start of Gambard's rise to a dominant position in the London art market.

Friday – May 12

Worked – Every day is now one of regular work. H. of C – paired till 10½ – to dinner – pleasant – then drove to the H. of C. Voted with the govt. on the Scotch Education Bill.[1] To the disgrace of the House, but to the relief, I suspect, of the ministers, we were beaten. The Ld Advocate[2] spoke excellently. I went home with Sir J Mactaggart.[3]

1. For TBM's own views on a system of national education, see his letter to Black in *LM*.
2. James Moncreiff.
3. Sir John Mactaggart (1789–1867) of Ardwell, Wigtownshire; MP for Wigton, 1835–57. His sister married T. F. Ellis. He lived at 69 Albany Street, Regents Park.

Saturday – May 13

Knocked up. Museum – dined at Strutt's. Pleasant party – The Milmans, Ld Lansdowne – sorry that he is getting deaf – Wood and Lady Mary.

Sunday – May 14

Worked in the morning – to W.T. – Then home. Ld L called to take me to Gordon Square.[1] A fine building, the chanting good, the dresses not bad, the preaching and prophesying execrable. The people very courteous to strangers. I heard the unknown tongue for the first time. It raises in me the strongest suspicions of deliberate hypocritic imposture. Home to dinner.

1. The Catholic Apostolic Church was founded by Edward Irving (1792–1834). The Irvingite Church in Gordon Square was built in 1854.

Monday – May 15

To Milnes's to breakfast. Walked away and worked – E to dinner.

Tuesday – May 16

To the Bp of O's to breakfast – worked – to dinner with Ld De Mauley. Cold weather and E wind. I did not feel at all well. However I dined tolerably – Lady Davy in grey hair which she should have worn two centuries ago – Lord Murray and Ly Murray – Ld de M's son, a dashing rattling young guardsman.[1] Glad to be at home.

1. The Hon. Ashley George John Ponsonby (1831–98) was MP for Cirencester, 1852–7 and 1859–65. He was a Captain in the Grenadier Guards.

Wednesday – May 17

Worked all the morning. At 3 Stafford House with B – an insipid lecture[1] – nothing but citations ill chosen from the Purgatorio and the Paradiso – with a great deal of *bello-bellissimo – magnifico mara viglioso* etc etc. Went with H and B in the carriage to W.T. and walked home. In the evening to dine with the Bp of Gloucester.[2] Most kind and hospitable but I had a vile irritation of the chest and coughed much. The girls handsome and pleasant. The party dull, the Bp of O excepted who is always agreeable. The Queen's Ball had thinned the company. Ld Saye and Sele[3] was there, very polite to me but not, I think very wise – G Bankes[4] – civil – The 2nd vol of Barker's absurd Parriana.[5]

1. By Lacaita.
2. J. H. Monk.
3. The Revd Frederick Twisleton Wykeham-Fiennes (1799–1887), thirteenth Baron Saye and Sele. He was a Canon of Hereford Cathedral.
4. The Right Hon. George Bankes (1788–1856), MP for Dorset, 1841–56. He had been a Bankruptcy Commissioner with TBM. He was the owner of Kingston Lacy.
5. E. H. Barker.

Thursday – May 18

By the bye yesterday I received from Longman a very handsome present, a good engraving of an early Reynolds of Dr Johnson. Wrote to thank him. Wrote to the Archbp of Canterbury to ask to see the corrected prayerbook of 1689. Worked. Letter from Edinburgh. In spite of my excuses they have chosen me President of the Philosophical Institution.[1] In the afternoon H and B called. We went to Greenwich – found the Ellises there – a splendid and luxurious dinner, as usual; and we were very cheerful and social. But I am not what I was. I feel it every month more and more. Home with the T's.

1. His letter of acceptance is in *LM*, vol. 5, p. 399, nn. 1 and 2.

Friday – May 19

Poorly, not from excess, for I avoided it, but in the regular course of things. In the evening much oppression of the chest – S.D.[1] – Worked however, and satisfactorily.

1. Perhaps *Stratagems Defeated*, by Mary Meeke.

Saturday – May 20

To breakfast with Mahon – pleasant enough. To Ld Ashburton's.[1] Our Committee met there on account of his gout. Lefevre was not with us – detained at the drawing room. We did not do much. To Hallam's – found him not so well as Mahon had led me to hope, yet better than he was a few months ago. I dare say that his life is a better purchase than mine. Worked well – S.D. – The twelfth Chapter[2] is now transcribed and the notes written.

1. Bath House, Piccadilly.
2. i.e. the second, Irish chapter of vol. 3 of *HE*, the last in *CW*, vol. 2.

Sunday – May 21

Worked – to W.T. I am a little low – not from apprehension; for I look forward to the inevitable close with perfect serenity, but from regret for what I love. I sometimes hardly command my tears when I think how soon I may leave them. Poor George again at home and on his couch. His bad foot hit by a cricket ball. Home – wrote – dined alone – SD – A mustard poultice. It did me good – Read Quevedo[1] while the poultice did its work.

1. Francisco Gomez de Quevedo (1580–1645) was a Spanish political writer and satirist.

Monday – May 22

Better. To VdW's to breakfast.[1] Very pleasant – Walked away with Milman – It rained and I gave him a letter – Then I worked hard – Interrupted not unpleasantly by calls. Stephen – Senior. Dined at Lansdowne House – Ld Stanley, D of Argyle, Ds of Sutherland, Stirling, Denison, Mrs Malcolm.

1. Van der Weyer's house was 3 Grosvenor Square.

Tuesday – May 23

Read some of Pichot's Charles the Fifth. To breakfast with the Bp of Oxford – pleasant enough – the old set. To the Athenaeum consulting papers. To W.T. – H brought me to Apsley House in the carriage. Home – by the way called at the Secy's office[1] and saw a very fine and spacious set of rooms in the Mansion facing Piccadilly. I think that I shall settle there. Home – worked – Dined alone – θαυμασιον τι.[2]

1. The Secretary to the Trustees of Albany is presumably meant. He was Alexander Copland Hemsley (1823–1906). TBM did not take them and stayed in F3 until his move to Holly Lodge.
2. (Greek): 'For a wonder'.

Wednesday – May 24

To the British Museum – Worked – H and B called – took B to Stafford House – Lecture on Petrarch – Heavy work – Told H of my plan about the new chambers – E to dinner – Sent for Bright today, who, in consequence of a blunder of his servant did not come.

Thursday – May 25

A day of work – θυγατηρ ἱερεως θεοδωρα. Bright Hydrarg.

Friday – May 26

Worked on – E to dinner again.

Saturday – May 27

Dear little Alice's birthday – Meeting of our Committee here – Ld A absent.[1] She came with her Mamma in the afternoon to see these chambers. On the whole I think that they will do. But there are difficulties and objections. Back with H and A to W.T. dined there and passed a happy evening.

1. Lord Ashburton.

Sunday – May 28

Work in the morning. To W.T. T. and H not returned. Jowett here. Gave him lunch. He went just as T and H came back. Home – Work – dined alone – Ελλεσμ[1] Horace Walpole's Memoirs.

1. Mrs Meeke, *Ellesmere*, 4 vols (1799).

Monday – May 29

Rain and sunshine – April at the end of May – staid at home all day reading and writing. Dined alone – E.M. H.W. Dodington[1] – Wrote to the Sec of the Albany about these Chambers.

1. Perhaps the *Diary of... George Bubb Dodington ...*, ed. H. P. Wyndham (1784).

Tuesday – May 30

Letter from Everett – very sad and kind. It brought tears into my eyes. Answered him[1] – Μακφ[2] at same time. Went to the library of the H. of C. in hope of finding the corrected Prayer Book. Shall not see it till tomorrow. Home through a tremendous shower. Wrote and read. Walked a little in the sunshine at four – Dined alone. Λαγγτων[3] Dodington. The Secy of the Albany called. I hope to get these rooms for 1200£ or less + ground rent of 65£.

1. *LM*, vol. 5, p. 400 and n. 2.
2. Macpherson.
3. TBM often used Greek to cloak his taste for the novels of his childhood. This seems to be *Laughton Priory*, by Gabrielli [Mary Meeke], 4 vols (1809).

Wednesday – [May 31]

Dodington. To the H of C – vexed to find everything shut up – Derby Day. I had been assured that I should find the M.S. I am really much disappointed. To W.T. sate an hour or two. Toothache and languid. Home – had to write letters to Edinburgh about a stupid Medical Bill which sets them all in an uproar on different sides.[1] A ridiculous letter from a Yankee with a ridiculous name – Hotchkiss. I did little today in the way of work – May however has not been ill employed. To dinner with Vernon Smith – Sate next Ly Mahon – Wm Harcourt[2] Ly Waldegrave Lady Morley[3] – Lord Dufferin – tolerably pleasant.

1. 23 March and 10 May 1854. A private member's bill to establish a register of all doctors qualified to practise had been introduced into the House of Commons. Nothing came of it, and the Medical Register was not established until 1858. C. E. Newman, *The Evolution of Medical Education in the Nineteenth Century* (London, 1957).
2. Revd William Granville Harcourt (1789–1891), Canon of York, Rector of Bolton Percy, Yorkshire. He lived at Nuneham Park. He had married Matilda Mary Gooch in 1824.
3. Harriet Sylvia Parker, Countess of Morley (1809–97), wife of Edmund Parker, second Earl of Morley (1810–64).

Thursday – June 1

Worked in the morning. To the House – found the M.S. of the correct Prayer Book, and made notes – presented a petition – home – worked – E to dinner.

Friday – June 2

Worked all the morning at the history of the Eccl. Commission in the Jerusalem Chamber – Read the Calder papers.[1] Not very well – excused myself to Ld Spencer for tomorrow Indeed I seldom am well now. Λαγγ[2] at dinner – Memoirs of George III by Walpole.

1. Robert Calder (*c.* 1650–1723), clergyman of the Scottish Episcopalian Church.
2. *Langhton Priory.*

Saturday – June 3

To W.T. Found B there – F called – H and A gone to Esher – home – looked into RI by the way – worked on – I began to flag.

Sunday – June 4

Worked – then to W.T. Walked across the Park with H and T to see the Conybeares.[1] He is in bed – poor fellow – worse a good deal, I am afraid than I. I saw quite a crowd of pleasant women – Mrs Rose,[2] Mrs Dicey,[3] Lady Stephen[4] – pity that they are not as young as they were. Walked home – worked a little more. Λαγγ – Yesterday by the bye I sent my page to attend his sister's funeral at Horsham and paid for his journey.[5] He thanked me at dinner – I told him that I was sorry for his loss. The poor lad burst out a crying. I felt for him much – H.W. Memoirs.

1. W. J. Conybeare (1815–57) was married to Eliza Rose (1820–1903), daughter of Mrs Rose, below.
2. Lydia Babington (1789–1880) married Joseph Rose, Vicar of Rothley.
3. Anne Mary Dicey, née Stephen (1796–1878), was wife of Thomas Edward Dicey (1759–1858). They were the parents of Albert Venn Dicey, the jurist.
4. (1793–1875). The wife of Sir James Stephen. She was Jane Catherine Venn, daughter of John Venn, Rector of Clapham.
5. Harriet Holland, née Hersee (*c.* 1789–1854) was the only woman buried at Horsham on 2 June. William Catchpole had left TBM's service in 1853. His successor may have been called Hersee, but I have found no confirmation of this.

Monday – June 5

Still March weather – cold N.E. wind. H and B called, pleasant half hour. Then walked to the Temple – E not there – back and saw the panorama of Berlin. It looks like what I supposed – the dullest of capitals. Home – worked on Chap XVIII. I am afraid that it will rather drag, though not ill-written.

Tuesday – June 6

Cold and dreary – my amanuensis[1] gone to Scotland in consequence of the death of an aunt. Bought some fine grapes – E to dinner – plagued by toothache. Fires in both rooms.

1. Cumin had four maiden aunts, and one, Miss Jane Cumin, died (intestate) on 3 June 1854.

Wednesday – June7

Still very bleak – wrote etc – walked to B.M. and made notes – Λαγ – d – Walpole's G III.

Thursday – June 8

Still cold – sent an excuse to the Hollands – to W.T. concerned to hear that F is unwell – a surgical case, I am afraid – with B to the British Gallery – very fine things – took her home – Back – Walpole, finished Λαγ.

Friday – June 9

To breakfast with Mahon – pleasant – Ld Lansdowne, Ld Carlisle, well and stout after his wanderings,[1] Cornwall Lewis, an American named Reid[2] – Lady Evelyn Stanhope,[3] rather a good-looking girl but I am afraid forward and given to public exhibitions of recitation etc. Walked away with Ld Carlisle to his door. On with Lewis. To the Ordnance about Edinburgh business. To the Admiralty about a job for Marriott – son of an old College Competitor of mine[4] – to W.T. – reassured about F. Home – wrote a little. It was warmer this morning but the wind is again north and it is very chill. To dinner, much against my will, at the Palace. Met Van de Weyer and Mme on the staircase – The D. of Newcastle – Wylde[5] – Ld Breadalbane[6] – the Palmerstons and a few other persons with whom I was acquainted. Soon came the Royalties – The Q,[7] K of Portugal and his brother. The K rather an amiable looking youth – not at all Portuguese in appearance. I sate between two foreigners – a Portuguese man, I believe, and a German woman, and said scarcely a word all dinner time. The music and pictures and the general gaiety of the scene made conversation less necessary. In the gallery I was bored by the compliments of the King and His brother – The King tells me that he was translating my history. His brother, the queerest little prig of fifteen, asked me if I knew Greek – whether I did not think it a pretty language – whether I did not admire Plutarch's parallels – K.T.L. The King I rather liked. He speaks English well, and seems to have sense and reading. The Queen, who was very gracious to me, told me that he had a great turn for science and natural history. She mentioned to me Ld John's appointment to the Presidency of the Council.[8] I like it well enough, unless it should cause some bad casting of parts among his colleagues. I agree with Her Majesty that the innovation is no evil at all. Glad to get away.

---

1. Since June 1853 Carlisle had travelled in the Levant. His *Diary in Turkish and Greek Waters* was published later this year.
2. Henry Hope Reid (1808–54). He was drowned at sea, returning to the US on the SS *Arctic*.

3. Lady Geraldine Evelyn Stanhope (1841–1914) was the daughter of Leicester Fitzgerald Stanhope, fifth Earl of Harrington (1784–1862). She married Edward Leeson, fifth Earl of Milltown, in 1871.
4. Presumably a son of William Henry Marriott (1800–*c.* 1832), who matriculated at Trinity in 1818, the same year as Macaulay. TBM calls him a competitor because he won many prizes.
5. William Wylde (1788–1877), Groom of the Bedchamber to Prince Albert, 1846–61.
6. John Campbell (1796–1862), fifth Earl and second Marquis of Breadalbane, was Lord Chamberlain to the Queen, an FRS and a Trustee of the British Museum.
7. Peter V (1837–61) came to the throne on the death of his mother Mary II in 1853. His father was Ferdinand of Saxe Coburg-Gotha, a cousin of Prince Albert's. His Queen was Stephanie (1837–59), a Princess of Hohenzollern-Sigmaringen. Peter V's brother was Louis (1838–89), who became King in 1861.
8. Lord John Russell, urging a Cabinet reshuffle on the declaration of war, became Lord President of the Council, as a result of which Granville left the Cabinet. See John Prest, *Lord John Russell* (1972), p. 366.

Saturday – June 10

A fine day at last. I am glad for the sake of the people who are gone to the Crystal Palace. Ellis called with Walter, went with them to the Temple – asked Thesiger what *causes célèbres* were coming on next week. Wylde had begged me to learn for the benefit of the most faithful King. I was glad to find that the great Manchester case[1] will be on. Wrote to Wylde – Read some of the trash in the Q Mag del Vag *bdo* [*sic*]. Worked – but not very heartily. Ld C's Lives of Chancellors[2] – Loughborough – Che sara sara.[3]

1. Perhaps the case, at the Liverpool assizes, of a burglary at James Howard's, the Manchester jewellers, in which John Goldsmith and an accomplice were charged with stealing, and with assaulting Howard's daughter, aged eighteen. I can find no other trial at this time that fits TBM's description.
2. Lord Campbell's.
3. Perhaps Mary Meeke, *What Shall Be Shall Be*, 4 vols (1823).

Sunday – June 11

Wrote to Brooks's – vexed by what I hear of the late arrangements and of the way in which Strutt has been treated[1] – To W.T. Jowett – dear children – very pleasant. Home and worked – Holland called. At dinner Loughborough.

1. Strutt became Chancellor of the Duchy of Lancaster in Aberdeen's government in December 1852. He had to resign in favour of Granville when Lord John Russell took over the latter's office of Lord President of the Council.

Monday – June 12

To breakfast with Hallam – delighted to find him better than I had expected – to the H. of Lords to look for the Bill ascertaining the salaries of Judges – disappointed – home – worked feebly. H and B called. I had just got an admission to the gallery for them from Ld CR.[1] I took them to the House and put them into the gallery – Home – CSS[2] – Lh – Erskine.[3]

1. Lord Charles James Fox Russell (1807–94). Lord John's brother was Sergeant at Arms in the House of Commons.
2. Che Sara Sara [*What Shall be Shall be*].
3. *Lives of the Lord Chancellors*: Loughborough and Erskine.

Tuesday – June 13

Busy rummaging and preparing – began working hard on Chap 20 – Bank etc.

Wednesday – June 14

To B.M. Bank – made a great collection of facts fit for my purpose – home – began to write, but was interrupted by a letter from Edinburgh asking me to be V.P. of an Anti-Slavery Socy. I had to refuse – which was matter of conscience with me – but delicately and dexterously. I was long working on my letter, short and simple as it at last was. Ward the painter came – Short chat – lent him a vol. of State Trials – The Dumont M.S. I am sorry that M. Dumont wrote a bad hand with bad ink and bad paper. It will try my eyes I fear – read a little – CSS – Erskine.

Thursday – June 15

Vile day – N.E. wind – rain as if the wind were S.W. I sate down to work and worked well – broke the neck of this business of the Bank. Ten days of shuch work wd do wonders – Then to the Dumont M.S.[1] which I had looked at while dressing. Valuable but not first rate. Wrote a letter of thanks to the Dean of Ossory[2] – Eldon ματριμ.[3]

1. The autobiography of Dumont de Bostaquet, a Huguenot refugee who came over with William III. See *HE*, ch. 14, *CW*, vol. 3, p. 128n, and C. H. Firth, *A Commentary on Macaulay's History of England* (London, 1938), p. 76.
2. Charles Augustus Vignoles, DD (1789–1877). He was appointed Dean in 1843 and held the post until his death. He too was of a Hugenot family.
3. Perhaps Mary Meeke, *Matrimony, the Height of Bliss or Extreme of Misery*, 4 vols (1811).

Friday – June 16

Another vile day; but I was forced, after finishing the rough draught of what I had to say about the Bank, to go to the H. of C at 12 – presented petitions – found that there was no more to be done today on the business which took me there. To the Lords. Saw the Judges Salaries bill – then to W.T. H at Esher – saw dearest B and A. Then to the India Board by appointment – explained my views and difficulties to Wood, and was glad to find that we agreed very well. I think that I shall be able to knock up Hayleybury. Home – looked through journals etc – Comyn[1] came back and wrote a page – I hope that he will stick to his work now. Eldon. Matr. Poor Tufnell is gone.[2] Who next? I very likely.

1. Patrick Cumin.
2. Henry Tufnell had been Secretary to the Treasury. He died on 15 June at Catton Hall, Derbyshire.

Saturday – June 17

No news of Cuming or Comyn – I am a good deal annoyed. Wrote – Judges Salaries Bill[1] – The Committee. Very satisfactory – E to dinner – Eldon.

1. *HE*, ch. 18, *CW*, vol. 3, pp. 505–6.

Sunday – June 18

Fine day. To Athenaeum. Looked at a history of the Grocer's Company[1] and found something – at a life of Ken[2] and found something more. To W.T. pleasant chat – walked across the Park to Senior's with T and A – Home – I have not walked so much this many a day. Mat. Eldon – Hydr.

1. William Ravenhill, *A Short Account of the Company of Grocers, from their origins, together with their Case and Conditions ...* (1689).
2. Perhaps J. L. Anderdon's *Life of Thomas Ken, Bishop of Bath and Wells* (1854), which was in TBM's Library.

Monday – June 19

At home all day – Cuming came – read and wrote. H and B called. I took leave of them somewhat sadly. Yet why? If it is to be I may as well go through it alone. Mat[rimony]. Gulliveriana – Wrote about Somers.[1]

1. *HE*, ch. 20, *CW*, vol. 4, pp. 53–5.

Tuesday – June 20

Miserable – As ill as I was on the 2nd May and in much the same way. Weak as a child, could hardly walk without holding the table. Sent for Bright. He prescribed tonics which did not at first seem to answer – I ate little and drank less. I could not write, but I read all day – Ruffhead's Pope[1] – and Walpole's letters etc – finished Mat. Ld Minto called. I was hardly able to converse. I was, sorry to hear so bad an account of the state of things in the cabinet. I hope that he sees matters through a discoloured medium. No head. No principle of union – Ld A opposed to Ld C.[2] Ld J out of his element and feeling himself to be so.

1. Owen Ruffhead, *The Life of Alexander Pope ...* (1769).
2. Aberdeen, Clarendon (Foreign Secretary) and Russell.

Wednesday – June 21

Better – much better – but not quite the thing – staid at home – wrote – Somers – finished. Now for Montague.[1] A deputation from Edinburgh about railway matters. I think of taking a house near Thames Ditton between Kingston and Hampton Court. Letter from Snow inclosing Australian newspaper puffs on himself – *The Hero* – The enthusiast – and such stuff. I have done with him. Kind letter from H – Lequel est l'Homme.[2] Walpole – Sir H.M.

1. *HE*, ch. 20, *CW*, vol. 3, pp. 55–9.
2. Perhaps Mary Meeke, *Which is the Man?*, 4 vols (1801).

Thursday – June 22

Sent W to see a house at Ditton which seems to promise well. Ld Lne called – very kind – To dinner with E – not amiss. Found W at home – very good account on the whole – determined to send him again to get H's opinion, as I cannot go there tomorrow. Lequel – HW – Sir HM.[1]

1. *Letters of Horace Walpole to Sir Horace Mann*, 3 vols (1833–4).

Friday – June 23

Sent W off again. He came back in good time in the afternoon. H approves, and I ordered the bargain to be immediately struck, unsight, unseen – Lequel – H.W. picked up Old W & YH.[1] I walk in the evenings again. Today Mrs S Montgomery[2] called with a parcel from Florence.

1. Mary Meeke, *The Old Wife and Young Husband*, 3 vols (1804).

2. Maria Gherardini (*c.* 1822–92), the wife of the James Montgomery Stuart referred to in *LM*, vol. 5, p. 380 and n. Presumably she brought the books mentioned on 25 June. See also Stuart's *Reminiscences and Essays* (1884), p. 20.

Saturday – June 24

To breakfast with Inglis – Sir G. Grey, The N. Zd Gov[1] – the Bp of New Zd,[2] Acland,[3] Ld Harrowby.[4] Worked and read. Snow has sent me a sensible answer. I hope that my severity has done him good. Lequel – H.W.

1. Sir George Grey (1812–98). He became Governor of New Zealand in 1846.
2. George Augustus Selwyn (1809–78).
3. Probably Sir Thomas Dyke Acland (1787–1871).
4. Dudley Ryder (1790–1882), second Earl of Harrowby, was Chancellor of the Duchy of Lancaster, 1854–5, and Lord Privy Seal, 1855–7.

Sunday – June 25

Wrote – Walked – I have done the characters of S[ome]rs and Montague with, I think, great spirit. Finished Lequel. Looked at a book sent me from Florence by Giudici, Savonarola's process[1] – and a Life of Beccaria[2] – not much in it – by Villari– walked in the evening H.W.

1. Paolo Emiliani Giudici (1812–72). He had translated TBM's *History*, vols 1 and 2, into Italian in 1852–3. He dedicated his *Storia della Letteratura Italiano* (1855) to TBM, whose letter of thanks for it is in *LM*, vol. 5, p. 404 and n.
2. Cesare, Marchese de Beccaria (1738–94) was famous for his *Dei delitti e delle pene* (1764). Pasquale Villari (1827–1917) wrote a life to preface an edition of Beccaria's works, published in Florence 1854.

Monday – [June 26]

Party to breakfast – Goulburn forgot – Mahon, Milman, The Bp of O and Milnes – very pleasant. Milman recommended me to read Photius.[1] I bought a copy at Natt's[2] and mean to take it to Ditton as a pièce de résistance. Tolerable. But I am not well. I wrote rather dejectedly to H about myself. And yet my spirits are little depressed. But I feel that the fund of life is nearly spent – Wrote – Harley[3] – not much. Began OW and YH. Walked in the evening. H.W.

1. A Byzantine scholar and Patriarch of Constantinople in the late ninth century. TBM seems to mean his *Bibliotheca*, which he read in an edition by Bekker.
2. Nattali and Bond, booksellers, 23 Bedford Street, Covent Garden.
3. *HE*, ch. 20, *CW*, vol. 4, pp. 63–7.

Tuesday – June 27

Worked. Wm's parliaments and his relation to them – walked – but not much – began Photius – astonished to find hardly anything but theology, and such theology. Herodotus, to be sure, he read – but he says little about Herodotus, nor indeed was much wanted – OW and YH. Walk – H.W.

Wednesday – June 28

To breakfast with Bp of O. Parsons – Bp of St D[1], Milnes, Sydney Herbert, D. of Argyle – not unpleasant. To the Athenaeum. Turned over the memoirs of Joseph Buonaparte[2] – dull poor stuff – home and wrote – Paul Foley[3] – not much but pretty well. More of Photius – read his abstract of Ctesias.[4] From the fulness of this abstract contrasted with the cursory manner in which Herodotus is despatched I infer that Ctesias was a very rare book and rare doubtless because it was a trumpery book. As to his account of the battle of Platæa it is palpably false. He has against him the voice of all antiquity, Æschylus to begin with. To prefer this obscure scribbler to Herodotus is mere love of paradox – OW and YH. Walk – H.W.

1. Connop Thirlwall.
2. P. E. A. Du Casse, *Mémoirs et correspondance politique et militaire du Roi Joseph ...* (1853).
3. *HE*, ch. 20, *CW*, vol. 4, p. 67. Foley (*c.* 1645–99) was Speaker of the House of Commons, 1695–8.
4. Doctor at Persian Court, late fifth century BC; author of books on Persia and India.

Thursday – June 29

Worked in the morning. Photius. To the House of Commons. Voted for the clause in the Oxford Bill admitting Dissenters to the AB degree. A complete victory.[1] Home to dinner – Spanish Campaign[2] – H.W. Hydr.

1. It was carried by 233 votes to 79. *PD*, 3rd ser., cxxxiv, 891–93.
2. Mary Meeke, *The Spanish Campaigns or the Jew*, 3 vols (1815).

Friday – June 30

Letter from Tauchnitz – £50 – Worked in the morning. Walk – Photius. B to dinner.

Saturday – July 1

Bank – The parson of Thornton's City parish[1] – a bore. To the Museum – paid Cumming. Then home. He has transcribed only 5 Chapters, and has been two months about it. On the whole I am glad to have done with him. The Committee – Melville[2] fierce for Hayleybury which he will not, I hope and trust, be able to save. I am to draw the report. I must and will finish it in a week. Macleod called – Longman too to consult me about some trash of Augustus St John,[3] or some such name. To dinner with Harcourt.[4] He has a delightful house and some interesting pictures. I was next to an M.P. whom I ought to have known but did not know, as often happens to me – Fortescue,[5] I think M.P. for Louth. The dinner was splendid and the company – Dukes of Argyle and Newcastle – Marquess of Lansdowne – Earls of Clarendon, Harrowby, Shelburne, Somers and Grosvenor – Ly Gr looking like an angel. Glad to get home.

1. St Mary's Woolnoth. Its Rector was the Revd Robert Dear (1810–72). He was a graduate of Trinity College, Dublin.
2. Revd Henry Melvill (1798–1871), Principal of Haileybury, 1843–57.
3. James Augustus St John (1801–75), a traveller and journalist; he wrote a Life of Sir Walter Raleigh (1868).
4. George Granville Venables Harcourt (1785–1861).
5. Chichester Samuel Parkinson Fortescue (later Lord Carlingford) (1823–98), MP for Louth, 1847–74. After Harcourt's death, he became Lady Waldegrave's fourth husband.

Sunday – July 2

Finished putting notes to what Cumin has transcribed as far as my M.S. enables me to do it. Went out – fine day. Walked to K. Wm's statue near Ln Bridge. Admired the view of St Paul's – home to work on the report – did not get on. I must work doggedly. Another no. of the Newcomes, very good – Finished Sp Camp, H. Walpole.

Monday – July 3

Went on putting notes to what Cumin has transcribed. Wrote some of the Boyne, packed books and papers – At dinner St GJ.[1] Walked in the evening – H.W.

1. Henry Cockton, *George & George Julian the Prince* (1841).

Tuesday – July 4

William went to Ditton today. To breakfast with Mahon – Ldy E Stanhope, as usual, Ly Craven,[1] Van de Weyer, – not unpleasant – finished packing etc. To dinner with Sir G. Philips – against the grain – but it was necessary – very stupid. Ld Harrington the great man of the party – [?Rich] a relief. Glad to be at home.

1. Lady Emily Mary Grimston (1815–1901) married William, second Earl of Craven.

Wednesday – [July 5]

To breakfast with Denison. The last time I am afraid that I shall breakfast in Burlington House – Senior, Drummond, Ld Carlisle – Drummond very amusing. We went down together to the H. of C. I presented a petition.[1] To the City by steam after a long interval – once a daily habit – saw my book. They have been blundering as they always are. To the Waterloo Station and thence to Kingston. To my house – pretty well pleased. The cabin – for a cabin it is – is convenient.[2] Then to Esher – found them happy and well – had a pleasant afternoon and dinner with them. In the evening we came in the carriage to Greenwood Lodge, as my country seat is called. I began Le Veau d'or.[3] To bed at ten.

1. From the Royal College of Surgeons, Edinburgh, against the Medical Graduates Bill.
2. Janet Ross recalled TBM taking 'an ugly little cottage on Ditton Marsh', and often walking over to Esher to see his sister; *The Fourth Generation* (1912), p. 36. The Trevelyans rented Sandown Lodge, which belonged to Lady Byron, the wife of Admiral George Anson Byron (1789–1858), seventh Baron, a cousin of the poet.
3. Frédéric Soulié, *La Vean d'or* (1853).

Thursday – July 6

Up to breakfast at nine – Rainy. To work – worked hard on the report – took a walk of an hour and a half in the afternoon – back and worked again till dinner – Dined – Veau d'or. In the evening walked an hour.

Friday – July 7

A fine day – Walked to H's – saw them all and was delighted to see them. – then home worked – then walked again – boat to Hampton Court and back – saw Ld St L's villa[1] from the water pleasant river and banks – Read Goldoni's Smanie per la Villeggiatura,[2] long a favourite play of mine. At dinner V d'Or. In the afternoon it rained in torrents. I had a wet dull evening walk.

1. Lord St Leonards (Edward Burtenshaw Sugden, first Baron, 1781–1875), Lord Chancellor in 1852; his villa was Boyle Farm, Thames Ditton, Surrey.
2. 'The Rage for Country Life' (1761). TBM's copy of *Delle Commedie de Carlo Goldoni, avocato*, 16 vols (Venice, 1761) is in Wallington.

Saturday – July 8

Began to write out my report. Got on well. Walked to H's at one. They were going to Roehampton and I went part of the way with them. By the way we called at Esher's peaceful grove.[1] I was interested by the woods, Kent's planting[2] and by the fine beeches. Kent loved the beech. I got out at Kingston Bridge and walked along the Middlesex side of the river to the Ditton ferry. There I crossed and came home – Goldoni Le Avventure della Villeggiatura.[3] V d'O. Walked on my lawn an hour and came in with my boots soaked through and through.

1. 'Pleas'd let me own, in Esher's peaceful Grove / (Where *Kent* and Nature vye for PELHAM's Love) ...'. Pope's 'Epilogue to the Satires', ll. 66–7.
2. William Kent laid out the gardens at Esher Place for Henry Pelham around 1733; also at Claremont nearby he designed garden buildings for the first Duke of Newcastle, which have now been restored. M. Jourdain, *The Work of William Kent* (1948), p. 78.
3. *Hazards of Country Life* (1761).

Sunday – July 9

A most absurd and impudent letter from some foolish boys who call themselves the Young Men's Protestant Association of Edinburgh.[1] Wrote a little – went out – fine – pleasant ramble – to Sandown Lodge. Read T my report. He seemed much pleased. Rain in torrents. Home by a fly. Wrote a little more. It cleared. But the ground is reeking with moisture. Goldoni – Avventure – At dinner V d'O. Finished the Avventure and the Ritorno.[2] The best scenes are those with the old miser. The In Tavola at the end is worthy of Shakspeare. It was very cold in the evening and I was forced to have a fire.

1. See *LM*, vol. 5, p. 408.
2. *Il ritorno della villeggiatura* ('The Return from the Country').

Monday – July 10

A good night – a foggy morning. Then it cleared and the sunshine was delightful. I wrote a little, and sallied forth – crossed by the ferry, and walked along the Middlesex bank to Hampton Court, sauntered an hour in the gardens and came back the same way. To work again: The report is almost finished. It will certainly be sent off tomorrow; and I shall be a free man again. Then I will go to work on Chap 20 and never rest till it is ready to be transcribed. Read Goldoni's Giuocatore not without merit, if the miserable ending did not spoil all – at dinner V d'O. The rain falling in torrents – Ordered a fire, and read the Impresario di Smirne.[1]

1. *Il Giuocatore* ('The Gambler') (1750); *El Impresario della Smirne* ('The Impresario from Smyrna') (1759).

Tuesday – July 11

Finished the report and sent it off to John Lefevre – walked and read V d'o. To Sandown Lodge – chatted with H and B and walked on to Claremont and Esher Common – a fine afternoon – back to S.L. – T came full of his grievances about the Commissariat.[1] I am vexed to see that he makes a personal question of it. Dinner. After dinner Selina came. She looks very poorly I am sorry to say. I walked home, as there were no flies at liberty in the neighbourhood. I was afraid that I should be caught in the rain, but I escaped pretty well.

1. Trevelyan was against the Commissariat being controlled by the War Office and wanted it under the Treasury.

Wednesday – [July 12]

Letter from the Royal Scottish Academy – returned what I thought a very good answer. To my History – worked all day – Chap 21 – liberty of the press. It is not right yet, but it can be made so. Rain – rain – v. cold – I was forced to have a fire. At dinner V d'O.

Thursday – July 13

Letter from Lefevre. He likes the report. Worked at the history – got the part about the press into tolerable form. V d'O.

Friday – July 14

Proofs of the report – corrected it and sent it back – a copy to Ellis – to H's. Met Lydia Price – talk about newspapers. The weather very unsettled, – V d'O.

Saturday – July 15

Worked all the morning – – H and B and A called in the carriage and sate some time. That pest James Mills came while they were here. He had just been annoying H after his usual fashion. Ld Aberdeen will not see him; and this is one of his monstrous grievances. He nearly plagued Ld Melbourne out of his life, after getting admittance by using my name with characteristic impudence. After they went I took a short walk but the rain soon came on heavy – St Swithin's. Began the Famille Recour.[1]

1. By De Bahr.

Sunday – July 16

I shall never believe in St Swithin again. A glorious day – a delightful walk to Hampton Court by the ferry – strolled in the gardens – finished the Famille Recour – poor stuff. Home – worked. Began Vanity Fair – Reconciliation of Wm and Anne.[1]

1. *HE*, ch. 21. *CW*, vol. 4, p. 145.

Monday – July 17

Still fine – a fig for St Swithin – wrote – then to H's sate there an hour or two. Home worked on. V.F. Trevelyan called a little before 7.

Tuesday – July 18

Still fine – wrote. Then to Hampton Court walked – at the pas de charge – through the rooms – looked into the Maze for the first time. Home by the Surrey bank – worked. Lady Gordon and her husband called.[1] VF. Not quite well today, though much better than when in London. I had meant to go to town this morning but was too late for the train by a minute.

1. Sir Alexander Duff Gordon (1811–72) married Lucy Austin (1821–69) in 1840. She was the daughter of Sarah and John Austin. Duff Gordon became Senior Clerk in the Treasury this year.

Wednesday – July 19

At breakfast, a letter from Law the solicitor[1] about this Medical business. A deputation from Edinburgh to see me. I went by the 10 o'clock train – bought Crabbe's poems – an imperfect and execrably printed edition – at the Station. To Fludyer Street – saw the delegates – to little purpose. They look at the matter from a point of view in which they will get nobody to look at it but themselves. Going to the Athenaeum met first Palmerston, then Thorneley.[2] Talked with both of them on the medical disputes and fancied that I saw a way of settling the matter quietly for the present. At the Athenaeum – Act Parl Scot – Glencoe[3] – then to the Station and home. After writing letters etc to H's to dinner – pleasant evening – walked home.

1. Probably James Law (*c.* 1800–67), Writer to the Signet 1825, who was the only writer of this name at this time. He was the son of a surgeon and he married a surgeon's daughter.
2. Perhaps Thomas Thorneley (1781–1862), a Liverpool merchant; MP for Wolverhampton, 1835–59; Chairman of the Public petitions committee 1844–53.
3. *HE*, ch. 18, *CW*, vol. 3, pp. 513–33.

Thursday – July 20

Glorious weather – working and walking – V.F.

Friday – July 21

Ditto ditto That pest James Mills? has been bothering H for money. I sent him 10£ with a letter such as he deserves.

Saturday – July 22

I had ordered a fly which never came. Walked to the Station. Very hot. To the Temple – E not there – left a few lines for him. To Cawthorn's – got Mrs Stowe[1] – to London Library ordered Huguenot Memoirs[2] – to Lefevre's. Satisfactory sitting – Carried almost everything – Dissente Jowetto. To the H. of C. paired for the rest of the session. Talked with Wood. Home reading Mrs S by the way, plagued in the railway carriage by people who knew me. A mighty foolish impertinent book this of Mrs Stowe. She puts into my mouth a great deal of stuff which I never uttered – particularly about Cathedrals.[3] A foolish woman to be taken in by such dunces as Joseph Sturge[4] and Elihu Burritt,[5] the very greatest asses living. What blunders she makes too. Robert Walpole for Horace Walpole. Shaftesbury the author of the Habeas C Act she confounds with Shaftesbury the author of The Characteristics. She cannot even see. Palmerston whose eyes are sky blue she calls dark-eyed. I am sorry that I met her at all and glad that I met her so seldom. V.F – walked on my lawn till late.

---

1. Harriet Beecher Stowe, *Sunny Memoirs of Foreign Lands* (1854). See *LM*, vol. 5, p. 412 and n. 2.
2. *Memoirs of a Huguenot Family, translated from the Autobiography of the Rev. J. Fontaines* (New York, 1853), SC, no. 719.
3. 'He said that all the cathedrals in Europe were undoubtedly the result of one or two minds; that they rose into existence very nearly contemporaneously, and were built by travelling companions of masons, under the direction of some systematic organization.' *Sunny Memoirs*, vol. 2, p. 4 (letter xix). See also Trevelyan, vol. 2, pp. 288–9.
4. Joseph Sturge (1793–1859) was a Quaker, an opponent of slavery and a Chartist.
5. Elihu Burritt (1810–79), a blacksmith by trade, and like Sturge an agitator for peace, was American consul at Birmingham, 1867–9.

Sunday – July 23

Tremendous heat – put the first vol of Wilberforce's Life[1] into my pocket and went by ferry across the Thames to Hampton Court – lounged under the shade of the palace gardens and of Bushy Park during some hours. Hot walk back. I do not know that I ever felt it hotter – worked – Glencoe – VF. Lawn in the evening.

---

1. By his sons, R. I. and S. Wilberforce (1838).

Monday – July 24

Not quite well – the heat, I suppose – I had yesterday sent the boy to H with Mrs Stowe's book. I sate at home almost all day – did some work. To the clergyman's.[1] He had called on me – finished VF – excellent – a fly came for me – to dine with the T's. Found dear A wild with delight at being mentioned by that foolish Mrs S.[2] – dinner – C Bendor[3] and Jowett. All shop – back by fly. The horse knocked up – began Voltaire's Correspondence with Frederic – a precious pair – great and little both of them.

1. See below, entry for 28 July 1854.
2. 'Some very charming young lady relatives seemed to think quite as much of their gifted uncle as you might have done had he been yours' (*Sunny Memoirs*, vol. 2, p. 3 (letter xix)). Mrs Beecher Stowe is giving an account of the breakfast party at the Trevelyans' on 11 May 1853 when she met Macaulay (see above, entry for 11 May 1853).
3. Unidentified.

Tuesday – July 25

After breakfast ventured out, but was soon driven in by the heat – worked. In the afternoon to dine with Sir A Gordon and my Lady.[1] A very bad dinner and very little of it. A good piece of beef and potatoes with Yorkshire pudding would have been the thing. But this was unsatisfactory fare. No wine but sherry – the company Tom Taylor, a Doctor whom Lady G called Charley and who seemed to me a very vulgar dog, Philips the painter[2] whom I met at Bowood in the winter, son of the R.A. H and B. We got on pretty well. In the evening B went with me in the carriage to my house. There was a change in the temperature. It was cool and windy. I rather apprehended rain.

1. They lived at Gordon House, Esher. This may have been the visit recalled by Lady Gordon's daughter Janet Ross in *The Fourth Generation: Reminiscences* (London, 1912), p. 36.
2. Henry Wyndham Phillips (1820–68), son of Thomas Phillips, RA, portrait painter who served for thirteen years as secretary of the Artists' General Benevolent Institution.

Wednesday – July 26

The weather good after all the menacing appearances. I worked at Glencoe. Jowett called. I walked with him to Kingston and back on the north side of the river to Hampton Court. Thence I was pulled down the stream to the landing place close to Mrs Horseman's.[1] Home – Marriage[2] – Voltaire's Correspondence.

1. Charlotte Louise Ramsden (*c.* 1815–95), wife of Edward Horsman.
2. By Susan Edmonstone Ferrier (1818).

Thursday – July 27

To H's – pleasant chat. Home worked at Glencoe again – Voltaire Marriage.

Friday – July 28

Worked at the report particularly with a view to some notes which T had left me. Walked to Hampton Court. Met Mr Pollard[1] who very kindly promised to lend me his private key. Home and worked again – Inheritance.[2] Wm went to town today to make purchases for E's reception.

1. Perhaps the Revd Henry Smith Pollard (1810–84), who lived at Thames Ditton and may have been TBM's visitor on 24 July (see above).
2. By Susan Edmonstone Ferrier (1824).

Saturday – July 29

After breakfast to town. Bank – All right – Plenty of money. I am anxious for Longman's letter. Not expecting much, I cannot be much disappointed. To London Library – to Athenaeum I dawdled a little – To Lefevre's.[1] Very friendly and pleasant. Surprised by L's account of a new geometrical school of mathematics which seems to be prevailing over the Analytical School – so absolutely dominant at Cambridge in my time and since. To Covent Garden – bought some peaches – to the Temple. With E to the station and thence to Kingston – walked to G.L. The baggage carried by a porter – chatted on the lawn pleasantly. Excellent turtle – good ham – good wine and plenty of it – good fruit then walk on the on the lawn.

1. 8 Spring Gardens, SW.

Sunday – July 30

After breakfast to the ferry – crossed passed some hours in the gardens of Hampton Court and under the elms of Bushy Park. Much fesc. Home – I read him a good deal of my M.S. He praised warmly; and I liked what I read, though I did not pick. I am confident of his sincerity. But he may be partial. Dinner – very good – much as yesterday. Walk in garden – Distant thunder.

Monday – July 31

Day gloomy at first. But it became fine. There was some little dropping which can do no harm. E went immediately after breakfast – I to H's reading the Times by the way – found Marianne Thornton and her niece,[1] A's little friend, on a visit there. Pleasant chat with H, B etc. Amused them by reading a bit of OW and YH – Home – worked – at dinner the Inheritance.

1. Henrietta Louisa Synnot (*c.* 1841–1924), daughter of Marianne Thornton's sister Henrietta Synnot (1807–53). Marianne was her guardian.

Tuesday – August 1

Fine day – worked in the morning at the report – to H's – found G there – delighted to find that he had done well in the examination and is third of his form. He is now in the highest form and will have more time to himself. I am sorry that W.E. is low; – very low. Dined there pleasantly and walked home.

Wednesday – August 2

Still the report – finished it. To H's – staid lunch – walked home with G – good boy, had a pleasant talk with him. Worked. Read Miss Austen's Sense and Sensibility at dinner. Excellent. Rain came on in the evening.

Thursday – August 3

I had meant to go to town to day but the rain was so heavy that I staid at home and wrote. Good news from Longman – £1500 next December. Ld Lne has asked me to dine and sleep at Richmond on Sunday. I must go. I made an excuse for H and T, who, I knew, would not go out on Sunday. Miss Austen – charming. Vile day.

Friday – August 4

A worse day than yesterday. However I went to town – attended a meeting at the Museum made some extracts from the Dutch M.S.S. Called on Ellis – went to the Bank, ate a basin of Birch's turtle,[1] finding myself very hungry, came home, and was glad to find a fire in the drawing room. I am seriously afraid for the harvest after all the brilliant promise of last week. Began Destiny.[2]

1. Frederich Birch, pastry cook, 9 and 10 Opera Arcade, Pall Mall.
2. By Susan Edmonstone Ferrier (1831).

Saturday – August 5

Rainy night; but in the morning it held up. Gloomy however and threatening. However I was able to walk to H's. There I met Mrs Austin,[1] a Mrs C Buxton,[2] neither of them so handsome as I remember them. We lunched and chatted long and pleasantly. Vexed by a note from Sir Alexander Gordon[3] which disturbs all my Richmond arrangements. Walked home. Worked hard and very successfully today – walked in my garden – Destiny – Forced to have a fire.

1. Sarah Austin (1793–1867), the wife of John Austin and mother of Lady Duff Gordon.
2. Charles Buxton's wife was Emily Mary (*c.* 1824–1908), the daughter of Sir Henry Holland.
3 TBM's reply is in *LM*, vol. 5, pp. 413–14.

Sunday – August 6

Huzza – the fine weather come back. The rain, after all, will have done more good than harm if the sunshine lasts now. Plagued all the forenoon with writing to the Rl Sh Academy about copyright in works of art. Worked, not long, but to the purpose. I see land as to this long chapter – the 21st. Walked and was delighted to feel the warm beams again – dawdled over Aulus Gellius. At six Lady Gordon – with her to Ld Lne's at Richmond. We got on very well during the journey. At Richmond found Senior, Tom Taylor, Philips, and a deaf Yankee and his pretty wife – Walked down to the river. Back and dressed in haste – pleasant dinner and evening. Tom Taylor is a good fellow and a clever one, but a little too much of Grub Street about him.

Monday – August 7

Fine day. All gone but Senior and Ly G. After breakfast she I and Ld L off for Hampton Court. Indelicate woman. Repeatedly saying things that made me ashamed for her. I can bear dissoluteness far better in ladies than such coarseness. Pleasant walk through the sights of the palace. But when we were looking at the Ds of Cleveland's portrait Lady G called out in a voice to be heard by fifty people (for there were many visitors) "Ld L – Mr M – do you remember how Pepys admired her smocks[1] when he saw them laid to dry – Sweet Lady Castlemain's smocks". Upon my word I hardly think that any wellbred strumpet would have said such a thing in such a voice. Dear Ld L would alight at Sandowne Lodge to shake hands with H and B. I cannot understand his liking for Ly G – whether I look at it as friendly or as amorous. Chatted a little with H and B, and then went home. Wrote – Newmarket etc. Finished Destiny – began Pride and Prejudice.

1. See Pepys's Diary for 21 May 1662.

Tuesday – August 8

Proof of Report from Lefevre. Corrected it and sent it back. Progress. Pliny's letters. Heard G construe the first 40 lines of the Plutus.[1] Very well he construed them. Home – work – P and P. Voltaire's letters to D'Alembert.

1. By Aristophanes.

Wednesday – August 9

Wrote to my colleagues. Was going to H's but met her servant with an invitation to dinner. Back – worked – Elections of 1695 – Went to Sandown Lodge – the Charles Buxtons. pleasant evening – walked home – moon rising.

Thursday – August 10

To London – worked a little at the Athenaeum – more at the British Museum – City – Birch's – bought Dickens's Hard Times and two other novels or rather novelettes. Home by the 4 o'clock train. H and B had called. Sorry to have missed them. P and P.

Friday – August 11

To H's – She and B took a long walk with me through the grounds of Claremont – Beautiful. I have not been in them since the summer of 1818 – when they were crowded with visitors. The poor Princess's death then recent[1] – I remember as if it were yesterday – the place and my thoughts, and the castles in the air that I was building. Home and then to work on the coinage business; but I was not in the vein – A book of Pliny's letters. A man certainly of very considerable abilities. V and D'A – Dickens's book – It has some merit, but is intensely disagreeable and affected. P and P – excellent – began Northanger Abbey – excellent too. How far inferior all our ranting, artificial romancers are to that woman. Heard from Lefevre that Wood is anxious to see the report. I sent it him, non-officially, as I found that a long time might elapse before I can hear either from Ld A[2]or from the Principal.[3]

1. Princess Charlotte Augusta, daughter of the Prince Regent, who died in 1817. Claremont was bought for her country residence on her marriage to Prince Leopold of Saxe-Coburg in 1816.
2. Lord Ashburton.
3. Henry Melvill.

Saturday – August 12

After some threatening a fine day. The harvest is in full progress and the contrast between the yellow sheaves and the green woods and meadows is beautiful. Wrote a little. Then to SL. Found Lady Malkin – Amusing chat of two hours – then home. By the bye G construed more of the Plutus and did it well. Wrote a little – Newton – Locke. I shall manage this matter at last.[1]Wrote to Longman. I think that I must take till October next. By that time the work may be, not what I wish, but as good as I can hope to make it. More of Dickens – One exceptionally touching, heartbreaking passage – the rest sullen socialism – the evils which he attacks he caricatures grossly and with little humour. Another book of Pliny's letters. Northanger Abbey – worth all Dickens and Pliny together; yet it was the work of a girl. She was certainly not more than 26.[2] Wonderful creature.

1. Evidently 'this matter' refers to the carriage. *HE*, ch.21, *CW*, vol. 4, pp. 184–97.

2. *Northanger Abbey* was published posthumously in 1818, but begun in 1798 when Jane Austen was twenty-three.

Sunday – August 13

Walk in Hampton and Bushy – read from novel or novelette. Green Fruit. Home wrote something – strolled in my garden – Pliny – N.A.

Monday – August 14

Beautiful weather – to H's – Lady M – chat – heard G's Plutus – very well – home – N.A – finished Dickens's book – disagreeable and overstrained. I like neither his jest nor his earnest. Persuasion – Wrote pretty well – Parlt – Nov 1695. Walk in evening.

Tuesday – August 15

Changeable weather – showers and sunshine – quite Aprilish – Wm went to town. Worked to good purpose – finished Pliny – Capital fellow Trajan and deserving of a better Panegyric. Persuasion – walk in the evening.

Wednesday – August 16

Odd enough – little Alice's letter a year old from Strasburg. Went to H's – made fun of the letter with them. We all walked together to Wolsey's tower[1] – that is to say as near as we could get to it. Very pleasant. Heard G's Plutus again – very well – Home – After a glorious morning we had some more April weather. I wrote – treason trials – Lucretius, glorious poetry – Emma – Walked in the evening – cool.

1. The surviving part of the Bishop of Winchester's palace at Esher, where Wolsey was seen by Henry VIII in 1529.

Thursday – August 17

Nothing from Wood – rather surprised. Worked – looked over the earlier part of this interminable 21st Chapter – Wrote something about the press. To dinner at F's – learned that Wood had been to Yorkshire and had gone thence to Scotland. This explains his silence. Read Milton to dear B. Then walked with her to Claremont – pleasant dinner. Heard G's Plutus. He does very well. Walked home after dark.

Friday – August 18

Fine day – wrote something – then walked to Kingston – took a boat there – down the river to Twickenham. Teddington Lock took me by surprise. The banks not in general pretty. Vexed to find a trashy tawdry Swiss cottage on the site of Pope's villa[1] – landed at Twickenham and walked a mile and three quarters to Kneller Hall, large and rather handsome building.[2] Found Jowett there in a room which would have been comfortable but for its nakedness. The shelves were without books. Chatted half an hour with him and his friend Temple[3] – then walked away, and Jowett with me. We went through Bushy Park and Hampton Court, and then along the river to the Ferry where we parted – Much talk about the Epistles of St Paul, the early history of Christianity, Bunsen's Hippolytus[4] etc. Jowett is certainly a superior man. Home – letter from E – read Emma at dinner. Walked in the evening. I must have walked twelve miles or more today – a rare thing with me now.

---

1. Pope's villa had been designed by William Kent about 1730; around 1810 it had been demolished and replaced by a house in Tudor Gothic, by H. E. Kendall (1805–85).
2. Kneller Hall, Whitton (Middlesex), originally built 1709–11 by Kneller as his country house; almost entirely rebuilt in neo-Jacobean style, 1848 (architect George Mair). It was a training college for workhouse schoolmasters, *c.* 1849–56; from 1859 it has been the Royal Military School of Music.
3. Frederick Temple (1821–1902), later Archbishop of Canterbury, was Principal, Kneller Hall Training College, 1849–55.
4. C. C. J. von Bunsen, *Hippolytus and his Age* (1852).

Saturday – August 19

Fine day again. Note from B desiring me to go at lunch time and take a drive with them – wrote on the press – infested by wasps. There must be a nest hereabouts. I was at last forced to exert a skill for which I was famous in my school days. I killed seventeen of them in a very short time, and they ceased to plague me – Perhaps the sight of the corpses deterred the survivors. I observed some of the living settle on the dead and examine them. To H's – lunch – T had taken a holiday and went out to shoot with G. H B and I in the carriage. Delightful drive through woods and over heaths – scenery which I love and air which made me feel younger. I really think that I shall settle at Weybridge after all. They brought me home, left me a brace of grouse and took away Hard Times. I hope the game which they have left is better than the book which they have taken away. A letter from my landlord asking for his rent for six weeks. Sent it him. At dinner – Emma.

Sunday – August 20

Fine – Hampton Court and Bushy – Too Clever by half.[1] Stuff to the last degree contemptible. Home – wrote – finished E – Mansfield Park.

1. Novel attributed to John Lang; published 1853.

Monday – August 21

Bad day. Staid at home only walking occasionally on my lawn when it held up – read Voltaire's and D'Alembert's Correspondence. Wrote a good deal and not amiss. A letter – not a very wise one – from Ld Ashburton – Mansfield Park – fine evening.

Tuesday – August 22

Letter from Wood. I am glad that he is satisfied. Surprised at not hearing from E. To Sandown Lodge – I find that E is come back and that Walter has answered G – walked with H and A – very pleasant. B and G were at Claremont on a sketching ramble. I see little of her now. But I will not be jealous. Back and wrote. Portland grant – must get the matter better up. I will go to London shortly for that and other purposes – M. P.

Wednesday – August 23

Long walk towards Ewell – read a trashy contemptible book by a Mr Samuel Laing[1] – a fellow without taste, knowledge or sense who undertakes to lecture the world on all the gravest questions. The weather became threatening, and soon after I came home it began to rain. I did not walk in the evening but finished MP and with MP Miss Austen's works. I admire her more than ever. Chap XVI.

1. There are two Samuel Laings, father (1780–1868) and son (1812–97). TBM probably meant the father, whose *Observations on the Social and Political State of the European People in 1848 and 1849* was published in 1850.

Thursday – August 24

Worked in the morning transcribing Chap XVI – then to Sandown Lodge – heard G's Plutus. Off with T, H and B for Lefevre's – beautiful journey – stopped at Ockham by the way – found Lushington[1] there amidst a crowd of relations male and female. How well I remember the house in old Ld K's time[2] – the dreary comfortless passages and bedrooms – the scant fare – the sordid neglect of which are provided for in every curate's little dwelling. Yet Ld K was a remarkably able man and had many good qualities. I remembered the Church, and was desirous to see the monument of the Chancellor – Roubiliac's.[3] It did not turn out as fine as I thought it had been but this was natural. When I saw it first I did not know that I was to see anything; and to find a Roubiliac in a country church delighted me. This time I went having prepared myself and others to be charmed; and I was disappointed. Lushington very kind and cordial. Off for Sutton – Lefevre's place – a most curious and interesting old place it is. An outlay of fifty thousand pounds would make it incomparable. As it is it is more comfortable than I could have expected from its date. Nothing could be kinder than Lefevre. A pleasant day. To Sandown Lodge. Dined there pleasantly. Walked home. In little doubt whether the road be quite safe late at night. We had a joking conversation about Cooper's Novels. I said that all his Indian talk consisted of "Hu Hu. There's a pale face" – G and M followed me along the garden palings and tried to frighten me by calling out Hu-there – etc.

---

1. Dr Stephen Lushington (1782–1873) was a barrister, a radical MP and an Admiralty judge. He lived at Ockham Park, near Ripley, Surrey – most of the house was destroyed by fire in 1948.
2. Peter King, seventh Baron King of Ockham (1776–1833), was an expert on currency questions and the first biographer of John Locke. He seconded Lord Lansdowne in TBM's election to Brooks's Club.
3. The monument in Ockham Church to Lord King, Lord Chancellor, 1725–33, is by Rysbrack.

Friday – August 25

This is a picnic day at Sandown Lodge. I walked to Richmond returned by a fly – then wrote out Chap XVI, a good deal and well. In the evening Les Belles de Nuit[1] – Stuff. Miss A puts one out of conceit with those paltry romancers. Walked in the evening.

---

1. By Paul Féval (1849).

Saturday – August 26

In the morning to Hampton Court – rambled through the palace – back by boat to Thames Ditton. Wrote Chap XVI and very nearly finished it. Dressed and to Sandown Lodge by fly. Heard G's Plutus. He cannot fail to do well, I think. Then with H and T to C Buxton's.[1] Nice house and grounds and not unpleasant party – Lushington his son from Bengal and his daughter in law,[2] a fine woman and an agreeable woman. In the evening Thomas[3] and John Austin. J.A. was wonderfully fluent and wonderfully conservative. He seems to have lost his taciturnity and his radicalism together. I remember when he was dumb and a Chartist or nearly so. However he is very clever and well informed. – Home – did not get to Greenwood Lodge till long after eleven. I had not been quite well all the day – Hydr.

1. Charles Buxton's house, Fox Warren, was designed by Frederic Barnes of Ipswich.
2. Stephen Lushington's son was Edward Harbord Lushington (1832–1904) of the Bengal Civil Service. He married Mary Jane (*c.* 1828–95), daughter of Colonel Michael Ramsay.
3. This is most likely to be Alexandre Thomas, the historian, who was a friend of the Austins. So far as I know, John Austin had no brother called Thomas.

Sunday – August 27

Letter from Jopp[1] – 50£ – Letter from E. He will be ready to start, I hope on the 8th – answered them both – to Esher. To Church – Naaman the Syrian.[2] I go seldom to Church; and scarcely ever without hearing something about Naaman the Syrian. Prayers very ill read – Sermon not contemptible. The T's were all there – walked with them to their house – and then home. Wrote – finished Chapter XVI – began the second volume. Belles de Nuit – It seems very insipid to me now.

1. John Jopp, WS (1805–57), was one of TBM's political supporters.
2. Luke 4:27.

Monday – August 28

Walked across the hill which is behind my house, and came by a circuitous road on Ditton Common – home wrote – H, F, and B called. They went on to Kingston. I walked in my garden and read – Voltaire's Correspondence, B de N.

Tuesday – August 29

Walked again across the hill and to Claremont – so to Sandown Lodge. Heard G's Plutus – chatted long and very pleasantly. Looked at Kaye's Life of Metcalfe.[1] Heavy I think. He has inserted my epitaph[2] – not bad, though not the better for the changes which Elliot forced me to make. Talk about Mrs E Cropper.[3] Odious woman – home – wrote and revised. Chap XVII all but ready. Finished B de N – Stuff.

1. J. W. Kaye, *Life and Correspondence of Charles, Lord Metcalfe* ... (1854).
2. *CW*, vol. 8, p. 593.
3. The wife of Edward Cropper, who had first married TBM's sister Margaret; she was the widow of TBM's brother Henry.

Wednesday – August 30

Again across the hill to Claremont and Sandown Lodge. Home – Chap XVIII. Looked again at the Life of Metcalfe. A pompous bad writer, Kaye. Voltaire's Correspondence. Cousin Pons.[1]

1. Honoré de Balzac, *Le Cousin Pons* (1847).

Thursday – August 31

Sent Wm to town to make purchases etc – worked at Chap XVIII, cutting carving and re-arranging – Voltaire. Cousin Pons.

Friday – September 1

To the Station – to town – to the Burlington Arcade – had my hair cut. It was as long as a Merovingian King's. To the Athenaeum – read Gunning's Memoirs[1] – frivolous, but amusing to a Cantab. Looked at some other books – bought the new No. of the Newcomes – got a Volume about Grimm from Cawthorn's – bought a watch for George at Dent's[2] – £16.0.0. To Peel's Coffee house[3] – long disused, and wrote a letter there. To the Temple. Saw the courier – not so goodlooking as Franz, but he will do well enough. With E to the station and to Greenwood Lodge. G and Walter came to call a little before dinner. They seem to be doing very well together. We dined well, but I felt not quite right – a tendency to headache.

1. Henry Gunning, *Reminiscences of the University, Town, and Country of Cambridge* (1854).
2. Edward John Dent, 33 Cockspur Street, Pall Mall.
3. 178 Fleet Street.

Saturday – September 2

I rose with a slight headache. It soon went off; and we had a long walk and a hot one to Claremont and through the beautiful grounds – round the piece of water, and so to Sandown Lodge. We found them at lunch – lunched with them. Then Walter departed. We – H, B, myself and E – set out for an airing or rather we went exploring like Mrs E in the barouche landau. To St George's Hill and over it. I had no notion that heath and furze cd be so beautiful. I was perfectly charmed and could wish to end my days in such scenery. Back by Esher Common. Sate on the lawn and chatted with Alice and George. Walked with E round the meadows. At dinner – T and Petrie of the Commissariat[1] – pleasant. In the evening home by a fly. The fly was open and the air cold. I suffered by this.

1. Samuel Petrie (1797–1871) was deputy assistant Commissary General.

Sunday – September 3

Disturbed at night by the symptoms of a cold coming on. The day very warm. I hoped that the heat would boil me or roast me well, and so it wd have done probably but for a vexatious East wind. We went down the river to Twickenham and then up again to Hampton Court walked through the apartments – lounged about the gardens – saw the famous vine. Boated back to Thames Ditton. I read to E a good deal of the XVIIth Chapter. He liked it pretty well, I believe – a good dinner. But my cold was not better – Hydr.

Monday – September 4

Poorly – partly from the disease, and partly from the remedy. I went, however, to SL and heard G's Plutus. Chap XVIII – Voltaire and Cousin Pons – I dined – wh I had better not have done. Hereafter, when I have a cold I will be abstemious from the very first.

Tuesday – September 5

Poorly – bad cough. However I was forced to go to SL in order to deposit my M.S.S. with H. The rest were all out – B and A sketching – T and G boating. Walked home. The day very cold after so much heat. Wind East. I was forced to have a fire. Chap XVIII – finished Cousin Pons. I read or rather looked at an exceedingly bad novel by a fool called Hannay.[1] A good deal of Voltaire. I did not dine but made a supper of tea, bread and butter and eggs. H had given me some wine of ipecacuanha and Paregoric Elixir[2] which did me some good.

1. Perhaps John Hanney (1827–73), author of *A Claret Cup* (1848) and *Hearts are Trumps* (1849), and other naval stories.
2. An analgesic derived from opium.

Wednesday – September 6

Pretty good night – better – little coughing – but the cold not quite gone – fine day – Walked a little – wrote a little – Voltaire – Pelham.[1] By the bye Warren has conveyed to me through Ellis a copy of Ten Thousand a Year.[2] I was vexed: for, though the book is clever, there are things in it which are open to objections more serious than those of mere criticism. However, I thanked him civilly. Packing.

1. By Bulwer-Lytton (1828).
2. Samuel Warren's novel was published in 1839. TBM's objections were made more fully to Ellis, *LM*, vol. 5, pp. 417–18.

Thursday – September 7

Off early sent my baggage to Bedford Place and drove to Bond Street – got some medical matters – then to Albemarle Street. R.I. – read some trifling books – Patmore[1] – what stuff! My cold plagued me. To Bedford Terrace and off for Folkestone. I do not much take to our courier.[2] A queer looking fellow and not alert. He began by losing my umbrella and Ellis's orange wood stick. We got to Folkestone by seven and had a comfortable dinner and good beds.

1. Coventry Patmore issued *The Betrothal* in 1854.
2. Kloss. *LM*, vol. 5, p. 420 n. 2.

Friday – September 8

Breakfasted and on board – delightful passage – the water very slightly ruffled – like the sea of the trades going out. From Boulogne off in a short time for Paris. All right till we got to the Hotel Wagram – very different reception from that of yesteryear – a garret miserably furnished. We got something to eat and went to bed in no very good humour.

Saturday – September 9

After breakfast to Galignani's – thence to the old Foreign Office – found it pulled down. The department has moved to the other side of the River. Went thither – found Dumont he very kind as usual. I learned that Ld Cowley[1] had applied on my behalf to the Foreign Office and the Foreign Office to the War Office – the War Office answer not yet returned. We rambled long – St Eustache – The Luxembourg – dined at The Frères – excellent regale not unreasonable bill.

1. Henry Richard Charles Wellesley, first Earl Cowley (1804–84), was Ambassador in Paris, 1852–67.

Sunday – September 10

Breakfast and off for Beauvais – got to Clermont by railway – there found a fellow who undertook to carry us to Beauvais and back in good time and kept his word. A capital English horse. We were an hour and a half in running twelve miles. I was delighted with the grandeur of the Cathedral, though less than the first time that I saw it. Ellis did not, I think, quite sympathise with me. Back to Clermont then by rail to Paris – F.P.[1]

1. Frères Provençaux.

Monday – September 11

Off this morning for Orléans. I had travelled the road before, but at dead of night. It was very pleasant till we left Etampes. When we got on the plain of La Beauce there was still an interest – but of a very old kind. Boundless fertility and utter desolation – a harvest like that of the seven plentiful years, and a bareness and solitude like that of the Great Desert. You look over a vast expanse bordered by the horizon – innumerable shocks of wheat and stacks of wheat, and scarcely a human being. Round the villages the piles of corn were immense. The houses were hardly visible. The people seemed to be buried in their food. So we got to Orleans. A burning afternoon. My cold surely must give way to this heat – lunched at a hotel – then to the Cathedral – such as I recollected it. A wonderfully clever imitation of the great old Cathedrals – Lucian to Plato. The towers are the least pure part of the building, and yet show most invention and talent on the part of the architect. On to Blois. Saw the Castle. I had seen it before it was decorated by L.P.[1] I did not think it much improved. Not that the decoration is not splendid and in good taste, if it had been meant to fit up the palace for use. But as it was meant to leave it merely a relique, I would have made no change except what might have been necessary to prevent ruin. Dined and slept comfortably at the Hotel d'Angleterre.

1. Louis Philippe.

Tuesday – September 12

A brilliant, burning, day. Walked to the Cathedral – not much, but a good old Church. Walked under the trees on the quay. When I walked there last, on a day nearly as hot eleven years ago, the fair was holding there. The fair was just over today, but the booths and placards still remained. To Chambord. The road different from what I recollected it – perhaps it took a different course; or perhaps the change might be explained by the wood cutting which had been most unsparing. The palace very much what I remembered it. We were greatly interested and pleased. On our road back we lunched on Beaugency and hard eggs. We stopped in the village of Chambord to buy a little salt for our eggs. From Blois to Tours by rail. The rail generally avoids the things which are best worth seeing and the steamers on the river have been knocked up. I shall never go down the Loire again. At Tours the Hotel de l'Univers – very good. My cold begins to give way.

Wednesday – September 13

A hotter day than yesterday. We however passed most of it on foot – The Cathedral – not large, but very good – the ruins of the rival Cathedral – St Martin's

– Lewis the Eleventh's palace at Plessis. What a take in. We dined at three and then off by rail for Paris. Got to our hotel at eleven. We are a little, and but a little, better lodged than at first.

Thursday – September 14

After breakfast to Dumont – found that the answer from the War Office had not come. Anxious lest I should be forced to stay here alone. I went to the Embassy – saw Ld Cowley for a minute. He very kind, and what was better, prompt – gave me a letter for the Minister of War.[1] I went and left it. To dinner at the F.P. Dumont dined with us. Luxurious and not very expensive.

1. Jean Baptiste Philibert Vaillant (1790–1872) was Minister from 1854 to 1859.

Friday – September 15

Received a most handsome letter from the M of War. After breakfast to the War Office. Very civilly received; but found difficulties for want of a formal admission. Returning at a later hour I found all difficulties removed. I was soon installed in a comfortable corner with pen ink paper and six or seven folios of records before me. I made a good day's work[1] and went away delighted. F.P. not so good.

1. In *HE*, ch. 18, TBM used an account of the second siege of Limerick 'in the archives of the French War Office'; *CW*, vol. 3, pp. 443, 444n.

Saturday – September 16

Again to the War Office – Finished my researches early and should have finished earlier but for the hospitable kindness of some functionaries who would do the honors of the office. A M. Turpin,[1] a friend of Dumont, showed me some interesting autographs of Napoleon – and one paper which fully established the truth of what I had heard asserted that Napoleon made himself a year and a half younger than he was in order to bring his birth later than the French conquest of Corsica.[2] Another officer of the department insisted on showing me a Commission granted to his bisaieul by James II. It was signed by the King and countersigned by Nagle[3] whose name the possessor of the parchment had never been able to make out. I was amused by the importance which he attached to this document. He offered me a copy, which I accepted very gratefully. To the Hotel. Went with E to the C de P to order dinner – then by cab to the Place of the Bastille – walked about my favourite Place Royale – then back to the C de P. Capital dinner – dear – but the last.

1. Étienne Louis Mathieu Numa Turpin (1802–73), an official in the Foreign Office.

2. Napoleon's birthday is now accepted as 15 August 1769, after the French occupation of Corsica in 1768. The belief that he had been born in January 1768 seems to be based on a confusion between himself and his older brother, who was baptized Napoleon but had his name changed to Joseph after the death of an elder child of that name.
3. Sir Richard Nagle (1636–99) was James II's Attorney General in Ireland, appointed in 1686. He followed James into exile. He is mentioned in *HE*, ch. 17, *CW*, vol. 2, p. 442. A direct descendant, Jean Marie Auguste, Baron de Nagle (1799–1878), was in the French army high command and may have been the officer mentioned here, though it is odd in that case that he could not recognize his own name in the signature of his *bisaieul* (great grandfather). The Baron is said to have encountered his Irish second cousin Richard Lynch Nagle, then only a sergeant, in the Crimea in 1855 or 1856 and rescued him from a court martial. See Basil O'Connell, 'The Nagles of Annakissey', *The Irish Genealogist*, 2:11 (July 1954), pp. 337–48.

Sunday – September 17

To Boulogne, – dull bad company. Yankees smoking and spitting. Left Boulogne half an hour before sunset – the wind fresh and the sea high. I had no qualms, but people were sick all about me and over me. At Folkestone no room in the Pavilion – got a bad supper – slept at the Paris Hotel.

Monday – September 18

Bad breakfast at ½ after seven. Off at eight – in London by ½ after 10. At Kingston by 12 – To Sandown Lodge – G and A – dear children – H and B out – To Greenwood Lodge. Answered letters – wrote journal – and walked on the lawn reading Warren's book. In the evening found Warren's print too small for my eyes and was forced to read Dunlap's Life of Cooke.[1] Nothing loth however: for it is a charming book and bears repeated perusal.

1. William Dunlap, *Memoirs of G. F. Cooke, Later of the Theatre Royal, Covent Garden ...* (1813).

Tuesday – September 19

A bad day. Staid at home all the morning. Looked through the alterations made by the Commissioners of 1689 in the Prayer Book. In the afternoon H and the rest called. It had cleared. We went to Hampton Court. I came back to a rendezvous with Kloss – paid him – then off for Sandown Lodge. Dined there – heard G in the evening another 200 lines of Plutus. I was quite satisfied with him. Bade him goodbye and home in a fly with my papers.

Wednesday – September 20

Looked through Chap XIV – pretty well satisfied. But there is much to do – I did a little. Sir H. Ellis[1] called to tell me that I need not go to the Museum on

Saturday. The day was bad till the afternoon. Then it became fine. I walked on the lawn and finished Cooke. At dinner Stokeshill Place.[2] After dinner fell asleep.

1. Sir Henry Ellis (1777–1869), Principal Librarian of the British Museum.
2. By Catherine Gore (1837).

Thursday – September 21

Fine day – To town – carried with me the abridgement of Grimm.[1] Too late for the train by which I meant to go. Came back – revised and wrote. To S.L. nobody at home – borrowed Pecchio's book on England[2] in a bad English Translation. Many years ago I read the original while wandering through the streets along the Thames as was then my habit. Ten Thousand. At dinner Stokeshill Place – Forced to have a fire.

1. Perhaps *Historical and Literary Memoirs and Anecdotes, Selected from the Correspondence of ... Grimm and Diderot ...* (1814); or the French version, which appeared 1813–14.
2. Giuseppi Pecchio, *Semi-Serious Observations of an Italian Exile during his Residence in England* (1833).

Friday – September 22

To London – Glad that the troops have landed on the Chersonese.[1] To Cawthorn's – got Le Gentil homme Campagnard[2] – to the Athenaeum – read Cole's Memoirs[3] got some information about the 3rd Earl of Shaftesbury. To Story's[4] – gave an order – to the Temple – settled with E about going down to Oxford on Saturday the 30th. To the station – thence to Kingston – to S.L. by fly – I was poorly and low. As I walked back a shower came on. Afraid for my chest, which, at best, is in no very good state, I turned into a small ale house and called for a glass of ginger beer. I found there a party of hop pickers come back from the neighbourhood of Farnham. They had had but a bad season, and were returning nearly walked off their legs. I liked their looks and thought their English remarkably good for their rank in life. It was in truth the Surrey English – the English of the suburbs of London which is to the Somersetshire and Yorkshire what Castilian is to Andalusian or Tuscan to Neapolitan. The poor people had a foaming pot before them, but as soon as they heard the price they rose and were going to leave it untasted. They could not, they said afford so much. It was but fourpence halfpenny. I laid the money down; and their delight and gratitude quite affected me. Two more of the party soon arrived. I ordered another pot, and when the rain was over left them, followed by more blessings than, I believe, were ever purchased for ninepence. To be sure the boon, though very small, was seasonable and I did my best to play the courteous host. Home – wrote – Shaftesbury – Had a fire early in the afternoon and at dinner. Read Warren – by candle light.

Used a new pair of spectacles which is stronger than that which I ordinarily use. At dinner C Bernard GC.[5] After dinner finished Stokeshill Place. Nothing but novels. But I have scarcely anything else that is at all amusing.

1. The Crimea. They landed at Eupatoria on 14 September.
2. By Charles de Bernard (1847).
3. Christian Cole, *Memoirs of Affairs of State ...* (1733).
4. Probably William Story, tailor and outfitter, 62 Fleet Street.
5. *Le Gentilhomme Campagnard.*

Saturday – September 23

Breakfast by fireside – Worked all the morning very pleasantly. Got to the end of Fuller's plot.[1] Another day should bring me near the end of Chap XVIII. Wrote to Glover. Walked on the lawn, and read Warren. A present of grapes – beautiful – I think from Bromley.[2] At dinner C.B. G.C. Dropped asleep by the fire in the evening.

1. *HE*, ch. 18, *CW*, vol. 3, pp. 500–5.
2. Presumably from the Misses Telford, cousins of Ellis's wife, who lived in Widmore, near Bromley.

Sunday – September 24

Began on the Judges Bill, and found it necessary to insert a long passage on the Veto,[1] Worked at it some time – then to Esher Church. The prayers ill read and a wretched sermon[2] – walked away with the T's. Very kind and pleasant – gave B 10£ dear child – walked home – and to work again, not unsuccessfully, I think, but we shall see. At five Warren – G.C.

1. *HE*, ch. 18, *CW*, vol. 3, pp. 505–8.
2. The Vicar of Esher was the Revd Wadham Harbin (*c.* 1797–1870), a graduate of Wadham College, Oxford.

Monday – September 25

Concerned to hear that Wm's niece is ill[1] – bilious fever. Saw the medical man who seems intelligent. He does not think her in danger. Walked to Kingston and back. Wrote – Wm's Veto. Finished Warren's book – G.C.

1. She was Louise Williams, b. *c.* 1837 and so about sixteen at this time. *LM*, vol. 5, p. 425 and n. 3.

Tuesday – September 26

Letter from Glover – determined to go to Windsor today. Wrote to H about Wm's niece – Fly – to Richmond. Thence by rail to Windsor – Found Glover[1] – examined the collection. Scarcely anything of earlier date than Geo I. A good hearing: I have now got to a point at which there is no more gratifying discovery than that nothing is to be discovered. Got the Sheridan M.S.[2] and found a few curious things in it. Back to Richmond – walked to Kingston – bought at the Station four novels by Cooper. On the way from Kingston to Greenwood Lodge I was overtaken by the carriage with B and her aunt Miss Neave.[3] H it seems was at Greenwood Lodge with Wm's niece. I got in. They took me home. H told me that all was going on well and went off with B and Miss N. Glad to find that there is no cause for uneasiness – Walked on the lawn read Mark's Reef.[4] Poor stuff and he repeats himself grievously. It is however above the mere rank and file of novels – G.C. excellent.

---

1. John Hulbert Glover (*c.* 1793–1860), Queen's Librarian.
2. Papers referring to Thomas Sheridan the Elder (1647–1712), Chief Secretary to Ireland in 1687, private secretary to James II in exile.
3. Caroline Hannah Neave (1781–1863) was the youngest sister of Harriet Trevelyan, wife of the Revd George Trevelyan, Archdeacon of Bath. She had lived in Clapham for much of her life.
4. By Fenimore Cooper (1847).

Wednesday – September 27

Fine weather but east wind – Worked – Ministerial changes. Introduction to Glencoe affair – Walked to Hampton Court through the gardens – back by ferry – wrote to Story who has forgotten to send my clothes and to the Miss Telfords to thank them for some delicious grapes. To dinner at S.L.

Thursday – September 28

Read – wrote – walked along the Surrey bank of the Thames to the Hampton Ferry – crossed – pleased with the villas – Wightmans amused by seeing Garrick's Temple[1] of which I had seen pictures when I was young – Home – Mark's Reef – Pathfinder[2] – G.C.

---

1. Sir William Wightman (1784–1863) was a Judge of the Queen's Bench, who lived with his wife Charlotte Mary, née Baird (1792–1891) at St Alban's Bank, Hampton Court, opposite Garrick's Temple to Shakespeare, built about 1768.
2. By Fenimore Cooper (1840).

Friday – September 29

My last day here – By the lane over the hill to the Common on which Claremont lies – went all round the parks paling to S.L. saw H. She took me home; packed – read Pathfinder etc.

Saturday – September 30

Up early off – to the Albany – left the papers there – to the Paddington Station. Ellis soon came. Off to Oxford – delightful weather. We found rooms at the Angel[1] – a dingy old place enough. Then walked about all the afternoon and were delighted with the Colleges and gardens. Enchanting city. Dined and chatted till near ten.

1. An old coaching inn that was to be part of the site of Jackson's Examination Schools. Its name survives in Angel Meadow, which was where its customers' horses were grazed.

Sunday – October 1

A day of fine sunshine – We rambled incessantly – Cloisters gardens – without end.

Monday – October 2

E off early – He was hardly gone when the Times came with news of the battle of the Alma. Reports of the fall of Sebastopol. Too good to be true.[1] I went to All Souls. Not one fellow in residence. I determined to write to the Warden[2] – Left a letter and card. Most civil answer. At 12 he took me to the Library. We soon found NL's Diary.[3] I got the seven vols which I wanted and was at a table in a back room with pen, ink, my notebook and blotting paper. I worked till past five – walked an hour or so and went to my inn – dined Pathfinder.

1. Sebastopol was considered the key to Russian power in the Black Sea, and early plans were for an armed raid that would destroy the Russian fleet. It was finally captured after a long siege on 9 September 1855.
2. Lewis Sneyd (1788–1858) had been Warden since 1827.
3. Narcissus Luttrell's Diary. Luttrell (1657–1732), bibliophile and chronicler, kept a journal called 'A Brief Historical Relation of State Affairs from September 1678 to April 1714'. TBM was the first historian to draw attention to its value, and an edition in six volumes was published by Oxford University Press in 1857.

Tuesday – October 3

To All Souls at ten – worked till five. The Diary in 1696 is dreadfully illegible. But that matters the less as by that time the newspapers had come in. Walk – Pottn Legy.[1]

1. By Albert Richard Smith (1849).

Wednesday – October 4

I have done with All Souls. At ten I went to the Bodleian. Had to wait a quarter of an hour for the librarian Dr Bandinel.[1] He came however and was most courteous and friendly. Got out the Tanner M.S.S.[2] Worked on them two or three hours then the Wharton M.SS.[3] – then the far more curious Nairne M.SS.[4] At 3 rung out. I do think that from 10 to 3 is a very short time to keep so noble a library open.

1. Bulkeley Bandinel (1781–1861). He was Bodleian's Librarian from 1813 to 1860.
2. The papers of Thomas Tanner (1674–1735); Bishop of St Asaph from 1732 until his death.
3. Thomas Wharton, first Marquis of Wharton (1648–1715).
4. The MSS of Sir David Nairne, first Bart (1655–1740). They are part of the the Carte MSS.

Thursday – October 5

Pamphlets – But pamphlets I can find at other places. So I fell on the Nairne MSS again – I got out a Volume which had been misplaced and found an infinity of curious things. I could amuse myself here ten years without a moment of ennui. Rang out at three – P.L. The Sea Lions.[1]

1. By Fenimore Cooper (1849).

Friday – October 6

To the Bodleian as soon as it opened. Passed three hours over M.S.S. and pamphlets and then to my inn. All was paid and I was off for town – Sea Lions. Came home between 4 and 5 – E to dinner.

Saturday – October 7

Looked over parts of the history. Pleased with the Bank. I shall put that to rights as soon as I am quite settled. Walked. Second part of Mr Verdant Green – not so good as the first part.

Sunday – October 8

To Brooks's – an interesting day. The Club not full of course at such a time of the year: but several persons there who were anxious about friends and relations. Ld Burghersh is come;[1] and everybody was impatient for the despatch. I went out at about one, and picked up in Pall Mall the Ext[raordinar]y Gazette – that moment out I took it in back to Brooks's. Ld De Mauley read it. Chief Justice Jervas,[2] Ebrington,[3] Ld Torrington,[4] these all interested for relations. A glorious battle. I am proud of our brave fellows, and could hardly help crying. Ld D did cry. Walked – Soho – At dinner κοκτων οικ.[5] To the Waterloo Station to meet H and B, Wm there too. They came – saw them off – Home and to bed.

---

1. Francis Henry William Fane (1825–91), later twelfth Earl of Westmoreland, was Lord Raglan's ADC. He brought home the despatch on the battle of Alma.
2. Sir John Jervis (1802–56). He had been Liberal MP for Chester, 1832–50; served as Attorney General, 1846–50; and was Lord Chief Justice from 1850.
3. Hugh Fortescue (1802–1905) became Viscount Ebrington in 1841, and third Earl Fortescue in 1861. He was at this time MP for Marylebone.
4. George Byng, seventh Viscount Torrington (1812–84).
5. Perhaps Henry Cockton, *The Steward* (οἰκονομος).

Monday – October 9

Up early and to the Euston Square Station. H and B came in good time, and we were off for Lancaster – pleasant journey. We had the carriage to ourselves – Stopped at Pratt's[1] – well remembered. An odd old fashioned dingy house, such as is rarely found in these days of railways. I walked with B through some of the dirty Streets, showed her my lodgings – then the Judges house[2] – took her to the terrace of the Castle – but it was too hazy to see much – back – dinner. In the evening, H read some of Don Manuel Espriella[3] – excellently written certainly.

---

1. So the manuscript, but *Pigott's Directory* of 1830 lists him as John Pritt, proprietor of the King's Arms in Market Street, Lancaster.
2. In Church Street, it dated from 1675.
3. *Letters from England by Don Manuel Alvarez Espriella ...*, by Robert Southey (1807).

Tuesday – October 10

Tolerable day – Walked with H to the Castle: – but saw little more than yesterday. Amused by a most absurd edition of the prayer book by Solomon Pigott Rector of Dunstable[1] – A special Ass he must be – "Rods was a Roman punishment" "The Apostle alludes to the Athenian games which were celebrated at Corinth" – "Enoch and Elias appeared with Christ at the transfiguration" "This prophecy was terribly fulfilled for we read that 1000000 Jews perished besides 296,490 who perished elsewhere". Off at 12 by railway to Milnthorpe – there found a carriage and four waiting for us. To Ulverstone – a fine country – but the weather did not show the scenery to advantage. At Ulverstone John met us.[2] We went on with a pair of horses to Aldingham. Very nice place. I hardly know a prettier or more commodious parsonage. If the library were well filled up and furnished with my 8,000 books there wd be nothing wanting – comfortable dinner and friendly quiet evening. The children are good; and Mrs J a woman of sense.[3] They were very kind and hospitable.

1. Solomon Pigott (*c.* 1779–1845), Rector of Dunstable, 1824–45.
2. TBM's brother John (1805–74) was Rector of Aldingham, near Ulverston, from 1849.
3. Jane Emma, née Large (*c.* 1809–92).

Wednesday – October 11

Fine day. I had a pleasant room and a good fire. The sea almost washed the walls under my window. After breakfast we lounged about the house, the shrubbery – the beach – the Church – the churchyard. In the afternoon I took us all to Furness Abbey – a fine ruin indeed – not so beautiful as Tintern Abbey but more extensive, solid and grand. I was much interested. We dined well at an excellent inn close by[1] and returned by starlight, had tea, and to bed.

1. Originally the abbot's house, and when TBM visited it, it was an inn, kept by one William Parker.

Thursday – October 12

A trying day – Up before six – hasty breakfast – kind adieus. Off at seven – posted to Ulverstone with two horses and thence Milnthorpe with four. The weather fine and the landscape beautiful. At Milnthorpe, much to my sorrow, we separated, H and B to Kendal, I to London – a long sluggish journey – that is today long and sluggish when compared to the speed of railway express trains. I read some of Deerbrook[1] by the way and liked it better than I expected. Did not get home till near eleven – Very cold – no fire. It seems they did not expect me. The fire was lighted and began to smoke enough to suffocate me. Wretched. Got to bed fast in no good humour.

1. By Harriet Martineau (1839).

Friday – October 13

Fine day – I had an excellent night and ate an excellent breakfast. I had a right to do so – for, except three sandwiches, I had eaten nothing for twenty seven hours. Wrote – Bank of England[1] – E to dinner – Edinburgh Review – Rogers on my Speeches[2] – very kind and judiciously so.

1. *HE*, ch. 20, *CW*, vol. 4, pp. 91–6.
2. Henry Rogers, in *ER*, 100 (October 1854), pp. 490–534.

Saturday – October 14

B.M. In the Chair – Dundas *and* Hamilton – Walked away with D – Home and wrote – At dinner – J Marryatt – K – O[1] – A little of Deerbrook – Diderot's works.

1. Frederick Marryat, *The King's Own* (1830).

Sunday – [October 15]

Brooks's Athenaeum – walked – wrote – K.O. Swift – Diderot.

Monday – October 16

Wrote on – Bank – walk – ιαπεσος Diderot and Swift.

Tuesday – [October 17]

Absurd letter from Weston Super Mare signed J.W. Croker. Some great fool – After breakfast finished Bank. To Woburn by railway. In the carriage with me were Lady Cranworth and Charles Howard. We were afterwards joined by C. Cavendish[1] and his wife. I found Lady C pleasant and sensible. At Woburn Sands some difficulty about carriages. I went on a fly with Lady C and sent her maid and William by the fly which I had ordered. I find that it is not the easiest thing in the world to get to Woburn. The Chancellor[2] and Ld J[3] are detained by a cabinet Council. On reaching the Abbey Howard and I went to the Duchess's tea table. There was old Sir R. Adair – 92[4] – wonderful old man – memory entire – he was upset in a carriage only yesterday and did not appear the worse for it. Howard and I then went to Dundas's room. I was warmly and pleasantly lodged near him – dressed – to the Saloon. Large party, though there were several blanks. I sate between Baron Parke and Lady P – Ld and Lady Howe were there[5] – Lady H charming. After dinner we were in the gallery. The Duke made me and some of the others entertain Adair all the evening. It was kind and hospitable of him and I willingly assisted, but was not much amused. Sir H. Seymour[6] – a great diplomate for ought I know but a poor companion. Glad to get to bed.

1. Perhaps Charles Compton Cavendish (1793–1863), later Lord Chesham; at this time he was MP for Buckinghamshire. His wife, Catherine Susan, née Gordon (1792–1866), was the daughter of the ninth Marquess of Huntly.
2. Cranworth.
3. Lord John was at this time Lord President of the Council.
4. Sir Robert Adair (1763–1855) was a diplomat, and a typical old Whig, ardently supporting Fox and sitting in Parliament for a rotten borough.

5. Richard William Penn Curzon-Howe (1796–1870), first Earl Howe and second Viscount Curzon. He married, as his second wife, the Hon. Anne Gore (1817–77), maid of honour to Queen Adelaide and a daughter of Admiral Sir John Gore.
6. Sir George Hamilton Seymour (1797–1880) was the grandson of the first Marquis of Hertford, and a diplomat. He was successively ambassador in Florence, Brussels, Lisbon, St Petersburg and Vienna.

Wednesday – October 18

The Chancellor came later yesterday night or rather early this morning in a dog-cart at the peril of his neck through pitchy darkness. He was pleasant and just as in old times. Rain – rain – a miserable day. So we wandered over the house and passed some hours very pleasantly in talking over the pictures. Then lunch. Some of the gentlemen went to see the Duke's farming apparatus – I had seen it, and was afraid of taking cold. So I staid in the library and in my own room reading. Before dinner I said two words to the Chancellor in favour of Edw Rose.[1] He told me to give him a memorandum in writing. The dinner but stupid – I could get nothing but water to drink and not much of that. Here the wine is poured out in thimblefuls and not more than twice in the course of a long banquet. In the last generation, I imagine Fox and Fitzpatrick[2] got larger measure. In the evening Ld J came with news – but not very important. The Ladies played a round game – Snap the Bundle. I looked on, but could understand nothing; nor indeed did the players in general seem to be wiser than I was. I read here some letters of the Sevigné family[3] – Gordon's Memoirs[4] – worthless. The Duchess today showed me her own suite of rooms, – charming – a beautiful flower garden which however did not appear to advantage.

---

1. See below, entry for 19 October 1854. He was Lydia Babington Rose's son.
2. Richard Fitzpatrick (1748–1813) was MP for Bedfordshire and a lifelong friend of Charles James Fox.
3. Perhaps Joseph Adolphe Aubenas, *Histoire de Madame de Sevigué, de sa famille et de ses amis* (1842).
4. Perhaps *Memoirs of John Gordon of Glencot ... who was thirteen years in the Scots College at Paris* (London, 1733).

Thursday – October 19

Breakfasted in company with Ld and Ly Howe and Lord and Ly J pleasant. Letter from Ld Howe's son[1] in the Crimea. Off at ten for the station – came safe to town – home – wrote letters. Snow has found a berth – an odd one – he is to command a Missionary Schooner bound for Patagonia – He will, ten to one, wreck the ship before he gets to his destination. If not he and his people will all be killed and perhaps eaten. I am sick of his idle romantic plans.[2] He cannot settle down to the common ['duties of life' erased]. I had just written the word common when a letter came from the Chancellor. He offers ER a living in Warwickshire worth 262£ a year.[3] Most kind and handsome. I am quite touched by it. Walked – bought several old tracts – E to dinner – He is going to the Session; and I shall not see him for ten days. He was at Harrow yesterday and amused me greatly by telling me that G had made an oration in the debating Society there and had acquitted himself excellently, according to W.E's report.

1. Howe had four sons in the forces. One, Leicester Curzon-Howe (1829–91), was at this time Military Secretary to Lord Raglan. He later changed his name to Smyth, on marrying Alicia Smyth of Drumcree, Co. Westmeath.
2. He actually spent two years 'carrying missionaries and their stores between Tierra del Fuego, the Falkland Islands, and different stations on the mainland' (*DNB*), about which he published *A Narrative of Life in the Southern Seas*, 2 vols (1857).
3. Edward Joseph Rose (1818–82). He evidently declined this offer and became Rector of Weybridge, Surrey, 1855–82, another living in the gift of the Lord Chancellor. See *LM*, vol. 5, p. 458 and n.

Friday – October 20

Diderot's Salon de l'Année 1765.[1] Amusing and clever criticism. After breakfast to W.T. delighted to find H B and A all, well walked with H to Macleod's – talk about Gibbon. She was greatly amused by G's oratorical success. To Ναυσικ – I am quite set up. To [illeg. ?WT and H]. Chancellor's Letter as I mentioned. To the Athenaeum to consult the Liber Eccl and the Topographical Dictionary. Wrote to Lydia – to the Chancellor – to H. Rogers. Sent H the Chancellor's letter – Diderot – Zizine.[2]

1. Diderot wrote an annual account of exhibitions in Paris for Grimm's *Correspondence Littéraire.*
2. By Charles Paul de Kock (1836).

Saturday – October 21

Walked – τω Διονvο ω αοδ. Then W.T. Talk about the Chancellor's kindness. Lydia Price much gratified – worked. Sent for Reine Margot. They sent me some trash instead – Flor Mac[1] – Diderot Grimm. Charles came – read a good deal of the history to him. He seemed pleased.

1. Lady Morgan, *Florence Macarthy* (1816).

Sunday – October 22

Wrote – W.T. – Charles pleasant – yet I was out of spirits when I went away. Wandered towards St John's Wood without getting there – home – Flor Mac – Grimm.

Monday – October 23

Walked – British Museum. Bought books – Coleridge's Biog[raphia] Lit[eraria] – the genuine article – not his daughter's adulterated edition.[1] Life of Hanmer[2] – called on Ellis. Vexed by some nonsense of Mrs Ommaney[3] – what a child I am in some things. Worked – Biog Lit – Grimm – Flor Mac.

1. Sara Coleridge (1802–52) published her edition in 1847. Presumably TBM means by 'the genuine article' the original edition of 1817.
2. Perhaps Sir Thomas Hanmer (1677–1746), who was Speaker of the House of Commons, 1714. His *Correspondence* was edited by Sir Henry Bunbury in 1838, but there is not a Life.
3. Susannah McTaggart (*c.* 1813–1902), elder daughter of Sir John McTaggart of Arwell, Bart, married John Orde Ommanney (1810–46) in 1829. She was Susan Ellis's niece, TF Ellis her uncle by marriage. She later resumed her maiden name, becoming Mrs McTaggart Ommanney.

Monday – October 24

British Museum. Returning overtook Senior going up my stairs and found B in my chambers. Chat with Senior. When he was gone with dear B. To work. Macleod called – Biog Lit – odious absurd, ill written, ill arranged book. What an over rated creature he was. And he to prate about *a whole* and the importance of unity of design! – And he to blame severe and one-sided criticism! – Was there ever such a heap of unconnected nonsense as this Biog – Or so brutal a critique as his on Maturin's play?[1] The minor blemishes of style in the parts which I understand are innumerable. The metaphysics I neither understand nor wish to understand. I see enough to see that they are worthless – Flor Mac.

1. Charles Robert Maturin (1780–1824) was an Irish clergyman, best known for his novel *Melmoth the Wanderer*. In 1816 Coleridge reviewed his play *Bertram* in the *Courier*, in five letters, one of which is reproduced in chapter 23 of *Biographia Literaria*. In the Princeton edition of Coleridge's *Works*, vol. 7 (part 2), the *Courier* letters are given in full, appendix B, pp. 257–79.

Wednesday – October 25

My birthday. Less cheerful than once. Yet far from cheerless. My health is gradually giving way. Yet I have many many comforts. I cannot walk as I once could. But I enjoy my friends and books. There is no decay in my affections, I am sure; – nor, I think, in my intellect. It rained; and I staid at home working till it was time to go to W.T. where I was to read some of my book. I went, and read most of Chap xix. They liked it and I liked it. I read myself hoarse. They were very affectionate, and I was glad to see them so happy.

Thursday – October 26

Fine morning. To the H. of C. to consult books. I have during some days been working on Chap XI.[1] I shall now get Chap XII into order. What work these two vols will have cost me. And perhaps to no purpose. But I hope better – Flor Mac – Grimm.

1. Ch. 11 is the first in vol. iv, and ch. 12 the Irish chapter, below, 31 October; ch. 13 is the Scottish chapter.

Friday – October 27

To the Museum – took my M.S. of the 12th Chapter and worked to good purpose. Grimm – finished F.M. Vexatious letter from Edward R.[1]

1. Edward Rose, presumably declining the Lord Chancellor's offer of a living in Warwickshire. See above, entry for 19 October 1854.

Saturday – October 28

The Museum again. Got on well. Home at two – CZ came – afterwards T – read to CZ the first part of Chap XII. I am better satisfied than I often am with my own compositions. La Reine Margot..

Sunday – October 29

Worked – To W.T. Walked with H and B across the park. Called on Hallam – still in the country. To Brooks's. Amusing chat with Ld De M – Ld Torrington, Jervas[1] and Blount[2] – Queer stories about Charles Warren and Pce Menschikoff[3] – Home wrote and read – RM.

1. Perhaps Sir John Jervis (1802–56), Lord Chief Justice, who was a member of Brooks's Club.
2. There were three members of Brooks's Club of this name – Edward, d. 1843; E. J., d. 1847; and Walter Aston, d. 1832.
3. An unlikely linkage with no evidence that I can find. Charles Warren (1798–1866) was commanding a brigade in the Crimea; he had been wounded at Alma, had taken part in the first assault on Sebastopol, and was shortly to be wounded at Inkerman. Prince Aleksandr Sergeyevich Menshikov (1787–1869) commanded Russian forces in the Crimea.

Monday – October 31 [30]

To the Temple. E not come – left a note. To the Museum – Met Dundas there – worked well. Home. Chap XII all but finished – R.M. Grimm.

Tuesday – October 31

To the Museum – went on – E to dinner – R.M. Fine weather.

Wednesday – November 1

Vile foggy morning and East wind. Lefevre – talked about our report. I had excused myself from dining with E on account of the weather. But the wind changed, the sun came out, the afternoon was lovely, true Martinmas. I went. Nobody but F., pleasant enough.

Thursday – November 2

Dull morning – breakfast party – H – B – E Dundas – Ld Glenelg – Macleod – Ryan – very agreeable. H and B found it so to my great joy. B looked very handsome. In the afternoon it became very fine. R.I. finished at last the Irish Chapter. To the Scotch Chapter tomorrow. Grimm R.M.

Friday – November 3

True Martinmas – beautiful. Began on the Scottish chapter. Then to the city. Account excellent – gave 20£ to the Patriotic fund.[1] To W.T. walked with dear B about the Park. Home – wrote – Grimm – R.M.

1. A fund set up in October for the relief of orphans and widows of soldiers and sailors who had fallen in the war.

Saturday – November 4

Worked in the morning. Charles in the afternoon. Read more of Chap XII. Liked it better and better. I really think that it will do. Grimm – R.M.

Sunday – November 5

Worked on the Scotch Chapter – To W.T. Grimm – RM.

Monday – November 6

Guy Faux in all his glory. To the Museum – worked at the Scotch Chapter – Grimm R.M.

Tuesday – November 7

Scotch Chapter – E to dinner.

Wednesday – November 8

Scotch Chapter – to W.T. – H and B out – Dear Little A – Going home fell in with the carriage at a shop door in Regent Street – drove about a little with B. While she was shopping read some of Von Ranke – Home – Grimm – R.M.

Thursday – November 9

Party to breakfast. Very pleasant – Ld Granville – Ld Glenelg – Lewis – Panizzi – La Caita – H and B – and the Milmans. We sate till one – then to work – Scotch Chapter – to dinner with E – Marian and Louise there.

Friday – November 10

Scotch Chapter – E to dinner.

Saturday – November 11

To breakfast with Inglis. Then to the Museum – then home – Charles – finished the Irish Chap and read him some of the Scotch. I shall be disappointed if the book does not succeed – Grimm – La Dame de Monsoreau.[1]

1. By Alexandre Dumas (*père*) (1846).

Sunday – November 12

Worked at the Scotch Chapter – to Brooks's – Ld De Mauley – Waddington[1] – to W.T. Charles Wood came – We had a long talk. All right – Home – Grimm – Dame de M.

1. Sir Horatio Waddington (1799–1867), Permanent Under-Secretary to the Home Office from 1848 until his death.

Monday – November 13

Bad day. Worked all the morning on Chap XIV. Well satisfied – To dinner at W.T. Anxious – as everybody is – about our brave fellows in the Crimea, but proud for the country and glad to think that the national spirit is so high and unconquerable. Invasion is a bugbear indeed while we retain our pluck. Charles and his wife[1] at dinner.

1. Mary Potter (*c.* 1821–1913).

Tuesday – November 14

The news makes me still more anxious this morning. However, I can do nothing. Worked hard on the 14th Chap. Schomberg – Nonjurors – Grimm – E to dinner.

Wednesday – November 15

Worked on – In the evening found my eyesight confused. My head perfectly clear. My tongue right. Impossible that there can be any general derangement. However, I took hydr. The confusion lasted only about an hour.

Thursday – November 16

Staid at home all day with hydr – bad weather. At six to dine with E – the ladies and F.

Friday – November 17

Worked in the morning – Lady Holland sent me the Life of her father[1] – E to dinner.

1. Lady Holland, the wife of Sir Henry Holland, was the daughter of Sydney Smith. Her *Memoir of the Reverend Sydney Smith*, to which she had asked TBM to contribute (see above, entry for 17 November 1853), was published in 1854.

Saturday – November 18

Sent the Life of Sydney to H – called at Berthes in Marlborough Street[1] and gave orders to Museum. To Museum. Worked there long – home and worked – Dame de Monsoreau. – Grimm – Collier.

1. TBM means Barthes and Lowell, booksellers of foreign books of 14 Great Marlborough Street.

Sunday – November 19

Worked – Collier – To W.T. – pleasant – Charles Wood came to W.T. – long talk – home and worked again to Museum. Dame de M. – Grimm.

Monday – November 20

To the R.I. Then to the Museum. Home and worked – Liaisons Dangereuses[1] – Grimm – D de M.

1. Pierre Choderlos de Laclos, *Les Liaisons Dangereuses* (1782).

Tuesday – November 21

Work – E to dinner.

Wednesday – November 22

Museum meeting – Goulburn – etc – worked.

Thursday – November 23

Worked all the morning. H and B called and took me to W.T. – dined there – pleasant.

Friday – November 24

Work again – D de M.

Saturday – November 25

Breakfast party – Milman and Mrs M, Dundas, Panizzi, C. Wood. I find that parliament is to meet in a fortnight. It now matters little to me. When they were gone I worked on – D M.

Sunday – [November 26]

Worked – to W.T. – pleasant chat – home and worked till E came to dinner.

Monday – [November 27]

Bad cold weather – worked all day – D de M.

Tuesday – [November 28]

Another bad day – worked. B called and sate an hour – very pleasant. I read her some of Herodotus into English – then H came for her. D de M.

Wednesday – November 29

A storm at night which woke me. The morning fine and mild. To the B.M. – Dutch Despatches. Home just in time to avoid another squall as violent as that of the night. A letter on the table from Leigh Hunt to ask for 12£. I had been wondering that I had been so long without hearing from him. Sent it him – D de M.

Thursday – November 30

[No entry]

Friday – December 1

E dined here. I am getting remiss about my journal. The truth is that I am working harder and harder at my history. The Rivalités[1] contains much that I am glad to see. But the writer has plundered me to an extent which his acknowledgments by no means cover – and, when he loses my guidance, blunders lamentably about English affairs.

1. Albert Laponneraye, *Histoire des rivalités et des lettres de la France et de l'Angleterre* (Paris, 1842).

Saturday – [December 2]

R.I. Work – Les 45[1] – [~~Sunday~~] Macleod called – disagreeable account of the Indian Law Commission.

1. Alexandre Dumas (*père*), *Les Quarante-cinq* (1848).

Sunday – December 3

Worked – to W.T. – pleasant chat for a short time. Charles walked home with me. 45.

[Monday – December 4]

[Portion cut out of MS] ... been curious. Home and made insertions and corrections. To dinner at W.T. read parts of the 16th Chapter. They seemed pleased.

Tuesday – [December 5]

Walked to the City. Longman has paid in my gains of the year. Ordered another 300£ to be bought for me in the 3 pc. To W.T. by the New Road. Dear little Alice not quite well and in bed. Sweet child. My dearest B too has a cold. Sate a little and walked home – Rainy afternoon – read the Histoire des Rivalités. E to dinner Life of Wilberforce – Molière.

Wednesday – December 6

Very fine day – quite like May – walked – [portion of MS cut out]. Met Longman – talk about a Dictionary of Fiction which he is thinking of. Advised against it. Home – work – The Irish part of Chap XVII. Dined at W.T. read the Boyne. They seemed to like it.

Thursday – December 7

Staid at home working all the morning. In the evening to E's to dinner. The ladies and Frank went out in the evening and left E and me tête à tête. I have done a good deal of Chap XVII.

Friday – December 8

Still Chap XVII – At dinner 45 – Macleod and Jowett called.

Saturday – December 9

Museum – looked at pamphlets etc – then board of Trustees. Walked away with Milman – worked – C called. I was not up to reading. At dinner 45 – Wilberforce.

Sunday – December 10

Cold – worked – W.T. Dear little Alice not quite well yet. Pleasant hour or two – home – worked – 45 – Wilberforce.

Monday – December 11

Very cold. To the Museum however; but could not find what I wanted. Home and worked – E to dinner.

Tuesday – December 12

Parliament to meet today – Went down – heard the opening of the debate. H and B in the ladies gallery. Home to an 8 o'clock dinner – 45 – La Harpe.[1]

1. Jean-François de La Harpe (1739–1803).

Wednesday – December 13

Wrote – still Chap XVII – B and G came. Excellent news – G has done very well. But I am sorry for Walter Ellis. Dined with Ld Granville, or rather at Ld G's – for he was at Windsor.

Thursday – December 14

[No entry]

Friday – December 15

E to dinner.

Saturday – December 16

Worked all day. To dinner at Lne House – Sir H Holland – Ld Carlisle – Milnes – pleasant.

Sunday – December 17

Worked – W.T. – read G's Comic Iambics – very good for him. He will do excellently – La H. 45.

Monday – December 18

Worked – bad day. At 12 to the Bd of Control – Lefevre and Lowe were there. Long discussion. I carried most points my own way – La H – 45 – finished.

Tuesday – December 19

Anxious about the foreign enlistment bill – a foolish affair. Wrote all the morning – Down to the House at 4 – staid till six. Hayter paired me[1] – Home. E to dinner. Hydr – Read him Aughrim – Pretty well. Hydr.

1. W. G. Hayter, Chief Whip.

Wednesday – December 20

Vile day – rain and sleet. Staid at home and worked. Still Chap XVII – La H and Gabriel Lambert[1] – Prince de Ligne.

1. By Alexandre Dumas (*père*) (1855).

Thursday – December 21

Worked on – Nothing particular. Very wet – carriage and to W.T. to dinner.

Friday – December 22

Work – walk – Temple – House of Commons – paired – F Mildmay[1] P de Ligne.[2]

1. *Frank Mildmay*, by Frederick Marryat (1829).
2. Charles Joseph, Prince de Ligne (1735–1813), Field Marshall, wit and military writer.

Saturday – December 23

Ld L called – Athenaeum – Franz, – Λει work Voltaire and J.B. Rousseau[1] – F.M. – P de Ligne.

1. Jean-Baptiste Rousseau (1671–1741), poet.

Sunday – December 24

Worked – Walked to W.T. – back – worked on – A novel of Elie Berthet,[1] J.B. Rousseau and David Hume.

1. 1818–91. Writer of thrillers and historical novels, he had just published *Le Garçon de Banque*.

Monday – December 25

Xmas day – Very wet and windy – Rousseau, Juge de Jean Jacques.[1] As mad as any man that ever bellowed in Bedlam. Worked. In the afternoon the carriage

– to W.T. pleasant afternoon – all good and happy. Pleased with some verses of G. He is turning out extremely well. I had sent S and F 20£ extra.

1. The *Dialogues* (1774). TBM plainly took the view of Diderot and Grimm.

Friday – December 26

Fine day – Worked and walked – Trois Mousq[1] – Rousseau.

1. Alexandre Dumas (*père*), *Les Trois Mousquetaires* (1840).

Wednesday – December 27

After breakfast T G and A called – G and A staid a little. I walked with them to the door of the R.I. Weather fine, but cold. Suffered for my rashness – Shivering pain in the limbs – no appetite – worked however – Rousseau – 3 M – hydr.

Thursday – December 28

Kept awake by rheumatic pains. Dull and low all day partly from the disease and partly from calomel. Did something, but not much – However the St G intrigues in Wm's cabinet[1] are beginning to take a far better form than before – 3 M – Rousseau.

1. St German's. For the relations between members of William's Cabinet and the exiled court, see *HE*, ch. 17, *CW*, vol. 3, pp. 408–17.

Friday – December 29

Another bad night – the pain not severe, but quite enough to spoil my rest. It left me in the morning. I sent for Bright and wrote a line to H – then worked – pretty well – 3 M – Rousseau Marmontel's Memoirs[1] – once my favourite book. With what rapture I read it the first time in a detestable translation at Cambridge. I think I was a freshman. It was my first glimpse of that singular society. I know a good deal about that breed of men now. M's book strikes me more now by its faults than by its beauties. Yet he tells a story well. H and B called and sate with me – Bright prescribed Colchicum etc.

1. Jean-François Marmontel's *Memoires d'un père* appeared in 1804. It was first translated into English as *Memoirs of Marmontel, written by himself* (4 vols) in 1805, and a third edition, in 1808, gives Hugh Murray as the translator.

Saturday – December 30

A better night – T and B – T went soon. B sate an hour. I went to work and found, to my great vexation that several sheets had disappeared from Chapter XVII. I cannot get over a suspicion that the charwoman had taken them. Wm and E, though much vexed, acquitted her on the ground that they could have been of no use to her – and I did not chuse to say that, to my certain knowledge, people had been willing to give five shillings and more for a scrap of my writing. However I did not choose to punish the woman on suspicion. I shall therefore be more cautious for the future about leaving M.S.S. in her way. It cost me almost a day's work to replace the lost sheets. – 3 Mousq – Finished Marmontel. Dumont's Memoirs.[1] Colch pills again – Mahon called.

1. Perhaps Pierre Étienne Louis Dumont (1759–1829), *Souvenirs de Mirabeau ...* (published in 1832).

Sunday – December 31

Tolerable night. Better. But a cold disagreeable day which kept me at home. Worked with much success – Mt etc finished. The Chapter, indeed, finished, except a bit here and there and a peroration. It has, I think, been greatly improved – Dumont – Excellent book and excellent man. E to dinner – Bright had called and recommended Hydr.

[This year is nearly a blank in the Journal. As in 1848, Macaulay was concentrating on the completion of the next two volumes of the *History of England* and there was little else to record. His illness, which in December confined him to his rooms but did not prevent him from writing, exempted him from attendance in Parliament. He missed the debates on the Sebastopol enquiry, which in September brought down the government of Aberdeen. There is not much sign in his letters that he followed the progress of the war in the Crimea. He later said that his chambers in the Albany 'were the only place where a man could pass a quarter of an hour in company without hearing the Crimea mentioned'. He realized that he was not being fair to his constituents in Edinburgh, and asked his friend Adam Black to look for another candidate. By the summer, however, he had recovered enough to take a house at Richmond from late June to late September. He also decided that his health would not improve while he lived close to the Thames fogs and in the densest of London's smoke. In November he corrected the proofs of the new volumes. They were published on the 17th, and he was relieved to read the reviews and find public reaction was favourable, as it had been to volumes 1 and 2.]

Monday – January 1 1855

A new year. May it be as happy as the last. To me, it will probably be more eventful, as it will see if I live and am well, the publication of the second part of my history.

Wednesday – January 10

I find that I am getting out of the habit of keeping my journal – I have indeed so much to do [?with] my history that I have little inclination for any other writing. My life too is very uneventful. I am a prisoner to my room or nearly so. I do nothing but write or read. I will however minute down interesting things from time to time – Some day the taste of journalising may return.

Monday – January 29

I open this book again after an interval of near three weeks – Three weeks passed by the fireside. Once I dined out – on Tuesday the 16th at W.T. to meet Gladstone. Nothing could be more lamentable than his account of affairs in the Crimea.[1] Tonight there will I suppose be a vote against the govt. Tomorrow a change of adm[inistrati]on. I am content that it should be so, and well pleased that my illness dispenses me from voting. I have made great progress with my book of late, and see no reason to doubt that I shall go to press in the summer. I am now deep in the 19th Chapter. Odd that here within a few yards of all the bustle of politics I should be as quiet as a hermit – as quiet as Cowper was at Olney – much more quiet, thank God, than my old friend Hannah More at Barley Wood – and buried in old pamphlets and broadsides – turning away from the miseries of Balaklava to the battle of Steinkirk on which I was busied today. The fates have spun him not the coarsest thread[2] etc as old Ben says. H, B, A, T, and G as kind as possible. I want no more. But I have other very kind visitors. I cannot think that this can go on long. But I hope that I shall bring out my two volumes. I am conscious of no intellectual decay. My memory I often try and find it as good as ever; and memory is the faculty which it is most easy to bring to decisive tests and also the faculty which gives way first.

1. *The Times* reports on the state of the British army after the battle of Inkerman had begun in late December 1854. Parliament met on 23 January 1855 and Roebuck gave notice of a motion for a Committee to enquire into the state of the army in the Crimea. It was debated for three nights and on the 29th the government lost by 148 to 345 votes. *PD*, 3rd ser., cxxxvi, 1230–3.
2. Ben Jonson's *The Poetaster, or His Arraignment* (1601). Epilogue 'To the Reader', l. 10.

Wednesday – February 14

The same story – still working on the history – still confined to my room by the cold weather. I sometimes feel a little depressed. But, everything considered, I do very well.

Wednesday – February 21

At last after the longest and severest frost that I remember so late in the year, the thaw has begun and is indeed nearly completed – the snow gone – the water which had been frozen in the pipes gushing in torrents. The wind S.W. The sun shining. Tomorrow I hope to emerge after a long and close imprisonment. I have worked hard and done much. The 19th Chapter is very nearly ready. I forgot to note one occurrence wh has added much to my comfort. A loose tooth which had plagued me two years, and interfered with my eating, talking and reading, fell out without the smallest pain and has left me a perfectly firm and sound set. It was the last grinder and therefore has made no visible gap.

Friday – March 2

A week of mild and moist weather – I am much the better for it – Tauchnitz came on Wednesday. I expect a comfortable addition to my income from that quarter. If I live, and the second part of my history succeeds tolerably, I shall enjoy what to me will be great opulence. I have been two days running at the Museum. But my work does not proceed quite so fast in this fine weather as when I was close prisoner. However I have got a fine start, and have no reason to doubt that I shall be free next Christmas. I had a breakfast party on Tuesday Ld Lne, The Dean,[1] Dundas, Denison, Mahon, Ld Glenelg, Van de Weyer. Yesterday Hobhouse called. By the bye Lewis called as soon as he had accepted his office,[2] and we had a long chat about finance and other matters. I have quite got out of the habit of keeping my diary.

1. Presumably Milman, Dean of St Paul's.
2. Sir George Cornewall Lewis succeeded Gladstone as Chancellor of the Exchequer on 28 February 1855.

[No entries from 2 March to 6 November 1855. TBM left a three-inch gap]

Tuesday – November 6

After an interval of eight months I begin my journal again. My book is almost printed. It will appear before the middle of December, I hope. It will certainly make me rich, as I account riches. As to success I am less certain. But I have a good hope, I mean to keep my journal as reg[ular]ly as I did seven years ago when the first part came out. Today I went to call on poor Hallam – how much changed! Then bought at a shop at Knightsbridge Sampson's account or the Irish Rebellion[1] read it as I walked across the Park to W.T. Found B H and A. Sate an hour – home – read Bisset's Plain English[2] – other pamphlets – some of Aristotle's Politics, at dinner Sir C Grandison. In the evening Courteney came from Spottiswoode's and brought me a proof of Chap XX.

1. The edition of William Sampson's *Memoirs* published in 1832 had an introduction detailing the causes of the Irish insurrection in 1798. Sampson (1764–1836) belonged to the United Irishmen.

2. William Bisset (d. 1747), *Plain English: A Sermon ... for Reformation of Manners ...* (1704).

Wednesday – November 7

Up at eight to work at Chap XX; – was at it the whole day, except during a short time which I spent at the Museum – pretty well satisfied. Sir C.G.

Thursday – November 8

Finished what I had to do to Chap XX before breakfast. Rainy day. Staid at home – read over a good deal of Chap XVIII and was pleased with it. I think the book must take. Read a volume of Shaftesbury's Characteristics[1] – often cleverly and gracefully written. Philo – Legation[2] – very interesting – Sir C.G.

---

1. Anthony Ashley Cooper, third Earl of Shaftesbury (1671–1713), *Characteristics of Men, Manners, Opinions, Times* (1715).
2. Philo Judaeus, *De Virtutibus, seu de Legatione ad Caium*. A writer of the first century AD, he pleaded for tolerance of the Jewish faith before the Emperor Caligula.

Friday – November 9

A rainy day. Staid at home working and reading till seven in the afternoon. Then to dine with Ellis. Chat about Spain with Frank.

Saturday – November 10

Worked in the morning – then to the Museum – Dundas – Goulburn – Milman. Walked away with Dundas – worked on till it was time to dress for dinner at W.T. A large and pleasant party. Sir C. Wood and Lady Mary, George Grey and Lady Grey, Ld and Lady Canning,[1] Merivale, Mangles and his wife, C. Buxton and his wife. I was in very good spirits and I thought, amused the party. I left with H. Chapters XIX XX and XXI.

---

1. Charlotte Stuart (1817–61), eldest daughter of Lord Stuart de Rothesay.

Sunday – November 11

Worked hard at Chapter XXII – Went to W.T. sate a little with H and B – home and worked again. E to dinner. Herrings, a turkey, a partridge.

Monday – November 12

Finished correcting Chap XXII and sent it back to the printer. To W.T. – then with H and B to see a house at Clapham which I have some thought of taking. A very nice house. The very thing for me. But the grounds far too large – grass for three cows a great extent of greenhouse. I gave up the plan unwillingly. To Loat the Builder[1] and explained what I wanted. H likes Chap XIX much better than I do. Home – read Turcaret.[2] Some of Locke's excellent Book on Language.[3] At dinner the Antiquary. A revise of Chapter XX came in the evening.

1. Christopher Loat (1802–76) lived in Clapham, where he was parish clerk of Holy Trinity. He was a neighbour of Marianne Thornton.
2. Comedy by Lesage, produced in 1709.
3. Bk III ('Of Words') in John Locke's *Essay Concerning Human Understanding* (1689).

Tuesday – November 13

Began to correct the revise of Chapter XX before breakfast, finished it by two. A dull day – clouds and east wind – staid at home – felt very well and comfortable. Sent off the revise – A letter from Μακφ. Invitation to the Grange – declined it. Cunningham of Harrow called[1] and sate an hour and a half. Note from Forster with another copy of his Life of Goldsmith.[2] Wrote a civil answer. Sent to a bookshop for two books which I had seen in a Catalogue – Sewell's Sermons[3] and a political work by Shebbeare[4] – both wretched and contemptible in different ways. Antiquary at dinner. Chapter XX returned at 11.

1. Presumably John William Cunningham, Vicar of Harrow, 1811–61.
2. John Forster's *Life of Goldsmith* appeared first in 1848 and again in 1854.
3. Perhaps William Sewell, *Parochial Sermons* (1832).
4. John Shebbeare (1709–88), surgeon and political writer.

Wednesday – November 14

Corrected Chap XX finally – to W.T. – saw William Trevelyan.[1] Then H, B and A came – pleasant hour. They seem to like the book. They carried me home and H took away Sewell. Some tracts from a bookseller's – trash – some of that wretched [illeg.] Pasquin among them. At dinner the Heart of Midlothian.

1. Probably William Pitt Trevelyan (1812–1905), CET's youngest brother, Rector of Calverton, Bucks.

Thursday – November 15

Corrected the earlier part of Chap XXI – finally. A terribly gloomy fog – my chest affected. A bad beginning of the winter. East wind – It cleared up – the sun shone; and I ventured out, but soon came back not the better for my ramble. Read Welsted's Life and Remains[1] – mostly trash. But Pope was certainly an odious fellow. At dinner that trashy Love Match.[2] In the evening Jesse's Selwyn Correspondence,[3] Skelton's Deism revealed,[4] a great deal of Bolingbroke's stupid infidelity. The close of Chap XXI come from the printers. I suffered so much from the weather that I was forced to have a mustard poultice and a fire in my bedroom.

---

1. Leonard Welsted (*c.* 1688–1747), *The Works in Verse and Prose of L.W. ... with historical notes ... and memoirs of the Author*, by J. Nichols (1787). Welsted satirized, and was satirized by, Pope.
2. There are two works with this title, by Catherine Charlotte Maberley (1841) and Henry Cockton (1845).
3. J. H. Jesse, *George Selwyn and his Contemporaries* (1843–44).
4. Philip Skelton, *Deism Revealed* (1751).

Friday – November 16

Better this morning – but a vile fog and East wind – worked at Chap XXI and sent it back. But I must have another revise of the later sheets. Trevelyan called – Milnes – Longman – all right. I am certain – as far as anything human is certain – of being what I should once have called a rich man – thrice as rich at least as when I first came to the Albany. Began Herodotus with great delight; read Clio[1] – Excellent. E came to dinner – unexpected but welcome. Late in the evening Chap XXII came.

---

1. Bk I.

Saturday – November 17

Chap XXII occupied me almost all day. I had to go to the Museum to work. Happily, though the fog and the East wind continue, my chest is wonderfully better. I finished correcting the Chapter, and also a revise of the last sheets of Chap XXI. I had no time however for Herodotus. To E's to dinner – Campbell, Ryan, Adolphus, Frank – pleasant party.

Sunday – November 18

Still fog and East Wind; and still I am well – strangely well. My hands too have quite ceased to plague me. Is this a constitutional renovation? Or is it a sign that my maladies will take some other form? At present it is welcome. Read Euterpe[1] – To W.T. pleasant hour or two there – Home. Euterpe. Looked at the Montrose case – a huge splendidly printed folio sent me by Ld Lindsay.[2] It has some interest. I never saw a clearer case in my life. The decision of the peers was perfectly right. How even an interested party can have had any doubt on the subject I hardly understand. Looked at the M.S.S. of Horace Walpole. E to dinner.

---

1. Herodotus, *Euterpe*, bk II.

2. In 1851 James Crawford (1783–1869), twenty-fourth Earl of Crawford and seventh Earl of Balcarres, claimed the Dukedom of Montrose. James Graham, the fourth Duke of Montrose (1799–1874), was confirmed in the title. The sender of the folio was Alexander William Lindsay, who was to become the twenty-fifth Earl of Crawford. The book, *The Lindsay Peerage Case* (1855), was no. 663 in SC.

Monday – November 19

H Walpole. Sent Chap XXII to the printer. Looked through earlier part of Vol IV. Pretty well satisfied. My spirits fluctuate. I do not think that this part can be thought a failure except by comparison with the first part. Certainly no other history of Wm's reign is either so trustworthy or so readable. A letter from Everett – poor fellow. He is sad and out of heart. I have a great kindness for him. I read a good deal of Walpole M.S. – κοκτωνος ψυχρ at dinner. My chest oppressed in the evening. The 2nd part of Chap XXII came. I forgot to mention a very odd absurd letter from Ld John, to which I hardly know how to frame an answer. He has taken it into his head – God knows why – that I wish to prevent Ward from painting a picture of Ld Russell's parting with Lady Russell.[1]

1. William, Lord Russell (1639–83), was executed for his alleged complicity in the Rye House Plot. There is a famous account of his parting with his wife ('the bitterness of death is past') in G. Burnet, *History of his Own Time*, 3rd edn, ed. O. Airy (Oxford, 1897–1900), vol. 2, p. 219. This particular subject does not seem to be recorded among Ward's paintings, but in 1874 he exhibited at the Royal Academy a different scene from the same story – Lady Rachel Russell pleading with Charles II for her husband's life. TBM's denial is in *LM*, vol. 5, pp. 470–1.

Tuesday – November 20

At work before breakfast – soon after breakfast sent off the first half of Chap XXII, finally corrected, to the printer. The day a vile one. I had meant to dine in W.T. But I sent an excuse. My cough and oppression of the chest, though not very bad, were quite bad enough to keep me at home in such weather. East wind and rain together. Herodotus. Ellis had sent me Blakesley.[1] I do not find that, as far as I have yet gone, Blakesley throws much light on the text. Dearest B to dinner – very pleasant. Good child. She read me one of Swift's Examiners in the evening with great interest and enjoyment.

1. Joseph Williams Blakesley (1808–85), *Herodotus, with a Commentary* (1854). He was at this time Vicar of Ware; he later became Dean of Lincoln.

Wednesday – November 21

Sent back the last half of Chap XXII corrected. I must see the concluding 20 pages again. Staid at home all day. Herodotus – finished Thalia – deep in Melpomene.[1] Excellent writer. I like Blakesley less and less – E to dinner.

1. Bks III and IV.

Thursday – November 22

Looked over and sent off the last 20 pages. My work is done – Thank God. And now for the result – On the whole I think that it cannot be very unfavourable. To the City – [page torn]. To W.T. With H to the Diceys'. H tells me of an odd letter of Inglis's in Bell's Weekly Messenger in which I come in. At the door of the Albany found the Duke of Argyle – showed him up – had a chat of half an hour with him – pleasant enough. We agreed perfectly. By the bye in the City I found my affairs prosperous. The Peninsular and Oriental goes on wonderfully well. Herodotus finished Melpomene. At dinner κν, afterwards Prescott's Philip II.[1] Well enough: but I read through half the first volume without finding anything that much altered my notion of the events on men of that time; and I have never studied that part of history deeply. Vile cough and oppression of the chest – the effect probably of going out – Sent Milnes an excuse – [page torn].

1. W. H. Prescott, *History of the Reign of Philip the Second, King of Spain* (1855). TBM's acknowledgement to the author is in *LM*, vol. 5, p. 474.

Friday – November 23

[illeg.] H and T. They came before ten with B. He has seen Brodie and Brodie thinks that the affection of his eye is not dangerous, but will be permanent. They seem pretty well satisfied. He is to have a silverplate over the wound. When they were gone Longman came. I had a note from him later in the day. All the 25,000 copies are ordered. The only doubt is about the solvency of two or three customers which must be well looked to. Monday Dec 17 is to be the day; but in the evening of the preceding Saturday those booksellers who take more than a thousand are to have their books. The stock lying at the bookbinders is insured for £10,000. The whole weight is 56 tons – It seems that no such edition was ever published of any work of the same bulk. If I had had this prosperity thirty years ago. But I ought not to complain. I earnestly hope that neither age nor riches will narrow my heart nor make me a miser., I had much oppression of the chest. The wind is from the West; but it is cold and foggy. I staid at home – read a good deal of my book Chap XIII. Not ill satisfied on the whole. Read Bissett's Modern Fanatic[1] – Much amused. Walpole and Parliamentary Debates on the 1st Regency Bill. At Dinner – Κν – then Prescott – σιναπι.[2]

1. William Bisset, *The Modern Fanatick* (1710).
2. (Greek): mustard, i.e. a mustard poultice.

Saturday – November 24

Staid at home all day. Read my book in its finally corrected form. Not ill pleased on the whole. Finished Walpole – Prescott – What strikes me most about Prescott is that, though he has had new materials, and tells his story well, he does not put anything in a light very different from that in which I have before seen it. κοκτων σιναπι.

Sunday – November 25

Again at home all day. Sent for Bright. H and T called in the afternoon. While they were with me Bright came – prescribed calomel. Soon after came Sir H. Holland – not unpleasant. E to dinner – Hydr.

Monday – November 26

Another day of confinement. Much affected by the medicine. My chest better. Read my book. Herodotus. Sir H. Holland has sent me the third edition of his Medical Essays,[1] interesting and curious. Ld Stanhope called and sate some time – κκτων.

1. *Medical Notes and Reflections* (1855).

Tuesday – November 27

Not so well as to the chest – vile East Wind etc – Read Holland's book – my own – some of W. Huntington S.S.[1] Correspondence Χηρ βαρν[2]– Received from Longman the first copy of my book in the brown livery. I sent him yesterday the list of presentation copies.

1. Sinner Saved.
2. Frances Trollope, *The Widow Barnaby* (1839).

Wednesday – November 28

Dawdled over my book most of the day – sometimes in good sometimes in bad spirits about it. On the whole, I think that it must do. The only competition which, as far as I perceive, it has to dread is that of the two former Volumes. H called and sate with me half an hour. In the afternoon my chest plagued me. I took a pill prescribed by Bright and was, I think easier. Looked over my accounts of several years with Longman and made calculations. More of Holland's Medical Essays – liked them. Herodotus – Erato[1] – the part of Herodotus wh I read first – indeed the only part that I ever read as school business. I do not know why Preston selected it. There are many better and more interesting things in the old fellow's book. At dinner βαρν. In the evening a Frenchman called for Perrotin's copy.[2] I gave it him. Hydr. Looked at Joseph Andrews.

1. Bk VI.
2. i.e. of TBM's *History*, vols 3 and 4. Charles Arthur Perrotin (1796–1866) was the publisher of the French translation.

Thursday – November 29

Another bad day – confinement to my room – calomel – again dawdled over my book. I wish that the next month were over. I am more anxious than I was about the first part. For then I had no highly raised expectations to satisfy. And now people expect so much that the Seventh Book of Thucydides would hardly content them. On the other hand the general sterility, the miserably enervated state of literature is all in my favour. We shall see – H and B called. Herodotus βαρν.

Friday – November 30

The weather better. Went out – met Ld Lansdowne in St James's Street – we chatted an hour. I sate by while he ate a sandwich at Brooks's, before starting for Bowood. He very kind and pressing: but I shall hardly venture out of town. Home – My book. Herodotus. H and T to dinner – very pleasant evening. B and A at Calverton.[1]

1. Their uncle William was Rector of Calverton, Buckinghamshire.

Saturday – December 1

Still fine – went out in the middle of the day – met Poodle Byng. D Coleridge called. Reading as yesterday. Looked at W.H.S.S.

Sunday – December 2

Fine – Read in the morning – to W.T. Sate with H an hour – went away with T and C ZM – walked all the way home – my chest oppressed at the time but soon recovered. Read as before – E to dinner.

Monday – December 3

Very dull and dreary – N.E. wind – staid at home and read. Anxious and sometimes low; yet on the whole I bear up. Odd that I should care so very little about the money, though it is full as much as I made by banishing myself for four a half of the best years of my life to India. W.H.S.S. βαρν.

Tuesday – December 4

Another bleak day passed in my chambers. I am never tired of reading. Invitation from the Duke of Bedford to Woburn. Declined it. Denison called. Chat about politics etc – I hope for peace – βαρν. Read some of Swift – Arbuthnot's John Bull.[1] One is never tired of these excellent pieces.

1. John Arburthnot's *History of John Bull* (1712).

Wednesday – December 5

Rather a pleasanter day – Walked to W.T. at lunchtime. Pleasant two hours. Dear H – Dear girls. Came with H and B to Piccadilly in the carriage. Read Brantome.[1] Longman called – 300£ from the Yankees. Good account of the Peninsular & Oriental – in fact 10 per cent income tax paid. At dinner βαρν – Brantome – The Queen of Navarre.

1. Pierre de Bourdeilles, Seigneur de Brantome (*c.* 1540–1614), left a series of manuscript portraits of famous men and women of his time. TBM may have been reading the two-volume edition by J. A. C. Buchon (Paris 1838).

Thursday – December 6

Fine but cold – wind North – staid at home all day. Read 10 Cantos of the Morgante Maggiore[1] – languidly amused. Read the preface to Thiers's new volume[2] and a good deal of the Volume – liked his narrative, absurdly partial as he is to the French soldiers. To the Duke of Wellington I think him not unjust. At dinner βαρν 2nd part – Swift – polite convn and some other pieces – I am in better heart about my book, though still anxious. A Yankee publisher sends me very coolly an enormous folio in two closely printed Columns – a Dictionary of authors – and this only a specimen, and asks me to give my opinion of it – that opinion of course to be printed as a puff. He has already used the opinions of Everett, Washington Irving and others in that way. I sent it back with a note saying that I could not form an opinion of such a work at a glance, and that I had not time for full examination. I hate such tricks. Àpropos of puffing – that great fool R. Montgomery is gathered to Bavius[3] and Blackmore.[4] How he pestered me with his alternate cries for mercy and threats of vengeance!

---

1. By Luigi Pulci (1432–84); published 1482.
2. Of his *Histoire du Consulat et de l'empire* (1855), vol. 12. It covers the period from April 1810 to May 1811.
3. Robert Montgomery, TBM's victim, died this month. Bavius was a poetaster of the first century BC, mainly known from a contemptuous reference to him in Virgil's third Eclogue (3.90).
4. Sir Richard Blackmore (1654–1729) was physician to William III and author of *Prince Arthur: an Heroick Poem in Ten Books* (1695). He was a butt of Pope and the Wits and appears in *The Dunciad*, bk II, ll. 247–56.

Friday – December 7

Another fine day, but very cold – staid at home. More of Thiers – More of Pulci. I forgot to mention that Guidici's Storia della Letteratura Italiana put it into my head to read Pulci again. I mean to get Tiraboschi[1] soon – read Herodotus's Urania[2] – βαρν 2nd part.

---

1. Girolamo Tiraboschi, *Storia della Letteratura Italiana* (1771–82).
2. Bk VIII.

Saturday – December 8

Another cold day. Staid at home. B called. While she was here Ld Carlisle came – chatted with him about this bible-burning[1] – blamed the prosecution. I am afraid that he is answerable for it. He went and then my darling B. I read Pulci – Herodotus – finished him – then Ctesias[2] – this brought me back to Photius, of whom I read a good deal with much gusto – I will go through him. βαρνβ. In the evening some of the pamphlets of that strange unprincipled blackguard Amyas Griffiths.[3] αυτος ναυσικ.

---

1. A Roman Catholic priest at Kingstown had exhorted his parishioners to give up any immoral books in their possession to him to be destroyed. The books were publicly burned, and it is alleged that they included at least one copy of the Authorised Version of the Bible. He was prosecuted by the Attorney General for Ireland, but acquitted by a jury consisting of five Protestants and seven Roman Catholics. Carlisle was Viceroy. *Annual Register* (1855), pp. 184–6.
2. See above, entry for 28 June 1854.
3. Author of *Miscellaneous Tracts*, published in Dublin 1787 and 1788.

Sunday – December 9

Colder and more gloomy than ever. Staid at home – enjoyed my liberty, though prisoner to my room. I feel much easier about my book – very much. Read a worthless Life of Hawker the Antinomian[1] – Photius – much interested – Pulci. E to dinner.

1. Perhaps John Williams, *Memoirs of the Life and Writings of the Rev. R. Hawker ...* (1831).

Monday – December 10

Another dreary day of East Wind. Staid at home. H called. Wrote to Montgomery Stuart and Emilio Guidici at Florence. Read Photius – His account of Isocrates induced me to take down Isocrates again. I have not read him since I was in India. I looked at several speeches. He was never a favourite of mine; and I see no reason to change my opinion. At dinner βαρν. I have found one serious mistake in my history. I wonder whether anybody else will find it out.

Tuesday – December 11

Trevelyan called. Lewis wants my opinion on two prints relating to the Museum – wrote to him. An Irish tract on Handel's visit to Dublin.[1] Pulci. At dinner βαρν 2 I shall not try 3 – Gulliveriana – looked at Gulliver. Warburton's Controvl. Tracts.[2]

1. SC, no. 79.
2. Ibid., no. 907.

Wednesday – December 12

At breakfast Cobbett – E.I.Cy – not ill pleased. Letter from the Chancellor of the Exchequer about the Museum. My hopes rise. B called – pleasant. Then Bouverie – glad to hear his account of the Cambridge business.[1] I shall not be unwilling to be on the Commission if it be such as it seems likely to be. I suggested Ld Stanley and Page Wood.[2] Read a good deal of Photius – much interested by his account of Theopompus and of the poetry of the Empress Eudocia.[3] I see that one of her poems was the origin of the best of Calderon's serious dramas El Magico Prodigioso.[4] Read Pulci – At dinner X Χεστ Τρολ[5] – afterwards Warburtonian Controversy – particularly Law's Behmenical attacks on DL.[6]

1. A bill to reform the University of Cambridge had been withdrawn in 1855 because it reached the Commons from the Lords too late in the session. Another bill was introduced and passed in 1856.

2. Both Stanley and Sir William Page Wood (1801–81; later Lord Chancellor) were appointed to the Statutory Commission to oversee the carrying out of the Cambridge University Act of 1856. Macaulay was not on the Commission.
3. Photius, ninth-century Byzantine scholar and Patriarch. His most famous work was the *Bibliotheca* or *Myriobiblion*. It is the main source of what is known about Theopompus of Chios (*c.* 378–320 BC), a rhetorician and historian. Eudocia was the wife of Theodosius II, Emperor of the West AD 408–50.
4. *The Wonderful Magician* (1637).
5. 'Ch. Chest Trol', i.e. *Charles Chesterfield: or the Adventures of a Youth of Genius* by Fanny Trollope, 1841.
6. For Law, see Volume 2, entry for 7 June 1849, n. 4. 'DL' is presumably *Divine Legation of Moses*.

Thursday – December 13

Still cold and frosty – staid at home – now the 8th day of imprisonment. Yet my spirits are good – Photius – Law v Hoadley.[1] Sent 5£ to Coutts's for Johnson's Goddaughter[2] – an absurd scheme of Carlyle's. But I could not say No. Read Lowth's letter to Warburton[3] – clever. H. T and G to dinner – Good news of G. He is 3d at Harrow. He brought some of his exercises, all fair, and one very good indeed – a Latin epistle from a Roman on Agricola's staff, to Tacitus about the state of our island. We dined pleasantly and passed the evening in chat. Longman had called, and had told me enough to show that my expectations of profit were rather too low than too high.

1. Bishop Benjamin Hoadly (1676–1761).
2. Ann Elizabeth Lowe (1777–1860). She and her sister Frances Meliora Lucia Lowe (*c.* 1783–1866) were the daughters of Mauritius Lowe, RA (1746–93). They were living in poverty in Deptford. Dickens, Forster and Carlyle raised a fund for an annuity for them of £30. See *The Times* of 1 November 1855, p. 7.
3. Robert Lowth, *A Letter to the Right Reverend Author of 'The Divine Legation of Moses demonstrated ...'* (1765).

Friday – December 14

A milder day – so much milder that, being very desirous to go to the City, I ventured out – made my arrangements at the bank – all right. It began to rain when I went out into Birchin Lane called a cab, and came home. Turton v Burgess.[1] A great ass Burgess was; and an able, cool, judicious writer Turton. Today my presentation copies go out. Letters will soon be coming in – but few of these much to be trusted. At dinner C Cest. Finished Turton.

1. Thomas Turton, *A Vindication of the Literary Character of the late Professor Porson from the Animadversions of the Right Reverend Thomas Burgess ... By Crito Cantabrigiensis* (1827).

Saturday – December 15

Woolston and Leland.[1] Rainy, and not cold – staid at home all the morning. Charles called. Vexed to find that he had not received his copy. Then a note from B to say that H's copy had not come. I was angry at the negligence and delay, and thought of writing to Longman. But I suppose the copies will reach their destinations today at latest. If not [words erased]. Leigh Hunt wrote to ask for a loan of a few pounds – Photius. Malden called. To dinner, not very willingly, at W.T. Large party – Dr and Mrs Vaughan,[2] the Merivales, the G. Denmans,[3] the Milmans. Oppressed and hardly able to breathe. Exerted myself and increased the oppression. Glad to be at home again. The copies are out – Hydr.

1. Perhaps Thomas Woolston (1670–1733), freethinker; and John Leland (1691–1766), nonconformist divine.
2. Charles Vaughan married Catherine Maria Stanley (1821–99), daughter of Edward Stanley, Bishop of Norwich.
3. George Denman (1819–96) was a barrister, the fourth son of Lord Denman, the Lord Chief Justice. He married in 1852 Charlotte Hope (*c.* 1829–1905).

Sunday – December 16

Staid at home all day – Better – Holland called – very kind. He had read the 1st Chapter and came to pay compliments which were the more welcome because my chief misgivings are about that Chapter. Read Photius – Cicero de Finibus – Excellent Parriana – incredibly absurd – in the afternoon T and G. In the evening E. to dinner.

Monday – December 17

Article on my book in The Times[1] – not very well written, but in tone very much what I wished, that is to say laudatory without any appearance of puffing. Bad day – cold, foggy with east wind. Staid at home – Ld Glenelg and R. Hamilton[2] called – R.H. going to the Crimea. I gave them copies of my book. Letters from Stephen and Adolphus, kind, but neither of them can have read enough to judge of the book – Cicero de Finibus. I always liked it best of his philosophical works; and I am still of the same mind. Began the Tusculan disputations – never great favourites with me. At dinner Trol X Χεοτ detestable – a wretched daub, not tolerable even as a caricature, for it is not even the caricature of anything that really exists. Longman came today. Told me that they must print more copies. He was for 5,000. I insisted that there should only be 2,000. He told me that there was a paper on my book in the Daily News.[3] I sent for it. Poorly written – but very favourable. Much oppression of the chest today. Hydr.

1. *The Times*, 17 December 1855, p. 4, col. 3.

2. Robert George Crookshank Hamilton (1836–95) was in the Commissariat Department. His father was Zachary Macaulay Hamilton (1805–76), minister of Bressay, Shetland, whose mother Helen was Zachary Macaulay's sister and so TBM's aunt. She married the Revd Gavin Hamilton (1780–1849).
3. *Daily News*, 17 December 1855, p. 2.

Tuesday – December 18

Times again – laudatory – but not particularly well executed. A heap of letters – begging letters, etc etc. – the proofs of my paper on Goldsmith from Black. After breakfast corrected the 2nd vol. and sent it to Paternoster Row. Ordered a copy to be sent to Walter Ellis – wrote to him. R.H. is going to the Crimea. He seems really a very deserving and promising young man. Corrected the proofs of the paper on Goldsmith. H. sate with me half an hour this morning. Most kind and full of affectionate sympathy. Daily News again – as laudatory as before.[1] Tusculan disputations – Parriana – at dinner X Xεοτ stuff beneath contempt.

---

1. *Daily News*, 18 December 1855. Four columns, mostly of quotations from *HE*.

Wednesday – December 19

Very cold though the wind from South or South East. A succession of calls – Charles's boy[1] – a nice fellow, blunt, frank and good humoured – John's boy[2] – not much to my taste. Clerk from Longman's with news that the two first vols must be reprinted – the sale has during the last few days been very great – H and B – I had meant to go with them to look at D'Orsay's house at Kensington:[3] but it was much too cold for me to venture out. Lefevre called. He had only begun the book and probably not seen his own name there.[4] He came to talk about the diplomatic examinations. Sir H. Holland to tell me that he had nearly finished the 3rd vol and liked it better than the two 1st. A rapturous letter about it from a lawyer in the Temple. The Scotch Free Press – not generally friendly to me and The Globe,[5] both loud in commendation. Wrote to S and F about money matters.[6] Glad that I am now able to make them quite comfortable. At dinner Ward of TC.[7] Read some pamphlets wh I bought from Brown in Oldthorpe & Smith[8] in Soho Sq – Mordecai[9] – Mouse turned Rat[10] – Vandeput and Trentham.[11] By the bye a letter from Captain Townshend[12] asking me to Raynham offering his ancestors' papers. Excused myself of course.

---

1. Probably Thomas George Macaulay (1842–64). He died of typhoid on his return from India. Cf. *LM*, vol. 6, p. 213 and n.
2. Henry George Macaulay (1837–69).
3. Presumably the small house occupied by Count Alfred D'Orsay next door to Lady Blessington, who lived at Gore House, Kensington, 1835–49. See M. Sadleir, *Blessington-D'Orsay* (London, 1933).

4. TBM refers to a note in ch. 11 thanking Lefevre and Thoms for their help with the archives of the House of Lords; see *HE*, ch. 11, *CW*, vol. 2, p. 468n.
5. *The Globe*, 19 December 1855, p. 1, gives reasons for the popularity of *HE*.
6. *LM*, vol. 5, pp. 479–80.
7. Frances Trollope, *The Ward of Thorpe Combe*, 3 vols (London, 1841), republished as *The Ward* in 1857.
8. Perhaps John Russell Smith, 36 Soho Square.
9. Perhaps by John Dunton (1659–1733), *Mordecai's Memorial: or, There's Nothing Done for him ... Writen by an Unknown and Disinterested Clergyman* (1718).
10. *The Mouse Grown a Rat* (1702), in TBM's Library SC, no. 647.
11. Sir George Vanderput, Bart (1729–84), wrote *A Dialogue between Two Free Electors, Dick and Tim, on a Certain Day of the Poll for L—d T—th—m and Sir G—e V—d-p—t* (1749). The contest in question was the Westminster Election.
12. John Townsend (1798–1863), MP for Tamworth, 1847–50, 1852–5; later fourth Marquess Townshend, of Raynham in Norfolk. He was a Captain in the navy; he later became Rear Admiral.

Thursday – December 20

Still very cold, though the wind rather southerly. Very sorry that I could not go to dine at W.T. Staid by my fire all day. Parriana[1] – Parr's Dedication to Hurd.[2] Milman's book – very good indeed. I have been neglecting Photius and Pulci of late. Bits of praise from time to time. No blame as yet. Plenty will come before long. Purchased some Spanish books read an act of a play of Solis[3] of which many years ago I read a bad prose translation at Clapham. It was quite different from the translation, not merely as to form but as respected the substance and the conception of the characters. At dinner Ward of T.C.

1. By E. H. Barker (1829).
2. *Tracts by Warburton and a Warburtonian*, published by Samuel Parr (1747–1825) in 1789, contained tracts by Warburton and Hurd that their authors had wished to suppress, prefaced by 'a bitter, biting Dedication to Dr Hurd' (1720–1808), who as Bishop of Worcester was Parr's diocesan. See W. Derry, *D. Parr* (Oxford, 1966), pp. 83–6.
3. Antonio de Solis y Ribadeneira (1610–86).

Friday – December 21

Another bitter day. Still by my fire. Letter from Ld Stanhope from a Mr Tighe at Limerick.[1] Read Solis and Fray Gerandio – looked into a history of the religious wars of France by a Mrs Marsh.[2] H and G called, very pleasant. E to dinner – Hydr – I saw Bright today.

1. Probably Robert Tighe (*c.* 1807–81), a graduate of Trinity College, Dublin, barrister, and member of Limerick's Library and Scientific Society, and benefactor of its Athenaeum.
2. Anne Caldwell became Mrs Marsh (1791–1874). She wrote *The Protestant Reformation in France* in 1847, as well as several novels and a translation of the *Song of Roland*.

Saturday – December 22

Still very cold – letters and papers. Praise in the Notes and Queries, in the Inverness paper,[1] from Jowett etc. Read Photius, Morgan's Essay on Falstaff,[2] Lady Morgan's Novice[3] and Sackville.[4] H and T to dinner. The Examiner – very favourable.[5] I was a little oppressed in the evening and coughed much.

1. *Inverness Courier*, 20 December 1855, p. 2, where TBM is praised for his powerful writings, and p. 5, where an article on 'Macaulay in the Highlands' is a little more critical of his stress on Highland poverty and primitivism. The editor was, of course, Robert Carruthers, who in June 1850 helped TBM with material for the *History* (see Volume 2, entry for 26 June 1850).
2. Maurice Morgann, *An Essay on the Dramatic Character of Sir John Falstaff* (1777) (new edn 1820, 1825 and 1912 (ed. W.A. Gill)). For Morgann, see *DNB* and Boswell's *Johnson*.
3. *The Novice of St. Dominick*, 4 vols (1805).
4. Perhaps *The Trial by Courtmartial of Lord George Sackville* (1760), *SC*, no. 888.
5. *Examiner*, 22 December 1855, pp. 803–5, praises TBM's 'perfect mastery of rhetorical skill'; he had 'the rare art of giving its meaning and weight to every word'. The writer then gives extracts on the origins of the National Debt, Swift's audience with William III, the trial of Lord Mohun for killing William Mountford, and the death of Mary.

Sunday – December 23

A change of weather. It blew and rained hard in the night. Today the air is mild and the wind westerly. I went out for the first time since Saturday week; walked to Brooks's and the Athenaeum. Very well satisfied with the criticisms which I saw. The Spectator growls, as it always does. But never was more innocent ill nature. Home – read some of Photius. He sent me to Lycias and I read with the greatest delight some of those incomparable speeches – incomparable, I mean, in their kind, which is not the highest kind. They are wonderful – Scarlett speaking in the style of Addison. Park's Travels in the old edition.[1] how familiar to me forty five years and more ago – not seen, I think, during the last thirty years and more. T and G called. E to dinner.

1. Perhaps Mungo Park, *Travels in the Interior Districts of Africa ...* (1799).

Monday – December 24

Another fine mild day – yet I felt little if at all better for it. Letters from Ld Lne and Ld Shelburne – very kind. But I feel that it will be impossible for me to go to Bowood. A bale of papers from Longman. Very eulogistic – with the usual allowance. Derwent called[1] – pleasant – H Rogers called. I am always glad to see him. Both praised my book highly. I am now quite at ease as to what I had dreaded – incurring the disgrace of a failure after such immense expectation. Read little that was solid today. At five Bright came, not summoned, but welcome – prescribed a new mixture. At dinner ΘK.[2] After dinner the Idler[3] – Mustard poultice. Bohn has sent me his edition of Addison.[4] I wrote to thank him, but pointed out the omission of the two delightful Spectators in the 8th Vol.

1. Presumably Derwent Coleridge (1800–83).
2. *The Ward of Thorpe Combe*, by Francis Trollope.
3. Dr Johnson's papers in the *Universal Chronicle* (1758–60).
4. *The Works of the Right Honourable Joseph Addison*, 6 vols (1854–6), with notes by Robert Hurd, DD, Bishop of Worcester.

Tuesday – December 25

Again – And in some aspects a happy Christmas – fame – fortune – affections – under these heads I have nothing to ask more, but my health is worse and worse every year. No acute suffering however; and nothing that menaces my head. Finished Photius. Cicero de Natura Deorum. The day mild, but very wet. To W.T. passed the afternoon pleasantly and quietly, though breathing with effort. Ellis and Frank to dinner. Snapdragon – the evening agreeable. – Home at ½ after nine.

Wednesday – December 26

Still mild and wet. My chest however still suffers, though somewhat less. A letter of praise from Ld John. Ld Duncan[1] had sent T a paper containing criticisms every one of which I victoriously refuted. I sent the refutation in a very civil letter to his Lordship – I do not think that he will have a word to say in answer. Cicero de Divinatione – The 2nd Book excellent. What a man he was! To think that the De Div, the De Fato and the De Officiis should all have been the fruits of his leisure during the few months that he outlived the death of Caesar. During those months Cicero was as busy a man as any in the republic, a leader of the Senate. The finest of his Senatorial speeches – spoken or not – belongs to that time. He seems to me to have been at the head of the minds of the second order. Bright came. H and B called. More criticisms. The Morning Herald of course hostile. Sir H. Holland full of praise – At dinner ΘK[2].

1. Adam Duncan (1812–67), later second Earl of Camperdown.
2. *The Ward of Thorpe Combe.*

Thursday – December 27

Still fine and mild. But I am not much the better for it. I went out however. Royal Institution – Then W.T. pleasant hour there. Home by Omnibus. Read miscellaneous trifles from the back rows of my books. Nathan's Reminiscences of Byron[1] – Colman's Broad Grins[2] – Strange's Letter to Ld Bute[3] etc. – Gibbon's answer to Warburton about the 6th Aeneid – Vindication.[4] At dinner ΘK. Great difficulty in finding the book. In the evening Middleton's Free Inquiry.[5]

1. Isaac Nathan, *Fugitive Pieces and Reminiscences of Lord Byron ...* (1829).
2. George Colman (the younger), *Broad Grins ...* (1802).
3. Sir Robert Strange, *An Inquiry ... into the Rise and Establishment of the Royal Academy ... To which is Prefixed a Letter to the Earl of Bute ...* (1775).
4. *Critical Objections on the Sixth Book of the Aeneid* (1770), in answer to Warburton's *A Dissertation on the Sixth Book of Virgil's Aeneid* (1753); and *A Vindication of Some Passages in the Ffifteenth and Sixteenth chapters ...* (1779).
5. Conyers Middleton, *A Free Inquiry into the Miraculous Powers ...* (1749).

Friday – December 28

Fine and mild – ought to have gone out. But staid at home expecting Bright and H to call. Neither came; and I lost my walk – read Middleton. Letters from various quarters – praise and corrections. Ld Duncan called – owned himself refuted. Tom Taylor wrote about a poor fellow named Chatto[1] of whom I have sometimes bought old pamphlets in Museum Street – sent 10£. A Miss Goble[2] asks me to buy a cabinet from her – a woman at Worthing of whom I never heard. At dinner ΘK. Middleton. By the bye I had today a letter from Derwent Coleridge about the Greek spoken in Calabria. I looked into the matter a little and sent him an explanation which must satisfy him.

1. William Andrew Chatto (1799–1854) was a miscellaneous writer and associate of Taylor. He edited a comic daily called *Puck*, which failed, but which might have inspired the launching of *Punch*.
2. There are several Gobles in the Worthing Census for 1851, none with any obvious connection with TBM.

Saturday – December 29

Still fine. After breakfast T and G. Then walked out – R.I. Athenaeum. The weekly Journals generally very laudatory – Home. Middleton's works – Milman called and sate half-an-hour. At dinner στρατ ησσ.[1] In the evening Fray,[2] Lavington, Rimius[3] etc., Morav.

1. A variant of *Strategems Defeated*, by Mary Meeke.
2. Perhaps José de Isla, *Fray Gerundio* (1758).
3. Perhaps Heinrich Rimius, *A Candid Narrative of ... the Herrnhuters, Commonly Called Moravians or Unitas Fratrum* (1753).

Sunday – December 30

Rainy and stormy. Read Cobbett's Register. It cleared up. To W.T. met there C Buxton, Charles, Price and his wife – bad account of George[1] – went to his house with Charles to inquire. I fear the end is approaching. Home – Cobbett – powerful and interesting: but the impression of a prolonged perusal of such venomous invective and gross sophistry becomes painful. Lavington's Methodists and Papists compared[2] – E to dinner.

1. G. O. Trevelyan's annotation 'Babington'.
2. George Lavington, *The Enthusiasm of Methodists and Papists compared ...* (1749).

Monday – December 31

Fine day. Longman called – promises me 20,000£ for the year. Letters and criticisms pour in. Praise greatly preponderates. but there is a strong mixture of censure. I can however see no sign that these volumes excite less interest than their predecessors. To W.T. – Susan there – Mary's daughter.[1] Came home with them in the carriage. George a little and but a little better. Fresh criticisms etc. – The Londonderry people seem to be in great glee. At dinner στρατ ησσ Cobbett – Hydr.

1. Susan Emma Parker (1836–1913), daughter of Mary Parker, née Babington. She had married in 1853 Archibald Smith (1813–72) of Jordan Hill, a barrister.

[Macaulay began the year by formally resigning his seat for Edinburgh. He was relieved to be succeeded by Adam Black. He decided it was a good time to leave the Albany, and he leased a house called Holly Lodge on Camden Hill in February, moving in (after a month of extensive repairs) on 2 May. He also resumed the spring tours with the Trevelyans, this time to Rochester and Canterbury from 20 to 24 March. His work on the *History* was suspended, but he finished a long essay on Dr Johnson for the *Encyclopaedia Britannica* in July. In the same month he made a short visit to the Stanhopes in Chevening. On 20 August he went with Ellis on an Italian tour, visiting Turin, Milan, Verona and Venice and returning on 27 September. Settling into Holly Lodge with his 10,000 books around him, he began writing the *History* again, and added to Chapter V the famous note against the criticisms of Dixon on Penn.]

Tuesday – January 1 1856

A new year. I am happy in fame, fortune, family affection – most eminently so. My health is very indifferent. Yet I have no pain. My faculties are unimpaired. My spirits are very seldom depressed; and I am not without hope of being set up again. Still reviews and letters pouring in – vehement praise, some censure, a little furious abuse. Fanny tells me that a sermon was preached at Brighton to my praise and glory last Sunday. Sent 10£ to a ruined bookseller Cochrane.[1] Made out, not without difficulty, a German letter from one of my translators, and wrote to him. Perrotin, the French bookseller, writes to tell me that the translation is proceeding at Paris and that Amédée Pichot is in raptures. Philo; The deputation to Caligula.[2] Looked through other works. I soon became tired – The Λογος was what I chiefly looked for, and I found something – though not much. Cobbett. E to dinner. After dinner a line from B to say that George Babington was dead.[3] Much affected.

1. Unidentified.
2. Philo Judaeus who in AD 39/40 led the mission to the Emperor Gaius (Caligula) that occasioned the *De Legatione ad Gaium*.
3. George Gisborne Babington. He died at 13 Queen's Garden, Hyde Park, and was buried in Kensal Green.

Wednesday – January 2

Put on mourning for poor G.B. Letters and critiques still pouring in. I hardly know where to store them – to W.T. – Lady Stephen and her daughter[1] – Home – Cobbett – At dinner στρατ ησσ.

1. Lady Stephen was Jane Catherine Venn (1793–1875). Her daughter was Caroline Emelia Stephen (1834–1909).

Thursday – January 3

Still letters, criticisms and bills – Cobbett στρατ ησσ. Wrote to Sir W. Craig and Black about the representation of Edinburgh.[1] My mind is made up: and so I told them. Went out – nothing of interest. Read a good deal of Cobbett. At dinner στρατ.

1. Cf. *LM*, vol. 6, pp. 6–7. TBM was succeeded by Black.

Friday – January 4

Breakfast party – Jowett, Ellis, H, B, Butler, and Hawkins' young Trin[ity] fellows[1] – a pleasant party. At least I thought so – After long silence and solitude I poured myself out very freely and genially. They staid till past one – a pretty good proof that they were entertained.[2] The day mild but wet. Read Cobbett – E to dinner – Sprats – I found on Tuesday that he liked them as much as I or more. In the afternoon Stapleton[3] called – a bore – told me that the Portuguese Minister[4] had spoken to him about my book. I must send a copy to the King. As S went out Adolphus came in. Very kind and complimentary. I really believe his compliments to be sincere.

1. Henry Montagu Butler (1833–1918) became Headmaster of Harrow, 1860–85, and Master of Trinity, 1886–1918. Francis Vaughan Hawkins (1833–1908) became a barrister.
2. Cf. Jowett, quoted in George Trevelyan's Introduction to E. Graham's *Harrow Life of Henry Montagu Butler*, ch. 24: 'Entertained! I should think we were entertained! Nobody ever talked like Macaulay.'
3. Augustus Granville Stapleton (1800–80) had been Canning's private secretary and became his biographer.
4. Count Francisco Lavradio (1797–1870).

Saturday – January 5

Still very mild and damp. Letter from Guizot. Kind compliments. Question about the place where the L[or]ds received C[harles] II on May 29 1660. Odd that a foreigner should trouble himself about so minute a matter. I went to the R.I. – got down the Journals, and soon found that the Lords were in the drawing room at Whitehall. The Commons were in the B[anquetin]g House – To W.T. H and B out – wrote letters, one to poor Sarah Anne,[1] another to Guizot. H and B came home to lunch. They have got the house in Gr Crescent.[2] I am glad of it. Home – wrote to the Portuguese Minister and sent him a copy for his master – The Revue Britannique very eulogistic as well it may be, seeing that the editor is translating my book[3] – Cobbett – at dinner strat.

1. Née Pearson (1786–1870), the widow of George Babington.
2. No. 8, Grosvenor Crescent.
3. He was Amédée Pichot.

Sunday – January 6

To my great sorrow the wind is in the East; And the day is foggy. However I am pretty well. I staid at home all day – read two or three good speeches of Lysias – heard from the Portuguese minister – very civil indeed – read old journals – Cobbett. E to dinner.

Monday – January 7

Another heap of criticisms – praise and blame. But it matters little. The victory is won. The book has not disappointed the very highly raised expectations of the public. The first fortnight was the time of peril. Now all is safe. Yesterday and today I have been reading over my old journals of 1852 and 1853. What a strange interest they have. No kind of reading is so delightful, so fascinating, as this minute history of a man's self. At dinner στρατ. Today Sir J Boileau sent me some game and a civil letter with an extract from a letter of Guizot – very laudatory. Butler called today a pleasing young man.

Tuesday – January 8

Slept till half after nine. Waked by Wm with the newspaper and letters. A letter from Craig. By the bye I had one from Black yesterday. Craig will not at present go into parliament. Black consents. An excellent Member he will make if his health can stand it. But he must be near 70; and how a man who at such an age goes for the first time into the H. of C can bear, even during a month, the hours and the air, I cannot conceive. Wrote to him and to Craig. Read my old journals with intense and even painful interest. A silly impertinent anonymous letter about Maurice the socialist divine[1] – Ld Campbell called – full of kindness and compliment. Pigot[2] the Irish Chief Baron about a son of his who wants to be a candidate for the Indian Civil service – at dinner στρατ.

1. F. D. Maurice (1805–72).
2. David Richard Pigot (1797–1873), Chief Baron of the Exchequer in Ireland, 1846–73. He had been MP for Clonmel, 1839–46. One son, James Quain Pigot (1835–1913), at this time a law student, became Puisne Judge of the High Court in Calcutta, 1882–96, and from 1892–3 Vice-Chancellor of the University of Calcutta.

Wednesday – January 9

Soon after breakfast T and G. G staid some time rummaging the Gazettes and Monthly Mercuries for accounts of the battles of La Hogue, Steinkirk and Landen – Journals – Greatly interested. Vile weather – East wind – snow – sleet, dull moist fog. Staid at home. Hawkins called – a clever young man, but not quite so pleasing to me as his schoolfellow Butler – At dinner finished στρατ.

Thursday – January 10

Fine and clear day but cold, and wind N.E. – staid at home – wrote with much labour a letter to Carruthers about the Cleland family[1] – Read some of Cobbett – his Intense Comedy of 1825. E to dinner.

1. Robert Carruthers (1799–1878). He was editor of the *Inverness Courier* and had helped TBM with information about the Scottish Highlands. Carruthers was writing a life of Pope (published in 1857), and the Cleland in question was likely to be William Cleland (*c.* 1674–1748), not the Colonel of the same name who appears in *HE*, ch. 13, *CW*, vol. 3, pp. 23–4.

Friday – January 11

Third article on me in The Times[1] – three columns of small cavils and a few sentences of the most high flown praise. It matters little – Staid at home all day – Cobbett – At dinner O φυγας εν Αμηρικη.[2] Today H, G and B called – pleasant hour.

1. *The Times*, 11 January 1856, p. 5, a very cogent critique of TBM's bias and exaggeration.
2. *The Refugee in America*, by Fanny Trollope.

Saturday – January 12

The day fine and bright. I ventured out to the Museum – but regretted my rashness when I found how cold it was – I went however – was in the Chair – long sitting – Dundas, Hamilton,[1] Milman, Murchison. Home with Dundas. Found my chest the worse for my excursion – mustard poultice – Ipec. and abstemiousness however set me to rights. At dinner read a little of the Dodd family abroad.[2] Cobbett. Absurd letter and Commission from M Stewart at Florence.[3] He is a perfect pest. I will be dry and concise with him.

1. William Richard Hamilton (1777–1869). He had been secretary to Lord Elgin. He arranged the transport of the marbles to the British Museum. He became a Trustee of the British Museum, 1838–58.
2. By Charles Lever (1853–4).
3. James Montgomery Stewart (1816–89) was an attaché of the British Legation in Florence. He was the Italian correspondent of the *Morning Post*.

Sunday – January 13

Very cold – staid at home – fully resolved not to go out till the wind changes – read my oldest journals. T and B called – very pleasant talk. H and G to dine with me on Tuesday – wrote some letters etc. Cobbett. E to dinner.

Monday – January 14

Very cold – Staid at home – T and G called – read a good deal – chiefly Cobbett. Longman, then Ld Stanhope and his boys[1] – at dinner 9 days mirac.[2] Letter from Twisleton. Rush's Embassy.[3]

1. Lord Mahon had just become the fifth Earl of Stanhope. His sons were Arthur Philip (1838–1905), Edward (1840–93), Henry Augustus (1845–1933) and Philip James (1847–1923).
2. Perhaps Mrs Mary Meeke, *The Nine Days' Wonder*, 3 vols (1804).
3. Richard Rush, *Memoranda of a Residence at the Court of London* (1833 and 1845).

Tuesday – January 15

Soon after breakfast a Mr Devon from the Record Office[1] called. He wanted to see the Legge papers in the Mackintosh Collection. He fairly owned that it was for the purpose of answering me. Ld Dartmouth, who knows, according to Mr Devon, nothing at all about the matter. who does not even know what his own family archives contain, takes this mode of vindicating the founder of the family. I most willingly showed Mr Devon the M.S. which did not serve his turn. He is apparently as ignorant as Ld D – For he had never heard of the Life of James published from the Stuart Papers, or the trial of Preston, or of Dalrymple. What folly in such dunces to undertake such inquiries. I showed him, with as much civility as I could, all the sources of information. I hope that my contempt was not perceptible. Cobbett. After he came into Parliament he was nothing. He spoke feebly there when I heard him which was often. He made, I believe, one successful speech – mere banter on Plunkett – when I was absent. He proved that he was quite incapable of doing anything great in debate; and his parliamentary attendance prevented him from doing anything great with his pen. His register became as stupid as the Morning Herald. In truth his faculties were impaired by age; and the late hours of the house probably assisted to enfeeble his body and consequently his mind. His egotism and his suspicion that everybody was in a plot against him increased and at last attained such a height that he was really as mad as Rousseau. Poor creature! I could write a very curious and entertaining article on him, if I chose. Read some of Sanchez – Poesias Castellanas[2] – Some hundreds of lines of the Cid – Very curious and interesting – Homeric – but by an artist far indeed inferior to Homer. Fray Gerundio.[3] T H and G to dinner – pleasant evening with them.

1. Frederick Devon (*c.* 1800–58). He was Assistant Keeper at the Public Record Office and Records Clerk at the Duchy of Cornwall in Somerset House.
2. Tomas Antonio Sanchez (1723–1802), *Collection de Poesias Castellanas anteriores al Siglo xv* (1779–82).
3. *Historia del famoso Predicator Fray Gerundio de Campazas alias Zotes* (1758), by José Francesco de Isla (1703–81).

Wednesday – [January 16]

Irving[1] – absurd affected creature – contortion without inspiration. Rainy foggy day – but mild. Staid at home. Note from Rawlinson. He wants to take my chambers – answered him civilly – read a good deal of Fray Gerundio. A good book – but the same situations are constantly coming over and over again. As a picture of the state of learning among the educated classes in Spain a century ago – the work has great value. The traits of manners are often interesting – There is something remarkable in the simple plenty and joyousness of the life of the rustics of Old Castile. James Stephen[2] called. His manners are certainly very queer. But I have an unconquerable liking for him. E to dinner. It seems that Walpole[3] is to be our MP for the University. I sincerely regret poor Goulburn.[4] He was a good gentlemanlike fellow; and we shall miss his financial skill and experience at the Museum.

1. Perhaps Edward Irving (1792–1834), founder of the Catholic Apostolic Church.
2. James Fitzjames Stephen (1829–94).
3. Spencer Walpole was MP for Cambridge University, 1856–82.
4. Henry Goulburn (1784–1856) died 12 January 1856. He had been Chancellor of the Exchequer in Peel's government.

Thursday – January 17

Very mild and rather fine. I thought this an opportunity not to be lost, and went by omnibus into the City, – stopped in St Paul's Churchyard – to the Deanery to set right a mistake about an invitation – then on to Birchin Lane. The City exhilarated by intelligence – true I hope to God, that Russia has accepted all the terms proposed by Austria. I long for peace. Did some business – then to W.T. by Paddington Omnibus – passed an hour there very happily, and home. Bored by a letter from Bannister[1] one of those indefatigable and unreasonable men with grievances who are the pests of the public offices. Fray Gerundio again. Finished him. Looked through some of the Controversial Tracts which his Adventures called forth. I do not think that, in the opinion of serious Protestants, Father Isla would stand altogether clear from the charge of having used Scripture with levity approaching to profaneness. He seems however to have been a sincerely religious man, as well as a man of wit and taste. He had by no means escaped from the bad effects of a Spanish education, witness the childish things which he says about mathematical and experimental science. At dinner finished 9 days – I was very much oppressed by phlegm all the afternoon. After dinner I coughed violently. My stomach relieved itself – σιναπι[2] Moore's travels.[3]

1. Saxe Bannister (1790–1877). Bannister had various grievances against the Governor of New South Wales, where he was Attorney General, 1823–6; he published his grievances in a series of *Claims* in 1853.
2. A mustard poultice.
3. John Moore, author of *A Journal during a Residence in France ...* (1793) and *A View of Society and Manners ... in Italy* (1781).

Friday – January 18

Better. Mild day, but rainy and misty. Staid at home. Craig called – pleasant hour with him. Ld Glenelg called. Longman sent me some more criticisms – favourable enough. Letter from the Ap of Dublin.[1] Wrote to Hayter and Lewis about the Chilterns.[2] Wrote most of my farewell Epistle to Edinburgh. Read some of Lessing – The Wolfenbuttle [*sic*] fragments[3] of which I had often heard – Dr Moore – at dinner – Myst Hus[4] Bower and Douglas.[5]

1. Richard Whately (1787–1863), Archbishop of Dublin from 1831.
2. W. G. Hayter was the Liberal Whip and Sir George Cornewall Lewis the Chancellor of the Exchequer. TBM was asking for the office of Steward of the Chiltern Hundreds to enable him to resign his seat in Parliament.
3. *Wolfenbüttelsche Fragmente eines Ungennanten* (Wolfenbüttel Fragments from an Unknown Man) (1774–8), by G. E. Lessing.
4. Most likely *The Mysterious Husband* by Gabrieli [Mary Meeke], 4 vols (1801), a copy of which was in TBM's Library (SC, no. 763).
5. Pamphlets dealing with the quarrel between Archibald Bower (1686–1766) and the Revd John Douglas (1721–1807), later Bishop of Salisbury. Bower, who had been a Jesuit, was accused of secretly belonging to the Roman Catholic Church while professing conformity to the Church of England.

Saturday – January 19

Mild but wet. Breakfast party – H, M, Twisleton, Glenelg, Milman and Mrs M, Ld Stanhope and Lady S – not unpleasant. Finished and sent off farewell letter to Edinburgh. Wrote to that pest Saxe Bannister. I hope that I shall quiet him – I was very plainspoken. Bower and Douglas. St Simon. At dinner M.H.

Sunday – January 20

A very mild day – went to W.T. a pleasant hour or two there. Home – St Simon – E to dinner.

Monday – January 21

Rainy. At home all day. Bannister has taken huff and sent back my subscription for his book.[1] Be it so. Charles's boy called to beg for autographs. Craig called – A most kind letter from Rogers. Too partial as he always is to me. St Simon. Surprised to find how much smaller the proportion of interesting matter to the mass is than I had imagined. Began Milman's Latin Christianity.[2] Bating the faults of style, it is most valuable. A letter from him about a house on Camden Hill – At dinner finished.

1. Presumably the book Bannister was writing, which appeared as *William Paterson, the Merchant Statesman and Founder of the Bank of England: His Life and Trials* (Edinburgh, 1858).
2. Henry Hart Milman, *History of Latin Christianity* (1854–5).

Tuesday – January 22

A letter from the Duchess of Argyll about this house on Camden Hill. Holly Lodge it is called. Wrote to her, to the Dean and to Hannah. The wind east but my chest not worse. Indeed I have gained and lost less this year by the changes of wind and weather than in former years. Read Lessing – five dialogues on Freemasonry.[1] Incredibly absurd. They lowered my opinion of him. Milman – read a good deal – more impressed than ever by the contrast between the substance and the style. The substance excellent – the style very much otherwise. At dinner the Nowlans.[2] Afterwards some of my Essays – Bacon – D'Arblay.

1. G. E. Lessing, *Ernst und Falk* (1777–80).
2. By John Banim (1826).

Wednesday – January 23

A beautiful day – almost like May – moisture and sunshine. S. West Wind. My farewell letter to Edinburgh is in The Times.[1] Invitation to Windsor for next

Monday – much vexed – must go, if possible; – To W.T. Found Mrs G.T.[2] there – went with H and B to see the house about which the Duchess and the Dean had written to me. It is in many respects the very thing. But I must know more and think more before I decide. Home – read a good deal of Milman – at dinner finished the Nowlans.

1. *The Times*, 23 January 1856, p. 11, col f. It is dated 19 June and printed, from the *Scotsman* of the same date, in *LM*, vol. 6, p. 9.
2. Frances Anne Trevelyan, née Lumsden (*c.* 1810–77), was the wife of Charles Trevelyan's brother George.

Thursday – January 24

My digestion not quite right – of late my stomach has plagued me little. My troubles have been from the respiratory organs. But I had at night some twinges and uneasy sensations once familiar. On the whole, however, my sleep has of late been very sweet and refreshing. A great blessing. At breakfast some praise and a little foolish abuse from Edinburgh. Busy correcting Vol 3 for another edition, whenever such an edition shall be wanted. Lessing[1] – I do not much take to him. His Laocoon seems to me far superior to anything else that he wrote. I have read his Nathan and Emilia Galeotti. I like neither; and, as they are universally allowed to be his best dramas, I do not mean to make acquaintance with any others. Milman – Social Religion Exemplified[2] – E to dinner.

1. G. E. Lessing, *Laocoön* ... (1766); *Nathan Der Weise* (1779); *Emilia Galotti* (1772). TBM's copy of *Laocoön* (Berlin, 1839) was in his library, SC, no. 399.
2. By Matthias Maurice (1750).

Friday – January 25

Fine day – To the Athenaeum – Saw some praise of myself where I expected none – in the Record.[1] Pestered by a foolish Sir James Riddell[2] about something which I had said of the Riddells in the 1st Vol of my history. Sent him Chapter and verse. To W.T. We talked about Holly Lodge. Yesterday Sir H. Holland called on me, and highly approved of the situation etc. I think and so do H and B that it seems to be the very thing. Home – found a most gracious autograph letter in English from His Most Faithful Majesty.[3] Finished Soc. Rel. Ex. Milman called – left me the Clementina[4] – very kind of him. A Yankee named Field[5] called. Very aristocratical in his politics, and abominating the whole system of government in his country. At dinner Βαρν Λμηρ[6] Life of Astley Cooper.[7]

1. The *Record*, 25 January 1856, p. 4, b, c and d. A very shrewd and penetrating article, much more informed than the paper's review of vols 1 and 2 (see Volume 2, entry for 23

January 1849, n. 4), and concluding with an estimate of TBM's position in modern British historiography.

2. Probably Sir James Milles Riddell, second Bart (1787–1861). In *HE*, ch. 5, TBM says that a Riddell arrested the Duke of Argyle, and 'on this account the whole race of Riddells was, during more than a century, held in abhorrence by the tribe of Campbell' (*CW*, vol. 1, pp. 436). The seat of the Riddells was Strontian in Argyllshire, and the second Baronet was Deputy Lieutenant for the County.
3. The King of Portugal, Peter V (1837–61).
4. See *LM*, vol. 6, p. 10 and n. 3.
5. Maunsell Bradhurst Field (1822–75). There is a description of his conversation with TBM in his *Memories of Many Men* (New York, 1875), pp. 140–2.
6. Barn Amer, i.e. *The Barnabys in America*, later shortened to Βαρν Αμ.
7. B. Cooper, *The Life of Sir Astley Cooper, BT* (1843).

Saturday – January 26

I am surprised to find that there is a clamour at Edinburgh about manoeuvring and surprise. A more absurd clamour never was got up. My conduct was even scrupulously fair; and it is the extreme of absurdity to pretend that three weeks is too short a time to give either Tories or Radicals an opportunity of looking out for a good candidate. But it matters little. To the R.I. – thence to W.T. I hear of puffs on me in the Herald and Chronicle. I see one in the Daily News.[1] Showed H and B a letter from the house agent – very encouraging as far as it goes. Lydia [Rose][2] came to lunch – as amiable and a cheerful as ever. Home – found a letter from Mrs Crinean[3] asking for a loan of 200£. I sent her 100£, not as a loan. But I told her that it was very inconvenient to me to do so, and that she must not expect similar assistance for the future. She no doubt has seen in the newspapers that I have been receiving mountains of gold lately. That wretched James Mills has sent a scurrilous begging letter in his usual style. He hears that I have made 30,000£ by my malignant abuse of good men. Will I not send some of it to him? Charles called. I dined at home and finished Βαρν Αμ.

1. The *Morning Herald*, 25 January, p. 13, gave more praise to TBM's colleague Craig. The *MC* for 26 January, p. 4 d, e, gave a long account of TBM's parliamentary career. *Daily News*, 25 January, p. 4.
2. The surname added by George Trevelyan.
3. Frances Barker Crinean, née Mills (*c.* 1797–1860), was TBM's cousin, being a niece of Selina Macaulay, TBM's mother. She lived at Bedminster, near Bristol. Her husband, the Revd James Crinean (*c.* 1794–1861), ran a 'classical academy' at Durdham Down, which did not pay its way. They had three children, Frances, Margaret and Richard.

Sunday – January 27

A cold day. I staid at home reading – E to dinner.

Monday – January 28

To breakfast with Ld Stanhope in his new house.[1] The wind West, but the day cold. I met Gladstone and his wife, Ld Stanley, Reeve.[2] Not an unpleasant party. A good house. Home in time to receive H and B who came to lunch. The house agent at one.[3] All very satisfactory. Gave him instructions. Lunch. When H and B were gone set out for the Waterloo Station. To Windsor. I was rather uneasy for the weather was cold and there was much rain and sleet. However I found myself at five seated by a warm fire reading Saturnin Fichet.[4] Dinner was at ½ before 7 on account of the play. I was glad to meet Ld and Lady Stanhope again. Ld and Lady John Russell were there, Ld and Lady Stanley of Alderley, Pemberton Leigh. The dinner got over pretty well. I sate by Lady John. Then to the Theatre. A Comedy of Tom Taylor's – Still Waters.[5] It was good – at least effective – and well acted. A trumpery afterpiece but prettily dressed – A set of smart romps in the powder and rouge of the old regime. The Queen spoke to me very graciously after the play. It was near one before I got to bed; and then it was long before I got to sleep.

1. 3 Grosvenor Place Houses.
2. Reeve's account of this occasion, and of TBM's conversation, is in *Memoirs of Henry Reeve*, ed. J. K. Laughton, 2 vols (1898), vol. 1, pp. 350–1.
3. Probably either William or John Mares, upholsterers and house agents, 21 Lower Belgrave Street, Eaton Square. John Mares (1809–91) is evidently the visitor mentioned below; see entry for 1 March 1856.
4. Frédéric Soulié, *Les Aventures de Saturnin Fichet* (1847).
5. *Still Waters Run Deep* (1850). This was a repetition of a production at the Olympic Theatre the year before.

Tuesday – January 29

A fine but cold day. Pretty easy. To breakfast at ½ after 9 in the well remembered room with the Tapestry of Meleager's adventures. Staid some time after breakfast chatting with Ld S of A and P L. Went with Ld Stanhope to the library Looked at Gilray's caricatures. Glover[1] was forced to go to a wedding at St George's Chapel. A lady of the household noosed.[2] Went back to my room read till lunch time. Joined the ladies at lunch. Lady John asked me to look in on Ld J. He has a very bad cold and is quite laid up. I went, and sate an hour with him – then to my room and read. Gibbs[3] came, and insisted on introducing me to the P of W. I had to go to H.R.H' s room – to stand before a boy of fourteen, sirring him and bowing to him. Wretched work! How much happier he would be with a more manly education. I feel too for that nice girl the Princess Royal.[4] To be betrothed to a foreigner whom she cannot care a rush for. And all from a senseless family pride unknown to the great old Sovereigns of England. Why cannot she marry as the daughters of the Plantagenets married? Dinner at 8. I sate between Lady

John and Lady S of A – not unpleasant. After dinner the Queen talked to me very kindly and agreeably. I got to my room just at midnight. I have suffered less from the cold than I had expected. I suspect that the cleanness of the country air has done me good.

---

1. John Hulbert Glover (*c.* 1793–1860) was the Queen's Librarian.
2. Maria Henrietta Phipps (1837–1915), daughter of the Keeper of the Privy Purse, Sir Charles Phipps (1801–56), married Captain Frederick Sayer (1831–68). *The Letters of Queen Victoria*, 1st series (London, 1907), vol. 3, p. 215
3. Frederick Waymouth Gibbs (1821–98) was tutor to the Prince of Wales, the future Edward VII.
4. Princess Victoria (1840–1901) married Prince Frederick William (1831–88), later Frederick III, King of Prussia and German Emperor, on 25 January 1858. The engagement was not formally announced until May 1857, but it was common knowledge before then. See Elizabeth Longford, *Victoria RI* (London, 1964), pp. 259–67.

Wednesday – January 30

After a pleasant breakfast off by the 10.25 train – Ld and Lady Stanhope in the same carriage. We were joined by an MP a great bore, Apsley Pellatt.[1] He talked. Ye Gods how he did talk. Ld and Ldy S took me in their carriage to the Albany. Found letters which I passed some time in answering. A Mrs Macknight[2] – mad or worse – who is separated from her husband and seems to wish me to take his place, a Mr Tupper[3] who wants room to be made for an ancestor of his in my book etc. etc. The house agent called – satisfactory – then H and B – very pleasant. Read some Spectators. At dinner – Saturnin Fichet. Fraser's Magazine[4] – very laudatory. The author evidently John Kemble. He is quite right in saying that I have passed lightly over continental politics. But was this wrong? I think that I could defend myself. I am writing a history of England. And as to grubbing, as he recommends, in Saxon and Hessian Archives for the purpose of ascertaining all the details of the continental negotiations of that time I should have doubled my labour, already severe enough. That I have not given a generally correct view of our continental relations he certainly has not shown.

---

1. Apsley Pellatt (1791–1863); MP for Southwark, 1852–7. For Emily Eden's reaction to Macaulay's railway carriage talk, see *Miss Eden's Letters*, ed. Violet Dickinson (1919), p. 368.
2. Sarah Thorne (1836–99), actress and theatre manager. She married Thomas Macknight, whom TBM disliked, see above, entry for 3 December 1853.
3. Perhaps Martin Farquhar Tupper (1810–89), a barrister and author of *The Proverbial Philosophy* (1838). He may have been pressing the case for an ancestor, John Tupper, who 'conveyed, at great personal risk, information to the English Admiral, Russell, which led to the Victory of La Hague' (*Burke's Landed Gentry*, 1921). But TBM makes no mention of him in *HE*.
4. *Fraser's Magazine*, 53 (February 1856), pp. 147–66. Signed 'J.M.K.'.

Thursday – January 31

Bad day. At home. Ld Granville called. Suffered a good deal. Read Spectators etc. – At dinner finished S.F. Mustard poultice.

Friday – February 1

Better. Weather still cold and dreary – staid at home. Ld Glenelg called – Lord Lansdowne. The Session has opened quietly and well. A great heap of monthly criticism sent me by Longman – generally laudatory – sometimes hostile – but, whether laudatory or hostile, for the most part very shallow. I could review myself better, whichever side I took, than any of my reviewers. At dinner Manners of the Day[1] – a Life of Munden.[2] By the bye I forgot – an odd forgetfulness – that today I read right through Cicero's Offices, and two books of the Metamorphosis. The Offices I do not rate high, except for the style which is, as usual, most pellucid. As a system nothing can be more wretched. Particular remarks and illustrations are often excellent. The second book of the Metamorphosis is as good as anything in Ariosto, to say the least.

1. By Henry Colburn; published anonymously (1830).
2. Perhaps *Memoirs of J. S. Munden*, by his son (T. S. Munden) (1844) (SC, no. 516). Munden (1758–1832) was an actor.

Saturday – February 2

A letter from the Ld Provost of Edinburgh[1] enclosing an Address from the Electors unanimously voted in a great meeting. I was really touched. Wrote to him. More criticism. Much correspondence with people who write about my last volumes. Sent 10£ to the sister of poor Sidney Walker.[2] I have got rid, thank God, of Mrs Macknight, who must be a fool or worse. Ld Hatherton sent me some portions of Ld Dudley's journal which had by chance been rescued from the common destruction, but are soon to perish. The loss will not be great. There is nothing in them except the information which they give as to the writer's character. That, to be sure, is of some value. A man of enormous wealth, high rank, in the prime of life, as he was when part of the journal was written, with considerable talents and learning, and a high reputation in society, ennuyé – sick of life – afraid of death – without a friend – and dying – as he thought of the pox. The only important historical part which I found was that in 1828 the Duke of Wellington left it to his colleagues to consider whether he could properly be at once 1st Ld of the Treasury and Commander in Chief. Lyndhurst, Dudley, Peel, Bathurst, Ellenborough against. Only one of the Cabinet for.[3] The name carefully scratched out, but certainly from signs which I discovered Aberdeen – and he hesitatingly and feebly. "He", says Ld D "hates liberty and the people overmuch." And I have seen this man the head of a

Whig Ministry, and a very respectable head he would have been, but for the war. Adolphus called. Wrote to Edinburgh – turned over books – finished Munden's Life – At dinner Manners of the Day[4] – Ovid's Metamorphoses ναυσ.

1. Sir John Melville (1802–60) was Lord Provost from 1854 to 1859; knighted 1859. TBM's reply is in *LM*, vol. 6, p. 13.
2. William Sidney Walker (1795–1846), poet and Shakespearean critic, who had been a Fellow of Trinity College and died in 1846 after being dependent on private charity since 1830. His sister Maria Essington Walker (1805–78) was a widow and ran a school in Chiswick.
3. According to Lady Longford, the cabinet was unanimous. *Wellington – Pillar of State*, (London, 1972), p. 154.
4. By Mrs Gore (1830).

Sunday – February 3

Cold day – the wind however southing – staid at home – read the Annals of Queen Anne's Reign – Boyer's[1] – some of the Metamorphoses – some of Talfourd's Life of C. Lamb.[2] E to dinner – vexed to find that his circumstances are less prosperous than formerly – the reports less in demand.[3] I wish I could serve him. Wrote to Fanny.[4]

1. Abel Boyer, *The History of the Reign of Queen Anne, digested into Annals*, 11 vols (1703–13).
2. T. N. Talfourd, *The Letters of Charles Lamb, with a sketch of his life* (1837).
3. Ellis and Blackburn.
4. *LM*, vol. 6, pp. 13–14.

Monday – February 4

C Lamb. Fine mild day – would gladly have gone out, but was kept at home by my promise to Ld Hatherton. The house agent. Everything must soon be settled. – There is little doubt that I shall have the house – Ld H – he seems uneasy at having let me see these remains of Ld D, and particularly nervous lest the expression about Ld A should get wind at present. I told him that he might rely on my discretion; and he may: for I shall mention the journal to nobody. H came and took me in the carriage with her to W.T., where I found my dear B poorly. She goes to Brighton tomorrow for change of air. Home finished the Annals of QA. They only go down to March 1713. At dinner Manners of the Day.

Tuesday – February 5

C. Lamb – De Foe's works – House agent again. All right. To the City. Ordered the sale of 1,000£ 3 per Cents. My affairs generally very thriving. The L. & S.W. stock rising and the dividend likely to be very good. To W.T. by omnibus along the new Road. Told H that I had yesterday some talk with William about the arrangements of my new establishment. H very angry and justly, I must say, at the encroaching spirit not of W but of E. I shall stand up against it firmly. Yet I wish to deal very kindly by them. Home – De Foe – I cannot understand the mania of some people about him. They think him a man of the first order of genius and a paragon of virtue. He certainly wrote an excellent book – the first part of RC[1] – one of those feats which can only be performed by the union of luck with ability. That awful solitude of a quarter of a century – that strange union of comfort plenty and security with the misery of loneliness was my delight before I was five years old, and has been the delight of hundreds of thousands of boys. But what has De Foe done great, except the first part of R.C.? The second part is poor in comparison. The History of the Plague[2] and the Memoirs of a Cavalier[3] are in one sense curious works of art. They are wonderfully like true histories. But, considered as novels, which they are, there is not much in them. He had undoubtedly a knack at making fiction look like truth. But is such a knack much to be admired? Is it not much of the same sort with the knack of a painter who takes in the birds with his fruit? I have seen dead game painted in such a way that I thought the partridges and pheasants real. But surely such pictures do not rank high as works of art. Villemain and before him Ld Chatham were deceived by the Memoirs of a Cavalier. But, when those memoirs are known to be fictitious what are they worth? How immeasurably inferior to Waverley or the Legend of Montrose or Old Mortality. As to Carleton's Memoirs[4] I see no proof that De Foe wrote them; nor do I believe it. As to Moll Flanders, Roxana, Captain Jack[5] and so forth, they are utterly wretched and nauseous – in no respect that I can see beyond the reach of Aphra Behn[6] or of Ward[7] who wrote the London Spy. As a political writer De Foe is merely one of the crowd. Nothing that he wrote of that sort has lived. His history of the Union is valuable only for the *pièces justificatives*. He seems to have been an unprincipled hack, ready to take any side of any question. Of all writers he was the most unlucky in irony. Twice he was prosecuted for what he meant to be ironical. He was so unskilful that everybody understood him literally. Some of his tracts are worse than immoral – quite beastly. Altogether I do not like him. At dinner finished M of the D.

---

1. *Robinson Crusoe* (1719).
2. TBM means either *A Journal of the Plague Year* or *Due Preparations for the Plague*, both published in 1722.
3. (1720).
4. According to James Sutherland, *Defoe*, 2nd edn (London, 1950), p. 268, *The Military Memoirs of Captain George Carleton ...* (1728) are 'frequently, but not quite conclusively, attributed to Defoe'.
5. The first two were published respectively in 1722 and 1724. *Colonel Jack* was published in 1722.
6. A dramatist and novelist, 1640–89.

7. Edward (Ned) Ward (1667–1731) was a tavern keeper and satirical writer. The *London Spy* was published from 1698 to 1709.

Wednesday – February 6

C Lamb – South W Wind and mild – but cloudy and windy. Montalembert's Book[1] – a present I suppose from himself. I read it rapidly. Good. But he is unjust to us as respects foreign affairs. He does not sufficiently consider how much his own countrymen are to blame – how much their conduct in 1848 did to justify the apprehension that they were unfit to enjoy liberty. Went out. Looked into Denman's Committee Room[2] – Kemble, Frank Ellis, Denman himself – their hopes high. E goes down this afternoon. Got the final Memoirs of Lamb[3] from the British Library. Home. At dinner. Le Testament de M. Chauvelin[4] – Pamphlets – Swift – Mis.

1. *De l'avenir politique de l'Angleterre* (1856).
2. George Denman (1819–96) was standing against Spencer Walpole in the Cambridge University Election, but when, in Cambridge, violent rioting occurred, he retired from the contest. Cf. *LM*, vol. 6, p. 29, n. 5. Denman was the fourth son of Lord Denman, Brougham's old colleague.
3. T. N. Talfourd, *Final Memorials of Charles Lamb ...* (1848).
4. By Alexandre Dumas (*père*). It appeared in 1850.

Thursday – February 7

Still mild – To W.T. H goes to Brighton tomorrow to bring back B. I had a letter from B – Dear Child – going on well. I am pestered by all sorts of absurd letters to which I sometimes have to write long answers. Here is a parson who sends me as a great and new discovery the old cock and bull story about Colonel Scott, Ld Sunderland, and Monmouth's intercepted letter. "Wondrous as is your research, this may have escaped you". Odd if it had. At dinner finished Le Testament. Life of Simeon.[1]

1. Perhaps *Memoirs of the Life of Charles Simeon ...*, ed. William Carrs (1847); or John Williamson, *Brief Memoir of the Rev. C. Simeon* (1848).

Friday – February 8

Fine day – Long at the Athenaeum – Read Miss Murray's trash[1] – New Life of Beaumarchais[2] – Villemain's recollections[3] – must read those again more carefully. I have finished Talford's last book about Lamb. The account of that villain Wainwright[4] is the most curious part – Simeon. A most absurd letter written apparently by a woman who can neither spell nor construct a sentence of English and signed by a man in a sprawling hand to ask whether I withdrew my accusations – (*this accusations* is the expression) against the lade (q late) Robert

Montgomery? A begging letter from James Mills – Mean as insolent and savage. That man's baseness is unfathomable. E to dinner.

1. Amelia Matilda Murray (1795–1884) was the Maid of Honour to Queen Victoria, whom TBM had met in Windsor on 28 May 1851. She wrote *Remarks on Education* (1847) and *Letters from the United States, Cuba and Canada* (1856). Murray's critical views on slavery led to her resignation from the royal household.
2. L. L. de Loménie, *Beaumarchais et son temps*, was published in 1856.
3. Perhaps Abel François Villemain (1790–1870), *Souvenirs contemporaires d'histoire et de littérature* (1854).
4. The account of Thomas Griffiths Wainwright (1794–1852) is in Thomas Noon Talfourd's *Final Memorials of Charles Lamb* (1848), vol. 2, pp. 9–27. For Wainwright's career, including his activities as poisoner and forger, see *DNB*.

Saturday – February 9

Very fine. As lovely a day as I remember at this season – May, if only the trees were not quite bare. Setting out, I met Bouverie[1] on the steps. We walked together to St James' Park, talking about the Cambridge Bill. I have a strong notion that the ministers, remembering how much I had to do with throwing out the bill of last year, do not wish me to be a Commr. And their wish quite agrees with mine. I hate turmoil; and to quarrel with Whewell would be particularly disagreeable to me. So when Bouverie hinted that if I really disliked the business, they would manage to do without me, I made haste to meet him more than half way. I like the intended Commission much – but I am sorry that they mean to have nobody who was in last year's list. Lefevre is a serious loss. Walpole of course could not be proposed, as he will be MP for the University. A miserable business this election. Grossly mismanaged. Some consolation from Edinburgh – Black victorious with flying colours.[2] Talked with Bouverie about the state of parliamentary business. The temper of the Commons good. Palmerston's speech yesterday excellent – grave, temperate, manly, satisfactory to all sensible men. In the Lords this question of life peerages – raised, I think, in a very unlucky way – seems likely to do no serious harm. On the legal question Granville and Cranworth made speeches which nobody has answered. But as to the question of expediency there is room for much debate. I am quite for creating life peers. But surely the wise course would have been to begin by some creation which should have had the plea of necessity or of great convenience, at least. To make Parke a peer for life – Parke who has a plentiful life income, who has no son and who will never have one, was to innovate for innovation's sake, – a thing always disliked in England.[3] To the Museum. Sir H. Ellis took his leave, or something like it. Ld J a little too formal and eloquent on the occasion. To W.T. A walk of half an hour, after a long interval, in Kensington Gardens with my dear B. Home – Simeon – At dinner Sue Famille Jouffray[4] – I do not like it Ναυσ.

1. Probably Edward Pleydell-Bouverie (1818–89), at this stage President of the Poor Law Board and MP for Kilmarnock.
2. Adam Black won the contest for the seat created by Macaulay's resignation, by 2,429 votes to 1,786.
3. There is an account of the Wensleydale peerage case by Olive Anderson in the *English Historical Review*, 82 (1967), pp. 486–502.
4. Eugène Sue, *La Famille Jouffray* (1853–4).

Sunday – February 10

Mild, but dull day. Read Simeon's Life. To W.T. – sate there two pleasant hours – Home – Finished Simeon. Sir Walter Scott's Life.[1] At dinner Harcourt.[2] Must begin work again tomorrow.

1. By J. G. Lockhart.
2. In four volumes (1799). Anonymous, but certainly by Mrs Meeke.

Monday – February 11

I did begin work. Went through the curious M.S. of Edwd Hopkins's[1] travels and abstracted it to good purpose. Sent Wm to W.T. In the afternoon he returned with a note from H promising to tell me all tomorrow. W is very much pleased with Holly Lodge. I think and hope that all will go right. I must not be pillaged or bullied – but I have every wish to deal liberally and kindly by old and faithful servants. Sir W. Scott's Life – Harcourt – Longman called – a lull in the sale. No wonder. What in heaven's name did he expect after selling more copies in a day than were sold of Marmion, not ½ of the price, in seven years? Ld Granville called. He spoke quite confidently about peace. Thank God! The day has been very rainy and misty.

1. Perhaps Edward Hopkins (*c.* 1675–1736), MP for Coventry and for Eye, diplomatist.

Tuesday – February 12

Rainy and misty again. Staid at home all the morning – Sir W.S. Old ERs – Excellent paper on Vaccination[1] – Lockhart praises Scott's Article on Beresford's Miseries[2] as a masterpiece of humour. But on my word I can see little in the paper to admire. It has all the worst faults of the early E.R, – and is by no means eminently clever, the Reviewer's miseries at the end always excepted. To dinner at W.T. after a long interval – pleasant – chatted with H and B over my plans and modified them considerably. I think that I shall be very comfortable and shall be able to manage on my certain income except for a tour of more than ordinary length, or for some extraordinary call on my liberality. The children most amiable and affectionate. As I went home, the sky was glorious after all the rain. Brilliant starlight. My old friend Orion again. I had lost sight of him a long time. He reminded me of the nights during which I stood watching him on the poop of the Asia twenty two years ago, as we were entering the beautiful sea of the Trades.

1. *ER*, 9 (October 1806), pp. 32–66. It was by Andrew Duncan and Francis Jeffrey.
2. Scott's article on James Beresford's *Miseries of Human Life* (1806) in *ER*, 9 (1806), pp. 184–96, is described by Lockhart in his life of Scott as 'that exquisite piece of humour' (ch. 16). TBM's eye for stylistic differences was acute: the passage on 'Reviewer's Groans' was by Jeffrey.

Wednesday – February 13

I had hoped for a fine day. But mist and rain again. It mattered less as I had taken calomel. Wrote to Dean Vignoles – returned the Hopkins M.S. to Mr Lenthall[1] – a letter from Everett with two copies of my book printed in America – the best and the meanest editions. The letter most kind.[2] Read a good deal of my book with a view to making corrections. Spent some time in calculations of expenditure. I have a great turn for finance, though few people would suspect it. I have a pleasure in carrying on long arithmetical operations in my head. I used to find amusement, when I was Sec. at War, in the Army estimates and indeed I generally went through my pecuniary statements without book except where it was necessary to come to pence and farthings. Then Scott's Life. Most interesting – as interesting as any Life except Boswell's Life of Johnson. At dinner – Harcourt.

1. There is a Francis Kyffin Lenthall (1824–92) in Boase, a barrister and Recorder of Woodstock, 1858–85. This may have been the MS TBM read on 11 February 1856.
2. TBM's reply is in *LM*, vol. 6, p. 18.

Thursday – February 14

A fine day. Party to breakfast – Ld Stanhope, Ld John, Lord Granville,[1] The Dean and Mrs M., Dundas, H and B. It was very pleasant. Ld J extremely gay and easy – not more so than I had often seen him, but so much so as to surprise others. Longman came with his little boy[2] while we were assembled. After the party broke up H and B remained till half past two, and lunched. With H's help I am fast approaching to a complete settlement of my establishment. A very good settlement. I calculate that every expense except that of a tour on the Continent will be completely defrayed for 2,850£ a year. And I may, I think, reckon on having at least 2,900£ a year certain. My casuel[3] has never since 1848 been less than 1400£. I may therefore live like an Emperor and lay up more than 1,000£ a year. At least such are my hopes. I walked half an hour in the afternoon – looked into the R.I. saw the Allgemeine Zeitung.[4] Found in it a long article on my book – very laudatory, and to me very agreeable: for I hold the judgment of foreigners to be a more sure prognostic of what the judgment of posterity is likely to be than the judgment of my own countrymen. Home – Sir W. Scott's Life – T called – E to dinner.

1. Lord Granville gives an account of the party in a letter to Lord Canning; see Lord Edmond Fitzmaurice, *The Life of... Earl Granville*, 2nd edn (London, 1905), vol. 1, pp. 164–5.
2. Thomas Norton Longman (1849–1930).
3. TBM uses this term for his earnings from writing. See below, entry for 4 March 1856.
4. 'Macaulay der Gerschichtsforscher', in *Allgemeine Zeitung* (Munich), 18 January 1856, pp. 281–2. It is in fact very critical.

Friday – February 15

Sent the Dean of Ossory his M.S.[1] – went out – very fine day – delicious – to Athenaeum – read Rogers's Table Talk[2] – a poor twaddling volume – less offensive than I inferred from what Milman said about it and very uninteresting. The best thing is a story of Porson. "Was not Bentley a Scotchman?" he was asked "Oh no, Sir, no: he was a very great Greek Scholar". Walked to the Houses of Parliament – admired the Clock Tower[3] – then by an omnibus to St Clement Danes – and walked back looking at bookstalls and dawdling. The weather quite like the end of a fine April. I have indeed seen much less genial weather in June. My chest has ceased to plague me. Home – Bought Tieck's works,[4] Thierry, and The Romancero Castellano[5] – William went to Holly Lodge – brought back a good report. I shall engage the coachman of my predecessor – a good arrangement. [gap] Sir W.S. [gap] Harcourt at dinner.

1. Charles Vignoles (1789–1877). He was appointed Dean of Ossory in 1843 and held the post until his death.
2. *Recollections of the Table Talk of Samuel Rogers*, ed. A. Dyce (1856).
3. 'Big Ben': it was completed in 1858.
4. Johann Ludwig Tieck (1773–1853). TBM may have bought his *Novellen*, published in seven volumes (1823–8); he can hardly have carried home his *Schriften*, published in twenty-eight volumes, between 1828 and 1854.
5. *Romancero Castellano, Colección de Antiguos Romances Populares de los españoles*, pub. with introduction and notes by G. D. Depping, new edn with notes by D. Antoine Alcalá-Galiano, 3 vols (Leipzig, 1844–6). Depping's collection of 1817 was the basis of J. G. Lockhart's *Ancient Spanish Ballads* of 1823.

Saturday – February 16

The wind has changed East. I soon felt it. However the day became fine and bright. The sun was warm; and I ventured out. R.I. Then to W.T. chatted – walked with B to leave a card at one of the Villas on the West of Kensington Gardens – Home – Read Tieck's Abdallah not very good[1] – Sir W.S. Harc[our]t.

1. J. L. Tieck, *Abdallah* (1785).

Sunday – February 17

The East wind in all the forms – vile fog – I must return to all my winter precautions. Thank God that I have got so well through the most trying part of the year. We shall hardly have very severe weather now. Read some of Tieck – The Brothers – The preface to the Collected Works. He complains that his countrymen are slow to take a joke. He should consider that the jokes which he and some of his brother writers are in the habit of producing are not laughing matters. Read the Gestiefelte Kater.[1] Heavy pleasantry in general, though now and then there is a good sneer at Kotzebue. Sir Walter Scott's Life. Had Rokeby[2] out, and turned it over. Poor work, yet gleams of genius few and far between. What an absurd blunder to make the scenery the foreground and the human actors the background of a picture of that sort. In the Lay the human actors stand out as they should and the Ail and the Tweed and Melrose Abbey are in proper subordination. In Marmion too. Even in the Lady of the Lake Loch Katrine does not throw Fitzjames and Roderic into the shade. But Rokeby is primarily a descriptive poem like Grongar Hill.[3] There was some foundation for Moore's sarcastic remark that Scott meant to do all the gentlemen's seats from Edinburgh to London. The only good thing in the poem is the Buccaneer.[4] Wilfrid is well imagined, but ill executed. Finished Αρκ [Harcourt].

1. Puss in Boots (1796).
2. Published 1813, it was Scott's tribute to the Palladian house and estate owned by his friend J. S. B. Morritt (1772–1843). The *Lay of the Last Minstrel* was published in 1805, *Marmion* in 1808 and *The Lady of the Lake* in 1810.
3. By John Dyer (1699–1758), published in 1726.
4. Bertram Risingham in this poem, whose career surely makes it much more than a poem of descriptive scenery.

Monday – February 18

I had sent an excuse to Hallam. Breakfasted at home and staid all day by my fire. A cold dreary day. Read a good deal of Tieck here and there – Sir W. Scott's Life – Some of Wordsworth – a silly book called Lives of Obscure (i.e. bad) poets.[1] Derwent Coleridge called last Friday to ask me to try to serve him. I wrote to Ld

Granville and got not only a kind but an encouraging answer. I sent it to D.C – and today he called again to thank me. God knows I should be glad to be of use to him. Read Lucian's φιλοψευδης[2] long a favourite piece with me. Calculations – Bage's Hermsprong[3] at dinner. Sir W.S. Dyer's Grongar Hill – could not find it on the map – near Golden Grove, I imagine.[4] Black called today. I was heartily glad to see him.

1. Perhaps *Sketches of Obscure Poets, with Specimens of their Writings* (1833).
2. Lucian of Samosata, *Philopseudes* ('Lover of Lies').
3. Robert Bage, *Hermsprong, Or Man as he is Not* (1796).
4. TBM was right. Golden Grove is 3½ miles south of Llandeilo. The Dyer family lived at Abergavenny, half a mile from Grongar Hill. For its relevance to Dyer's work, see *A Garden Lost in Time* by Penny David (London, Weidenfeld and Nicolson, 1999), ch. 4.

Tuesday – February 19

A good night. All my nights are good now – deep sweet sleep. The wind still east, the sky still foggy, and some rain falling. Staid at home reading and calculating. Finished the φιλοψευδης liked it better than ever. Then the διαλέταιρ and φιλσπατρις.[1] Trevelyan called. My receipts from the duties on books in the West Indies *and* at The Cape are, it seems, 37£ – The other colonies may make it up to 100£ – Hermsprong. Sir W.S.

1. Lucian, *Aetairikoi Dialogoi* ('Dialogue of Courtesans') and *Philopatris* ('Patriot').

Wednesday – February 20

Still cold and dreary weather: but I must go out volens nolens. At one to W.T. with the boy. William I left at home because he had a cold in one of his eyes – From W.T. to H.L. with H and B. Certainly a delightful house and garden even seen under all disadvantages. I really doubt whether I could have found in England anything that would have suited me better – looked through the rooms and the ground floor and settled about bookcases, carpets, etc. – got home a little before 4. Read Peregrinus again[1] with much interest and profit. You see there how a false religion gets into vogue – Ἑρμσπρωγ[2] Finished the life of poor Sir W. It is a sad story. Ld Glenelg called this afternoon to talk with me about his motion for asking the op[inio]ns of the judges[3] – I told him what I thought; and he seemed to take in what I said very well.

1. Lucian, *De Morte Peregrini*.
2. *Hermsprong*.
3. Glenelg's motion asking for the opinions of the judges on the question of life peerages was defeated by 142 votes to 111. *PD*, 3rd ser., cxl, 1121.

Thursday – Feb 21

Soon after breakfast came the house agent to measure the bookcases and to make other arrangements. Then Kemble who wants to be Principal Librarian and Secretary to the Museum. I should prefer him to Panizzi.[1] They both have much the same faults and much the same merits. But K's appointment would be much the more popular of the two. Then Ld Lansdowne on the same matter which brought Ld Glenelg here yesterday – Ld and I agreed perfectly. Lucian – The Lapithæ. Then the True History[2] – not so good as Gulliver's by a great deal. E to dinner. Sad and anxious. I feel much for him, and the more because I am afraid that, before I knew of his vexations, I exulted in my own recent prosperity in a way which must have hurt him, generous and friendly and unenvious as he is. I offered him anything in my power; and I shall make my arrangements in such a way as to have some hundreds at his service without inconvenience to myself. It is only denying myself a few fine engravings and sets of books and other trifles which I had thought of buying.

1. Kemble and Panizzi were the names put before the Cabinet by the Trustees, and Panizzi was chosen. See E. Miller, *That Noble Cabinet* (London, A. Deutsch, 1973), pp. 189–90.
2. *Vera Historia*, by Lucian of Samosata.

Friday – Feb 22

Woke uneasy about E. I wish to God that he would speak quite openly to M – I fear too that, for want of plain speaking out on his part, W may be extravagant.[1] The wind west, but the weather still cold. I thought of going to W.T. but dear B and A came to me with Cora and sate some time. So I staid at home. Twisleton called and, while he was here, Derwent Coleridge. I wrote to Rawlinson about the chambers. Read Lucian's Alexander – most curious and interesting – several pamphlets of Anne's reign – Finished Ερμοπ. Life of Byron.[2]

1. M: Marian; W: Walter.
2. Moore's *Life of Byron*, published in 1830.

Saturday – Feb 23

Fine day – West Wind. To the Athenaeum – thence to the Museum. The Archbp[1] in the chair. I find that Panizzi is certain to have the Principal Librarian's place. He has great qualifications: but there are drawbacks; and there will be a perfect storm of obloquy. I said a word for Kemble: but Milman spoke so strongly about K's habits that I was silenced. I am glad that I have not to give a vote on the question. Home. Wrote to Mr Kennedy of Maryland on a historical question about which Thackeray had asked me.[2] Answer from Rawlinson about the chambers

– pecuniary calculations. As far as I see, I am upon velvet. Van de Weyer called – told me that Hepworth Dixon's book was out[3] – and that the man complains of my not noticing his former attack on me. He will go to his grave with that grievance. A pretty life I should pass if I were to wrangle with every tenthrate scribbler who has a fling at me. At dinner Les Catacombes[4] – Moore's Byron – the wind north – felt it painfully.

---

1. John Bird Sumner.
2. John P. Kennedy (1795–1870) was a politician and writer and Speaker of the House in 1846. See *LM*, vol. 6, p. 17, and notes for TBM's letter and explanation. The historical question concerned a Colonel George Talbot of Virginia, who was indicted for murder and pardoned by James II. TBM was evidently not aware that he was killed fighting for Louis XIV in the Irish Brigade. The episode was used by Kennedy in a historical novel, *A Legend of the Chesapeake* (1871).
3. William Hepnorth Dixon, *William Penn, an Historical Biography ... New edition, with a New Preface in Reply to the Accusations of Mr Macaulay* (1856).
4. Élie Berthet (1818–91), *Les Catacombes de Paris*, 4 vols (Paris 1854).

Sunday – February 24

Dawdled over Beaumont Fletcher – to Brookes's – amused by seeing that some fool has made an article against me in the Atlas[1] by simply copying all the attacks, reasonable and unreasonable, that he could find in all the other periodical works. To W.T. – there learned that Dixon's preface is out and saw an article on it in the Illustrated London News.[2] From that article I judge that he has made nothing of his attempt to defend Penn. I was certain that nothing would be made of it. I shall not buy such rubbish. If Longman thinks it worthwhile to send it me he may. I have really no curiosity. Walked home with Charles. Calculations. Life of Byron. Les Catacombes. I shall certainly get into my new house cheaper than I expected.

---

1. *Atlas*, 1554 (23 February 1856), pp. 122–3.
2. *Illustrated London News*, 23 February 1856, p. 199, says that TBM is not willing to admit his error over Penn.

Monday – February 25

People busy from eight o'clock in the dining room. I breakfasted in the sitting room. At eleven Rawlinson came. Glad to find that he wishes to take the book-cases. He shall have them; and I will have new ones at Holly Lodge. I shall be saved a residence of a month at a hotel which would have been both uncomfortable and expensive. I hope to be at Holly Lodge by the 21st April. A dull day, but not cold – Wind WSW. To W.T. – walked half an hour in Kensington Gardens with B and A. Home and put some time in writing to a person who has very civilly objected to some of my doctrines about currency. He is high Anti Birmingham[1] and indeed seems to think money unnecessary. E to dinner in the sitting room. It was not unpleasant.

---

1. Presumably this means hostile to the 'soft money' doctrines of Attwood and his followers who opposed the return to gold.

Tuesday – February 26

A lovely day. Quite May. After breakfast to the Athenaeum – thence to the City. Looked at my book in Birchin Lane.[1] All well. The city exulting in the armistice.[2] Walked – now a rare thing with me – two miles through places once familiar – Bishopsgate Street – Shoreditch – Hoxton Square – Charles Square – so on to the City Road where I bought Thackeray's Miscellaneous Works.[3] I had seen at a bookseller's in Bishopsgate Street Dixon's new Edition of the life of Penn with the preface in answer to me. But, as I was certain that the answer could be no answer did not chuse to give the fellow seven shillings, and went on. Got into an omnibus – to W.T. – found H and B just starting for Clapham – went with them to Thurlow Lodge, a pleasant ride – back by omnibus. Hair cut – read Moore's Life of Byron – Les Catacombes – Calculations.

---

1. There was only one bookshop in the lane, no. 27, owned by Thomas Benjamin Bumpus, Jr.
2. In the Crimean War. The peace congress opened at Paris on 25 February, and the Peace Treaty was signed on 30 March.
3. *Miscellanies in Prose and Verse*, 4 vols (1855).

Wednesday – February 27

A dull day, but not cold – Went to breakfast at H[alla]m's Alas! D. of Argyle, Ld Stanhope, Murchison, Cater. We got on tolerably: and that was all – Home – Calc[ulatio]ns – Owen called. Talk about his position and the possibility of doing something for him in the Museum.[1] I really felt for him – for the nation too which is disgraced by the distresses of a man so eminent. When he left me I wrote to the Chancellor of the Exchequer[2] and to Ld Stanhope – about him. Longman called and brought his boy!! Read Byron's Life. A dull cold day – wished that I had not been forced to go out but there was no help – to W.T. Large party and not one that I cared for. Lushington I was glad to see however. There was Monsell[3] who went to sleep and snored – The Buxtons – The Haweses all except the gentleman now Sir Benjamin.[4] Captain Peel did not come.[5] But there was my old friend Black, and Sir S. Northcote and his wife[6] and one or two people whom I did not know. I got near Lushington and

H and managed pretty well. In the evening a violent fit of coughing. Glad to be at home again.

1. See below, entry for 2 March 1856 and n. 1.
2. Sir George Cornewall-Lewis. TBM's letter is in *LM*, vol. 6, pp. 20–1.
3. William Monsell (1812–94) was Clerk to the Ordinance and MP for Co. Limerick, 1847–74. He was made Baron Emly in 1874.
4. Hawes (1797–1862) had been Deputy Secretary at War, and was created KCB in 1856. He married Sophia Brunel (1802–78). They had four children, three daughters and one son.
5. Sir William Peel (1824–58) was the son of the Prime Minister. He distinguished himself in the Crimea at Sebastopol, and later in the Indian Mutiny. He died at Cawnpore.
6. Cecilia Frances Farrer (1823–1910).

Thursday – February 28

Cold and very dreary and foggy. N.E. Wind. Staid at home reading Byron all the morning. Often affected even to tears, but as much, I think, by old recollections as by the power of the poetry. Many passages I had never, to the best of my remembrance, looked at since my college days. I was much struck by the poverty of many things which I once admired, by the general want of finish; by the incorrectness of the diction and versification. Yet here is true genius. At dinner Les Catacombes – Then Byron again.

Friday – February 29

A fine day but wind East. Staid at home – Wrote to Ld Lne about Owen – favourable answer from the Chancellor of the Exchequer. I hope that the thing may be managed. Byron – my own book. Some more criticism – favourable and unfavourable. The most scurrilous attacks on me have been made by the Papists and the High Presbyterians – The Rambler[1] and the Witness.[2] Fortunately those attacks are even more stupid than scurrilous. Longman called. Necessary to reprint. This is wonderful. Twenty six thousand five hundred copies sold in ten weeks. I should not wonder if I made 20,000£ clear this year by literature. If so I shall have 60,000£ besides my copyrights, worth a good 15,000£ more, at least. Pretty well considering that, twenty two years ago, I had just nothing when my debts were paid; and all this, with the exception of a small part left me by my uncle the Gen[era]l, made by myself, and made easily and honestly, by pursuits which were a pleasure to me, and without one insinuation from any slanderer that I was not even liberal in all pecuniary dealing. E to dinner. I wish from my soul that he were as well off.

1. *The Rambler*, xvii (February 1856), pp. 140–57, amd (March 1856), pp. 208–28. The review was by John Moore Capes, who had also reviewed *HE* vols 1 and 2.
2. *Witness*, 17:1737 (27 February 1856), p. 2.

Saturday – March 1

Fog and East Wind. Did not go to breakfast with Milnes. W. Ellis called as I was going to breakfast. His father soon came. I hope to God he will turn out well. Soon after they were gone came B and G who is out on Exeat. Pleasant chat – Mares came. Gave some orders. To R.I. Nothing. I cannot find that anybody has taken the smallest notice of the Defence of Penn. I therefore shall certainly not buy it. Home. Some fool sent me an anonymous letter to say that the Glenmore Highlanders have burned me in effigy[1] – I suppose for saying that their ancestors had the itch. Wise people they must be! Busy correcting for the new edition. There is not much to do. I doubt whether any work of equal bulk ever escaped with as little injury after going through such a gantelope.[2] H and B in the carriage – went with them to two or three places, and finally to W.T. – Pleasant. Coming home I found a letter from a brazen fellow in Scotland who says that he wants to publish a novel, that he is 23 years old and that he will come up and show me his M.S. if I will only send him fifty pounds. Really I can get better novels cheaper. Byron – I sent an excuse to Lady Mary Labouchere[3] – read Les Catacombes at dinner and Byron in the evening.

1. See *HE*, ch. 13, *CW*, vol. 3, p. 46. There is a *Times* report on the burning – 6 March 1856, p. 11 col. f.
2. Gauntlet.
3. Formerly Lady Mary Howard.

Sunday – March 2

Cold and Dull. At home all day finished Byron's poems and Life. Lewis called, and – told me, to my great delight, that my letter to him was read in the cabinet yesterday and generally approved, and that, in all probability, the arrangement suggested by me would be adopted. I am glad to find that there is a chance that Hawkins may be pensioned off.[1] Then we shall have good humour I hope and ability in our staff. Finished Moore's Life. Very interesting; but it raises neither the hero nor the writer in my opinion. At dinner Les Catacombes. Then Leigh Hunt's book.[2] Amusing but certainly there never was a happier epithet than that of Cockney. Clever as he is, and observant, there is a shabby genteel air, a frowziness about his style, which produces ridicule and a slight disgust. I was much amused by a passage which I thought very indicative of the laxity of his notions of meum and tuum – a laxity which he owns and glories in. He speaks of the smallness of Ld B's head. Shelley's head too it seems was small. So was that of Keats. "They were the only three of my acquaintances whose hats I could never get on". His account of Cs Guiccioli[3] "A buxom parlour boarder".

The Appenines "enormous puddings" are specimens of the singular vulgarity of his mind.

1. Richard Owen became Superintendant of the Natural History Collections of the British Museum in May 1856. Edward Hawkins (1780–1867), Keeper of Antiquities since 1826, did not retire until 1860.
2. *Lord Byron and Some of his Contemporaries*, 3 vols (1828). The phrases Macaulay mentions are in vol. 1, pp. 68 and 105, and vol. 2, p. 131.
3. Countess Teresa Guiccioli, born Teresa Gamba Ghiselli (1799–1879).

Monday – March 3

Still cold – still a prisoner – Finished the corrections for Vol 3. Read a good deal of Shelley and Keats. Liked Shelley less than formerly and Keats not at all, though there are fine lines and even stanzas in both. Kemble called and sate long. His name is before the ministers. I held out no hopes to him. Indeed I could not without gross insincerity hold out any. Leigh Hunt – E to dinner.

Tuesday – March 4

An American newspaper – The Tribune – which calumniated me grossly two or three years ago – now full of eulogy.[1] After breakfast H – then Mares – long consultation. H very kind and judicious. I think, that I shall effect my removal for an expense which will be within 1800£ *and* that, by selling out 2200£ of 3 per Cs. I shall be able to go on most comfortably till Michaelmas when I hope to be able to invest about 20,000£. That will raise my regular income to more than 3000£ – besides a *casuel*, which, judging from the experience of the last seven years, I should estimate at not less than 1500£ a year. I am therefore a very opulent man, and well able to help others, which I will do as opportunities offer.[2] Read and corrected Chap XVII for the 2nd edition – Longman called – gave him the corrections of Vol 3. There is ample time for the 2nd edition will not appear till after the trade sales of April. At dinner Les Catacombes. Thackeray's Miscellanies – often clever and spirited, but a little overcharged. The endless false spelling and Irish blarney become tiresome. A page of cockney English or Tipperary eloquence is very well in Punch. A single Character like the drunken old Irish reprobate in Pendennis[3] is very well. But a whole book in that style is too much of a good thing; not to say that the cleverness which Thackeray himself furnishes does not harmonize with the vulgarity and ignorance of such a fellow as Yellowplush and thus the dramatic effect is marred. Galt's Parish Minister and Lawrie Todd[4] are characters of a higher sort than Yellowplush and they may, without any inconsistency, be sensible and even eloquent. However Thackeray is an excellent writer and shows his ability even in these trifles.

1. *New York Daily Tribune*, 8 January 1856. The reviewer quotes copiously from set pieces in *HE*. The review notes TBM's contempt for Quakers, and specially praises the account of the National Debt.
2. Cf. *LM*, vol. 6, pp. 25–6.
3. Captain Shandon.
4. Mr Balwhidder, in John Galt's *Annals of the Parish* (1821) and the hero of *Lawrie Todd: or, the Settlers of the Woods* (1830).

Wednesday – March 5

When I got up the wind was west; and I hoped that my captivity was over. But while I was dressing the weathercock shifted first to North and then to North East – By the bye – what shall I do for a Weathercock at Holly Lodge – I shall say like Wordsworth's little boy

At Campden Hill's no weathercock
and that's the reason why.[1]

A weathercock is quite a necessary of life to me. I spent the morning in putting up parcels of pamphlets etc. to be bound. Read more of Thackeray. Read and corrected Chap XVIII for the second edition. Looked through Crabbe's Tales.[2] Very good – finished the Catacombes at dinner. William and Elizabeth have been at Holly Lodge, and are much pleased with it. They are making out lists of what will be wanted. My present inclination is to be moderate at starting. I can add whenever I think fit. Letter from Ld Lne. Owen's business is most satisfactorily settled to my great joy.

1. The reference is to Wordsworth's 'Anecdote for Fathers' (1798): 'At Kilve there was no weather-cock; / And that's the reason why.'
2. Crabbe's *Tales in Verse* (1812) or *Tales of the Hall*, 2 vols (1819). The latter was in TBM's Library SC, no. 543.

Thursday – March 6

Still Wind N.E. Another day of confinement – Westley, the bookbinder,[1] came. I shall employ him to arrange the books at Holly Lodge. Showed him the books which are to be bound immediately. Thackeray. A very clever writer certainly. At dinner Granby[2] – Good but not powerful. My Pocket Book.[3]

1. Perhaps William Russell Westley (1796–*c.* 1889), of Westley and Co., Friar Street, Doctors' Commons.
2. By Thomas Henry Lister (1826).
3. Perhaps the burlesque by Edward Dubois (1807) on Sir John Carr's *The Stranger in Ireland* (1806), for which the publishers were unsuccessfully prosecuted by Carr.

Friday – March 7

Weather worse and worse – black sky and bleak wind. Staid at home – Corrected Chap XIX for the new edition. B called and sate half an hour chatting very pleasantly. Scarcely was she gone when Longman came, with a very pleasant announcement. He and his partners find that they are overflowing with money and think that they cannot invest it better than by advancing to me – on the usual terms of course – part of what will be due to me in December. We agreed that they shall pay 20,000£ into Williams's Bank next week. What a sum to be gained by one edition of a book – I may say gained on one day. But that was harvest day – the work had been near seven years in hand. I was however much pleased. I feel relieved from some anxieties which would now and then obtrude themselves. I wrote to Thornton to desire him to add 1,000£ to my balance which is already a large one, and to invest the remaining 19,000 in the 3 per Cents *en attendant.* I wrote also to W.T. At dinner finished Granby and looked through the introduction to the Chronicles of the Canongate.[1] Letter from dear B in the evening. They are all much pleased. They have indeed as much reason to be pleased as I, who am pleased on their account rather than on my own, though I am glad that my last years will be comfortable. Comfortable however I could have been on a sixth part of the income which I shall now have.

1. Sir Walter Scott. The first series of *Chronicles of the Canongate* (1827) contained *The Highland Widow*, *The Two Drovers* and *The Surgeon's Daughter*. The second series contained *Saint Valentine's Day*, or *The Fair Maid of Perth* (1828).

Saturday – March 8

Wind North – then turned to West. But as yet there is little or no mitigation of the cold. Determined to stay at home and sent an excuse to the Duchess of Argyll. The weather improved – so much that I went to W.T. and passed a couple of hours there. Then with H and B in the carriage – left them and went home. Cottle's Coleridge[1] – at dinner Pinmoney.[2] Solis uno bobo[3] far the best book of the set.

1. Joseph Cottle, *Early Recollections; Chiefly Relating to the Late Samuel Taylor Coleridge ...* (1837) (revised as *Reminiscences of ... Coleridge ...* 1847).
2. By Mrs Gore (1831).
3. Antonio de Solis (1610–86), *Uno bobo hace ciento* ('One fool makes many'), from the first part of *Comedias Escogidas* (1652).

Sunday – March 9

West wind – but dull day and not warm – corrected a good deal of Chap XX – To Brooks's – Found Cadogan[1] and Hobhouse – nothing except an article in the

Press[2] on Dixon's book about Penn, from which I saw how miserably helpless the fellow was. To W.T. two pleasant hours. H has chosen for me carpets, curtains etc. She is particularly vain of the library carpet; and, I do not doubt, with reason. How kind and good they all are. Home – Cottle – Pinmoney – Mathias and his Impostures.[3] Marshall[4] and a Mr Arthur Bigg,[5] an All Soul's Man – called. Not unpleasant – I am now so much secluded that I have less objection to callers than I had. At dinner Pinmoney – Mathias.

1. The Hon. Frederick Cadogan (1824–1904), fourth son of the third Earl Cadogan. A barrister and member of Brooks's, he became MP for Cricklade, 1868–74.
2. *The Press*, 4:149 (8 March 1856), p. 234.
3. William Loete Stone, *Matthias and his Impostures; or, the Progress of Fanaticism, Illustrated in the ... Case of R Mathews ...* (New York, 1835).
4. Perhaps William Marshall (1796–1872), MP for Carlisle, 1835–47, and East Cumberland, 1847–67, who married Christiana Hibbert, daughter of George Hibbert.
5. Arthur Bigge (1818–85), Fellow of All Souls, 1843–58. He was a stipendiary magistrate in Brighton from 1855.

Monday – March 10

Still West Wind. Went out – R.I. – Athenaeum – Colnaghi's[1] – Home – Note from Rawlinson. He cannot make up his mind about the Chambers, but offers to reimburse me for the expense to which his change of purpose has put me. I civilly excused myself from accepting anything. But he has certainly used me in a provoking way. I shall be put to a charge of 250£ merely on his account. However – by way of set off – Longman writes to say that the 20,000£ will be paid in on Thursday. He sent me a M.S. of Ld Normanby about the French Revoln of 1848[2] – the style so so, The reflections so so, but the facts curious. I wish that he were less bitter against Guizot whom I cannot help admiring with all his faults. Looked through two volumes of a Diary of a Mr Raikes.[3] Greater stuff I never read. A mere old club twaddler – with no information beyond what the newspapers afforded – a Tory of the most stupid sort, just the man that would sit all day in the window of the Conservative Club reading the Morning Herald and The Standard. If the Diary were dug up five hundred years hence it might be worth reading. But every observant man of this generation knows all that Raikes can tell him. Miserable! Derwent called and brought his son – I hope a son who will be a greater comfort to him than the first born.[4] This vile wind – North East again – Alas! – Solis – Matthias – Pinmoney – Soirées de N[euilly].[5]

1. Paul Colnaghi & Dominic & Co., 13 and 14 Pall Mall East.
2. Lord Normanby was Ambassador in Paris 1846–52; his *A Year of Revolution. Paris Journal for 1848* was published in 1857.

3. Perhaps *A Portion of the Journal kept by T. Raikes Esq from 1831–47* (1856). Thomas Raikes (1777–1848) had been an associate of Beau Brummel. He was a London merchant and a Governor of the Bank of England.
4. Derwent Coleridge's first-born son, Derwent Moultrie Coleridge (1828–80), emigrated to Australia and died before his father, who was survived by his second son, Ernest Hartley (1846–1920), and a daughter Christabel Rose (1843–1921).
5. Attributed to 'M. de Fongeray'; actually by Adolphe Dittmer and Edmond Cavé.

Tuesday – March 11

East Wind. However I must go out. Saw a man from the silversmith's – from Sharpus's[1] – Mares. I shall have something to pay for these things, but I can well afford it. To the City by omnibus – Young – I never see him without thinking of that unlucky business of 1832 which Napier was such a blackguard as to make public. Gave instructions to my bankers. Passed half an hour very pleasantly. They laughed, and affected to consider me as a great capitalist. I said that I should go to the Chancellor of the Exchequer to bid for the next loan. I have ordered things so that I shall henceforth have an income of 3,000 a year – 10,400£ or so in the 3 per Cents – this exclusive of the *casuel.* To W.T. by a Paddington omnibus – passed a pleasant hour there – laughing at them and laughed at – very pleasant. Home. Got the Handbook of the North of Italy,[2] and formed plans for the autumn – Wrote to Ellis. Finished S de Neuilly. At dinner Pinmoney. Letter from Thornton. Everything done already, except as to two thousand pounds in the Bristol & Exeter. Sir H. Holland sent me a German book on English literature and a letter from the author[3] which I must acknowledge. Read some of Scribe.

1. Perhaps John William Sharpus, china and glass manufacturer, 35 Oxford Street.
2. *Handbook for Travellers in Northern Italy*, by Sir Francis Palgrave, one of John Murray's guides (first published in 1842 and frequently reprinted; a sixth edition appeared in 1856).
3. Hermann Hettner (1821–82), *Literaturgeschichte des Achtzehnten Jahrhunderts* (1856), vol. 1; cf. *LM*, vol. 6, p. 26, n. 2. This is in SC, no. 430.

Wednesday – March 12

East wind and very cold. I went out before I knew how sharp it was. But I suffered less than I might have expected To Brown's in Old Street – made some purchases, and home. Read Haldane v Drummond[1] – Clarkson's eulogy on Robt Montgomery[2] – a trashy volume called Cambridge Conversations[3] of which I had never heard till I saw it in Brown's Catalogue. It came out while I was in India and dropped, as it deserved, dead-born from the press. I therefore was not aware that it existed, though it contained some trash about me. Scribe. Looked at Herr Hettler or some such name on English Literature. The man has read a good deal of English; but he does not at all understand us. He attributes a powerful influence on our philosophy and theology to Freemasonry, which may have produced some effect in Germany, Spain and other countries where truth could be spoken only in secret, but which here has never been considered by men of sense in a serious light, and which no eminent English writer, I am confident, has ever treated except as a jest. Then in this book such writers as Tindal, Toland, Morgan, Chubb[4] whose very names are unknown to the great majority of educated people and whose works are seldom inspected even by the most curious students are ranked among the master spirits of our literature. I wrote a short civil letter to the author, praising, as I could with truth praise, his knowledge of our writers, but saying nothing about his taste and judgment. A letter from Ellis with a strange circuit story.[5] At dinner – Pinm[oney] – Soirées de N.

1. Perhaps J. A. Haldane, *Answer to Mr Henry Drummond's Defence of the Heretical doctrine promulgated by Mr [Edward] Irving ...* (1830).
2. Perhaps Edward Clarkson, *Robert Montgomery and his Memories* (1830); Clarkson had praised Montgomery's poems in the *Sunday Times* and the *British Traveller*, comparing him with Milton.
3. R. A. Willmott, *Conversations at Cambridge* (1836).
4. Matthew Tindal (1657–1733); John Toland (1670–1722); Thomas Morgan (d. 1743); Thomas Chubb (1679–1747) – all Deists.
5. *LM*, vol. 6, p. 27, and n. 2, indicate that this concerned a barrister named Preston. Of the two men of that name on the Northern Circuit, Charles James Preston (1818–96) married a woman much younger than himself; the other, William Thomas Preston (1813–77), died unmarried.

Thursday – March 13

Still very cold and dreary – staid at home all day – Read the Craftsman[1] which I bought yesterday for 7s. Pleased to find that it was Bp Douglas's copy and contained notes in his hand – valuable notes – for he was intimate with Pulteney the author of many of the papers. Solis. Lord John called. Thank God, Owen's business has been done. Ld Malmesbury's Correspondence.[2] At dinner – Pinm[oney] – Malmesbury again.

1. Started by Nicholas Amhurst (Caleb D'Anvers) in 1726, it was an anti-Walpole production. Bishop John Douglas (1721–1807) was Bishop of Salisbury from 1791.
2. *Diaries and Correspondence of James Harris, 1st Earl of Malmesbury* (1844).

Friday – March 14

Colder than ever – but bright. Staid at home. B came and sate half an hour. Glad to see her, dear child. Read Malmesbury sent Longman a receipt for 20,000£ – gave instructions to buy 2,500 of S. Eastern Stock. I find that Bristol & Exeter is not to be had. What odd letters I get. This morning a woman writes to say that she is possessed of some curious information about James II, but that, as she is poor, she shall expect something handsome for communicating it. Πινμ.[1] Ordered the purchase of 2,500£ of South Eastern instead of 2,000£ Bristol & Exeter.

1. *Pinm(oney).*

Saturday – March 15

Still a prisoner – finished Malmesbury's Diary. A great scoundrel and far from a wise man. Stapleton called.[1] We are to be neighbours. He gave me some advice about tradesmen etc. Charles called. Then Longman. It seems that Blackwood's Magazine is to fall on me.[2] With all my heart. Calculated my means, now that everything is invested. Sixty thousand pounds yielding 3,000£ a year, and Copyrights which cannot be rated at less than 1,500£ a year for a long time to come. In bank above 2,400£ and more coming in daily. I wish to God that Poor E were as well off. Read Mrs Fitzherbert's Memoirs[3] – They are interesting – that is Ld Stourton's narrative is so. The editor Langdale is a sulky solemn ill-tempered bigot as ever I knew. Read Fox's letters beginning in 1783 – I like them better than before.[4] Πινμ.

1. Stapleton lived at 3 Hornton Villas, Kensington.
2. Perhaps a rumour of the article on *HE*, by Margaret Oliphant, in *Blackwoods* for August 1856.
3. Edited by Charles Langdale (1856), brother of Lord Stourton, a near relative of Mrs Fitzherbert, whose Narrative is one of the principal sources for Mrs Fitzherbert's Life.
4. Perhaps *Memorials and Correspondence of Charles James Fox*, ed. Lord John Russell (1853–7).

Sunday – March 16

The weather still the same, but I was so curious about the Empress that at twelve I went out to Brooks's. A prince born.[1] God help the poor child! The probability is that he will go after the king of Rome and the Duke of Bordeaux. To W.T., long and pleasant chat. T. has made it up with Hayter. But I apprehend that they can never be friends. Home. Today I wrote to E – strongly – about the pusillanimity with which he seems to sink down under what, after all, is no such ponderous load of misfortune. I feel for him extremely. Finished Fox's letters. Read some of Romilly's Memoirs[2] – Πινμ.

1. The Empress Eugénie (1826–1920) had married Napoleon III in 1853. The Prince Imperial, Napoleon Louis, died in 1879 fighting in the British army against the Zulus. The King of Rome, styled Napoleon II (1811–32), was the son of Napoleon Bonaparte by Marie-Louise of Austria. The Duke of Bordeaux, Henri de Bourbon (1820–83), also

known as the Duc de Chambord, was the Pretender to the French crown. His 'Legitimist' supporters called him 'Henri V'.

2. Perhaps *Memoir of the late Sir Samuel Romilly ...* (1818); or *Memoirs of the Life of Sir S. Romilly ...* (1818).

Monday – March 17

Rain – yet the wind still East, veering indeed occasionally towards the south. Staid at home. Read a great deal of Cicero – the 1st and second Philippic particularly. They have great merit: yet they are not what I once thought them. Romilly. Πινμ.

Tuesday – March 18

Delmar[1] – the Solicitor of the Shaws[2] – with the assignment lease and bond. I executed them. He took away the assignment and the Lease to get them registered. I paid his bill. Then to W.T. settled about our Easter excursion. Then to the City – all going on as well as possible – Home – Romilly – Πινμ.

1. Perhaps George Delmar of 46 Lincolns Inn Fields, or James Frederick Delmar of 7 Finsbury Square.
2. William Ambrose Shaw (1796–1867) of Wycombe Lodge, Camden Hill.

Wednesday – March 19

Featherstonehaugh's Travels.[1] Most interesting book – a strange fellow – clever, coarse, daring, made for lawless societies and desperate adventures, yet not himself lawless or desperate. Went at one to W.T. – saw F. Walked a quarter of an hour in Kensington Gardens with B – home – finished Featherstonehaugh – Finished Πινμ. William ill, to my great vexation.

1. G. W. Featherstonehaugh, *Excursion through the Slave States ...* (1844).

Thursday – March 20

William still ill. I cannot take him with me. Wrote to H, begging her to bring her man. Barham's vulgar blackguardly ill-written Life of Theodore Hook.[1] Delmar came. The deeds registered – paid him the 500£. Looked over Crabbe's Tales of the Hall. At ½ after two started for the station. They soon joined me – A cold dull day – But we got comfortably to Stroud.[2] Thence by a fly to Hotel – Ordered dinner and walked out – saw the Close – the Castle – the outside of the Cathedral – Home – chatted and dined pleasantly. Read some of Featherstonehaugh's Excursions in the Slave States. A little of Pickwick's adventures at Rochester. To bed.

1. R. H. Dalton Barham, *Life and Remains of Theodore Edward Hook* (1849).

2. Strood, now part of Rochester.

Friday – March 21

Good Friday – cold east wind. They went to Church – I staid by the fire. Cathedrals do not suit me in such weather. In the afternoon we walked. Pleasant dinner and evening. B read some of Pickwick excellently. I was quite pleased with the spirit and propriety of her reading. T is studying the Iliad and enjoys it thoroughly.

Saturday – March 22

After breakfast we took a walk – had a view of the fortifications of Fort Pitt[1] and again visited the close of the Cathedral. At about twelve off with horses for Canterbury. Changed at Sittingbourne. A pleasant journey. It is seldom that I now travel so far in that way. Reached the Fountain[2] at Canterbury at about four. Excellent house. After securing rooms and ordering dinner went to the Cathedral and walked over it. The cold was so severe that I put on my hat. The show woman objected and said that Archdeacon Harrison's[3] orders were positive. A fool! However I would not contend. The Cathedral is a very fine one, the nave inferior in grandeur to several, but to none, I think, in grace and in beauty of proportion. The choir I admire less – too much black and white. It reminded me of the magpie look of the Cathedral of Pisa. Long stroll with H through the Precincts. Full of interest as might have been expected from the antiquity and dignity of the Church. Home to dinner – Pleasant evening. B. read beautifully.

1. Built between 1805 and 1819 as a fortification between Chatham and Rochester, it became a hospital in 1828.
2. In Rose Lane, Canterbury.
3. Benjamin Harrison (1808–87), Canon of Canterbury and Archdeacon of Maidstone, 1845–87. His marriage to Isabella Thornton (1803–93) meant that he was well known to TBM. Cf. *LM*, vol. 6, p. 29 and n.

Sunday – March 23

Easter Sunday. I should have liked to go to Church: but it was bitterly cold and I could not venture. I sate by the fire all the morning. They went to the Cathedral and lunched with the Harrisons. In the afternoon the Harrisons called on me. I was very civil, though not in good humour with the Archdeacon for his absurdity in forcing invalids to remain bareheaded in all parts of his Church, however cold the weather. Pleasant dinner. H read Cowper's Task – It pleased me less than formerly.

Monday – March 24

Soon after breakfast we were off by railway. We all got into one carriage – not without some difficulty and altercation with a very ill-mannered damsel who tried first to block up the entrance of a carriage, and then to take possession of all the seats. At two we reached London Bridge. Home – passed the afternoon in answering letters. Glad to find Wms better, if not quite well. Sent 5£ to Sedgwick for his geological Museum.[1] Wrote to Ellis. The Times has of late been lauding the Indian Commission and what I wonder at more, lauding my Penal Code. Lowe,[2] I suppose. But I should not have expected that Lowe would praise me. At dinner Ledby.[3] – Modern Philosophers. Theodore Hook.

1. Adam Sedgwick (1785–1873), Woodwardian Professor of Geology at Cambridge, had appealed for funds to provide show cases etc. for recently acquired specimens. See J. W. Clark and T. M. Hughes, *The Life and Letters of ... Adam Sedgwick* (Cambridge, 1890), vol. 2, pp. 320–2.
2. Robert Lowe (1811–92), then a leader writer on *The Times*.
3. Albert R. Smith, *The Adventures of Mr Ledbury* (1842).

Tuesday – March 25

I am today master of my new house. After breakfast I read Cicero's speech against Piso – then the speech for Ligarius. To Holly Lodge, though the day was cold and the wind N.E. I find that there will be much to do in the way of painting and whitewashing. The place looked well, the weather considered. To come tomorrow with H and F. Home. Stapleton called and Longman – read the De Claris Oratoribus – much interested – then a good deal of the De Oratore. Began Ward's Memoirs[1] – Λεδβ.[2]

1. Perhaps *Memoirs of the Political and Literary Life of Robert Plumer Ward*, ed. E. Phipps (1850).
2. *Ledbury.*

Wednesday – March 26

Article in The Times on Penn[1] – some person of Dixon's clique. Trash. Read Cicero's Orator and De Optimis Genera. Ward's Memoirs. Letters of another Ward, Ld Dudley.[2] Went to W.T. and thence with H and F to H.L. Gave orders and made arrangements. They brought me home. The two Wards and Λεδβ.

1. *The Times*, 26 March, p. 4, col. 8. This lists and demolishes eight charges made by TBM, in the *HE*, against William Penn, and challenges Penn to reply to them.
2. Robert Plumer Ward (see above, entry for 6 December 1853) and John William Ward, Earl of Dudley, *Letters ... to the Bishop of Llandaff* (1840).

Thursday – March 27

Still this weather – the sun brighter however. Finished the Wards. Went out, bought some books in King Street Holborn.[1] The house agent came with the valuation of the things which I am to take. Very moderate £281.2.6. – There may be a little appendix – Will Marshall called. More like what he was and less like what he has become – this pleased me. But n'importe. Perhaps I am at this moment a little irritable, galled by the petty attacks which a great and indeed unprecedented success has called forth. But I ought to have, and I will have, self command enough not to be disturbed by such trifles. Next week will, I suppose, produce plenty of abuse; and then it will be over or nearly so. Read Monk's Life of Bentley,[2] stopping to read Bentley himself from time to time. Read a good deal of the Epistola ad Milliam, excellent – some of the Boyle lectures[3] – less striking. Λεδβ. In the evening the books which I had bought in the morning came. I turned some of them over – a Life of Curran[4] – almost – not quite – as bad as Charles Philipps's[5] – a collection of tracts by and about Shebbeare,[6] with a portrait of his impudent face.

1. Perhaps from the Mr Salkeld whose story is given in Trevelyan, vol. 2, pp. 450–2.
2. J. H. Monk, *The Life of Richard Bentley D.D.* Macaulay's copy of the second edition (1873) is in the Library of Trinity College, Cambridge.
3. (1691). Richard Boyle (1627–91) had endowed an annual series of sermons in proof of the Christian religion. Bentley was chosen to give the first, which he did in 1692–3.
4. Perhaps W. H. Curran, *Life of J. P. Curran* (1819).
5. *Curran and his Contemporaries* (1850).
6. John Shebbeare (1705–88), a political writer patronized by Bute. TBM, in his essay on Chatham, calls him a wretched scribbler, contrasting the favours he received with the neglect of Dr Johnson. *CW*, vol. 7, p. 231.

Friday – March 28

Still, still, N.E very bleak. But I have got wonderfully through the winter – always valetudinarian – but never positively ill – never a positive cold. Bentley's Horace.[1] Finished his epistle to Mill. Read his Emendations on Menander and Philemon[2] – really a wonderful work – though many of the emendations are mere original Iambic lines. The second part of his answer to Collins[3] – Very good, though sometimes sophistical. Λεδβ.

1. (1711).
2. (1710).
3. Richard Bentley, *Remarks upon a Late Discourse of Free-Thinking* (1713). *A Late Discourse of Free-Thinking* (1713) is by Anthony Collins.

Saturday – March 29

Bentley – to W.T. – though the wind was still East – gave H 100£. She seemed not unwilling to let B go with me to Italy in the autumn, if E cannot go. I hardly like to take such a responsibility, much as I should enjoy the dear child's company. Home – Letter this morning from E – answered him. He is more cheerful, I think. Read a volume of tracts – The Ireland forgery[1] – Paull's duel with Burdett[2] – Trial of Mitford for perjury in 1812[3] – Vincent in defence of the Westminster education[4] – Λεδβ – Monk's Life of B.

1. Presumably an account of William Ireland (1777–1835), the forger of Shakespearean manuscripts. They were exposed by Edmund Malone in 1796. See SC, no. 580.
2. James Paull (1770–1808) and Sir Francis Burdett (1770–1844) fought a duel after a disagreement in the course of the Westminster Election of 1807.
3. John Mitford (1782–1831), miscellaneous writer. See SC, no. 881.
4. William Vincent (1739–1815), *A defence of Public Education* ... (1801). Vincent was Headmaster of Westminster, 1788–1802, and later Dean, 1802–15. This was no. 788 in SC.

Sunday – March 30

The wind a little veering towards south – the weather bright not cold – to Brooks's. Thence to W.T. – Home – Bentley – Hare's Epistola Critica.[1] Finished Monk's Life – Bentley's fame rests chiefly on what he did during the first half of his long life. The Epistle to Mill, the Corrections of the Comic fragments,[2] and above all the Treatise on Phalaris[3] are his great performances. The Horace is much less valuable. The Terence I have not seen. But the Phaedrus[4] seems from Hare's quotations and Monk's admissions to have been nearly worthless. The Manilius is not worth much. The Milton is utterly contemptible and detestable. The latter to Mead on the Sigean Inscription[5] was all in the wrong. The discovery of the Digamma[6] was, no doubt, a great thing. But Bentley left no written account of the discovery. To be sure even in his worst works, the Milton excepted, traces of his genius may be detected. But he seems to me an eminent instance of the extent to which intellectual powers of a most rare and admirable kind may be impaired by moral defects. It was not on account of any obscuration of his memory or of any decay in his inventive faculties that he fell from the very first place among critics to the third or fourth rank. It was his insolence, his arrogance, his boundless confidence in himself and disdain of everybody else that lowered him. Instead of taking subjects which he thoroughly understood, which he could have treated far better than all the other scholars in Europe together, he would take subjects which he had but superficially studied. He ceased to give his whole mind to what he wrote. He scribbled a dozen sheets of Latin at a sitting, sent them to the press without reading them over, and then, as was natural, had to bear the baiting of word catching pedagogues who were on the watch for all his blunders. The way in which he drew up his proposals for the New Testament is most characteristic. His saying that no man was ever written down but by himself was excellent, and was proved to be so, both by his victory over Christ Church[7] and by the defeats which he sustained in his encounters with Middleton, Hare, and other antagonists less formidable. I forgot to mention that last week, on Saturday, I think, I read Tunstall on the letters of Cicero and Brutus.[8] I read also the letters, which convinced me much more than Tunstall's arguments, that the whole correspondence is spurious, a rhetorical exercise of the third century probably. Λεδβ. Life of Morland.[9] Just as I was going to bed, I heard the guns – Peace – Thank God.[10]

1. By Francis Hare (1726).
2. A letter by Bentley to Tiberius Hemsterhuys on Julius Pollux and Greek Comic Metres (1708).
3. *Dissertation on the Letters of Phalaris* (1799).
4. Phaedrus was a freed slave who compiled books of verse fables in the reign of Augustus.
5. For Richard Bentley's letter to Dr Richard Mead (1721), see J. H. Monk, *Life of D. Richard Bentley D.D.* (London, 1830), pp. 458–60.
6. For a lucid explanation, see R. C. Jebb, *Bentley* (London, 1882), p. 150.
7. Concerning the authenticity of the Letters of Phalaris. TBM tells the story twice, in the essay on Sir William Temple and in his essay on Atterbury; *CW*, vol. 4, pp. 320–3, and vol. 7, pp. 224–89.
8. James Tunstall, *The Epistles of M.T. Cicero to M. Brutus ...* (1743).
9. There is a *Life of George Morland* by G. Dawe (1807) in SC, no. 222.
10. The salute of guns from St James's Park at 10 p.m., for the news of the signature of the Treaty of Paris, marking the end of the Crimean War.

Monday – March 31

A fine day at last – bright sun and the wind almost south – To the City – Saw my book. Crowds round the Mansion House where the letter of George Grey[1] to the Ld Mayor was exhibited. Still greater crowd in front of the Exchange – bought the British Quarterly Review – an article on my book[2] – praise and blame – like other writers I swallow the praise and think the blame absurd. But in truth I do think that the fault-finding is generally unreasonable, though the book is, no doubt, faulty enough. It is well for its reputation that I do not review it, as I could review it. Home. Finished the Life of Morland, very curious and instructive. Wilkes's controversy with Horne[3]. Mares called to take orders about paper. H had chosen patterns and I of course ratified her choice. Λεδβ.

1. Sir George Grey (1799–1882), the second Baronet, was Home Secretary.
2. *British Quarterly Review*, 23 (April 1856), pp. 297–325. 'The art of history: Macaulay', by G. H. Lewes (Wellesley Index).

3. Presumably the controversy printed in the *Public Advertiser* for 1771, between John Wilks and John Horne Tooke concerning, inter alia, the use of the funds of the Society ... of the Bill of Rights to pay Wilkes's debts.

Tuesday – April 1

Very fine day – Wind south west. After breakfast to the Athenaeum and R.I. – Saw articles on my book in the Dublin Review,[1] and the National Review.[2] Very well satisfied to find that the whole skill and knowledge of Maynooth could make no impression on my account of the Irish War. The National Review contains some just criticism, but in a bad, obscure mystical style. To W.T. – Diana Babington dead in a strange sudden way.[3] She had a brute of a husband – and he had a jade of a wife. He used to beat her; and she richly deserved it. I went with H to the house where the corpse was. But just as we stopped – it was in South Audley Street, a party walked up to the door – T G B her father, and his wife, Arthur and his wife.[4] I did not know any of them. Tom, once well known, I have not seen, I should think, these eight and twenty years and more. But H knew them and made haste to order the carriage to drive on. Home – Wilkes – Porson's Letters to Travis[5] – I am never weary of them. Λεδβ.

1. C. W. Russell reviewed the volumes in the issue of the *Dublin Review* for March 1856, vol. 11, pp. 156–200. He had reviewed the earlier ones in June 1849 (vol. 2, pp. 33).
2. *National Review*, 2 (April 1856), pp. 357–87; by Walter Bagehot. Reprinted in *Collected Works of Walter Bagehot*, ed. N. St John Stevas (London, 1965), vol. 1, pp. 396–428.
3. She was Augusta Diana Babington (b. 1815), daughter of the Revd Thomas Gisborne Babington (1788–1871) of Rothley Temple. She died on 28 March at 69 South Audley Street. The cause of death given was 'heart disease terminating in apoplexy'. Her husband was Frederick Mortimer Lewin (1799–1877), who had been in the Madras Civil Service.
4. Thomas Gisborne Babington had married a second time; his wife was Augusta Teresa Vecqueray (1812–90). The Revd Thomas Arthur Babington (1820–96) was his son; his wife was Katherine Mary Bolton (1821–81). They had married on 19 August 1847.
5. R. Porson, *Letters to Archdeacon Travis ...* (1790).

Wednesday – April 2

Another delightful day. Went to the R.I. – walked long – picked up some books. Public Characters[1] – Life of Matthews the Actor[2] – Life of P. Ward.[3] Home – H and B called – then Mrs Macleod to look at the rooms for Ld Rollo.[4] Plenty of competitors – I finished Porson's incomparable letters – looked at Turton's Vindication[5] – Λεδβ.

1. TBM had two collections of portraits under this title; see nos 743 and 744 in the Library SC.
2. *Memoirs of Charles Mathews, Comedian*, by Mrs A. Mathews (1838).

3. Perhaps *Memoirs ... of Robert Plumer Ward ...*, ed. E. Phipps (1850).
4. John Rogerson Rollo (1835–1916), tenth Baron. Mrs Macleod had been Catherine Greig (b. 1822). Her sister Agnes (1806–55) had married the eighth Lord Rollo, and she was therefore the young man's aunt.
5. Thomas Turton, *A Vindication of the Literary Character of the Late Professor Porson ... by Crito Cantabrigiensis* (1827).

Thursday – April 3

The morning cloudy. The rain no doubt is coming up after the long drought. Went out. Returned after a long ramble just in time to escape the rain. I ordered Dawes's Mis Crit[1] of Mott. Longman sent me a heap of reviews of my book, two which I had not seen, the Christian Remembrancer[2] and the London Quarterly[3] – both quite as laudatory as I could have expected. A little acid does no harm. But the London Quarterly Reviewer is so ignorant as to believe that Wn III gave T Oates Church preferment, and this on no better authority than poor Miss Strickland's. Looked at the 1st Vol of Public Characters. I remember reading it at Edinburgh in July 1817 near 39 years ago – I forgot to mention that the editor of the Lit Gaz[4] wrote to ask me for Memoranda about Penn. I thanked him, but declined. I will not stoop to controversy with Dixon. But if I did, I would write something and put my name to it. I am sorry that I did not always follow this rule. E to dinner after a month's absence. Glad to see him so well and cheerful. We sate till near 12 – Hydr.

1. Richard Dawes, *Miscellanea Critica ...* (first published 1745).
2. *Christian Remembrancer*, April 1856.
3. *London Quarterly Review*, 4 (April 1856), pp. 205–63, by W. C. Yonge.
4. Lovell Reeve (1814–65). The journal closed in 1862.

Friday – April 4

A true April day. Having taken physic I staid at home till late in the afternoon – read Public Characters. To dine, after a long interval, at W.T. Sanford[1] called in the morning about the chambers. I have little doubt that I shall get rid of them comfortably. Pleasant quiet evening in W.T. George there. He has done excellently. He is now second, and first of all the boys of his standing. His composition, both Greek and Latin has improved surprisingly; and he shows a real taste for classical learning. The next year and a half, well spent, will send him up to Cambridge a good scholar.

1. Perhaps William Ayshford Sanford (1818–1902), a colonial civil servant, whom TBM had met at Woburn in 1850 (*LM*, vol. 5, p. 144n.).

Saturday – April 5

Letter from a poor author named Cole whom I assisted some months ago. He protests that he is not the author of some attack on me in Sharp's Magazine or some such work of which I never heard. To the Museum. lounged among the bookcases during an hour or two, – then to the Board Room. Long sitting. Walked away with Dundas. Home – Public Characters – Λεδβ – April weather.

Sunday – April 6

Still true April weather. To Brooks's – to W.T. – Batten, a civil servant of the E.I.C. and a son of the old Principal of Hayleybury,[1] called and lunched there. Home in a cab through the rain. Finished P C. Began the Buckingham papers.[2] The most vilely edited collection that I know – yet valuable. The Duke is the prince of fools. Λεδβ.

1. Joseph Hallet Batten (1778–1837), Principal of Haileybury from 1815, and his son, John Hallet Batten (1810–66).
2. Perhaps *Memories of the Court and Cabinet of George the Third ...*, edited by the Duke of Buckingham (1853).

Monday – April 7

Fine day. Forced to go to the City, having been weak enough to let myself be importuned into being photographed for some periodical work. I had to climb to the top of a house in Gracechurch Street[1] – half the height of the monument. Then I was smothered and stunk to death with æther and other chemical abominations. I was hard put to it to keep my temper. Walked back by Holborn – bought Burke's Correspce[2] of which I had only the first two vols. The Buckingham Corres. Scott and Liddell's Dictionary.[3] Coming home found a letter from Germany. Six translations of my new vols into German are coming out at once.[4] Buckingham Correspondence. E to dinner. Glad to see him so well and cheerful. We talked of Italy with hope.

1. *LM*, vol. 6, p. 33, shows the importunity was from Herbert Fry (1830–85), who was putting together a series of photographs of celebrities with accompanying biographical notes. The photographers Maull and Polyblank at 55 Gracechurch Street were used for the photographs.
2. Perhaps the edition published in 1844 by the Earl of Fitzwilliam and Sir Richard Bourke.
3. A. G. Liddell and R. Scott, *A Greek Lexicon*, 1st edn (1843).
4. *LM*, vol. 6, p. 35, n. 6.

Tuesday – April 8

G and B to breakfast. very pleasant – took them to the Museum – passed two hours in rambling through those immense galleries. Home – finished The Bm Correspondence. The Duke must be the greatest dunce and fool that ever had the ordinary advantages of education. Not a page without solecisms, anachronisms, blunders of all kinds. A most hopeless idiot! The correspondence however very curious. Wrote a few lines of my article on Johnson.[1] It is good to break the ice. Old newspapers with great zest. At dinner finished Λεδβ.

1. For Black's *Encyclopaedia Britannica.*

Wednesday – April 9

Wet – but I went to the City. All right. Home – wrote a little for Black – read Morning Chronicles of 1803 – Malden called and sate long. At 7 H and B called for me. We took up T at the Treasury and went to the Deanery of St Paul's. Ld and Lady Monteagle – K. Howard and Lady Louisa[1] and Twisleton, Ford and Mrs Ford,[2] were there. I have not dined out this long time. The Trevelyans went to an evening party at the Admiralty. I got into a cab opposite the Horse Guards and went home.

1. Hon. James Kenneth Howard (1814–82). He had been MP for Malmesbury, 1841–52. He married Louisa, Lord Lansdowne's only daughter (1813–1906).
2. Perhaps Richard Ford (1796–1858) and his third wife, Mary (1816–1910), daughter of Sir Arscott Molesworth.

Thursday – April 10

I went again to the City today in consequence of a report about forgeries[1] on the G.S.W. Railway of Ireland. I found that I ran no risk worth naming. Back, through Covent Garden etc. – wrote a little – read Burke's Correspondence and Morning Chronicles 1803–4. Looked into Dawes's Miscellanea Critica. A German translation of part of my third Volume. E to dinner. The Longman sent me The Morning Advertiser containing an absurd article about George Fox by that great fool Howitt.[2]

1. James Montgomery Knighting, a transfer clerk in the Great South Western Railway, had created, from 1853, fictitious transfers of stock and pocketed the money. He was indicted at Dublin's Court of Queen's bench on 20 June 1856.
2. 'Macaulay and George Fox', *Morning Advertiser*, 8 April 1856, p. 4e (a half-column). William Howitt was the son of a Quaker.

Friday – April 11

Burke's Correspondence – To the R.I. I see that there is to be no article on me in the Quarterly, but that there is to be one in the Edinburgh. I looked at several books – Merivale's History of Rome[1] – Tiberius – Washington Irving's Life of Washington.[2] To W.T. Went with H and. B to Grosvenor Crescent where they took up Mrs Buxton. Then to Chelsea Hospital. There the ladies alighted to hear the examination on Crimean matters.[3] I went home, wrote a little, and read old newspapers and Burke's letters – At dinner Κοκτ οικον– By the bye I have lost this week two old acquaintances – one friend, I might almost say – Evans,[4] whom I have known thirty five or six years, and with whom I have always been on a footing of kindness – and William Melville,[5] a surly, dull impracticable man, always maundering and unsatisfied, yet not without good points.

1. Charles Merivale, *History of the Romans under the Empire* (1850–64); or possibly an earlier version, *A History of Rome under the Emperor ...* (1841).
2. Washington Irving, *Life of George Washington*, 5 vols (1855–9).
3. A Commission of Enquiry had been appointed to consider the report on the breakdown of various military departments in the Crimean War, which concerned in particular Lord Lucan, Lord Cardigan and Colonel Gordon. The report of the commision published in July exonerated these officers.
4. William Evans (1788–1856), for many years MP for North Derbyshire, 1837–53. He married in 1820 Mary, daughter of the Revd Thomas Gisborne, of Yoxall Lodge, Staffordshire. Gisborne had married a sister of Thomas Babington. Cf. *LM*, vol. 1, p. 198n.
5. William Harry Leslie Melville (1788–1856), Director of the East India Company. He was the third son of Alexander Melville, the seventh Earl.

Saturday – April 12

A long sitting at the Museum – wrote a little about Johnson. Read Burke's Correspondence – οικ – Malden called and sate long.

Sunday – April 13

Delightful day – Walked in the Park and Kensington Gardens to – W.T. made arrangements for tomorrow – Home – Burke – Paul Feval Les Bandits.[1]

1. (1847). TBM was amused that this work contained a character, 'a charming Englishwoman, Miladi Ophélie Dog'. *LM*, vol. 6, p. 31.

Monday – April 14

Up at six. H, B, A and G called for me at 7. To the Shoreditch Station. An East wind and not a very genial day. However we had a pleasant journey to Cambridge and a comfortable breakfast at The Bull.[1] Then walked – through King's saw the Chapel – through Caius. Then into Trin Coll by the great gate – through the Great Court and Nevile's Court – saw the Library – then the gardens, then through St John's and into Trin again. I called on W E. Then the ladies came up to see his room – a well remembered room.[2] It was poor Stainforth's in 1819 – Malden's in 1822. But W E had furnished it much better than his predecessors – too well indeed, all things considered. Asked him to dinner. Met H. Parker. Asked him too – I had not seen him since his accident. Dreadful. Called on Buxton, and asked him to join us. Then to our inn. Sate some time – then set out again. Walked through Corpus Christi, Pembroke, St Peters, Cath Hall, saw as much as we could of Queen's which was under repair, then went by the backs of the Colleges to Clare and so to Trinity just at dinner time. G was with his young friends. H was tired and went to the inn. I took the dear girls to Jesus, and then to the Bull. I enjoyed little Alice's delight and surprise. It is her first journey of the kind. We met old Sedgwick[3] in Trumpington Street. He greeted us warmly, and made little Alice an offer in form, for which she was very grateful. "What a good-natured old man!" At ½ after 5 dinner. Our three young guests were punctual. I gave them as good fare as The Bull afforded, and that is not saying much, and some Champagne. At 7 we were off. Reached London at ½ after 10 and separated. A most pleasant day. I love them all dearly. Home and to bed much tired.

---

1. In Trumpington Street.
2. Walter Ellis, at no. 3 Great Court. George Stainforth (1796–1820) was a high flyer who had taught TBM and who died tragically young. Cf. *LM*, vol. 1, pp. 18n, and 145n.
3. Adam Sedgwick, of Trinity.

Tuesday – April 15

Had meant to go to the levee today, but finding that there will be another levee in May I changed my mind. The wind was sharp; and I did not like to expose myself to it without a great coat. Dr Carpenter called about this Registrarship.[1] Longman – talked about reprinting. Ordered some books – Walked – crossed the Thames by Blackfriars Bridge and back by Bridge – bought Tasso's works in 12 Vols qo. Home – finished Burke's correspondence – most interesting – Johnson. To dinner with Denison – a fine house.[2] The dining room painted with frescoes. Bad art – but good upholstery. The Duke and Duchess of Argyle, Gladstone and his wife, Dallas the American Minister,[3] a venerable whiteheaded old gentleman, Stephenson the engineer,[4] Wentworth from Australasia.[5] The party not particularly lively.

---

1. William Benjamin Carpenter (1813–85), appointed Registrar of the University of London, 1856–79.
2. 7 Carlton House Terrace.

3. George Mifflin Dallas (1792–1864), former Vice-President of the USA, and Minister to Great Britain from 1856 to 1861.
4. George Robert Stephenson (1819–1905), son of the inventor of the Rocket. He built railways all over the world.
5. Presumably William Charles Wentworth (1783–1872), the Australian statesman.

Wednesday – April 16

Fine day, but cold east wind – to the R.I. and Athenaeum – to W.T. Nobody but Alice at home – The rest gone to the Crimean examination. Home – Johnson – Parliamentary examination and debates about the D of Y.[1] 1809 – E to dinner – He very fesc.

1. In January 1809 Gwyllm Lloyd Wardle (*c.* 1762–1833) brought forward a motion in the House of Commons attacking the Duke of York, the Commander-in-Chief of the army, for corruption over the sale of commissions, in which Mary Anne Clarke was involved. The proceedings in committee lasted from 1 February to 20 March, and led to the Duke's retirement.

Thursday – April 17

At breakfast B and G came and sate a short time. They are all going to Buxton's Brewery[1] today. A Mr List called – a clerk from Weigel's house at Leipzig[2] – he brought me the translation of my new vols published by that House. His report very encouraging. He tells me that Tauchnitz has sold already from four to five thousand copies of the English edition. That ought to bring a handsome sum to me. I went to the Athenaeum. The Bp of Exeter[3] most kind and laudatory, to my surprise, I own. Walked into the City merely for a walk. – along Bishopsgate Street into Spitalfields and back by Whitechapel, thinking of old times when every corner of that part of London was as well known to me as Regent Street. Home – wrote a little about Johnson – finished the D of Y's affair. At dinner the Bandits. Began a queer book called the Whale by Herman Melville.[4] Absurd – yet better than I had expected from a glance which I gave to a thing of his called Mardi which seemed to me a bad imitation of the worst part of Rabelais. Today I called on Dallas in Portland Place. Sir H. Bulwer called on me.

1. The Black Eagle Brewery, Brick Lane, Spitalfields. It was run by Truman, Hanbury and Buxton, and was one of the largest in London.
2. Cf *LM*, vol. 6, p. 35, n. 5.
3. Henry Phillpotts.
4. *Moby Dick; or The Whale* (1851). *The Whale* was the title of the English edition, also published 1851. *Mardi, and a Voyage Thither* was published in 1849.

Friday – April 18

Again fine and again cold with N.E. wind – Holly Lodge – thence by Bayswater Road to W.T. – with H and B to Grosvenor Crescent – Home – Whale – Morning Chron. – The exposure of Wardle. Very interesting. At dinner finished the Bandits – poor stuff – an incredibly absurd picture of English Society.

Saturday – April 19

Dull day but not cold. Walked – Athenaeum – Read the new Quarterly. Bought Selwyn's Memoirs and Correspondence.[1] Home and passed the day in burning and arranging papers. Some things that met my eyes overcame me for a time – Margaret! Alas Alas – And yet she might have changed to me – but no that could never have been. To think that she has been near 22 years dead; and I am crying for her as if it were yesterday. But sursum corda. To dinner with Labouchere. Ld and Lady John, Ld and Ly Stanhope, D. and Duchess of Argyle, Ld Elgin,[2] Charles Greville – etc. Not unpleasant. A crowd in the evening. Stole away.

---

1. Probably *George Selwyn and his Contemporaries, with Memoir and Notes*, ed. J. Heneage Jesse (1843).
2. James Bruce (1811–63), eighth Earl of Elgin.

Sunday – April 20

Fine though the wind east. To Brooks's. To the ['Athen' deleted] W.T. Charles, T, G and James Cropper[1] who is on a visit at W.T. wished to see my new house. We walked thither – but nobody was at home. A great neglect, though there was little risk: for there is no furniture as yet and the shutters were closed. We got into the garden and walked there. It is really a very pretty place. Home – Sir H. Holland called – Morning Chronicles of 1810. At dinner finished the Whale – a most absurd book[2] with here and there a curious passage.

---

1. James Cropper (1823–1900). He was the eldest son of John Cropper (1797–1874) and nephew of Edward Cropper, Margaret Macaulay's husband.
2. It was in fact based upon the true story of the whaler *Essex*, which was sunk by a sperm whale in 1820.

Monday – April 21

Wms woke me before eight. The moving of the books was beginning – I gave orders – breakfasted and sate in the small room. Oddly enough on this day – the last day on which it suited me to have callers, I had a most unusual number – Ld Glenelg, Ld Hatherton, Cavour the Sardinian Minister,[1] a very superior man – a vulgar ignorant fellow, Secretary of the St James's Literary Association,[2] who came to pester me for a donation, and to ask how he could get ordained. Then came Fry[3] bringing me a hideous photograph of myself, ugly beyond all names of ugliness, and begging me to go again to have this delicious likeness retouched. I was thoroughly provoked and gave him a piece of my mind. He had the face then to ask me for a sketch of my life. Brazen impudence! A fool named Chapman has been writing to the Longmans to say that he is going to lecture about me, and wished them to send him a description of my person, manners, etc. These vagabonds ought to be whipped at the cart's tail. To W.T. B walked with me. I brought her to the Albany and then took her back to W.T. with the photograph. How she and her mother laughed at it! I then went by an omnibus to London Bridge. Thence by railway to Greenwich – dined at the Trafalgar and ordered dinner for ten on Saturday. Read the Pucelle de Belleville[4] but found it heavy. Home – Letter on the table from a Quietist merchant in the City who has got some of my grandfather's Behmenite M.S.S. and wishes to know whether I care about such theosophic lore, as he calls it.[5] I answered him very civilly, but in a way to show that I was no follower of Jacob and Law. Nollekens's Life.[6]

1. Camillo Benso, Contedi Cavour (1810–61).
2. The St James's Library and Scientific Institution, 1 Cork Street. The Secretary was Sidney Corner (*c.* 1816–84), a watercolourist. Its president was the Earl of Carlisle.
3. Herbert Fry (1830–84), author of *National Gallery of Photographic Portraits* (1858). See above, entry for 7 April 1856.
4. Charles-Paul de Kock, *La Pucelle de Belleville* (1843).
5. This was Christopher Walton (1809–77). TBM's letter to him is in *LM*, vol. 6, p. 36.
6. J. T. Smith, *Nollekens and his Times* (1828).

Tuesday – April 22

I see that there has been a debate on the Museum and that Milnes exposed himself,[1] as I might have expected. I sent an excuse to him for not going to a lunch which he gives in honor of his child's christening.[2] I had much to do. To the Museum – looked into King's Book[3] – found that I was right and the Dublin Review wrong on every point. Saw Panizzi – talked about the debate. Went to the new reading room – a splendid rotunda[4] – very nearly as large as the Pantheon. To the Strand and by omnibus to Campden Hill – found the people from Wesley's busy putting up the books. The day was dull, but the garden looked pretty, and the whole aspect of things was cheering. While I was there Derwent Coleridge called. We walked together in the garden during some time – chatting as we used to do thirty five years ago. Then away together by the lane which skirts the grounds of Holland House – We discussed Southey, Wordsworth etc. etc. Home. The books are gone – my shelves empty – tomorrow I take final leave of this room, where I have spent most of the waking hours of near ten years. Already its aspect is changed. It is the corpse of what it was on Sunday. The shelves look like a skeleton. I am a little sad, though with many many reasons for joy. I hate partings. Shall I be as happy at Holly Lodge as I have been here? E to dinner – The last of probably four hundred dinners or more that we have had in these chambers. We sate in the small room all the evening. I hate to see the large room as it now is.

1. In a debate on the management of the British Museum, Monckton Milnes stated that an Englishman should be Principal Librarian. Panizzi had just been appointed. *PD*, 3rd ser., cxli, 1346–52.
2. Monckton Milnes's second daughter, born in December 1855, was christened Florence Ellen Hungerford, in honour of Florence Nightingale, whom Milnes had tried to marry six years before. She died in 1923. J. Pope-Hennessey, *Monckton Milnes, The Flight of Youth* (London, 1951), pp. 82–3.
3. Perhaps William King's *State of the Protestants of Ireland under the late King James's Government* (1691). King (1650–1729) was Dean of St Patrick's and later Bishop of Derry. In 1703 he became Archbishop of Dublin.
4. The reading room was Panizzi's idea. See Miller, *That Noble Cabinet*, pp. 187–8.

Wednesday – April 23

The day of the Naval Review. Odd that I remember nothing particular about this day except that I read Nolleken's Life and the Pucelle de Belleville. I ordered a set of the State Trials.

Thursday – April 24

Breakfast with the Bp of Oxford – Gladstone, Heathcote,[1] Gordon,[2] Stafford,[3] Ld Stanhope. Stafford talked the Young England gossip – now a worn out cant. Walked away with Ld S. He showed me a malignant lying ill written libel on Ld Rutherfurd which Brougham, has scribbled and wished to tack to a report of the H. of L. To W.T. All out except Alice. To H.L. pretty well satisfied with the look of the books, but vexed by the delay of the painters. Home. State Trials sent – Parr – Bellendenus[4] Warb and Warbn[5] – Belleville.

1. Presumably Sir William Heathcote, Bart (1801–81); MP for Oxford University, 1854–68.
2. Perhaps Sir Alexander Duff Gordon, third Bart (1811–72).
3. Augustus Stafford, formerly Stafford O'Brien, Secretary of the Admiralty, 1852.
4. Bellendenus is William Bellenden (d. *c.* 1633); like Samuel Parr, a classical scholar.
5. Perhaps *Tracts by Warburton and a Warburtonian*, two of William Warburton's tracts published by Parr in 1789.

Friday – [April 25]

Beautiful day – bored in the morning by callers – one man wanting to be Registrar of the London Univy – another pestering me about the Marriages Bill.[1] Went to the Athenaeum – there met Ryan – walked with him in search of Lefevre – to the H of L – to the Civil Service Exn office. To the Treasury Talked much about the Civil Exams. The division in Ld G[oderic]h's motion[2] yesterday is a great feather in T's cap. I hope he will not be rash. Strange folly of the Tories, or worse than folly in absenting themselves on the gravest occasions in order that the Govt may be beaten by Liberals and Peelites. The punishment will soon come. The division is, on the whole, a happy event for the country. Home – Longman has sent me the 2 last vols of Tom Moore's Life.[3] I read them with some interest – My own name often recurs, and always agreeably. Memoirs of George Selwyn. Le Serpent[4] – Hydr.

1. Perhaps the Marriage Law Amendment Bill, presented by Brougham in the Lords on 28 April, to remove inconsistencies in the laws governing marriages in England and in Scotland. *PD*, 3rd ser., cxli, 1587 (28 April 1856).
2. Viscount Goderich's motion in favour of entry to the civil service by competitive examination was passed by 108 votes to 87. The debate is in *PD*, 3rd ser., cxli, 1401–44.
3. Vols 7 and 8.
4. Perhaps Charles Leslie's *A Snake in the Grass* (1696).

Saturday – [April 26]

Weather changing – some rain. Staid at home till 12 – saw Wesley and Mares. Two fresh men have been sent to put the books in order. Mares assures me that within 24 hours after the books are in order everything will be ready. I have made up my mind to sleep at H.L. next Saturday. To the R.I. To the Museum – Long sitting. To Greenwich. Handsome dinner and pleasant party – C Z M, T, H, B, G, E, F, M, L[1] – Home with the T's.

1. i.e. Charles Macaulay, all of the Trevelyans, and Ellis and his children, Frank, Marian and Louisa.

Sunday – April 27

A cold disagreeable day. However I went to W.T. and in the evening, much against the grain to Lne H. I took Ld Glenelg with me. We found Ld L gouty and Lady S laid up with cold. Senior was there, Twisleton and his Squaws[1] – Arnold. I had a short conversation with Ld L about a disagreeable matter [heavy erasure] – the attack which Brougham has made on Rutherford in a paper which has been printed and circulated among the peers who form the Committee on Life Peerages. Dundas mentioned it at the Museum yesterday. I was glad to find that there was no chance that the paper would be published. Should it be published poor R will not want defenders or avengers.

1. Edward Twisleton (see Volume 3, entry for 11 August 1851 and n. 1) had married an American wife, Ellen Dwight (1819–62), of Boston, Massachusetts. She had three sis-

ters, one of whom, Elizabeth (1830–1901), was then staying with the Twisletons in London. She later became Mrs J. Elliot Cabot.

Monday – April 28

Staid at home waiting for Westley. He came with good news. His men will be out on Wednesday. I shall sleep in my new house on Friday. Walked long. I forgot to mention that on Saturday on my way from the Museum to the Greenwich Station I looked in at Longman's and saw W. Longman. My affairs are going on as well as possible – 5,000 copies of vols. 1 and 2 sold since June last. Today I picked up a treatise of Andrew Fuller's[1] on what is called among the Baptists the Modern Question. A treatise which I had long wished to see; but I was sorry to find that it had been mutilated in the controversial part. Home – Selwyn – Cooper's Wyandotte.[2] To dinner at Fox's – Van de Weyer and Mme V – Dundas – a Dr Jackson, an Indian medical officer.[3] Tolerable but tolerable. Fox has excellent qualities. But he is one of the oddest of human beings. He told me that I had hurt his feelings – that he had a complaint to make. I could not conceive what he meant. He took me apart and showed me a passage in my History in which I contemptuously mention the Duke of Maine as the bastard. He really took this as a reflection on himself and all other bastards. I should never have been guilty of the indecency of referring to the misfortune of his birth. Indeed, I should have expected to be knocked down, as I should have deserved to be, if I had done so. I did not know which way to look. However I said that, as he wished the word to be changed, I would change it; and I will.[4] But what strange weakness! I took Dundas back to town – We talked of Fox's eccentricity.

1. Andrew Fuller (1754–1815), *The Gospel Worthy of All Acceptation* (1785).
2. J. F. Cooper (1843).
3. Perhaps John Jackson (1804–87), who married Marie Pattle, was a Member of the Royal College of Physicians and had just returned to England. There are four other Jacksons in the IMS at this time but this man seems the most likely. He wrote *Forms of Tetanus in India* (1856).
4. Charles Richard Fox was the son of Lord and Lady Holland, born before their marriage. Louis Auguste de Bourbon, the Duke of Maine (1670–1736), was the natural son of Louis XIV and the Duchess of Montespan. In the first edition of vol. 4 of the *History* (ch. 21), Macaulay wrote of Maine's conduct in 1695: 'At the first glimpse of danger the bastard's heart had died within him' (p. 587); in later editions, 'bastard' was altered to 'dastard' (*CW*, vol. 4, p. 160).

Tuesday – April 29

To the City – not without difficulty: for the Heralds are out today in all their glory.[1] The crowd immense – the Temple Gates shut. I found that Thornton had got 450£ of Rl Exchange Stock for me. Walked with him from the Bank in

Birchin Lane to St Paul's. To the Temple. E not at home. Found myself a prisoner in consequence of the crowd at the gates – forced to make my escape by the Blackfriars Gate. Back by Holborn – to Piccadilly. Ordered new cards. To W.T. – H, B and G soon returned from Oxford where they had been passing a day. Chatted, came with them in the carriage to Oxford Street. Home. Wrote nine or ten letters to tell people my new address. Longman has sent me the new vols of the D. of Buckingham's Papers – fell upon them eagerly and read till it was time to go to the Club, my first dinner at the Club this year. I found a pleasant party. Dundas in the Chair – Ld Aberdeen, Senior, Sir H. Holland, Milman, Hawtrey,[2] Pemberton Leigh, Van de Weyer, the D. of Argyle, Ld A., Dundas, P L and I remained till half after eleven.

1. To announce the proclamation of peace in the City of London and Westminster. There is an account of the traditional ceremony in the *Annual Register* (1856), pp. 100–1.
2. E. C. Hawtrey, Provost of Eton.

Wednesday – April 30

To breakfast with Ld Stanhope – Ld Stanley – the Duke d'Aumale, Lady Evelyn Stanhope etc. – Not amiss. Then to the City – transferred 1200£ 3 per cent Stock in order to buy Rl Exchange Stock.[1] To H.L. The books very nearly put up: but there will still be much to do before they are arranged as I wish to have them – several rooms almost ready for use. The garden charming. Gave orders, and home. Read Wyandotte. By the bye I first finished the Duke of Bm's 2 new Vols. Contemptible below all words which express contempt. A few letters from his family repositories – perhaps five or six interesting pages in those letters – the rest of the two large octavos made up of extracts taken with the scissors from Wraxall, Lady C Bury, Brougham, etc. etc. All joined by ungrammatical twaddle, the work of his Grace or his Grace's hack. It seems almost incredible that the editor should have confounded the D. of York with the D. of Gloucester. Yet the fact is so; and a letter signed William Frederic and in all things opposed to the known sentiments of the D of Y is ascribed to the D of Y. To dinner with E. Nobody but F.

1. The Royal Exchange Assurance Co.

Thursday – May 1

The change draws very near – After near 15 happy years passed in the Albany I am going to leave it, thrice as rich as when I entered it, and far more famous, with health impaired, but with affections as warm and faculties as vigorous as ever. I have lost nothing that was very near to my heart while I was here – kind friends have died, but they were not part of my daily comforts. H, B, A, G – all well and good and happy. Dear little A is an enjoyment added since I came hither. I do not at all expect to live 15 years more. If I do I cannot hope that they will be so happy as the last 15. The removal makes me sad, and would make me sadder but for the extreme discomfort in which I have been living during the last week. I have today burned some papers, packed and arranged others, sent a dozen letters to acquaint Secretaries of Railway Companies etc. of my change of domicile. Read Wyandotte. Corrected some fifty pages of my 4th Vol. Ld Glenelg called to talk about a speech which he is to make on Monday next. Went out. to the Athenaeum. Then into the City – dined at the Ship and Turtle[1] – very cold disagreeable day – finished Wyandotte – began Satanstoe[2] which I like better than most of Cooper's. It has a historical interest for me. Home. Thought, as I climbed the endless steps, panting and weary, that it was for the last time; and the tears would come into my eyes. I have been happy at the top of this toilsome stair. To bed – everything that I do is coloured by the thought that it is for the last time. One day there will come a last in good earnest. Be it so – I do not complain.

1. 129–30 Leadenhall Street.
2. James Fenimore Cooper, *Satanstoe* (1845), a historical novel of manners.

Friday – May 2

Breakfasted and waited till past 12 in hope of seeing Mares. He did not come; and I went from the rooms for ever in all human probability. To the R.I. To W.T. Went with H and B to the R. Academy. Less crowd of great people I thought, than usual. A good exhibition. Much pleased with Ward's Marie Antoinette[1] and glad to meet him there and to praise and congratulate him. A pretty picture by Paton[2] – very affecting and good. An excellent Stanfield[3] – indeed more than one. Two or three by Roberts very good. Millais, Hunt[4] etc. execrable to my thinking. After all I could only catch a glimpse of the pictures. Back with H and B to W.T. – dined – pleasant evening. At ½ past, 9 my carriage came. To H.L. to bed – The room very comfortable: but the bells not yet hung; and many things still to do.

1. E. M. Ward, *The Last Parting of Marie Antoinette and her Son* (1856).
2. Joseph Noel Paton (1821–1901). His picture was called *Home*.
3. There were paintings by both William Clarkson Stanfield (1793–1867) and his son George Clarkson Stanfield (1828–78). TBM may have meant *The Abandoned*, by the father, which was especially admired.
4. Holman Hunt's picture was *The Scapegoat*.

Saturday – May 3

Charmed by the first view of the turf, trees, and flowers from my bedroom window. I really am delightfully lodged. Breakfasted in the Library – too many signs that things are still in an unfinished state. But the place is really delightful. I could not have found one more exactly suited to me. The day Aprilish, showers of rain and sleet, followed by splendid sunshine. Longman called. At ½ after 2 H, B and A – all much pleased with the house, furniture and garden, H made a list of what was still wanted. We then went to the private view of the French pictures in Pall Mall: but the crowd was such that we could see nothing, and we came out almost as soon as we had gone in. To Bond Street – bought Parian ornaments and lustres for the drawing room chimney and blotting books and inkstands for the drawing room and bedrooms. Then we parted – Home – read Parr's tract against Combe[1] – mighty absurd, yet the man showed parts, and learning even in his absurdity. At dinner Satanstoe.

1. Samuel Parr, *Remarks on the Statement of D. Combe ...* (1795).

Sunday – May 4

East wind and ungenial weather, yet, in some sense fine. After breakfast went out meaning to go to church. Fell in with Stapleton at his own door putting his wife and daughter into a cab.[1] Got into the parish Church – Service not till ½ past eleven. The Church as ugly as the suburban Churches of the last century generally are. The congregation numerous and attentive. Thanksgiving for the peace. I did not think much of the sermon. But it was tolerable. The Archdeacon[2] very like his brother Sir George but not so absurd – Sir George the vilest speaker in parliament that I ever heard. A collection for the parochial charities. I gave a Sovereign, and I saw that such a donation from a person in the free sittings surprised the quêteur. Got into an *omnibus* at the Church door and to Brookes. No news – Across the Green Park to Hallam's. A duty – Alas! no pleasure now. Home – called at Argyll Lodge and left cards. Their Graces at Clifden.[3] At H.L. found my brother Charles – walked, sate and chatted with him some time. When he was gone, put my papers in order – a business which occupied the whole afternoon – At dinner Satanstoe. Then Parr v Combe.

1. Stapleton's wife was Catherine Bulteel (1800–56). His daughter was Theresa (1842–1929).
2. John Sinclair (1797–1875), Archdeacon of Middlesex and Vicar of St Mary's, Kennington. His brother was Sir George Sinclair (1790–1868), MP for Caithness, 1811–41.
3. TBM means Cliveden, where Argyll's father-in-law, the Duke of Sutherland, had established his summer residence.

Monday – May 5

Wrote to the D. of Argyll. Answer from the Duchess, very kind – The ornaments for the chimney of the drawing room came. Stapleton called – chatted with him. At five to the Athenaeum. Thence to the University Club – took in E and his bag – to H.L. It was not a very brilliant day – East wind and no sunshine. Yet the place looked pretty: and the comforts of the house were more perceptible than if the weather had been more pleasant. – He liked it much. Dined – then went to the Library and passed the evening there – Sate rather late.

Tuesday – May 6

Breakfast at ½ after nine. Walked with E by the Holland House lane to the High Road. He by an omnibus to Charing Cross – I across Kensington Gardens to W.T. – chatted with H and B and A. Went with H to Chelsea, taking up young Coltman[1] by the way. Left them at the Hospital and by a cab to H.L. read etc. all the rest of the day – Tasso's works – The Cruscan Controversy.[2] Much interested – At dinner Satanstoe – H J B G and A have sent me some pretty ornaments of Bohemian glass as a present. God bless them all!

1. Presumably a son of Sir Thomas Coltman (1781–1849), a justice of the Common Pleas. He had three sons, two of whom were at Trinity College, Cambridge.
2. The Accademia della Crusca was founded in 1582 to purify the Italian language. It published in 1612 the first Italian dictionary, the *Vocabolario degli Accademici della Crusca*, which in successive editions established an authority among Italian writers. It is not clear which controversy TBM meant, perhaps the debate in 1584 on the respective merits of Tasso and Ariosto.

Wednesday – May 7

Wind and rain. Up to greet my guests. Found H and B already come – the others pretty punctual except Dundas who did not come, in consequence of a mistake. The D and Ds of Argyle, The Earl and Ly Stanhope, Ld Glenelg, the Bp of Oxford, Milman and Mrs M – The breakfast, very handsome – the talk less pleasant than I have known it – yet not amiss, especially when the breakfast was over and we got round the library fire. I staid at home all the rest of the day. At five or soon after E came. We dined on the reliques of the breakfast and passed the evening on the hearth of the library over our wine and olives.

Thursday – May 8

Breakfast at ½ past 9. E to town, I staid by appointment. Soon after eleven Carruthers of the Inverness Courier called. I was very civil – the least that I could be; for he had been very kind and useful. Then Archdeacon Sinclair – extremely polite. I went at two into town – my coachman not well acquainted with London – he did not know Cockspur Street – left E's bag in Bedford Place – paid a bill for old pamphlets in King Street Holborn. Home. I have finished Tasso's works – that is, as far as they are interesting to me.[1] An odd light these volumes throw on the state of Italy in the 16th Century. I read Ælian[2] for the first time. Odd that it should be the first time. I despatched the whole Volume in a few hours – skimming and reading sometimes the Greek and sometimes the Latin translation which I thought more than usually well written. The most interesting fact which I learned from this very miscellaneous collection of information was that there were said to be translations of Homer into the Persian and Indian languages and that those translations were sung by the barbarians. I had never heard this mentioned. The thing is really not improbable. The conquests of Alexander must have made the Greek language well known to men whose mother tongue was the Persian or the Sanscrit. I wish to heaven that the translations could be found. At dinner Satanstoe – looked into Adolphus's Life of Jack Bannister,[3] but thought it heavy from very lightness. In my bedroom I turn over while dressing and undressing the Memoirs of old Mrs Carter,[4] a book which is heavy from a different cause.

1. Torquato Tasso (1544–95), *Opere e Commentario*, racculte per G. Mauro, 12 vols (Venice, 1722–42). This set was in TBM's library, SC, no. 966.
2. Claudius Aelianus, a classical writer, AD 165–230.
3. John Adolphus, *Memoirs of John Bannister, Comedian* (1839).
4. Perhaps *Memoirs of the Life of Mrs Elizabeth Carter* ... by Montagu Pennington, 2nd edn (1808). Mrs Carter (1717–1806) was a friend of Johnson and a miscellaneous writer.

Friday – May 9

To breakfast with Hallam – poor fellow – Dundas, Milnes, Murray the bookseller. We did very well – walked away with D – to W.T. – H and B out – Mary Parker and then her daughter Susan came. At last H and B. Home after calling on Stapleton and the Archdeacon and leaving cards. Dreary weather – the old joke of January and May has ceased to have a meaning – Bannister – Withers's trash – Satanstoe. My chest affected by the vile weather.

Saturday – May 10

After breakfast to town by omnibus. To the Pay Office about 60 or 70£ which I am to receive from the Colonial Customs received on account of my book. Some hitch – the people most civil – promised to send me the needful papers as soon as possible.[1] To the Museum – by the way bought a volume containing some of the best modern Latin poetry – Sannazarius, Fracastorius and Veda.[2] Two hours at the Museum – asked Ld John and Dundas to breakfast next Saturday. At after ½ went away in my own carriage, called at two or three places and home. The wind north; but the sun warm and bright. My chest not the thing, and some cough. Read Kotzebue's Deutschen Kleinstädter.[3] Very good – the most successful specimen that I know of German pleasantry. Some of Sannazarius and Fracastorius. The painted table and the remaining bookcases came – At dinner Satanstoe. Finished it afterwards.

1. TBM's thanks for this service is in *LM*, vol. 6, p. 42.
2. Jacopo Sannazaro (1458–1530), a Neapolitan, author of *Arcadia* (1485). Girolamo Fracastoro (1483–1553) was a physician who wrote a poem on venereal disease. Marco Girolamo Vida (1480–1566) was Bishop of Alba.
3. Auguste Frederich Ferdinand von Kotzebue, *Die Deutschen Kleinstädter*.

Sunday – May 11

Much milder. Wind still N.E. and my cough not removed. After breakfast Davies's Life of Garrick.[1] To Church – I have a seat very well situated in the front row of the Gallery looking right towards the pulpit. A Whitsunday sermon in which I could have pointed out not a few *non sequiturs*. Home – walked on my lawn – read Davies's Life of Garrick and Miscellanies. Ld Lansdowne called – very kind as usual. Then Longman and his brother in law, an officer,[2] Arbuthnot. Hayley's absurd Memoirs.[3] The Chainbearer[4] – heavy and not equal to Satanstoe. Spring soup and veal cutlets for dinner. Both good.

1. Thomas Davies, *Memoirs of the Life of David Garrick Esq ...* (1780).
2. Colonel Robert Bates (1813–94).
3. *Memoirs of the life and Writings of William Hayley ... Written by Himself ...* (1823).
4. By James Fenimore Cooper (1845).

Monday – May 12

Still North East wind. And the sky which yesterday was bright and clear as sullen as in November. Not quite well, and felt no inclination to work – Read several books – Pompey the Little[1] – Sandeman's Letters on Theron and Aspasia[2]. The clock came today. H B and T to dinner. Very pleasant evening – The soup etc. all very good.

1. *The History of Pompey the Little; or, The Life and Adventures of a Lap-Dog*, by F. Coventry (1751).
2. Robert Sandeman (1718–71), *Three Letters on [James Henry's] Theron and Aspasia*, 2 vols (1757).

Tuesday – May 13

I never saw so gloomy a May morning – It was like the very blackest days of November. Old May day too. But old May day vindicated its character. For soon the wind changed and blew from the South West. There were gentle showers and gleams of sunshine; and it was plain that at last Summer was coming. I corrected a good deal of my 4th Vol. – read many pamphlets of Q. Anne's time. To dinner with the Club. Small but agreeable party – Milman, Ld Aberdeen who now never fails, Ld Overstone and Ld Glenelg.

Wednesday – May 14

Rain and strong South West wind with gleams of sunshine. My chest quite at ease. Corrected Vol 4. Read a good deal in a desultory way – looked through the controversy between Sherlock and South – the Dean and Prebendary of the song.[1] The reasoning on both sides trash, never was greater nonsense talked. In style, wit and eloquence South is decidedly superior: but his malignity is infernal. I do not know that I ever read works which gave me a worse notion of the writer's heart. Ld Stanhope sent me the 1st vol of the Peel papers.[2] I devoured them. The Volume relates entirely to the Catholic question. It contains some interesting details which are new; but it leaves Peel where he was: I always noticed while he was alive and I observe again in this his posthumous defence an obstinate determination not to understand what the charge was which I and others who agreed with me brought against him. He always affected to think that we blamed him for his conduct in 1829, and he produced proofs of what we were perfectly ready to admit, that in 1829 the state would have been in great danger if the Catholic disabilities had not been removed. Now what we blamed was his conduct in 1825 and still more in 1827. We said – either you were blind not to foresee what was coming; or you acted culpably in not settling the question when it might have been settled without the disgrace of yielding to agitation and to the fear of insurrection; and you acted most culpably in deserting and persecuting Canning. We also said that a man who, in 1827, had declared himself the champion of the Test Act and the C[atholi]c disabilies and who repealed the Test Act in 1828 and removed the Catholic disabilities in 1829 ought not to complain if we attached little value to his authority on the subject of parliamentary reform. To this – which was our real point – he does not even allude. He is a debater even in this book. To dinner with the Lewises at Kent House. V Smith and Mrs V.S. Ld and Lady Goderich, Lady Dalmeny, Panizzi, Sir E. Lyons,[3] D and Ds of Argyle, Lady Morley. Pleasant enough. Finished Peel before I went to bed.

1. A Dean and Prebendary
Had once a new vagary,
And were at doubtful strife, Sir,
Who had the better life, Sir,
And was the better man,
And was the better man, etc.
'A Battle Royal', printed in *The Original Works of William King*, 3 vols (London, 1776), vol. 1, pp. 221–2.

2. *Memoirs of the Rt. Hon. Sir Robert Peel*, eds Lord Mahon and E. Cardwell (1856), vol. 1. For the difficulties they faced as editors, see William Thomas. *Quarrel of Macaulay and Croker: Politics and History in the Age of Reform* (Oxford, 2000), pp. 24–5.
3. Sir Edmund Lyons (1790–1858), created a peer 25 June 1856.

Thursday – May 15

Fine mild day. Sun and rain – Went out when it was fine and without my great coat for the first time this year. W.T. H and B gone to Chelsea. Chat with A. To the City – drew 20£ and saw my book – back by omnibus – and [illegible word] Read old Morning Chronicles. E came early – pleasant dinner etc. Fesc. [top part of page cut away] Athenaeum – found some books lying there for me – Guizot's R Cromwell[1] – A life of Kitto[2] – left a note at Ld Stanhope's home. Hallam called – poor fellow – I could not but ask him to breakfast here tomorrow, But – Stapleton called – [reverse of cut away page] action is destroyed ... would have been hooted out of society instead of holding an honorable place in it. At dinner the Chainbearer. A note from H reproaching me for not dining in W.T. I quite forgot that I was engaged to dine there. She invited herself, T, B and Butler who was of their party to tea. I gave orders. They came at half after eight, and had tea and coffee – a very pleasant evening.

1. M. Guizot, *History of Richard Cromwell and the Restoration of Charles II* (translation published 1856).
2. J. E. Ryland, *Memoirs of John Kitto* ... (1856)

Saturday – May 17

A party to breakfast – H, B, Ld John, Dundas, poor Hallam, Vernon Smith and Mrs V.S. Very pleasant, except that poor Hallam's infirmities made us all sad. H and B staid till near two. Went with them to W.T. to meet G who came from Harrow to see a dentist. A good lad and getting on excellently. Home by cab – called on my neighbour Shaw who had called on me – wrote to Lewis[1] in favour of Panizzi's plan of gilding the dome of the reading room at the Museum – Capefigue Consulat et Empire – Wagram – the divorce. At dinner Chainbearer – the weather genuine April – gleams of sunshine – then black clouds and storms of rain and hail. My garden is becoming charming.

1. *LM*, vol. 6, p. 42.

Sunday – May 18

Stormy and rainy all the morning – I staid at home – C I wrote a little for Black. T called and brought his crazy cousin Sir Walter,[1] looking very wild. I did a little towards putting in order the books in the room adjoining my bedroom. Read an odd fragment of Wesley's Journal published in 1848. The case of that wretched Sir Eyre Coote[2] – At dinner Chainbearer. Beaumarchais.

1. Sir Walter Calverley Trevelyan (1797–1879), sixth Bart, who later bequeathed Wallington Hall, Northumberland, to Sir Charles Trevelyan.
2. *A Plain Statement of Facts relative to Sir Eyre Coote ...* (1816). This is an account of the proceedings that led to the dismissal of Sir Eyre Coote from the army.

Monday – May 19

The weather better. Into the city by omnibus – paid a subscription for the life of a Dr Kitto[1] in Paternoster Row – looked in on the Longmans. Home – wrote for Black – Macleod called – carriage at ½ after 5. To the Athenaeum – to the University Club – Carried E to H.L. – pleasant dinner and evening.

1. J. E. Ryland, *Memoirs of John Kitto, DD ...* (1856).

Tuesday – May 20

After breakfast walked into town with E through Kensington Gardens and the Park – a charming walk, and a lovely summer day. To Brookes's – thence to W.T. Dearest little A confined with the mumps. With H and B to Grosvenor Crescent – admired the new house. They to Clapham. I by omnibus home. Wrote a little for Black – Cooper's Jack Tier[1] – Wraxall's Memoirs[2] – second part.

1. J. F. Cooper, *Jack Tier* (1856).
2. Wraxall, *Historical Memoirs of my Own Time*

Wednesday – May 21

I began today to keep my journal in this huge volume.[1] Shall I live to fill it? God knows. Glorious weather. Before breakfast I employed myself during about an hour in putting pamphlets etc in order. After breakfast I took a long walk. I wished to ascertain the geography of the wide extent of country which I see from my bedroom window. I walked to the West London Cemetery.[2] The impression made by the cypresses and monuments sad, but not unpleasing. Saw the outside of St Mark's.[3] Very ugly by Derwent's leave – Cremorne Gardens – Battersea Bridge – Chelsea Church – took a cab there and home. Wrote a little for Black – put some pamphlets and books in order. At ½ past 3 to Burlington House. We were nineteen – the Chancellor, Ld Burlington in the chair. I was between Ld Overstone and the Bp of St David's. The ballot was several times repeated as an absolute majority was necessary. The final result was Carpenter 10 – Heaviside 9.[4] I voted for Heaviside to the last. Home – dressed. To Longman's – met there H, B and T, Lady Teresa, Reeve and his wife, Milman. The children pestered everybody. Two or three of them were in the dining room through the whole dinner and dessert – eating of everything at side tables, squeezing themselves between the guests, making Milman very nervous, and others, me among the rest, very angry. I never saw anything of the kind at any other house. Surely it is a strange want of savoir vivre. Glad to get home.

1. Vol. 11 of the MS.
2. In West Brompton.
3. St Mark's College, Chelsea, where Derwent Coleridge was Principal, 1841–6. It was designed by Edward Blore (1787–1879).
4. William Benjamin Carpenter (1813–85) was a biologist, an FRS and, after this vote, Registrar of London University, 1856–79. James William Lucas Heaviside (1808–97) had been Professor of Mathematics and Registrar of Haileybury.

Thursday – May 22

A miserable rainy morning. However I went into the City – paid in to my bankers' hands a bill for £67.10.[1] – the fruits of my copyright in the colonies. Home. The day cleared up – began looking through Johnson's Shakspeare[2] in order to verify what I fully believed, that he never once quotes any of Shakespeare's contemporary dramatists. Looked also into the Dictionary and after turning over many pages could find no citation of Massinger, Ford or Fletcher – Jack Tier[3] – Johnson's Shakspeare again in the evening.

1. See above, entry for 10 May 1856.
2. Samuel Johnson's edition of Shakespeare was published in 1765; the Dictionary in 1755.
3. By James Fenimore Cooper. Published as *Captain Spike* in 1848; as *Jack Tier* in 1856.

Friday – May 23

A doubtful day – to W.T. H and B – Walked a little with dear B. Alice still *au secret* with the mumps. Home – Shakspeare – At ½ after 7 to Lansdowne House – Ld Minto, Milman and Mrs M – Mr and Mrs Brookfield. I had forgotten her. She was Miss Elton[1] – a very handsome girl and is still a good looking woman. I liked her much fifteen or sixteen years ago.

1. William Henry Brookfield (1809–74) married Jane Octavia (1821–96), daughter of Sir Charles Elton, brother-in-law of Henry Hallam. He was made an Inspector of Schools in 1848.

Saturday – May 24

Tolerable day – Museum – Covent Garden – bought some grapes and left them at the Athenaeum – new Vol of Thiers[1] – Consulat et Empire – read it while walking home. Today I finished my examination of Johnson's Shakespeare and found that I was quite in the right. At six to the Athenaeum for my glasses – then to the U Club for Ellis. Home with him – pleasant evening.

1. *L'Histoire du Consulat et de l'Empire*, vol. 13 (March 1811 to 1812).

Sunday – May 25

Fine morning. To Church with E. Home and walked in the garden. Cameron called – then Trevelyan and Collier.[1] While we were talking in the verandah I slipped from the mat and sprained my ancle. In falling hurt my wrist – the pain at first great. But I soon became easier. However I must expect much annoyance and confinement. Dined however and chatted with E all the evening.

1. Perhaps Robert Porrett Collier (1817–86), later first Baron Monkswell; MP for Plymouth, 1852–71; judge, 1871.

Monday – May 26

I had a bad night. The wrist plagues me more than the ancle. Could hardly wash or shave. Wrote ill and with difficulty. H called early with A – both very kind. Later in the day Adam Black. I read a great deal. Finished Thiers. Finished Wraxall.[1] Marrow of Modern Divinity[2] – Toplady v Wesley[3] – very clever. Jack Tier at dinner. After dinner B and my brother Charles – Tea and Coffee – pleasant talk – Much easier.

1. Wraxall, *Historical Memoirs of his Own Time.*
2. E. Fisher, *The Marrow of Modern Divinity* (1645).
3. Perhaps A. M. Toplady, *A Letter to the Rev. Mr. John Wesley ...* (1770).

Tuesday – May 27

A good night – but not quite right – Dr Browning Smith by Aikin's recommendation.[1] All going well – Toplady. Shrubsole[2] – Barry O' Meara[3] – finished Jack Tier.

1. Thomas Browning Smith (*c.* 1809–73) was a surgeon and member of the London Medical Society. Arthur Aikin (1773–1854) was the brother of Lucy Aikin, the writer. He was a geologist and writer on science.
2. Perhaps *Christian Memoirs* (1776), by William Shrubsole (1729–97).
3. Barry Edward O'Meara, *Napoleon in Exile*. TBM's copy of the fifth edition of 1822 is at Wallington.

Wednesday – May 28

Breakfast party – H, B, Van der W and Mme V, Mrs Drummond, the Bp of St David's, and Longman – pretty well – fine morning. After the party broke up the weather became stormy – violent hail. It mattered little to me because I could not walk. Wrote several letters – to Edinburgh to excuse myself from making myself a show at the Philosophical Institute – to a person who wishes to put up Rogers[1] – volentem nolentem[2] – for the Chair of Moral Philosophy at Edinburgh. Read O' Meara then Forsyth.[3] E came early – we dined and chatted pleasantly.

1. Henry Rogers (*c.* 1806–77), theological writer and Edinburgh reviewer.
2. i.e. without consulting him.
3. Probably William Forsyth (1812–99), a Trinity man, a lawyer and a prolific writer. He edited the *Annual Register* from 1842 to 1868. Among his non-legal writings, he published a *History of the Captivity of Napoleon at St. Helena, from the Letters and Journals of the late Sir Hudson Lowe*, 3 vols (1853), which TBM seems to have consulted as a corrective to O'Meara.

Tuesday – May 29

The day of fireworks and illuminations.[1] People seem uneasy, I hardly know why. I never knew any mischief take place on such occasions. The day is dull – the wind N.E. The rockets in the park will hardly be seen here. My servants will be at the top of the house. I shall not stir. Dr Browning Smith came – put an elastic sock on my foot. I find it a great support. My hand suffers more. I write with pain at this moment. E to town – read and corrected part of my first vol for the smaller edition. Forsyth – At dinner Easy[2] – Thiers. At half after nine the fireworks began. I had a view from my bedroom window of part of the show in the Green Park. Very beautiful it was. The servants in the top of the house saw all the display in both Parks and on Primrose Hill. But I, sprained as I was, could not venture to climb so high.

1. To mark the treaty of peace with Russia. There were displays in Hyde Park, the Green Park, Victoria Park and Primrose Hill (*Annual Register*, pp. 115–16).
2. Frederick Marryat, *Mr. Midshipman Easy* (1836).

Friday – May 30

Glad to find that all had passed over without an accident. Into the City to move 7,000£ stock from Consols to new Threes – Home. Had to walk more than suited my foot. It was hardly possible to get a cab. The racketting of yesterday had knocked up drivers and horses. In the evening to dine with Ld. Harry Vane – the Dean,[1] Dundas, Lady Marianne Alford,[2] the D and Duchess of Argyle. Milman, it seems was at the top of his Cathedral yesterday night. So was Dickens. It was a fine sight no doubt. Today the weather has been as cold and ungenial as in January.

1. Milman.

2. Lady Marianna Alford (1817–88), daughter of Lord Northampton, was a gifted painter, writer and patroness of artists. Her husband, Viscount Alford, had died 1851.

Saturday – May 31

Cold and rainy. To the Duke of Argyle's to breakfast – George Grey, Labouchere, Ld Stanhope, Dundas, Milnes, a Mr Palfrey[1] from New England, looking for historical materials. Home and ordered the carriage – to W.T. chatted there a short time and back. Looked at a specimen of an index which Longman left here. Detestable beyond belief. Read in a rambling way – Afloat and Ashore[2] – Capefigue – etc, etc.

---

1. John Gorham Palfrey (1798–1881), a Boston Unitarian Minister and historian. He had owned and edited the *North American Review* and was in London researching his five-volume history of New England.
2. By James Fenimore Cooper (1844).

Sunday – June 1

Wretched morning. The surgeon came to look at my foot. All going on well. The weather so bad that I did not go to Church. Ld Hatherton called. Left me four vols of Ld Dudley's correspondence with Coplestone.[1] Then T and B. T. vexed at some new Treasury arrangements. I soothed him as well as I could. While they were here the weather cleared up. Fine sunny afternoon. I put on boots and clogs and walked in my garden after a week of confinement. Ld Dudley – Afloat and Ashore.

---

1. *Letters of the Earl of Dudley to the Bishop of Llandaff*... (1840) was in one volume, so these four volumes must have been the original manuscripts. Coplestone was Provost of Oriel, Ward's College.

Monday – June 2

Glorious day – to call on Ryan – met him a short way from his house – took him into the carriage and went with him to the Athenaeum talking about E – home. Finished Ld Dudley's letters. I own that they have made on my mind an impression very unfavourable to him. He talks of his love of truth. He speaks with just severity of the dirty tricks of low hackney writers. Yet for such writers there are excuses which he could not plead; and yet he practised tricks as dirty as any of theirs. It appears that, while living on terms of civility with Sydney Smith he conveyed through a private channel to Gifford an anonymous attack on Sydney's honor and morals – the most savage that ever appeared in the Q.R. It appears too that this lover of truth, while passing for a Whig and a follower of Lds Grey and Grenville, while voting with them, while speaking on their side, while looking forward to office under them, secretly wrote attacks on them in the Q.R. It cannot be said in his favour that even in these attacks in the Q.R. he spoke his real mind. For he says that, in order to adapt his writing to the QR, he affected to be more Anti Whiggish than he really was. What unutterable baseness! I looked at his papers in the Quarterly. That on Sydney is worth nothing – nor that on Roscoe's Letter to Ld Grey. That on Horne Tooke is much better. That on Rogers is just – but not striking. The best of his papers is that on Fox's correspondence with Gilbert Wakefield.[1] I wrote to H Rogers about the Chair of Moral Philosophy at Edinburgh. Paced my lawn reading Don Quixote after an interval of, I think, twelve years – nay, thirteen – with great delight; – read till I settled him in the inn where Maritornes was chambermaid.[2] Wrote a little for Black. Miles Wallingford[3]. In the evening walked in my portico till near ten. Baretti's crazy work entitled Tolendron.[4]

---

1. Dudley's papers in the *QR* are reviews of the following books: Sydney Smith, *Visitation Sermon 1809* (3:5, February 1810); William Roscoe, *Observations on the Address ... by Earl Grey* (5:9, February 1811); W. Hamilton Reid, *Memoirs ... of Horne Tooke* (7:14, June 1812); Samuel Rogers, *Poems* (11:17, March 1813); *Correspondence of Gilbert Wakefield ... with Charles James Fox ...* (9:18, July 1813). Identifications by Hill Shine and Helen Chadwick Shine, *The Quarterly Review under Gifford, 1809–24* (Chapel Hill, NC, 1949).
2. *Don Quixote*, bk III, chs 16–17. Maritornes is an Asturian chambermaid.
3. James Fennimore Cooper (1814). It was the sequel to *Afloat and Ashore.*
4. Giuseppe Marc' Antonio Baretti, *Tolendron. Speeches to John Bowle about his Edition of Don Quixote* (1786).

Tuesday – June 3

To breakfast with Milnes. Two Yankees, Palfrey and Kennedy,[1] The Ds. of Sutherland, the Bp of St D[avi]ds, Hunter the Antiquary.[2] Walked away to Lansdowne House – asked Ld L to breakfast with me on Saturday. Home by Omnibus – wrote for Black – read Don Quixote. At six B came – at half past six the Ellises. They admired my turf and flowers amazingly. I gave them a good simple dinner; and we had a pleasant evening.

---

1. John Pendleton Kennedy (1795–1870). Cf *LM*, vol. 6, p. 17, n. 1.
2. Presumably Joseph Hunter (1783–1861).

Wednesday – June 4

After breakfast to W.T. Found them in the agonies of moving, took B in my carriage to Grosvenor Crescent with a hamper full of glass and china. Home. Read Whately's edition of Bacon's Essays.[1] My neighbour Mr Vincent[2] called – gentlemanlike agreeable man I think. – Don Q – Wrote for Black – Don Q again.

Very kind letter from Rogers – Don Quixote. Miles Wallingford – disagreeable letter from J.

1. Richard Whateley's edition was published in 1856.
2. Henry William Vincent (1796–1865), of nearby Thornwood Lodge. He was Queen's Remembrancer in the Exchequer.

Thursday – June 5

Went to W.T. to consult H about J's letter – Home – wrote an answer though with pain and difficulty. My hand plagues me much – Read D.Q. – T, H, B, C and Mrs C to dinner. Good and well served – Pleasant evening.

Friday – June 6

Into town. Bought Hogg's poems[1] – not seen for forty years or so – Home – read – wrote a little – DQ – dined at home – M.W.

1. If TBM's memory is accurate, this must mean Hogg's volume of parodies or imitations, *The Poetic Mirror: or the Living Bards of Britain* (1816). However, he read that on 16 October 1849.

Saturday – June 7

Breakfast party. Senior, Labouchere, Grey, C. Howard, Ld Hatherton – H and B – Agreeable. Talked about Ld Dudley's letters and read some of them. H and B staid to lunch. They went home, and I into town – DQ – MW.

Sunday – June 8

To Church. I have been put into a worse seat – indeed one on which I can hardly sit. In the afternoon T, B and A came – DQ – Ramblers – MW.

Monday – June 9

Into town to order wine – Left some cards – Home – read and wrote – E to dinner – A letter to the Globe in defence of my account of Penn from a Mr Blundell.[1]

1. Benson Blundell (1806–84) was a barrister of the Middle Temple. See *LM*, vol. 6, p. 45.

Tuesday – June 10

Took E into town – Home – read a good deal. Made, as well as I could with my maimed hand, some changes in the distribution of my books. To dinner with Ld Broughton – seated next MacCulloch[1] and rather bored.

1. Perhaps J. R. McCulloch (1789–1864).

Wednesday – June 11

Into town again about the wine. Got Villemain's account of Narbonne[1] and read it with great interest. Kennedy – the American – called. Long talk and not uninteresting. Don Q – Wrote a little – At 6, T, H, B and A. Their house all in confusion. Pleasant dinner and evening. Sent them home to G. Crescent in my carriage. Invited them to come again tomorrow.

1. Abel François Villemain, *Souvenirs Contemporaires d'histoire et de littérature* (Paris, 1854), contains an account of Louis, Comte de Narbonne (1755–1813), War Minister under Louis XVI, later ADC to Napoleon, and French Ambassador in Vienna 1813.

Thursday – June 12

To breakfast with Ld Stanhope – Ld Stanley, Mrs Gaskill,[1] the writer of a book which I have not read and am not likely to read. Sir C and Lady Lyell – thence to G.C. Found them all in confusion – Home. The weather changed. Rain and wind. Went to the U. Club at 6 for E. Dinner of six – pleasant – At ½ past nine the Ts went – E staid.

1. Probably Elizabeth Gaskell (1810–65). She had already published several novels, including *Cranford* (1853) and *North and South* (1855).

Friday – June 13

Took E into town and home – a vile cold rainy day – sate indoors and had a fire in the evening. Did what I could with a maimed right hand towards arranging books. DQ – Diversions of Purley – Villemain's Souvenirs – at dinner – Snowdon.[1]

1. An ode, published in London (1837).

Saturday – June 14

To the BM. Thence to Mahomet's in Little Ryder St[1] – Took a douche. I hope that it may answer. Home – to dine with Heath[2] in Russell Square. Fine house and fine dinner – they were very kind and hospitable: but I had rather be at home. I hardly knew anybody, and nobody well.

1. It was at no. 7. Sake Deen Mohamed (1759–1851) advertised himself as a shampooing surgeon. He died in Brighton, where he was buried. His son Arthur Mohamed (*c.* 1820–72) succeeded to the business. A grandson, Frederick Henry Horatio Akbar Mohamed, became a pathologist and physician.
2. John Benjamin Heath (1790–1879) was a London merchant and banker. He married in 1811 Sophia Bland (1793–1863) and died at 66 Russell Square.

Sunday – June 15

After Church to G.C. sate half an hour and to Brooks's to talk about the news – had a quiet chat with Hawes. I am strongly for peace; and I really think that the Yankees, little as I love them, are *dans leur droit*. Nothing known yet. Another douche and home – finished the Diversions of Purley. Surely a very extraordinary book; – a really great book. At dinner – Snowdon – Walked in the Evening.

Monday – June 16

To Grosvenor Crescent – H and B out – on to Athenaeum – Walked. M πρειχ[1] No douche today. To G.C. again. Went with H to leave cards as far as Addison Road. Home – Lady Morley called. Stapleton's wife dangerously ill[2] – Spanish Campaign[3] – Senior's Egyptian M.S. – put books in order as well as I could with my left hand. Walked in the evening.

1. Perhaps Marryat's *The Phantom Ship* (1839).
2. A. G. Stapleton, now TBM's neighboor, was rumoured to be the illegitimate son of John Parker, first Earl of Morley.
3. Mary Meeke, *The Spanish Campaign or The Jew*, 3 vols (1815).

Tuesday – June 17

To breakfast with Milman – Took the Duke of Argyle. All will go right, I am glad to find, with the U.S. At the Deanery Twisleton and Mrs T.,[1] Ld Lne – Kennedy – pleasant enough. Got a douche and home. Palfrey called. Put books in order – called on Stapleton – sorry to hear that there is little hope. To the University Club for E – brought him out. Walter in the 2nd Class[2] – I fear that he will do nothing. But E is resolved, I see, to keep him at Cambridge. Dinner pleasant Fes. Walk by moonlight on the terrace.

1. Ellen Dwight (1819–62), daughter of Edmond Dwight of Springfield, Massachusetts, married Twisleton in 1852. Mrs Twisleton described a breakfast party with the Milmans in 1854 in which Macaulay was present in *Letters of the Hon. Mrs Edward Twistleton Written to her Family, 1852–62* (London, 1928), pp. 254–6.

2. In the annual college examination held in the Easter term.

Wednesday – June 18

Party to breakfast – Ld Stanhope, Ld Broughton, Twisleton, Macleod, Ellis, Heath, Whewell. I doubted how these elements would mix. But mix they did; and the morning was very pleasant. I took E to the Temple – got a douche and home. Called at Stapleton's by the way. All is over.[1] Put books to rights – Mrs Veal[2] – Don Quixote – At dinner Sp. Camp.

1. Augustus Stapleton's wife (Catherine Bulteel) died on 18 June.
2. Perhaps *A True Relation of the Apparition of one Mrs Veal the Next Day after her Death to One Mrs Bargrave* (1707) by Daniel Defoe.

Thursday – June 19

Bad weather. To breakfast at Stafford House.[1] Splendid party – Prince Albert, the Duke Regent of Baden,[2] the Argylls, Ld Grosvenor and his beautiful wife,[3] beautiful indeed beyond words, Gladstone. I saw for the first time the Le Noir portraits[4] and admired them greatly. Thence to the British Gallery – good, but not so good as usual. Two noble Ruysdaels.[5] Had my douche and home – forced by the rain to take a cab. In the afternoon to the U Club – brought out E to dine and sleep.

1. The town house of the Duke of Sutherland, now Lancaster House.
2. Friedrich I (1826–1907), sixth Grand Duke of Baden, was made Regent on the mental illness of his brother Ludwig II in this year. He was a liberal constitutionalist.
3. She was Constance Gertrude Leveson-Gower (1834–80), youngest daughter of George Granville, second Duke of Sutherland.
4. Alexandre Le Noir (1762–1839) was Conservator of the Musée de Beaux Arts, whose collection of French portraits was bought by the second Duke of Sutherland in 1838. It was sold in 1876 to the Duc d'Aumale, who deposited the portraits in the Chateau de Chantilly.
5. Algernon Graves lists seven pictures by Ruysdael in his *Century of Loan Exhibitions 1813–1912*, vol. 3, p. 1179. They were shown at the British Institution.

Friday – June 20

Breakfast at 9. Took E to Westminster – my douche – home – put books to rights etc. Wrote a page or two for Black with difficulty. In the afternoon by omnibus to the neighbourhood of G.C. The walk was short – but it rained hard and I should have been soaked had I not met Cator who protected me with his umbrella. The house all at sixes and sevens – pleasant chat however. CZM dined with us – Uneasy about ... [ms torn] and seems to become [tear in ms]. G has the English essay prize.[1]

1. The Headmaster's Prize for an English Essay (*Harrow School Register* 1801–92).

Saturday – June 21

Bought some books – Bill – Douche – Home – wet cold evening. Forced to have a fire – Sp Camp – Huetiana.[1] I have read again that strange book of F Barrett, The Lefevre of No Fiction[2] – A religious novel which made a noise near forty years ago. A most curious business.

1. Pierre Daniel Huet, Bishop of Avranches, *Huetiana; ou, pensées diverses de M. H., Evesque d'Avranches* (1722).
2. Francis Barrett, *Memoirs of Francis Barrett, the Lefevre of 'No Fiction'* [A novel by Dr Andrew Bell ...] (1823).

Sunday – June 22

A better day – To Church – then to town and had my douche – back to H L – put books to rights – wrote a little – Huetiana – to dine at Lne House – the Strutts, I had not seen them since their calamity.[1] She very much altered in looks by grief, and so woebegone that she almost made me cry. Senior, Dr Waagen the Connoisseur.[2]

1. The elder son William (b. 1838) had died at Bonn on 19 January 1856, aged only seventeen.
2. Gustave Friedrich Waagen (1794–1868), German art critic and historian.

Monday – June 23

To town. The douche – My wrist still a great torment to me. E to dinner.

Tuesday – June 24

Midsummer – Wages – Took E into town – to Birchin Lane and gave orders – to Jeffs in the Burlington Arcade and ordered books. To Brooks's – Douche – G C – Nobody but dear little Alice – Home – wrote a little – read a good deal – At dinner the Entail.[1]

1. John Galt, *The Entail* (1823).

Wednesday – June 25

Wrote – My neighbour Shaw[1] called on me. We went together to the D. of A – had a meeting to little purpose. Dressed and went to the levee [MS torn] anti-room. A Yankee came in a costume evidently intended as an affront to the Queen – frock coat, yellow waistcoat, black stock.[2] Everybody – English or foreign – was disgusted by the fellow's senseless impertinence and vulgarity. However when he was informed that he could not be admitted in that garb, Dallas, who was himself very properly dressed, fired up and went away in a pet. I had hoped from Everett's letters that D was a man of good sense and good feeling. I am sorry to be undeceived. The Queen was very civil to me. I was glad to be at home again. In the evening I had to dress a third time that day and to go to Ld Burlington's. Not a very brilliant party, though there were some good men. I had some interesting talk with Graham and Thirlwall. My hand better though I had no douche today.

1. William Ambrose Shaw (*c.* 1794–1867) of Wycombe Lodge. A wealthy man of independent means, he was the previous occupant of Holly Lodge.
2. The offensively dressed Yankee was Denis Hart Mahan (1802–72), Professor at West Point Military Academy, and father of A. T. Mahan, the naval historian. The incident is described in George M. Dallas, *Letters from London* ... (London, 1870), vol. 1, pp. 72–7.

Thursday – June 26

To breakfast at G.C. Then to Harrow with dear H and B. The Hall crowded to overflowing. G was the hero of the day. All his exercises had merit. I was much pleased with the Latin verse. The English verses too were good and very well received. I hope and believe that he will turn out a distinguished man. He is most amiable; and I never saw such perfect harmony in a family as there is between him and his sisters. In truth none of the three ever, as far as I am able to discover, says or does anything inconsistent with perfect love and kindness to the others. There was, after the speeches, a ceremony at which Sir W Williams[1] was to officiate. I was knocked up and did not mix in the crowd. I got Dr Vaughan's permission to take G with me to dinner on condition that he should go back early tomorrow. We had a joyous journey from Harrow to H L though I was oppressed with cold, the effect of some chill in this hot weather. As a set off my wrist is certainly better, though I have intermitted the douche two days running. At H L T. and Marianne Thornton joined us. A pleasant dinner and evening.

1. Sir William Fenwick Williams (1800–83) was the hero of the defence of Kars in Anatolia.

Friday – June 27

To breakfast with Hallam – Sir F. Williams, Ld Lansdowne. He tells me that the Yankees have made a sort of apology. To G.C. Home – wrote a little – read Joanna Southcote. E to dinner. Festivities at the D. of A's in honour of his clansman Sir Colin.[1] The Ds wrote very kindly to invite me but my cold and E's visit prevented me from going.

1. Sir Colin Campbell (1792–1863). He had commanded the Highland Brigade at the Alma, and in 1857 he was to be sent out to India, as Commander-in-Chief, in preference

to Sir Patrick Grant. He was a kinsman of the Duke of Argyll, but he was born a MacIver; his mother was a Campbell of Islay, and he changed his name in 1807.

Saturday – June 28

Took E into town – called for a few minutes in G C – T, H and B go to Harrow today and stay till Monday. To the Burlington Arcade and took on board a cargo of French novels – set down E at Somerset House – to Birchin Lane – procured six notes each for a hundred – ordered 500 £ 3 per cent to be sold. To the Museum – sate there two hours – to the R.I. – now very seldom visited by me – to Mohammed's and had a douche – Home – wrote – read – dined – walked – Entail.

Sunday – June 29

My arm worse than it has been since Wednesday – heaven knows why. Did not go to Church – Brookes's – wrote on Johnson. Adolphus called – then Sir H. and Lady Holland. Read Joanna – Entail – Walk.

Monday – June 30

My wrist a little better. Staid at home writing and reading – E to dinner. Gave him 600 £ in notes. Very dark threatening weather.

Tuesday – July 1

Fine again – To Senior's to breakfast. Dicky[1] very absurd about Nineveh, Hebrew learning – and other matters of which he is profoundly ignorant. To Birchin Lane – sold out 500 £ 3 per C for 481. To Bond Street – paid my tailor's bill. R.I. To G C. Sate with them a short time and home – G was there on *exeat*. Wrote – Savage[2] – not ill – Lawrie Todd[3] – Mare's Bill more by 200 £ than I expected. But no matter.

1. Richard Monckton Milnes.
2. Presumably the passage on Richard Savage, in TBM's essay on Johnson. *CW*, vol. 7, pp. 333–4.
3. *Lawrie Todd* (1830), by John Galt,.

Wednesday – July 2

Staid at home and wrote – read Lexiphanes.[1] Ticknor called – Then R Mackintosh – improved I thought – to dinner with E – nobody but F.

1. Archibald Campbell (*c.* 1726–80), *Lexiphanes, a Dialogue. Imitated from Lucian and Suited to the Present Time. Being an Attempt to Restore the English Tongue to its Ancient Purity*, 2nd edn (1767).

Thursday – July 3

Bad night. Cold hanging about me. To breakfast with the Bp of O, Bp of St D[avi]ds. Ld Lne, Trench, Van de Weyer etc – pleasant. To the Athenaeum. Mahan – the unfortunate Yankee of last Wednesday's scene – has written a letter to the Secretary of the Athenaeum[1] which is put up in the reading room. The poor man has really been very badly used by Dallas, who is the only person to blame in the whole business. Home – wrote – to G.C. – Took B to Milman's. Miss Thelluson's recitation.[2] A ballad of Hogg's – bad. Speech of Ulysses from Shakspeare – worse. Dalilah's speech from Samson Agonistes – pretty good. But the whole thing disappointing. Took B to H.L. – Her Mama and Alice already there. T. came – pleasant dinner and evening. Mares's bill surprised H.

1. James Claude Webster (*c.* 1819–1908), FSA, barrister of the Middle Temple.
2. She was Sabine Matilda (1823–82), eldest of the three daughters of Thomas Roberts Thelluson (1801–69) and his wife Maria, née Macnaughton (d. 1881). She became Mrs Richard Greville.

Friday – July 4

£250 from Tauchnitz on account. Beautiful morning. Party to breakfast – Mackintosh, Ticknor, Panizzi, Jowett, Milman, Ld Lne, Van de Weyer, Senior. We mustered on my lawn. Pleasant enough. When they were gone, to the Bank. Sold out 500 £ more. I am now, I think, on perfectly solid ground – Home – wrote – Lawrie Todd.

Saturday – July 5

To breakfast with Van de Weyer – the old set – Ticknor – away to H.L. wrote – Matrimony.[1] Walked in the evening. Not very well cold in the head.

1. *Matrimony, the Height of Bliss, or the Extreme of Misery*, by Mary Meeke, 4 vols (1812).

Sunday – July 6

Fine morning – to Church – good sermon from Sinclair – to G.C. – Home – wrote – to Richmond to dine with Ld Lne – Ld John and Lady John, Lady Shelburne, Ticknor, Ld Minto, La Caita – not unpleasant, except that Ticknor insisted on going back in my carriage merely for society – his own cab to follow. The cab and we parted company – I had to take him home late at night and through rain.

Monday – July 7

Bad weather coming – to breakfast with Ld Stanhope – Ld Stanley, Dr Waagen or some such name, Ticknor of course. Walked away with Ld Stanley whom I much like. Home – wrote and read G. Stephen's Attorney in search of Pce.[1] Mat[rimon]y.

So cold that I had a fire in the evening.

1. Sir George Stephen, *Attorney in Search of Practice* (1839).

Tuesday – July 8

Paid Mares's bill. Rainy day. But I was forced to go into the City. Called at G.C. Saw H, and took leave. They go to Oatlands tomorrow. To Paternoster Row. Discussed matters with Longman and Rees – Home – wrote and read. To dine with the Club. Full and pleasant meeting. Brought the D of Argyll home.

Wednesday – July 9

The day fine. Staid at home – read – Parr v Curtis[1] – Law v Mandeville[2] – wrote – J's Shakspeare – At dinner Mat[rimony].

1. Samuel Parr, *A Sequel to the Printed Paper ... by Charles Curtis ...* (1792).
2. William Law, *Remarks upon a Late Book Entitled, The Fable of the Bees* (1724).

Thursday – July 10

Into town by omnibus. Athenaeum – home – wrote and read. To dine with the D of Argyll – Teesdale from Kars,[1] Ticknor, Labouchere and Lady M, the Blantyres. Pretty Well.

1. Sir Christopher Charles Teesdale (1833–93), distinguished in the defence and battle of Kars, 1854–5, for which he was awarded the VC.

Friday – July 11

To breakfast with Milnes – Ld Lne, Ticknor, Palfrey, Ld Stanley, Browning and Mrs B, Hawthorne,[1] author of The Scarlet Letter, Butler.[2] Went away with Butler – drizzling rain – took him to his office in a cab – then home. Much oppression of the chest. Weather uncertain – wrote – Club – Thrales. Read Cowper's letters. At dinner Mat[rimony] – walked on the lawn till past ten.

1. There is an account of this party in Hawthorne's *The English Notebooks*, ed. Randall Stewart (New York, 1941), pp. 380–3, quoted in *LM*, vol. 6, p. 47n.
2. Henry Montagu Butler, later Headmaster of Harrow, and Master of Trinity; appointed private secretary to William Francis Cowper, Vice-President of the Committee of the

Council on Education in July 1856; also Secretary to the Royal Commission for rebuilding the National Gallery.

Saturday – July 12

On my breakfast table a line from Lady Holland – They are at H house. Answered her. Walker the engraver[1] came and forced me to subscribe for one of this prints much against my will. To the Museum. Silly vexatious conduct of Hawkins[2] and Madden.[3] The Ld Chancellor[4] not quite so judicious or courteous as he should have been. Want of thought no doubt for he is the best fellow living. Home – to Holland House – wrote – At dinner Mat[rimony], walked.

1. Perhaps William Walker (1791–1867).
2. Edward Hawkins (1780–1857); Keeper of Antiquities at the British Museum, 1826–60.
3. Frederick Madden, Head of the Department of Manuscripts at the British Museum, 1837–66.
4. Lord Cranworth.

Sunday – July 13

Did not go to Church. Into the City and back by omnibus – old places long unseen – Charles called – then Panizzi – Wrote – At dinner St G J.[1] Walked on the lawn till 10.

1. Henry Cockton, *George St. George Julian, the Prince* (1841).

Monday – July 14

Shaw called about the rent. It seems that the upper landlord Broadhurst[1] is inclined to be disagreeable. As he chuses. Why he will not take the rent directly from me passes my comprehension. However I went into the City and gave the necessary orders. Home again – read some of my 3rd vol. Read Cobbett's America.[2] Yesterday by the bye I read the Trial of E G Wakefield.[3] Wrote. To dine at Holland House at half past eight. I see that it will be necessary for me to be cautious and resolute in order to prevent the kindness of my good neighbours from becoming importunate, and yet to remain on a friendly footing with them. My lady takes the tone of her mother in law and seems to expect that her summons is to be obeyed at the shortest notice. Now I never was very complying even with the mother in law; and I am not at all inclined to be the Allen of the new Hd House. However this is ungrateful – for they are very kind and cordial.

1. John Broadhurst (*c.* 1778–1861) was a Derbyshire landowner, who now lived in Richmond. He was the head lessee while TBM and Shaw were sub-lessees.

2. Perhaps *Cobbett's American Political Register* (New York, January–June 1816, May 1817–January 1818).
3. *The Trial of E. G. Wakefield ... for the Abduction of Miss E. Turner* (1827).

Tuesday – July 15

Wrote and read till past two. Then started for Chevening with post-horses. The stupid postboy at Bromley took me to a wrong place and set me down at the door of Perkins the brewer.[1] At last I got to Chevening. Lord and Lady S very kind and hospitable. No company – the Bp of Oxford had disappointed them. The afternoon fine. The woods and water looked well. But in the evening came thunder and hail. We got on pretty well without the help of company.

1. Frederick Perkins (1780–1860) of Chipstead Place, Sevenoaks. His father John (1731–1830) had founded the family brewery, and was a friend of Dr Johnson.

Wednesday – July 16

After breakfast Ld S very kindly and sensibly left me to rummage his library. A fine old library it is of, I should guess, fifteen thousand volumes, much resembling a college library both in appearance and in the character of the books. I was very agreeably entertained till two in the afternoon. Then we set out for Mountstuart Elphinstone's six miles off.[1] The weather looked dubious when we started. But all doubt was soon over. Down came such a storm of hail as I have not seen since August 1 1846 – near ten years ago. We were dry: but the servants were thoroughly soaked. We got to Elphinstone's however; and I saw him, probably for the last time – still himself, though very old and infirm – a great and accomplished man as any that I have known. Home – the weather a little better. Darwin a geologist and traveler,[2] and Sykes[3] the parson of the parish came to dinner – Very well.

1. Mountstuart Elphinstone (1779–1859) lived at Hookwood, near Limpsfield, Surrey.
2. Charles Darwin (1809–82), the author of *The Origin of Species*.
3. Thomas Sykes (*c.* 1805–88), a Queens' College graduate. He became Rector of Chevening in 1854.

Thursday – July 17

The morning again in the library. Poems – plays – etc etc – Bentley's Milton. Pamphlets in answer to De Foe's White Staff.[1] In the afternoon to a pretty spot of common land which has fallen to Ld S under a late inclosure act – fine wood and heath – fine prospect. My Valentine with us, dancing about among the flowers, gathering foxglove and whortleberries, and very gay and happy. I love all little girls of that age for the sake of my own nieces. And Lady Mary is a very amiable child to all appearance. Back – Sir A Campbell[2] and somebody else to dinner. Mrs Mildmay I believe.[3] In the evening Ld S produced a tragedy written by Pitt and his brother Ld Chatham in 1772 – detestable of course – but well enough for a boy of thirteen. Odd that there was no love at all in the plot – a dispute about a Regency during the absence of the King and the minority of his son Prince Florus. There were several passages which reminded me of 1789.[4]

1. Daniel Defoe, *The Secret History of the White Staff*... (1714).
2. Perhaps Sir Archibald Islay Campbell (1825–66), third Bart, MP for Argyllshire, 1851–7.
3. Perhaps Marianne Frances (*c.* 1815–73), only daughter of Granville Harcourt Vernon (1794–1879), MP, who had married Humphrey St John Mildmay (1794–1853), MP for Southampton and a Director of the Bank of England.
4. The piece was 'Laurentius, King of Clavinium': see John Ehrman, *The Younger Pitt* (1969), pp. 6–7; and TBM's essay on William Pitt, *CW*, vol. 7, pp. 358–9, where this passage is elaborated.

Friday – July 18

Off after breakfast. Glad to get home though my host and hostess were very kind and agreeable. Letter from Tauchnitz with £242.11.6 in addition to the former £250. Pretty well, yet little, the sale considered, which has amounted to nearly ten thousand – an immense sale for an English book on the continent. Wrote – Johnson's establishment in Bolt Court. At dinner – Sea Lions[1] – Walked in the evening.

1. By James Fenimore Cooper (1849).

Saturday – July 19

After breakfast into the City – paid in the £242 from Leipsic. E has paid £300. The Yankees are going to pay me off my 30 000 Dollars of U S Stock. Very good of them. I was going to sell out. Home – Letters and Journal – then wrote for Black. Leigh Hunt called – paid me £10. To dinner at Holland House – Ld Lne, Lady Morley, Lady Ashburton, Senior etc. Still plagued with cough and oppression of the chest. The summer has not done much for me as yet. My wrist however is getting better.

Sunday – July 20

Read Boswell's Tour to the Hebrides. To Church. Collection for the National Society.[1] Doubted – but gave a trifle – Home – wrote and read. Rainy and cloudy. Then it cleared and was fine. At dinner Sea Lions. Walked in the evening, but not much.

---

1. The National Society for Promoting the Education of the Poor in the Principles of the Established Church (founded in 1811).

Monday – July 21

Worked some time in the forenoon – then off for the Waterloo Station – to Walton. There the carriage met me with H and the dear girls. We called on E Rose.[1] He was out – I saw his wife and his mother. A pretty and most pleasant parsonage. To Oatlands.[2] Much disappointed. I had imagined Oatlands a noble country seat, and I expected that even in its decay and partitioned as it is it would be worth seeing. A miserable piece of piecrust – true Wyatt and Walpole Gothic – everything in short that is meanest and most tawdry. The rooms however are not amiss. The grounds are well enough for a small villa, and the air and scenery of the neighbourhood are delightful. I was much vexed by learning from H that this Crimean report throws much blame on T.[3] I suppose that the officers did their best to screen their brother officer at the expense of the civil departments. I do not think that the report will attract much attention or command much respect. Still the thing is very disagreeable. I hope that it may tend to sober him. The only thing that he wants is sobriety of mind. The evening pleasant, though less, than it would have been but for this business.

---

1. Edward Joseph Rose, Rector of Weybridge, 1855–82.
2. Formerly the residence of the Duchess of York.
3. The Report, by Sir John McNeill and Colonel Tulloch, into the Quartermasters department and the Commissariat during the war, had been resented by the army, who demanded their own Court of Enquiry, which had met and heard witnesses in Chelsea Barracks. This was their report, and is in *Parliamentary Papers* (1856), xxi. But see below, entry for 26 July.

Tuesday – July 22

I had not a very good night. In truth my respiration is not much better than in the winter. But I can now go into the open air freely, which I could not do then. I am much in the same state out on my lawn in which I was last Christmas by my fireside with every window closed. H made me breakfast at ½ after 9. T and the rest had breakfasted an hour before. Walked with B and A to a most singular monument of human folly. The Duchess of Y had made a cemetery for her dogs. There is a gateway like that under which coffins are laid in the Churchyards of this part of the country. There is a sort of chapel. And there are the gravestones of sixty four of Her R H's curs, with the names inscribed – Presto – Ginger – Poor Devil – etc etc. On some of these mausoleums were inscriptions in verse.

I was disgusted by this exceeding folly. Humanity to the inferior animals I feel and practice I hope, as much as any man. But seriously to make friends of dogs is not my taste. I can understand however that even a sensible man may have a fondness for a dog. But sixty four dogs. Why it is hardly conceivable that there should be any warm affection in my heart for 64 human beings. I had formed a better opinion of the Duchess. Back to Oatlands. Talked and looked at prints till the Roses came to lunch. I took much to Edward. His mother I have loved ever since I can remember. I like his wife too. Took leave very affectionately of the girls. H took me to the Weybridge Station. Back to town by the railway – By cab from Vauxhall to H.L. Absurd anonymous letter imploring me to give up taking opium. At dinner O'Donnel.[1] Walk in the evening.

1. *O'Donnel: A National Tale*, by Sydney, Lady Morgan, 3 vols (1814).

Wednesday – July 23

Wet day – Wrote – Letter from H. The report strong against T. But he will be supported; and perhaps we may make these fellows ashamed of themselves. E came soon after 5. We walked and talked till dinner, and walked again a little in the evening. My nights are but bad.

Thursday – July 24

After breakfast with E to the British Gallery. My first impressions confirmed. Excellent Ruysdaels – A fine Hobbema – some other good Dutch and Flemish landscapes. Good interiors by Teniers. Excellent Vandykes.[1] Took E to The Temple. Home – wrote – letter from T. It is a disagreeable affair, but it will end well, I trust. Villiers held most proper language in the H. of C. yesterday.[2] Fortunate that the prorogation is close at hand. O'D. Excellent – E came soon after six. Dinner and walk as before.

1. For the details, see A. Graves's catalogue; above, entry for 19 June 1856, n. Graves lists two Hobbemas, three David Teniers, and six Van Dykes.
2. C. P. Villiers, Judge Advocate General, complained that he had been accused by Lord Lucan in the House of Lords of delaying publication of the Report of the Chelsea Commission on the conduct of the Crimean War. See *PD*, 3rd ser., cxliii, 1115–18 [Villiers]; 1176–80 [Lucan]; and 1273–4 [Villiers] (all 23 July).

Friday – July 25

Took E to the Temple, and home – Wrote – I see land – read my fourth vol – pretty well pleased. To the U Club at 6. brought E out – dinner and walk – Fesc τον. Letter from Thornton. The Royal Exchange stock up at 270 – A thousand for sale.

Saturday – July 26

Took E to the Temple and went on to the City. Thornton not at the bank. Made inquiries, and determined not to buy Rl Exch which is now up at 275. On my way back crossed Longman in a cab near Hyde Park Corner. We stopped, and had two minutes talk. Glad to find that I am likely to have still something to receive in December. T's business is thought important, as far as I can yet judge, by nobody but himself. The report of the Chelsea Comrs. appears to be very slightly thought of. Nothing is said about the part which relates to T either in the H of C or by the Times. Bought a new Vol of Thackeray's Miscellanies.[1] Home – Read and wrote – Adam Black called. To dinner at H[ollan]d House rather against the grain. The party dull as all parties are where there is a prince to be called Sir and Royal Highness. The Duke of Aumale however is sensible and does not want vivacity or information. Ld Lyndhurst – Ly Lyndhurst – a miserable falling off from the last Ly L in person at least.[2] Odd that I should never have met either except at Holland House – 23 years interval – Vernon Smith and his wife – Ld Stanley of Alderley – stupid evening.

1. Thackeray's *Miscellanies* were published in four volumes (1854–57).
2. Lyndhurst's glamorous first wife was Sarah Garay Thomas (*c.* 1794–1834), daughter of Charles Brunsden, and widow of Lt-Col. Charles Thomas, killed at Waterloo. His second wife was Georgiana Goldsmith (*c.* 1807–1901), whom he married in 1837.

Sunday – July 27

Night a little better. To town hoping to see the Chancellor. Left a card and note for him. To Brookes's and Athenaeum. Anxious about the Sunday papers. Glad to see scarcely any mention of T. and none of an unfavourable kind. The report has fallen quite dead. Wrote to H. Read Colls's trash about Bentham.[1] Bentham was sufficiently open to censure. But Colls is the dirtiest dog that ever turned up his leg against a dead lion. The Rejected Comedies.[2] Very good. Turned over Joe Thompson[3] an old novel and a bad one – Lydia by that rascal Shebbeare.[4] Wrote – Jack Ashore.[5] Bad weather in the afternoon; but it cleared up at least and I walked between 9 and 10.

1. John Flowerdew Colls, *Utilitarianism Unmasked …* (1844). Colls was one of Bentham's Secretaries. He became a Christian minister.
2. Perhaps *The Rejected Theatre, or A Collection of Dramas which Have Been Offered for Presentation but Declined by the Managers of the Playhouses* (1814).
3. *The Life and Adventures of Joe Thompson*, by Edward Kimber (1750).
4. John Shebbeare, *Lydia, or Filial Piety* (1755).
5. By Edward Howard (1840).

Monday – July 28

Letters from H – G has got the Gregory with much honor.[1] Thank God, His letter to his mother is excellent. A good boy. Wrote to congratulate them from my soul. Wrote for Black. To B M – Read Baretti's[2] Strictures on Mrs Piozzi in the European Magazine for 1788. Blackguardly beyond even the Tolondron.[3] Baretti must have been a hateful fellow. The lady was, if not a whore, the very next thing to it. Home by Shepherd's Bush omnibus. Read a good deal of the Indian penal Code. Old Reviews and Magazines. Muggleton – At dinner J[ack]. A[shore]. Walked.

1. The Gregory was a leaving scholarship for Latin composition, endowed by Richard Gregory, the great-uncle of Sir William Gregory of Coole Park, Co. Galway. See C. Tyerman, *History of Harrow School 1334–1991* (Oxford, 2000), p. 234.
2. Presumably Giuseppe Marc' Antonio Baretti, who edited a collection of Johnson's letters.
3. Also by Giuseppe Baretti (1786).

Tuesday – July 29

My nights wretched. Why I should have this difficulty in breathing now that the weather is warm I cannot tell. However my general health and spirits keep up. Wrote – at 12 Pistrucci – he sate an hour and a quarter.[1] We talked. I got on wonderfully, – much better than I at all expected. When he was gone I looked over and corrected much of this paper on Johnson. I read Goldoni's Bottega del Caffè[2] with much pleasure. But the character of Eugenio is too vile to be reclaimed. Such a fellow should be left, in poetical justice, to ruin himself, and hang himself. Goldoni is too fond of converting such creatures into honest men. Mazio is excellent. The dialogue about the watch is as good as anything of the sort. A most lovely day – Walked. At dinner J.A. – Walked. Read Foot's Life of Bowes.[3]

1. Valerio Pistrucci (1827–83). By 1859 Pistrucci was Professor of Italian Literature at King's College, London. See *LM*, vol. 6, p. 51 and n.
2. Carlo Goldoni, *La Bottega del Caffè* ('The Coffee Shop') (1750–1).
3. Jesse Foot, *The Life of Andrew Robinson Bowes ... and the Countess of Huntingdon ...* (1812).

Wednesday – July 30

Last night rather better. A fine day, but too hot for walking. Once I cared little either for heat or cold. Then I was young and poor and obscure. Opulence has come and fame with the infirmities of advancing life. Yet I have as clear a head, thank God, and as warm a heart as at twenty. Pistrucci at 11. Got on very well. I am pleased to find how quick and how retentive my memory is. I catch every hint and bear it in mind as well as I could ever have done. When P was gone I wrote. The paper is finished with the exception of a sentence or two, and a few corrections. It will probably go off tomorrow. Walked and read old vols of the Gentleman's Magazine. To dinner with Vernon Smith. The Duc d'Aumale again. But the party more pleasant than on Saturday – Ld Lne – And I was seated very agreeably between two clever women Lady Morley and Lady Dufferin.[1] Lady Dufferin talked about Oatlands. It seems that she and Mrs Norton were often there when they were girls of 12 or 13, and that the Duchess of York was very kind to them. I mentioned the dogs, and was greatly amused by the information which I obtained. It seems that the epitaphs which I had guessed to be Monk Lewis's were written by Mrs N and Lady D. But the best part of the story is that the Duchess was plagued to death with presents of dogs, which she did not like to refuse, and which would have turned her house into a kennel if she had not poisoned the beasts and sent them to the cemetery. This is quite a new view of her tenderness for four footed animals. The weather is intensely hot. Everybody complains. But the harvest promises wonders.

1. Helen Selina Sheridan (1807–67). She married in 1825 Price Blackwood, fourth Baron Dufferin, who died in 1841. She was Mrs Norton's sister.

Thursday – July 31

A burning day. At eleven Pistrucci. Sate under a tree with him and talked Italian glibly. Ugo Foscolo.[1] Then wrote and revised. Finished this article except a concluding sentence. At five to the Chancellor's[2] in Brook Street. Very anxious on E's account. But nothing could be more satisfactory. He was kindness itself, and will, I feel confident, do whatever he properly can. To the Athenaeum – then to the U.C – brought E home – told him what had passed to his great contentment. We dined and sate in the verandah after walking a little – pleasant evening.

1. Ugo Foscolo (1778–1827) was an Italian patriot and poet. He lived in England from 1816. He was a friend of Panizzi and of Bayley Wallace, who challenged TBM to a duel.
2. Cranworth.

Friday – August 1

Took E into town – back – Pistrucci. Got on better than ever. Talked about Tasso – about the United States. When he was gone, finished my paper on Johnson and sent it off to Black. By the bye there is a poor trumpery article about my book in Blackwood[1] – praise and blame – but neither judiciously bestowed. Looked over Buckingham's absurd Volume about his Institute.[2] Goldoni – Il Cavalieri e la Dama.[3] To dine in Bedford Place, Frank, Walter, a Mr Watson[4] a fellow of Trin and a 2nd Wrangler. But I did not much take to him – he talked of his intention of climbing Mont Blanc by a new track and without guides. He had no earthly object, he said, but to risk his life. The danger was the attraction. Madness, if it were true. Coxcombry of a miserable sort, if, as I suppose, it is false.

1. The first of two articles on Macaulay by Margaret Oliphant (1828–97), in August 1856; vol. 80, pp. 127–41. Another followed in September 1856; ibid., pp. 365–78.
2. James Silk Buckingham, *An Address to the British Public on the Slanderous Articles ... in Punch, against the British and Foreign Institute ...* (*c.* 1846).
3. By Goldoni.
4. Henry William Watson (1827–90), second Wrangler 1850; Fellow 1851. He became a master at Harrow, 1857–65. He was one of the founders of the Alpine Club.

Saturday – August 2

The weather has during the last week been intensely hot. On the whole it agrees with me. I have had a good night – better than for some weeks. Up and ready soon after six. Gentleman's Magazine. D. Wilson's dialogue with Bellingham.[1] After breakfast Pistrucci. Read Il Bugiardo.[2] Far inferior to Corneille's Menteur[3] and to Foote's Liar.[4] At a quarter after one to the Waterloo Station – thence to Weybridge. There B was waiting for me with the carriage – To Oatlands, happy quiet afternoon among those whom I love best. All content and peace and cheerfulness. Dear G in high spirits. Looked over his papers. Very good indeed. He must do well at Cambridge. Much laughing about the Duchess of Y's dogs. At eight to Weybridge and back to town. This morning I heard from Longman. His calculations had been too sanguine. There will be an arrear instead of a surplus. But nothing to speak of. I am not disappointed, not having expected anything else. Letter from that vagabond James Mills threatening what he calls a personal application. He thinks that I am still at the Albany, where it would have been much easier for him to cause annoyance than here.

1. D. Wilson, *The Substance of a Conversation with J. Bellingham, the Assassin of the Late Right Hon. Spencer Percival ...* (1812).
2. *The Liar*, by Carlo Goldoni.
3. *Le Menteur* (1643).
4. *The Liar* (1762).

Sunday – August 3

Burning day. Staid at home and read. Corrected Chap 1 for the small edition. Charles M called – Then Senior – at dinner 10 000 a year. Walked in the evening.

Monday – August 4

I had a wretched night. I must try the effect of calomel. The liver must be concerned in all this. Hot – but not quite so hot. Corrected Chap II. Pistrucci – we read some poems of Giusti[1] – a name unknown to me – vigorous, a little coarse, and not highly finished. Many modern phrases which were new to me. Read a good deal of Daru[2] and Sismondi to revive my recollections of the history of Lombardy and Venice. At dinner – 10 000 etc – I see that a jury at Edinburgh has found a most shameful verdict against The Scotsman.[3] I am not fond of newspapers, or averse to the reasonable use of the law to restrain their licentiousness. But here the comments complained of did not come up to the ordinary freedom of English electioneering controversy. A most scandalous verdict! 400 £ – Hydr.

1. Giuseppe Giusti (1809–50), poet and member of the Tuscan Legislative Assembly.
2. Piérre Antoine Noël Bruno, Count Daru, *Histoire de la republique de Venise* (1819).
3. The *Scotsman* had in 1852 attacked Duncan McLaren, the Lord Provost, for supporting Brown Douglas, a Conservative MP, against Adam Black. McLaren was described as 'deserting principles, and traducing friends, and acting for ... his own malignities'. McLaren sued and was awarded £400 damages. See *The Times*, 4 August 1856 (p. 10e), 12 August 1856 (p. 7c) and 14 January 1857 (p. 4f).

Tuesday – August 5

Better for the hydr; I think. Another burning day; but the harvest promising excellently, trade thriving, the value of stocks rising, the dividends of railway companies increasing. Pistrucci – we chatted pleasantly near an hour. Daru. To the Chancellor's to dinner – Sir H. Holland and the Speaker – No other guest that I knew. Dana, the Yankee, Author of Life before the Mast.[1] The dinner very bad – No wine to be got. I certainly did not drink as much as would have filled one large claret glass. Odd, considering that Rolfe, in his bachelor days, was rather a connoisseur in wine. I remember tasting several sorts which I have never tasted since at his house in Spring Gardens. They were very kind – as kind as possible. I attribute the deficiencies not to any narrowness, but to want of housekeeping skill on the part of the lady. What a dessert. Apricots like bricks – strawberries a mere mash!

1. Richard Henry Dana (1815–82). His *Two Years before the Mast* was published in 1840. There is an account of this dinner in *The Journals of Richard Henry Dana Jr*, ed. R. F. Lucid (Harvard, 1968), vol. 2, pp. 772–5.

Wednesday – August 6

Still hot, though a little less so – corrected part of Chap III. I am puzzled what to do about it. Pistrucci for an hour. Read Daru. I have got my Italian history in tolerable order for the journey. Looked at St Real.[1] At dinner 10,000 a year – Walked in the cool of the evening. Hydr.

1. César Vichard, Abbé de Saint-Réal (1639–92), was a savant and diplomat. TBM probably read his *La Conspiration des Espagnols contre la république de Venise en 1618* (1674).

Thursday – August 7

Pistrucci did not come today. It was intensely hot. I staid at home all the morning and read the three parts of the Villeggiatura again. I know them well. I prefer them on the whole to any of Goldoni's pieces. The Impresario delle Smirne.[1] E came – Pleasant evening – walk after dinner in the garden.

1. By Carlo Goldoni.

Friday – August 8

The morning cool. A little rain fell. Went with E to the photographer in the Quadrant, rather against my will.[1] Spent some time in sitting. Took E to the Temple. Home – finished the Impresario. Went on with Chapter III. To the University Club to take up E. Brought him back through heavy rain. Dinner – No walk in the evening.

1. Antoine François Jean Claudet (1797–1867) had a studio at 107 Regent Street. He became Photographer in Ordinary to Queen Victoria.

Saturday – August 9

A great shock. A letter from John's son Henry[1] to say that John had had a terrible accident – a fall into a mine pit, and is in a precarious – I fear a hopeless – situation. Much distressed, though the tie was not a very close one. After breakfast to the Treasury to consult T. He was not expected today. Left E at the Temple and home. Hoped to hear from C or to see him. Wrote to H, to Aldingham – to Ld Lne to excuse myself from dining with him on Monday. God knows what may come of this. One of the least serious consequences is the unsettling of all my plans for travelling. Very sad. However I had to go to work and corrected the proof of my paper on Johnson, which I think a very good one. Looked through a volume of one of the German translations of my history. Poorly done, I think. In the afternoon Charles. He had been summoned up from Ramsgate by a Telegraphic despatch, and had seen Charles Gore[2] who had been at the accident &, it seems, had been so much shocked as to faint. Charles had better hopes than Henry's letter had led me to form; and just as he was going came a line to me from Gore, with a telegraphic despatch saying that a favourable turn had taken place and all was going on well. Thank God! – 10, 000 a year[3] – Walked in the evening.

1. Henry George Macaulay (1836–69). He became an official in the Treasury.
2. Charles Alexander Gore (1811–97) was Commissioner of Woods and Forests.
3. The novel by Samuel Warren.

Sunday – August 10

Staid at home all day waiting for news but got none which I hope is a good sign. H sent a servant from Oatlands. Read one of Goldoni's Venetian Pieces – C called. In the evening 10 000 and Ld Hervey[1] – Walked.

1. Presumably the *Memoirs of Lord Hervey* (1696–1743), edited by J. W. Croker (1848).

Monday – August 11

No letter from Aldingham. To the Treasury. T. not expected – but a letter from Gore. All going on well. Home. Read a silly contemptible book about Curran, better than Charles Philips' however.[1] By the bye a letter from Lady Malkin. She wants 100 £. I sent it her with real pleasure. No news of Franz.[2] If I do not hear of him in a day or two, I must take somebody else. Read a play of Goldoni's, Female punctilios.[3] Tolerable. The weather intensely hot, with a short shower now and then. The Gentleman's Magazine of 1785. A queer volume which I remember picking up just after my return from India – Edwin and Julia.[4] Ld Hervey – At dinner 10 000 – Walked in the evening.

1. There were three memoirs of Curran besides Phillips's.
2. Courier for his trip. (George Trevelyan's note).
3. *La femmine puntigliose* (1750).
4. Perhaps *The Interesting Story of Edwin and Julia* (1788) or *Edwin and Julia: or, Weyhill Abbey: A Romance* (1806).

Tuesday – August 12

A letter from H M – All going on well at Aldingham – Nothing yet from Franz. Wrote part of a note on Penn – Read Goldoni's Vedova Scaltra[1] – Fra Paolo's History of the dispute between the Venetian govt and Paul V.[2] I read that work last on a burning Sunday in India, and got through the whole at one sitting. An interesting story, and more honorable to the Venetian Aristocracy than anything else that is recorded of them from the closing of the Grand Council to the destruction of the republic. At dinner 10 000 – Ld H. Walked.

1. *The Shrewd Widow* (1748).

2. Perhaps Paolo Sarpi, *Trattato dell' Interdetto della Santita' di Papa Paolo V* (Venice, 1687).

Wednesday – August 13

Staid at home again. Sent Wm to see Pierotti[1] – and desire him to call tomorrow. Finished the History of the dispute of 1605. Ld H – 10 000 – Walk. Corrected the revise of my article on Johnson.

1. Courier.

Thursday – August 14

Pierotti – Very handsomely he behaved – settled things with him as far as they can be settled. – To town – British Museum – Extracts from Bp Cooper's works[1] – to the City – settled money matters – made some purchases – to the Royal Institution – Brooks's – Willis's rooms where the Athenaeum is sojourning during the repairs. The carriage came. Took up E at the U C and brought him out – pleasant dinner and evening.

1. Thomas Cooper, Bishop of Lincoln and of Winchester (1584–94). Macaulay added a note quoting from Cooper's answer to Martin Marprelate, *An Admonition to the People of England* (1641), to the later editions of *HE*, ch. 1, making the point that forms of church government are not divinely ordained.

Friday – August 15

E read my paper on Johnson and liked it. Into London with him. At the photographer's. A hideous likeness of me produced at last.[1] Codsfish, as Charles II said, I must be an ugly fellow.[2] Home by omnibus. At three set out for the Waterloo Station. A little before 5 reached Oatlands – all kindness and happiness. E Rose, Buxton and their wives came to dinner. Pleasant though too much theology.

1. See *LM*, vol. 6, p. 16, n. 2.
2. For the source of this, see *LM*, vol. 3, p. 257, n. 5.

Saturday – August 16

A bad night. My chest much oppressed – the morning fine. Delightful talking and rambling. How happy they are and deserve to be, thank God. T. is reading Greek with the energy with which he betakes himself to every pursuit which seizes his fancy. G will be an excellent scholar. Left them, somewhat sadly, not expecting to see them again till October, and not knowing whether I may ever see them again. Read in the railway carriage Foudras Les Hommes des bois[1]

– poor work. Reached H L at ½ after 7. 10 000 – Saw Pierotti, – Nothing from Franz – The passports all right. Hydr.

1. Théodore Louis Auguste, Marquis de Foudras, *Les Hommes des Bois* (1856).

Sunday – August 17

A rainy day – Staid at home, having taken calomel, wrote letters, read Ld H – 10 000.

Monday – August 18

A dull day. Letter from Franz to Wm. Franz will not be here till the 22nd or 23rd – Pierotti – gave orders for Wednesday – To town in the carriage. Bank. Looked in at Murray's to buy the last edition of the Handbook of France.[1] Murray came in while I was opening my purse, and very civilly insisted on giving me the book. Home – Finished Ld H – G[entlema]n's Mag[azi]ne. Trevelyan's evidence about the public offices. 10,000. Walk in the evening.

1. *Handbook for Travellers in France, 6th ed. Revised and Corrected, with an Account of the Island of Corsica* (1856).

Tuesday – August 19

Dull drizzling day. Preparations for departure – packing – locking up – calculating – etc etc. Longman called – wrote a few letters – Finished 10 000.

(I shall keep the journal of my tour in a separate volume.)

[Vol. 10 of the MS contains three journals of TBM's three tours abroad, the first of which begins here.]

Wednesday – August 20

Up early. P. came by eight o'clock. Off to S E station met E there, and away. Read in the railway carriage Plutarch's Life of Theseus – curious. Got on board at Folkestone – A short and smooth passage, but made disagreeable by the rain. We did not know our good fortune. We afterwards learned that late in the afternoon it began to blow hard, that vessels were lost, the mails stopped, the railway station at Dover damaged. We, meanwhile, were whirling away to Paris, having dined at Boulogne. We reached Paris at eleven and were well accommodated at the Hotel de Bristol. I was much exhausted and could hardly draw my breath. We resolved however to go on tomorrow.

Thursday – August 21

I had but a bad night. However we set off betimes for Dijon. April weather till we got to the highlands of Burgundy. Then storm and rain in torrents. We were as well lodged as we could be at Dijon. For we had the apartments which the Emperor occupied a few weeks ago when he went to visit the parts of France which had suffered from the floods. We walked in the evening, but were not much struck by anything that we saw. I had expected more. The Cathedral but mean.

Friday – August 22

I walked a little about the town, and was better pleased with it. I had had a much better night than usual. Off for Lyons. Arrived pretty early in the afternoon. To our old inn The Hotel de L'Univers, and were lodged in our old rooms. Walked a little. April weather. Engaged a carriage to Susa for 200 francs. Bought the 14th vol. of Thiers[1].

1. *Histoire du Consulat et de l'Empire*; vol. 14, on the Russian Campaign, June–December 1812.

Saturday – August 23

A doubtful morning. We started soon after nine. The first twelve or fifteen miles were dull. But soon the country became richer and bolder. After we had passed the Pont de Beauvoisin the scenery was really magnificent. At one moment things looked ill. At Echelles we found that the horses were all out, and that a heavy storm was brewing among the mountains. We sate disconsolately in our carriage with the glasses down under a heavy rain. But the horses came: the rain blew over; and we had a delightful journey to Chambery through fine rocks, ravines and woods. We reached Chambery just after sunset, dined not very luxuriously and got to bed much tired.

Sunday – August 24

A lovely day. I was much better. I have slept well ever since we left Paris. We had a most delightful journey of about 70 miles to Modane – At one point a noble view of Mont Blanc in all his glory. Many mountains with snow on their summits. A river, murmuring and raging close to us the whole way. Modane, a small country town among the mountains. The inn very clean and the people civil. But the accommodation moderate; and the wine of the neighbourhood bad. However it was but for a night. We sent on to Lans le Bourg to order breakfast, and made our arrangements for starting at half past 6.

Monday – August 25

Another glorious day. Some delay about the horses. However we got off, and reached Lanslebourg before ten. At half after ten we began to ascend Mont Cenis. During the next four or five hours the pleasure which the scenery gave me mounted almost to pain. The ascent grand. But the descent far grander. I never shall forget Mont Roche Melon. I really never before saw a mountain – I mean near: for Mont Blanc I have seen only at the distance of some forty miles. But Roche Melon was divided from me only by a glass: and I saw the whole huge mass from the head covered with snow and rising above the clouds down to the feet where they rest on the plain of Piedmont. I must have taken in at one glance a good eleven thousand feet of perpendicular height. And then the surpassing loveliness of the valley of Susa. It looked like the garden of Eden. We got to Susa soon after three. No train to Turin till seven. Ordered dinner, and walked about the town. To the Arch of Augustus. Curious, particularly the sculptures which were executed on the principle that every figure was to be of an equal height – man, horse, ram or pig. The effect is very grotesque. A tolerable dinner – then to Turin. Well accommodated at the Europa, an excellent house. Coffee and iced water and to bed, much exhausted – my face blistered by the sun, but my general health improved.

Tuesday – August 26

A fine, but very hot day. Read Thiers. His account of the Russian campaign good, but less striking than other accounts which I have read. He is a little too fond of parading his love of truth: and like most people who are loud and boastful in laying claim to a particular virtue, he is rather deficient in the very point on which he wishes to be thought unassailable. Galignani with London news a day later than what we brought with us. Walked two or three hours in the heat of the day, or rather out of the heat of the day. For we kept under the arcades which run through the city for miles. A fine town – something like the modern part of Brussels. Better shops than I remember to have seen at Genoa, Florence, Rome or Naples, or even at Leghorn. Churches rich to gaudiness. Marochetti's statue excellent[1]. We went over the Gallery of pictures at the Castle. Some very good indeed. Back to our inn, wrote and read – out again in the cool of the afternoon. Struck by the Palace Carignan. I never saw such brickwork; nor had I the faintest notion that brick could be made to produce such an effect. Dined better than since we came to the Continent. P's bill, about fifty guineas in six days – But then we have travelled more than 800 miles; and the mere cost of locomotion has amounted to near forty pounds.

1. The statue of Duke Emmanuel Philibert in the Piazza San Carlo.

Wednesday – August 27

Galignani again. Glad to see that the weather in England is fine again and the harvest promising. No letters. I think that there ought to be by this time. Wrote to H – read some of Cicero's letters at the great crisis – most interesting. To the palace – great state rooms – splendid gilding and mirrors and pictures, but all daubs. The suite of apartments finer, I think than that of Buckingham Palace – Strange that George IV who had a great wish to be magnificent and an immense command of money could not give us a tolerable palace. To the Chapel. Not in very pure taste – to the armoury. No catalogue. No historical information. Wax dolls in armour on stuffed horses – a mere show for children. The cuirass which Eugene wore at the battle of Turin dinted with bullets.[1] By the bye, I wonder that there are not more memorials of him here. He was far the greatest man of the House of Savoy. Back to our inn. In the afternoon off to the Superga.[2] A heavy pull of two hours up hill. Nothing to be seen of the Alps or next to nothing. They were buried in cloud. The immense plain of Piedmont however was a striking object. We went down to the vault where the coffins of the Princes of the House of Savoy are arranged, then round the cloister and through the refectory of the religious house once occupied by ninety priests, now by only two. The Church, the dome at least, is rather fine. Down much faster than we came up. At the hotel found a letter from H. All well at Oatlands. Thank God – John quite right. Another reason for thankfulness. Dinner – a very good dinner and excellent Chambertin.

1. On 7 September 1706.
2. It was from this hill that Victor Armadeus and Prince Eugene were able to survey the state of the French army beseiging Turin and to decide where best to attack it.

Thursday – August 28

Up early, breakfasted, and at the Station before eight. Off for Novara. There found an open carriage provided for us. While the baggage was coming from the railway, we walked about the town. These third rate and fourth rate Lombard towns seem to me very superior to towns of corresponding rank in the other countries with which I am acquainted. I am quite sure that no town of not more than 16,000 inhabitants in England contains such stately piles of building as are at Novara. We posted thence under a burning sun and along a dusty road, crossed the field of battle where the Austrians beat the Piedmontese[1] – then the Ticin, not as Silius describes it a languid stream, but almost as impetuous as the Rhone.[2] After all that we had heard of the Austrian frontier police we passed as easily as we should have passed out of Middlesex into Surrey, The trunks were not even opened. E had been trembling for his Fra Paolo. But we might have brought Mazzini's and Kossuth's trash with perfect safety. The country most richly cultivated. Indian Corn and Mulberry trees everywhere. The hedges as thick on both sides as those of the Devonshire and Somersetshire lanes. But the tree which predominates, and indeed forms most of the hedges is the Acacia. After a time one of the springs of our carriage got out of order; and we had to wait till a smith could be got to put it to rights. It was past four when we reached Milan, and were driven to the Hotel de la Ville – an excellent house to all appearance. We are in large rooms with painted cielings – cornices, Mosaic floors, Venetian blinds and balconies high above a gay noisy showy street. From the balcony we caught a glimpse of the Cathedral which made us impatient to see the whole. We went. I never was more delighted and amazed by any building, except Saint Peter's. The great façade is undoubtedly a blunder; but a most splendid and imposing blunder . I wish to heaven that our Soanes and Nashes and Wilkinses had blundered in the same way. We walked round this most magnificent Temple. The inside we kept for tomorrow. Back to our inn – dined excellently – much amused by looking down from our window on the crowd of equipages with ladies in all their finery or the Austrian officers swaggering about in their white uniforms, and on the innumerable idlers in light dresses who were seated each with his cigar and his cup of coffee or glass of lemonade at tables in the street. I have been reading occasionally of late those most interesting letters of Cicero which were written just after Caesar had taken up arms. What materials for history! What a picture of a mind which well deserves to be studied!

1. On 23 March 1849. The Austrian General Radetzky routed the Piedmontese army under the Polish General Chrzanowski.
2. See Silius Italicus, *Punica* IV.82: 'caeruleas Ticinus aquas et stagna vadoso'. TBM's comment echoes that of Joseph Addison, *Remarks on Several Parts of Italy* ... (London, 1705).

Friday – August 29

Slept well. I always sleep well now. But my nose is like Bardolph's[1] and the sun has put his brand on both my cheeks. These eruptions are salutary though not very becoming. After breakfast to the Duomo. It is, or might easily be made, quite as fine inside as outside. We saw the service very solemnly and splendidly performed. Then to the Ambrosian Library. Worth seeing; but far inferior to what Panizzi's talk in old times had led me to expect. A hundred and forty thousand volumes – few new purchases – and those of Theological works, all no doubt, Roman Catholic. Some very interesting M.S.S. Some interesting pictures with many daubs. Back to our inn. Wrote to B – Journal – read Cicero's Letters. After a very good dinner we walked half an hour or more in the cool of the evening.

1. *Henry IV, Part I*, III.iii.30–48.

Saturday – August 30

Still fine, but terribly hot. After breakfast sent for a carriage and made a circuit of Churches. San Alessandro richly coloured and gilded. It contains no good painting: but the general effect reminded me of the great Roman interiors. E much struck. Disappointed by La Madonna. San Lorenzo interesting only on account of the Columns before it – noble remains of antiquity, San Ambrogio highly curious and interesting – the *atrium* especially, and the superb carved work of gold and jewels round the high altar – undoubted work of the 9th century. The *atrium* might, I think, with advantage be used in ecclesiastical and even in domestic architecture by ourselves. Then to Sa Maria delle Grazie. By the civility of an Austrian soldier we were directed to the refectory which contains the only thing that we wanted to see the famous Leonardo.[1] I was agreeably surprised to find so much of it left. It is certainly even in decay, a very fine painting. The art of the perspective struck me particularly, not because it is the highest excellence of the picture, but because there is no trace of it in any of the many engravings which I have seen. Back to the inn. E went to the Brera[2] to see second rate and third rate pictures. I being tired and knocked up by the heat preferred passing an hour or two in the coolness and gloom of the Duomo, into which the sun can scarcely find a way through the thickly painted windows. I admired the Duomo as much as before, but I felt the faults a little more strongly. So we are made. I easily found out the famous St Bartholomew which I had not noticed before. I might as well not have noticed it now: for I saw nothing to praise in it. It may perhaps be a good imitation; but a good imitation of what ought not to be imitated is a bad thing. To the inn. Cicero's Letters – Dined – Letters from B and A. All well.

1. *The Last Supper*.
2. Palazzo di Brera, housing the picture gallery; now the Pinacoteca di Brera.

Sunday – August 31

After breakfast to S Fedele, celebrated here as a fashionable church. Then to the Duomo with E, admired it more than ever; heard high Mass and a sermon of which I understood very little. Met Hayward[1] in the nave – sorry to meet him – I was afraid that he might be going our way; and I had no wish to have such a companion[1]. To my great joy I found that he was bound for Genoa. He told us, to do him justice, one good story about that very absurd Luigi at Naples. Off for Como. The railway carriages very pleasant. Como an agreeable town; but the first aspect of the lake, though agreeable, not very striking. We walked through the chief streets and into the Cathedral, dined tolerably and had some very fair claret. Cicero's Letters. No novel ever interested me half so much, and often as I have read them, every sentence seems new.

1. Abraham Hayward (1801–84).

Monday – September 1

Breakfasted and on board of the steamer by eight. A most beautiful day, but intensely hot. The voyage however delightful. There was a remarkably handsome and graceful Italian family seated near us on the deck. The eldest daughter, a girl of twenty eminently beautiful, with the sweetest voice and pronunciation and with the semblance at least of vivacity and good temper. I never saw a damsel with whom I could so easily have excused a young fellow for falling in love at first sight. The scenery of the lake glorious: the hills on both sides are, near the base, rich with cultivation and whitened by numerous neat villages clustering round church towers – then they rise into bold barren heights and precipices of rock. It is a more fertile Kent below, and a ruder and wilder Glencoe above. We landed at Bellagio, got a boat, were rowed into the eastern branch of the lake – came back, took some little refreshment under a thick grove of acacias overlooking the lake, were bored by a boy, the brother of our beauty, who pulled about E's telescope, and wanted to catch fish without a bait to his hook – crossed to Cadenabbia and had a view of the lake from that side. The steamer from Colico took us up and we reached Como in time for dinner, much pleased with our trip.

Tuesday – September 2

After an early breakfast off in a carriage with posthorses for Bergamo. The day dull, and occasionally rainy. The scenery however, pleased me. At Bergamo we found a fair open and the whole town in a bustle. The new town, I mean, which is on the plain: for there is on an eminence an old town, like that of Boulogne, but much finer and more interesting which is peopled by the Bergamasque aristocracy and is quiet and dignified in spite of the tumult below. The view from the ramparts of the old town over the boundless plain of Lombardy is wonderful. It is a rich green ocean of rice, vines and mulberry trees, out of which the dark hills rise like islands. We dined indifferently, as usual and were glad to get to bed. But the noise in the town was incessant and louder at midnight than that of Ludgate Hill at noon. Then came a storm of wind and thunder louder even than the noise of the merrymakers in the streets. The rain came down in torrents; and the cold was such that I found it necessary to throw my dressing gown over my bed.

Wednesday – September 3

The day pretty good after the storm, but cold, so cold that I put on my great coat and was glad that I had done so. We went in a carriage with 2 horses to Brescia. The higher hills on our north were covered with snow which had fallen in the storm of last night. The temperature was that of England in April. Forty eight hours ago it was like that of Bengal. Brescia less interesting than Bergamo but by no means without interest. We went to the Museum and saw some remarkable

Corinthian columns on the spot on which they were discovered. The Cathedral fine, in the St Genevieve style. Curious old municipal buildings. The glimpses which we caught of the courts of private houses were very pleasing and striking. I love those arcades built round little gardens of flowers and acacias. We dined, very ill, and set out for the station. There we found that, under some absurd rule, the people would not receive our baggage. We were forced to leave Pierotti[1] in charge of it for the night and to go without him to Verona. We managed very well however. We were expected at the Duc Torri, found a very good suite of rooms – though rather high up – waiting for us. We were glad to go to bed after a busy day.

1. Their courier.

Thursday – September 4

Very fine. Pierrotti came with the baggage before we were up. After breakfast we sallied forth to see the town. A most interesting place – more so than any that I have seen in the course of this tour. There is nothing like the Duomo of Milan to be sure. But on the whole Verona interests me more than Milan. Here are three quite different kinds of interesting objects, Roman remains, Mediaeval remains and fine works of the renaissance, and all crowded thick together. The amphitheatre has not the immensity and grandeur of the Coliseum; but it is more perfect, and is one of the very finest things that the dark ages have spared. The piazza dei Signori, the Council hall, the tombs of the great turannoi who ruled the City in the 13th and 14th Centuries delighted me. By far the finest picture here is the Assumption by Titian in the Cathedral I was charmed by it. E did not see anything in it. In truth he did not see it. In the afternoon we had a carriage went to St Zeno, a fine old conventual Church with a remarkable cloister. To San Bernardino, another conventual Church turned into an Austrian magazine. There is a small chapel of San Bernardino which is considered as a gem of Italian art of the best age. We made our way to it by a path choked with rank grass and jungle, and found it to be the almost exact likeness, indeed evidently the model of the pretty ante-chapel of Clare Hall.[1] To Juliet's tomb, rather as matter of duty than as matter of pleasure. For no doubt the tomb is a humbug devised for the purpose of getting a few lire out of English travellers. I was struck by the intense hatred of the people here for the Austrians a hatred of which I saw no sign at Milan, Como, Bergamo or Brescia. The sacristan of St Zeno, the old man who showed the chapel of San Bernardino, the old woman who showed the tomb of Juliet, all, without any hint or question from us said things which indicated the utmost bitterness of feeling against the German tyrants. Yet Verona has gained at the expense of other places by the events of 1849. The seat of government has been removed from Milan hither, and there must be a great expenditure of money among the population. To be sure they, on the other hand, see their masters very close. We drove to a garden attached to one of the old palaces of the city. It was worth seeing. Gigantic cypresses, said to be many centuries old. I never saw such huge pyramids of black vegetation. Home. A letter from H. All well Thank God. A good dinner and good Claret. In the evening three nos. of Galignani which our courier had managed to borrow from Lady Walpole.[2] The D. of Newcastle whom I remember hearing sing and play at the D of Somerset's. Alas! Not much in Galignani, but all good. The English harvest, the French vintage going on well. Wrote to H and A.

1. Clare College, Cambridge. The Ante-Chapel was designed by James Burrough and built 1763–9.
2. Harriet Bettina Frances Pellew (1820–86).

Friday – September 5

A letter from H. All well. Walked again round the Piazza de'Signori and the Herb Market, looked at the Amphitheatre once more, and off for the Railway Station. Saw the Euganean Hills at a distance on the south of our road, and remembered a very bad poem on them by Shelley[1] which I read in Jesus Lane when I was a freshman, and which still runs in my head. Padua. Strange old town. Endless arcades under the houses. A very good inn – too good, I should have thought, to be supported at such a place. Sallied out. Saw the Church of Saint Antonio, then found our way to Santa Maria in Arena. The Arena nothing. The Chapel highly curious, as being covered with frescoes by Giotto, said to be in his best manner. I spent a long time in looking at them, and, though I allow them some merit I must say that to put in such things above or even near Paul preaching at Athens or the three Maries,[2] seems to me pitiable absurdity, if indeed it be not mere affectation of singularity. To our inn after some wandering. I have not been quite well since I drank some sour vin du pays at Brescia. I took here what was called by Madeira, but what I strongly suspect to be Cape.

1. *Lines Written among the Euganean Hills* (1818).
2. By Raphael and Annibale Carracci.

Saturday – September 6

Better. Long walk about the City – saw the Prato della Valle, the Church of San Justino, the university – the Caffé Pedrocchi, the Piazzas, which are the real wonders of Padua, the huge hall especially and back to our inn. Then off for Venice. A dull journey till we approached the lagoons. The view of Venice rising out of the sea or rather out of a great smooth lake; for the water has none of the character of the sea, is very striking. When we had alighted, we were for the first time since we left England plagued about our passports. We had to pass muster before some official men and to answer to our names. What danger this foolish government apprehends from travellers like us, and why, if we are thought likely to be dangerous, we were not inspected at Milan or Verona, I cannot imagine. If we had landed at Venice from some other country the thing would have been at least intelligible. But we must have come through a great extent of Austrian territory. In fact we were at the end of our course, before these precautions were used. All that I have seen of arbitrary governments leads me to think that they are even more silly than oppressive. With a tenth part of the trouble which they give they might provide ten times as well for their own security. However we got through and were soon in a Gondola, on the Grand Canal. In a short time we turned out of the Grand Canal into a bye street – a street of water. I had been as well prepared for what I was to see as a man could be. I had read and heard about Venice ever since I was a child. I had also been long familiar with the best Canalettis and Stanfields; and yet this voyage between lofty houses – the doors opening upon the water, without any place beyond the threshold on which a foot could rest, the turning out of one of these sea alleys into another, seemed strange to me beyond all words. At last we came to the Albergo d'Europa – once a palace. We are well lodged, and everything seems clean and comfortable as well as stately. We dined at six and sallied forth. We found ourselves in a few minutes on the Place of St Mark. I was delighted. It is a nobler, graver, more ancient Palais Royal. We wandered about it and the adjoining Piazzetta during near two hours. The music – the singing – the shops – the crowds at the doors of the Coffee houses, everything in short interested and pleased us. Back to the inn and to bed in good humour.

Sunday – September 7

After breakfast to St Mark. The piazzas looked as well by sunlight as by gaslight. St Mark's Church very strange. I do not know how it fascinated me. I do not think it – nobody can think it – beautiful. Yet I never was more entertained by any building. I never saw a building, except St Peter's, where I could be content to pass so many hours in looking about me. There is something in the very badness of the rhyming monkish hexameters, in the queer designs and bad drawing of the pictures, which has an attraction. Everything carries back the mind to a remote age; to a time when Cicero and Virgil were hardly known in Italy, to a time compared with which the time of Politian and even the time of Petrarch is modern. There is a Byzantine air about the whole. I returned in the course of the day and spent an hour in making out the histories of Moses and Joseph, and the mottoes. They amused me as the pictures in very old bibles used to amuse me when I was a child. In the course of the day we got on board of a Gondola which is in waiting on our orders, and went up the Grand Canal, stopping to walk about the Rialto and returned through the Giudecca. At four in the afternoon we went out again, and were rowed to a garden where we lounged about and saw the gaieties of a religious festival celebrated by the common people. Saw the Lido, Ld Byron's riding ground. We had passed his palace in the morning.[1] At 6 dined. Thunder and rain kept us from going out.

---

1. Byron took a lease of the Palazzo Mocenigo on the Grand Canal in 1818.

Monday – September 8

We remained at home till eleven. Then the Gondola came to take us to the Palazzo Manfrini, renowned for its pictures. Two of them I had particularly set my heart on seeing Titian's Juan of Cyprus and his Ariosto. Both were sold. I was quite out of humour, and could hardly look at what remained. Indeed almost all the gems are gone. There was however the Giorgione which Ld Byron extolled in verse and prose.[1] I thought it hardly worthy of such praise. To the Jesuit Church – fine to tawdriness. To San Giovanni e Paolo. There saw the death of Peter the Martyr[2]. A noble painting indeed. I admired it most heartily. The Church interesting But we were pestered by a crowd of children who were undergoing catechization – then a priest preached an execrable sermon on "Give us this day our daily bread" I did not think it possible for a human being to utter such a mass of trash in so short a time. All utter platitude and tautology, made more contemptible by vehement action and raised tones. "Men are of two kinds the rich & the poor. The rich have money; they have land, they have houses, they have clothes, they have horses, they have carriages, they have cattle, they have furniture, they have good food, they have good wine, etc etc etc The majority are not rich. Sono poveri, sono miseri, sono bisognosi, non abbiano case, non abbiano danaro etc etc" After being bored for half an hour, I stole away while he was insisting much on the mysteries contained in the word quotidianum. I stepped into the Church again some time after; to have another look at the Titian; and I heard the fellow still bawling quotidiano, quotidiano. Back to the Inn. At ½ past 4 the Gondola again. Along the Grand Canal and back by a circuitous route. The gondolier asked for some beer. I wondered that he did not ask for wine. Indeed the great consumption of beer in Italy has surprised me. I remember nothing of the kind in 1838. I was told that a succession of bad vintages had made the wine so dear that beer had become the common drink of the working people. Home just in time for dinner. In the evening St Mark's. Felt a bad cold coming on.

---

1. The *Famiglia di Giorgione*, later removed to the Palezzo Giovanelli. The picture is praised by Byron in a letter to John Murray, 14 April 1817, *Byron's Letters and Journals*, ed. L. Marchand (London, 1973–82), vol. 5, pp. 212–14, and in *Beppo*, XII: 'That picture (howsoever fine the rest) / Is loveliest to my mind of all the show.'
2. It was by Titian. It was destroyed in a fire in 1867.

Tuesday – September 9

A wretched night – convulsive cough then pains in the neck and throat and soreness of the trachea. A little better towards morning. Took some pills which E had brought with him. Rhubarb Ipecac and Squills. To the Academy – a magnificent collection. Titians Assumption. First rate. Many interesting pictures and generally a blaze of colouring. To Schielers the Bankers with my letter of credit. It took me some time to get forty pounds worth of Napoleons. They are not quick in business on the Continent. Left a letter and pamphlet from Ld Stanhope with Mr R. Brown[1] a resident here. Back to our inn. At five rowed towards the Lido. Had a fine view of the City – Dined, I sparingly. In the evening R. Brown called and sate with me an hour. E walked in the Piazza San Marco and heard the band. Hot water for my feet – so hot that they were nearly scalded. More pills and to bed. Pierotti poorly.

1. Rawdon Lubbock Brown (1803–83), resident of Venice 1833–83; he was commissioned by Palmerston to calendar Venetian State papers relating to England and published eight volumes of his *Calendar* (1864–84).

Wednesday – September 10

Fine day. Much better. Pierotti well again. After breakfast to the Place of St Mark. To the Ducal Palace. I was delighted. The hall of the Great Council is magnificent. I do not know that any particular painting was much to my taste. But there was a blaze of Venetian colouring which provided the most splendid effect. Then the Scala d'Oro, the hall of the Council of ten, of the Senate, of the College, of the four doors. Everywhere gorgeous tints and fine carving. Some really noble paintings. It is a pity that so many of the subjects are absurd. Huge pictures of fifteen feet by ten representing one Doge worshipping the Virgin, another witnessing the marriage of Christ and St Catharine, a third kneeling before Faith who is holding the cross and the chalice, a fourth – surely no harmony or splendour of colouring can make such works thoroughly pleasing. But if the painting be considered as a sort of upholstery – a degrading view, I admit – the effect is perfect. I have seldom been more pleased than with the Doge's palace. Home, and out again with the gondola. To St Maria in Salute, San Georgio Maggiore, San Redentore in Giudecca – not much pleased with any of them. To Santa Mara Glorita de'Frani. Very striking indeed. The largest monuments that I ever saw. A huge pile to the Doge Giov Pesaro[1]. Another to the Doge N Tron[2]; another to Titian – another to Canova. Looked at Titian's grave. One of his most famous pictures is here, and justly famous as far as mere colouring and execution go. But the Virgin, the Babe, St Peter, St George carrying a banner with the Pesaro arms, and five persons of the Pesaro family kneeling make such a jumble that I derive but a very slight pleasure from the work. I begin to feel weary of the eternal recurrence of the same subjects. In a single sacristy, of no great size, I this day saw six pictures of the Virgin and child, three from one hand. The most fertile genius must be exhausted by such constant repetition. I suppose that it is speaking with compass to say that almost every great Venetian painter must have painted a hundred Virgins with Babes, fifty Ecce homos, twenty crucifixions, twenty depositions, twenty Annunciations, twenty Assumptions. Art, however exquisite, employed on these subjects moves me more and more faintly every day. From the Frari to the Scuola di San Rocco. The S di San Rocco is, on a smaller scale, much like the Ducal Palace – walls and ceilings blazing with gorgeous Venetian colouring. The paintings not generally very fine, in my opinion, if considered merely as painting, but admirable when considered as architectural decorations. The scuola is an odd institution, a kind of guild for religious purposes. It once, our guide told us, had 60,000 Ducats a year, which Napoleon took away. The members who are generally mercantile men and about two hundred in number, meet there on a few great feasts, hear service, and have a banquet. It is a fine sight: I am glad that I did not miss it. Back to the Inn – Dined. St Mark's place – a most pleasant lounge.

1. Giovanni Pesaro, Doge 1858–9.
2. Nicolo Tron, Doge 1471–3.

Thursday – September 11

Staid at home reading Cicero and Plutarch till Mr Rawdon Brown called – Went with him to the Doge's palace to see a picture of Fra Paolo by Bassano. An expressive head. Then to the Archives by water. A rainy day – our first rainy day at Venice. The Archives of immense extent and well arranged. A great part of them consists of judicial papers, revenue accounts, reports of surveyors, etc etc – But the diplomatic correspondence contains much that is valuable. The Keeper the Cavalier Mutinelli very civil.[1] I was introduced to a young Frenchman who is toiling in this mine – a protegé of Guizot, a M. Armand Baschet.[2] To Rawdon Brown's residence – the 2nd floor of an old palazzo – the climb high, but the rooms excellent – indeed noble – and a fine view over the Grand Canal. He has been very kind and civil. He would not dine or breakfast with us, but promised to call on Saturday and take us to the Library. To the Lido. Saw the Adriatic and back. Read Cicero's letters and Plutarch – dined – St Mark – Austrian Band – wonderful for a military performance. Beautiful night. The Grand Canal in the moonlight was a sight beyond words.

1. Cavaliere Fabio Mutinelli was Director of the Archives, 1847–81.
2. (1829–86). The author of *Les Archives de Venise* (Venice, 1857) and *Les Princes de l'Europe au XVIe Siècle, d'après les Rapports des Ambassadeurs Venitiens* (Paris, 182).

Friday – September 12

Our sojourn here is drawing to a close. A pleasant one it has been and will leave us ideas and reflections for the rest of our lives. The gondola soon after ten. To San Giovanni and Paolo again. Admired the Peter Martyr more than before looked over the Church with more pleasure than while that old ass was bawling quotidiano, quotidiano. To the Rialto. Our Gondolier tried to make us buy some gold chainwork. He was doubtless to have his percentage. But I was on my guard, and a little provoked, and would buy nothing. To the Pisani palace – fine entrance and staircase. Fine rooms above, but a little too low. A celebrated Paul Veronese of Alexander with the women of Darius's family after Issus.[1] Fine colouring – but little expression and absurd costume. Then to the Academy for the second time. The Assumption glorious – much superior, I think, to the Peter Martyr. In general I should say of the collection that the glow, the blaze, of warm Venetian colouring produced a wonderful effect. But there are few pieces which, considered separately as works of art, give me much pleasure. There is an eternal repetition of the same subjects – nine holy families, for example in one small room. Then the monstrous absurdity of bringing Doges, Archangels, Cardinals, Apostles, persons of the Trinity and members of the Council of Ten into one composition shocks and disgusts me. A spectator who can forgive such faults for the sake of a dexterous disposition of red tints and green tints must have improved his eye I think, at the expense of his understanding. Scarcely less absurd are those paintings in which the marriage of Cana and the supper given by the converted publican to Christ are represented as taking place in gorgeous halls such as could hardly have been found in Nero's Golden House; not to mention that the company and the servants in attendance are all dressed like splendid and opulent Venetians of the sixteenth century, while our Lord wears quite a different garb. I ought to say that the miracle wrought by St Mark – a Tintoretto of which Rogers had the sketch – pleased me more than, from the sketch, I should have thought possible. Home. E staid at the Europa. I walked into the Mercaria and rambled during three quarters of an hour through what seemed an infinite labyrinth of Cranborne Alleys. I lost my way repeatedly, but found it again, got to St Mark's, spent an hour in the Church very pleasantly. What an entertaining quiet old place. Back to the Europa – wrote to H – E engaged in a Milesian tale. Cicero's Letters. Dinner. We had meant to have gone out in the gondola by moonlight. But the evening proved wet and stormy and we contented ourselves with a walk under the arcades of St Mark.

1. The battle at which Alexander defeated Darius in 333 BC.

Saturday – September 13

My last day of Venice. Spent the morning in rowing without any definite object, through the labyrinth of small water streets and lanes. At two went with R. Brown to the Ducal palace to see the Library. Some interesting things – Bessarion's copy of the Iliad,[1] some curious autographs and M.S.S. But the collection was not what it should have been. I was more indignant than I chose to show when I found, not only that Petrarch's legacy of books had been suffered to perish but that the public library of Venice did not contain a copy of one of Aldus's great editions of the Greek Classics. To the inn. Cicero. Dined. The gondola. A beautiful night. The water like glass. The moon at the full and glorious. The two rows of palaces which line the Grand canal were as bright in the mirror as they were above. We went the whole length of the canal, and returned by a somewhat devious course. We landed at the Piazzetta and had a last lounge about the Place of St Mark – I am sorry to leave this fascinating city – for ever, I suppose. I may now often use the words for ever when I leave things.

1. Johannes Bessarion (1403–72), fifteenth-century Greek archbishop, who became a Roman cardinal.

Sunday – September 14

A miserable day. Cold, rainy, stormy. Venice in kindness put on her worst looks at parting that I might regret her less. It was so cold that I was glad to put my great coat on. A dull gloomy journey to Coccaglia – thence in the coupé of the Malle poste[1] to Treviglio, a wretched hour of delay in a room crowded with smokers: for it was so wet that I could not venture out. We got to our inn at Milan before 8. Dinner had been ordered: and we were very comfortable, except that my respiration had been affected by the weather and the travelling.

1. The mail coach, limited to two or three passengers with not more than 55 lb of luggage. *The Gladstone Diaries*, ed. M. R. D. Foot and H. C. G. Matthew, 14 vols (Oxford, 1968–94), vol. 2, p. 571, n. 6.

Monday – September 15

A most beautiful day after the rain. Breakfasted early and off for Novara. The road the same which we had travelled a fortnight before or so. But then the Indian corn was growing, now it was cut or cutting. Then too the Alps, Monte Rosa excepted, were blue. Now the whole ridge was white. When there was cold rain on the plain of Lombardy there was no doubt snow on the mountains. We got with perfect ease, through the hot custom houses. At Novara we found that there were no first-class carriages between Aroni and Alessandria. We were forced to go by a wretched carriage which had no convenience for keeping out the heat and which was crowded and even disagreeably crowded. At one time our company left us, and we hoped that we should have had elbow room. But we were immediately told that we must turn out and go by another vehicle which was so full that we could hardly get in. Things are so arranged that we had to wait two hours at Alessandria for a train coming from Turin. We had not time to see the tower which is some way from the station – especially as no fly was to be had. We dined as we could at the station – the food better than might have been expected. The wine absolute poison. I drank water. At last the train came and away we went. During the latter part of the journey an Italian lady and her daughter, a goodlooking engaging girl named Giuseppa, were in our company. The evening was beautiful, the scenery as far as we could discern by twilight and moonlight, very fine. The engineering of the road certainly wonderful – I do not know that I ever saw a railway on which greater physical difficulties had been overcome. Reached Genoa at nine – a carriage was waiting for us and brought us to the Quatre Nations. I was extremely exhausted and wretched. I lay for some time on the sofa gasping for breath after I had clambered to our apartments, apartments situated very low for a Genoese house, but very high for me. Took some coffee and eggs and to bed.

Tuesday –September 16

A bad night – Difficulty of breathing. In the morning a tremendous din of railway carriages roaring past my window. After breakfast discussed our plans, and found that it will be absolutely necessary to pass two days here, and to take five days for the journey to Marseilles. I am content. We sallied forth. I was impatient to see whether the impressions of 18 years ago would be revived. The Annunziata. I well remember how the Annunziata affected me in October 1838. It was the first Italian Church that I had entered. It opened a new source of pleasure to me. I was instructed and delighted in one instant. Nothing but St Peter's afterwards gave me more pleasure. The Church has been superbly embellished. Yet I could wish to see it as I saw it at first. At present the pictures and the marbles are thrown into shade by the gilding; and the effect, though richer, is perhaps less beautiful. Still it is very fine. The Strada novissima, the Strada nuova, and the Sta Balbi, though very fine, – astonished and pleased me less than formerly, the natural effect of enlarged experience. Perhaps it may be the same if ever I see St Peter's again – That Genoa is very much more prosperous and busy than when I was here last is not a matter of doubt. The improvement is immense. Alone in Italy this place reminds me of the bustle and incessant progress which are characteristic of England. A new Genoa is springing from the decay of the old Genoa. No new Venice, I am afraid, will rise out of the Lagoons. In the evening E and I walked on the terrace lately erected between the port and the huge houses in one of which, the Croix de Malte, I lodged formerly. The terrace is, in itself good: but I cannot think it on the whole an improvement. The old line of towering palaces along the beach was a grand thing. Dined at 8 and early to bed.

Wednesday – September 17

Had a better room and slept better. After breakfast we went to several churches – I called at my banker's and got 70£. We went to the red palace and saw the state apartments. They were not large, but numerous and most sumptuous. The marble pavements beautiful. Some good pictures. But the discomfort extreme. To the Doria palace. Much interested by the frescoes and other decorations. Whatever could be removed is at Rome. E went out in a boat. I read a good deal of the Promessi Sposi. We walked again on the terrace – Dinner and to bed, as we had a hard day's pull before us.

Thursday – September 18

A hasty breakfast. Off by eight. The post in a wretched state. At Aranzana we could get no horses, and were forced to go on with the poor beasts which had brought us from Genoa. However we got to Oneglia by daylight, after seeing a succession of glorious views, at once soft and sublime. I do not know a more charming road; and there never was a more glorious day. At Oneglia we found a clean and comfortable inn. The dinner was not very good; and in truth I have not dined luxuriously since Milan. But the people were civil and meant to please.

Friday – September 19

Off by half past eight. At San Remo no horses – Forced to go on a weary pair to Ventimiglia. This however was the only mishap of the kind today. The ascent to Turbia magnificent. Indeed I have never seen more charming scenery. Till we got to the head of the pass of Monacus the weather was very fine. Then it became stormy and we were driving a short time among clouds and rain. But soon the sun broke out, and we had a magnificent view of the Maritime Alps, some of them capped with snow. One which was preeminent we supposed to be Monte Viso. Long before we had descended to the level of the sea the weather had become quite fine again. The evening was falling when we drove into Nice and were welcomed to the Hotel de la Grande Bretagne. Pierotti manages excellently about providing accommodation for us at inns.

Saturday – September 20

At Nice for the first time I was seriously infested by mosquitoes, so seriously that I could hardly get any rest. Off by nine – got easily through the Douane

– the country not equal in interest to that which we have lately traversed, but, still agreeable. Passed Lord Brougham's house, not very attractive in any way.[1] We had an accident which would, I was afraid, have proved fatal to our postilion. The third horse who, according to a senseless practice is here put on in front, fell down – the wheelers fell over him, We got out; but it was some time before we could, with the help of a peasant who was going by extricate the postilion from his disagreeable and dangerous situation. I do not think that he was much hurt, but he seemed quite unnerved. He was very grateful for a Napoleon which I gave him by way of solace. The peasant who had assisted us was still more grateful for a five frank piece, wished me all sorts of good luck and went home wishing no doubt that a Milord might meet with some accident in that neighbourhood every day. I may well be thought a Milord: for the carriage which I hired at Genoa to take us to Marseilles – a very comfortable and handsome carriage – was Lord Warwick's and retains an earl's coronet. We reached Frejus at about four. The mistral was blowing – an execrable wind as cold and ungenial as the English north east wind of March, but much more violent. Between the cold wind and the hot sun I was distracted. The wind forced me to put on my great coat and the sun to keep up my umbrella. The sun baked the earth into dust and the wind blew the particles into my eyes and nose. I was divided between fear of a rheumatism and a sunblow. We managed however to see the ruins of the Amphitheatre and of the Aqueduct, which have very considerable interest. We had a poor dinner and wine just drinkable. I was determined not to spin out our journey in this part of the world, particularly with the Mistral blowing, and insisted positively that we should make a push and reach Marseilles tomorrow. The thing may be done with a little exertion, and must be done.

1. Brougham built the Château Eleanor Louise, named after his daughter, at Cannes, and passed some part of each year there from 1840 until his death.

Sunday – September 21

Up before five – swallowed a mouthful of bread and a cup of bad coffee – off at a quarter to six. We had generally good road, good cattle and good drivers, and got on at the rate of seven miles an hour. The country was at first insipid, particularly when compared with the country which we had left behind. But in the afternoon things improved. The rocks, valleys and brooks would have seemed delightful to us five weeks ago, and, though not so striking as the scenery of Mont Cenis of the Lake of Como, and of the Cornice, were very well worth seeing. The Mistral was sufficiently disagreeable all day, but did not become violent till the evening. Then the dust was driven into our faces with such violence and so unintermittingly that we could hardly see or talk or breathe. I was glad when we got to the Hotel de L'Orient at Marseilles. The improvement is great here since 1838 and

1839. I still remember with horror the filth of the inns of those days. We are very comfortably and cleanly lodged – Middling dinner – Good Cote Rotie. We have long been drinking such poor wine that I notice this. To bed much tired. Letter from dear B.

Monday – September 22

Good night. Comfortable breakfast. Walked out. Saw the old port, well remembered – the new port – the principal streets – and after wandering about during three or four hours returned to our hotel to write letters etc. Marseilles is a far more cleanly town than it was eighteen years ago. Then the old streets were really impregnable in their stench. I could not bear to enter them. Now they are drained. The port is purified by a stream of fresh water; and the nose is not more offended than in many other towns. My own nose which has lost much of its power of discriminating I should not trust. But E tells me the same. Dinner and to bed.

Tuesday – September 23

Off for Lyons – Read Manzoni's Promessi Sposi. Much pleased – particularly with the fine description of the methods by which Gertrude is brought to take the veil. The day was not brilliant. We caught some fine glimpses of the Rhone scenery. But it struck me less than in 1838. I had not then seen the Rhine; and perhaps I over-rated the beauty of the Rhone – I ought to remember also that then I saw both banks from the middle of the river. Today the left bank, which I thought the finer, was invisible. To the Hotel de L'Univers at Lyons, but not to our old quarters. The house very full – our rooms high up. A hard climb: but it mattered the less as I shall not have to repeat the exertion. Dined and to bed.

Wednesday – September 24

Up early – off to Paris – a hard pull of eleven hours. Finished Manzoni's novel, not without many tears. The scene between the Archbishop and Dom Abbondio is one of the noblest that I know. The parting scene between the lovers and Father Cristoforo is most touching. If the Church of Rome really were what M represents her to be, I should be tempted to follow Newman's example. Reached Paris at seven – to the Hotel de Bristol through heavy rain. Fortunate enough to find comfortable rooms. Dined well and to bed.

Thursday – September 25

Passed the morning in walking about Paris. Met Hayward again. He now boasted that he had been pimping for a Yankee at Milan. He told us before that he had pimped for two Englishmen at Berlin. If I did such things I would at least keep my own counsel. He did one good thing however. He advised us to see the Bois de Boulogne. Accordingly I engaged a fiacre. We drove thither. To be sure this government has done wonders.[1] The Bois de Boulogne may fairly rival our Parks. I have seen nothing of the kind more skilfully executed or in better taste. Back to Paris. Dined at the Trois Frères luxuriously. We were entitled to one feast after many fasts. Walked long about thc Palais Royal and the Boulevards in the evening.

1. The Bois de Boulogne, and much of the rest of Paris, laid out by Baron Haussmann, from 1853 onward.

Friday – September 26

Started at noon for Boulogne – a tolerable day – Read by the way Disraeli's absurd Sibyl – or, as he spells it, Sybil[1] – bad and silly. He is a poor creature. Began Soulié's Lionne.[2] Not much better. When we reached Boulogne it was raining hard, and I anticipated a most disagreeable passage. The cabins were crowded like the Black Hole – and we should have been even worse off than Suraja Dowla's prisoners. For they at least were not seasick. However just as we started the rain ceased: the stars came out: I went on deck, and had a most delightful voyage; the breeze a little fresh, the sea just enough up to be pleasant. But E suffered a good deal. We reached Folkestone in good time: for the clouds were again gathering, and a gale was beginning to blow. We were lodged at the Clarendon[3] – a sort of appendage to the great Hotel and supported apparently by the overflowings of that huge receptacle. We dined at near eleven, and after five weeks of thin potations, had Sherry again.

1. *Sybil; or The Two Nations* (1845). Disraeli may have initiated what is now convention, that a sybil is a prophetess and Sybil a girl's name.
2. Melchior Frédéric Soulié, *La Lionne* (a novel).
3. Tontine St, William Smith, proprietor.

(Here ends the Journal of my tour – I go on in the large Volume).

Saturday – September 27

Left Folkestone by the railway at a quarter past nine. A vile day. Torrents of rain; and cold which I felt the more because, only five days ago, the heat was such at Marseilles that I could walk only on the shady side of the street. Read the Lionne[1] – poor stuff. At London Bridge parted with E and Pierotti. In a cab to H L. Found all well and right – great heaps of letters and parcels, but little which required notice. Wrote to H – Read. My respiration very much oppressed during the afternoon. In the evening I became better. Dined comfortably – Comtesse de Morion – Stuff.

1. Frédérick Soulié, *La Comtesse de Mourion* (1847); *La Lionne* is the first part.

Sunday – September 28

Staid at home the whole day – a day of rain and wind – wrote several letters. Read a good deal of Horace Walpole's Memoirs and compared them with the M.S. Read with them Sir C.H. Williams's squibs.[1] Galt's Member – Annals of the Parish.[2] Much better today.

1. A comprehensive edition of Sir Charles Hanbury Williams's writings was published in 1822.
2. John Galt, *The Member* (1832); *Annals of the Parish* (1821).

Monday – September 29

A better day, though not without menacing indications which however ended in nothing. After breakfast came Pierotti. Settled accounts. Paid him handsomely. He deserved it. An article in the Times about burglaries hereabouts.[1] Talked with William on the subject. I find that there is some real danger. I shall take precautions. It is hardly worth my while to learn the management of firearms at this time of day. I never loaded a pistol, and scarcely ever fired one. If I had an opportunity, however, I would take a lesson. Into the City. Saw my book. All well. How rich I am! Sent poor Z 20 £. Home by omnibus. Walked in my garden for the first time since my return. It is really charming. The flowers are less brilliant than when I went away. But the turf is perfect emerald. All the countries through which I have been travelling could not show such a carpet of soft rich green herbage as mine. Read desultorily. Tomorrow I will positively set to work. At half past five went into town, got Walpole's letters to Lady Ossory[2] from Cawthorne's – called for E at the U.C. and carried him out – Dinner and pleasant chat.

1. 29 September 1856, p. 8d. The writer's description of burglaries in the Notting Hill area compares them with the description of similar dangers in TBM's third chapter in *HE.*
2. *Letters addressed to the Countess of Ossory from 1769 to 1797*, ed. R.V. Smith (1848).

Tuesday – September 30

Carried E into town – City – signed power of Attorney – home – read about the fire of Whitehall. Galt's Annals of the Parish – etc Walpole's Letters to Lady Ossory.

Wednesday – October 1

To the Museum – turned over the Dutch despatches for information about the fire of Whitehall.[1] Saw Panizzi – Home – wrote a sheet of foolscap – the first of Part III. God knows whether I shall ever finish that part. I begin it with little heart or hope. Soon after 6 T came – then H, B and A. Pleasant dinner and evening. I am always happy with them.

1. January 1698. *HE*, ch. 23, *CW*, vol. 4, pp. 379–81.

Thursday – October 2

After breakfast I called in Grosvenor Crescent – handsome house – handsomely furnished – an hour pleasantly passed. Home – finished writing about Whitehall – Galt – Young Duke.[1] – H.W's Letters. His Memoirs of G II – corrected my copy from the M.S. Life of R. Robinson today.[2]

1. By Disraeli (1831).
2. Probably G. Dyer, *Memoirs of the Life and Writings of Robert Robinson* (1796).

Friday – October 3

Staid at home reading – and writing a letter to a Mr Barter who has sent me a strange translation of Homer[1] – much harder to understand than any Greek – could not satisfy myself as to the letter and lost much time. To the U Club at ½ past 5 – brought E out – Evening as usual – Roberton.[2]

1. William George Thomas Barter, *The Iliad of Homer* with Notes (1854). Barter (*c.* 1810–72) was a barrister of Gray's Inn.
2. Perhaps Robinson's *Life*; see above, entry for 2 October 1856.

Saturday – October 4

Took E into town – Home and studied books about Russia for my account of the Czar's visit. I think that it will do. Macleod called. Then I walked on my lawn reading W. Huntington's Forty Stripes[1] etc – D Coleridge found me thus employed and walked an hour with me. Read H. Walpole's Correspondence with Mason, at dinner the Y[oung] D[uke] – In the evening H.W. and my own paper on Moody – not much pleased with it.[2] How it pleased my father near thirty years ago! Quando era in parte altr'uom daquel ch io sono.[3] Hydr.

1. W. Huntington, *Forty Stripes Save None for Satan ...* (1792).
2. TBM's paper reviewing reports by Major Thomas Moody on the conditions of liberated slaves appeared in *ER*, 45 (March 1827), pp. 383–423. It has been reprinted with an introduction by John Clive and Anthony Lester in *Race* (the journal of the Institute of Race Relations), 13 (1971–2).

3. *Quand'era in parte altr'uom da quel ch'i'sono* (Italian): 'When I was in part another man, and not what I am now'; Petrarch, *Canzonieri*, ed. and tr. A. Mortimer (Penguin Classics, 2002), pp. 2–3.

Sunday – October 5

The calomel and weather kept me at home – Read Shaftesbury's Characteristicks[1] – H W and Mason – Gray's Letters, and made further preparation for the Czar: but I will not write till I have been to the Museum lest I should have to do the whole over again. Y.D. In the afternoon the weather became fine; and I walked a little in the garden.

1. Anthony Ashley Cooper, Earl of Shaftesbury, *Characteristics of Men, Manners, Opinions, Times* (1711, rev. 1713).

Monday – October 6

A thick fog – such as, in London, would have forced me to light a candle to dress by. After breakfast went to G.C., saw the two dear girls, chatted with them ten minutes, then to the Museum and staid there till three collecting information from L'H,[1] Van Cleverskirke, and a crowd of old books of travels about Russia and the Czar Peter's visit to England.[2] Home, and read the first chapter of my history and corrected for the small edition. At dinner Y.D. – Finished H.W. and Mason – Read H.W. Ld Hd. A review of my book in a Catholic newspaper. The Papists are furious because I do not believe the story about the discovery of the Cross.

1. L'Hermitage.
2. *HE*, ch. 23, *CW*, vol. 4, pp. 381–7.

Tuesday – October 7

Foggy and dreary. Staid at home – Wrote – Russia – the Czar – Corrected Chapter II. Y.D. Sexagenarian[1] – Hateful fellow.

1. William Beloe, *The Sexagenarian ...* (1817).

Wednesday – October 8

Foggy and rainy – Still at home – Wrote – began to correct Chap. III – Y.D. Sexag.

Thursday – October 9

A little better weather. Wind N.E. but less cold than that wind generally is. Wrote – finished Y.D. – read Porson's Miscellanies by Kidd[1] – read a good deal of the Lysistrata[2] – Excellent. It is called licentious, precisely because it is the most moral of the Attic works of that age. Just as Ovid's poems are called licentious, precisely because there is no "Corydon ardebat Alexin"[3] no "puerorum mille furores",[4] [3 lines crossed out] in Ovid. The Iliad itself is not more pure than the Lysistrata from that cursed taint which poisons so much of Greek history, poetry, even philosophy.[5] To the UC. Brought E out – dinner and pleasant evening.

1. *Tracts and Miscellaneous Criticisms ...*, collected by Thomas Kidd (1815).
2. The play by Aristophanes.
3. Virgil, *Eclogues* II; Formosum pastor Corydon ardebat Alexim.
4. Horace, *Satires* II, 3.325.
5. TBM means homosexuality.

Friday – October 10

Took E to the Temple. By the way gave orders about a stove for the hall. Called on G.C – Saw my dear girls. I forgot to mention that B and Gertrude Malkin[1] called on me yesterday and sate half an hour. Home – walked an hour in my garden under a delightful sun – then the East wind brought clouds and fog; and I was driven in. Wrote – At dinner V Grey 2nd part[2] – very poor and extravagant. W[alpo]le's Letters.

1. Lady Malkin's daughter (*c.* 1833–1903).
2. Disraeli's first novel (1826–7).

Saturday – October 11

The Museum. Sate till past 3. Nobody but the Duke of Somerset, Hamilton, and myself. Home – read desultorily till dinner – finished D'Israeli's trash – trash indeed – utterly execrable – Walpole.

Sunday – October 12

A gloomy morning. Staid at home – finished Czar Peter, for the present at least – read a good many pamphlets – among others Whiston's account of his expulsion from Cambridge and his correspondence with Bp Lloyd and other divines.[1] I have been reading a new no. of the E.R. Not much amiss; but nothing striking. There is an article on American politics which must be by an American.[2] The article on Conybeare is severe, but I am afraid, just.[3] At dinner and afterwards looked through the later vols of Sir C. Grandison.

1. William Whiston (1667–1752), who was Newton's successor as Lucasian Professor at Cambridge, was expelled from the University for Arianism in 1710. In 1711 he published his *Historical Preface to Primitive Christianity Reviv'd, with an Appendix, Containing an*

Account of the Author's Prosecution at, and Banishment from, the University of Cambridge. Whiston was ordained by Bishop Lloyd of Worcester; he had scruples about taking oaths to William and Mary, and therefore did not apply for ordination to bishops who had taken the places of deprived non-jurors.
2. 'The Political Crisis in the U.S.', ibid., pp. 561–97, was by William Henry Hurlbert (1827–95), a journalist then on the staff of *Putnam's Magazine.*
3. The review of W. J. Conybeare's anonymous novel, *Perversion, or the Causes and Consequences of Infidelity*, in *ER*, 104 (October 1856), pp. 518–31, was by Richard Monckton Milnes.

Monday – October 13

Foggy moist morning – but fine day. Read about the standing army question – Charles's boy called to beg for autographs. Gave him a scrap of the D of W and a scrap of Canning. Looked at the old vol – a favourite of my childhood – God's Revenge on Murder[1] – found, after long and vain search, the Tully which I value as a curious relique. I walked on the lawn during two hours, and was then driven in by the moisture which found its way through my clogs. Read many curious and amusing pamphlets, chiefly relating to Anne's reign. At dinner Danvers.[2] After dinner pamphlets – Drake's savage attack on Whigs and dissenters[3] – looked into Merton.[4] Line from H inviting me to dinner tomorrow – dear B's birthday. Tonight there was an eclipse of the moon. I sate an hour watching it with much interest.

1. Perhaps John Reynolds, *God's Revenge against Murder and Adultery* (1770).
2. By Theodore Hook, in *Sayings and Doings*, 1st ser. (1824).
3. Perhaps James Drake, *The History of the late Parliament* (1702).
4. In Hook's *Sayings and Doings.*

Tuesday – October 14

B is twenty one today. God bless her. She has made a great part of the happiness of twenty one years of my life. Standing armies. I see my way pretty well: but I must go to the Museum before I begin to write – corrected Chap 3. – To G.C. Found H B and A. Delightful afternoon and evening with them – T came just before dinner. Glad to see him so well and in such spirits. Talked about Conybeare and his critics, Dred,[1] J Wood's death[2] – the probable appointment to his place, etc. Dearest B with some reluctance took 21 £ – a small present compared with what I owe her for twenty one years of love and kindness. They are to dine with me on my birthday. Home by ten. The stove has been put up today in my hall.

1. Harriet Beecher Stowe, *Dred: A Tale of the Great Dismal Swamp* (1856).
2. John Wood (1790–10 October 1856). He had been MP for Preston in the unreformed Parliament; and he became Chairman of the Board of the Inland Revenue from 1849.

Wednesday – October 15

Rain and wind with gleams of sunshine. To the R I – looked at magazines etc – home – not much inclined to work but forced myself to begin on the Army Question[1] (1698). Corrected Chap 4 – Walked in the garden. Walpole to Mann. At dinner the F[rien]d of the Family[2] – H and B called – God bless them.

1. In *HE*, chs 23 and 14, *CW*, vol. 4, pp. 347–9, 457–60.
2. Theodore Hook *The Friend of the Family* (*Sayings and Doings*, 1st ser. (1824)).

Thursday – October 16

Delightful day. Walked a good deal. Corrected Chaps. 4 and 5. To U.C. – Brought E out – Kind present of excellent grapes from Widmore.[1]

1. Widmore Place, near Bromley, Kent. The Miss Telfords, cousins of Ellis's wife, lived there; Ellis's house, Old Cottage, was nearby.

Friday – October 17

E. deep in Sir C. Grandison. His avidity amuses me exceedingly. Into town with him. Left him at the Temple. Bought a pair of Goloshes said to be waterproof. To G.C. and left most of the Widmore grapes there. Home – beautiful day – walked and read. The Sutherlands.[1]

1. In Theodore Hook's *Sayings and Doings*, 3rd ser. (1824–8).

Saturday – October 18

After breakfast to the Museum. Staid there till 3 – made extracts from the Dutch despatches of 1698. Very valuable. Indeed invaluable. Turned over books and looked at marbles – At 3 home – walked a little in the garden and read Wle and H. Mann – At dinner The man with many Friends.[1]

1. Theodore Hook, *The Man of Many Friends* (*Sayings and Doings*, 2nd ser. (1825)).

Sunday – October 19

Thick moist fog in the morning – then a glorious day for the season. To Church. A collection as usual – I doubted about giving anything as the charity is one to which I subscribe annually; and it is rather contrary to principle to let a preacher get out of you more than, on full consideration, you thought it right to appropriate to this particular purpose. However, I gave something. By the bye, yesterday Leigh Hunt borrowed 30 £ of me. He always borrows in such form – sends long epistles explaining why he wants money just at present, and employs such queer Ambassadors. This time it was his daughter.[1] He seems to distrust the post strangely. A queer fellow! He had genius disfigured by a vile vulgar affectation. The genius seems to have taken flight: and the affectation remains. To return – walked two or three hours in my garden finishing the perusal of Vol I. The wet soaked through my goloshes – so that I must try some other device. Wle and H Mann – At dinner Passion and Principle.[2] T. called this afternoon and walked in the garden with me during half an hour. It is pleasant to see with what enthusiasm he takes to Greek.

1. Probably Julia Trelawney Hunt (1825–72).
2. By Theodore Hook, in *Sayings and Doings*, 2nd ser. (1825).

Monday – October 20

Into the City – At the corner of St Paul's Churchyard the horse stumbled and fell. The shafts of the brougham were broken – I sent the coachman home with the carriage and walked on to Birchin Lane. All right. Walking back near Paternoster Row met Longman and had a little chat. Told him to send me Dixon's last edition.[1] I must write a note about the Taunton girls,[2] – Home by Omnibus – Walked and read. At dinner Passion and Principle.

1. TBM had noticed Dixon's book in Penn earlier in the year (see above, entry for 23 February 1856, n. 3) but thought it unworthy of a reply. He now realized he must write one.
2. Among the reprisals that followed the failure of Monmouth's rebellion, some girls from Taunton who had made and presented him with a standard were thrown into prison. Some Court ladies saw the chance of spoil and demanded £7,000 for the girls' release. In *HE*, ch. 5, TBM claimed that William Penn was the man they chose to extort the money. Dixon claimed that it was not the Quaker leader but a local man called George Penne. TBM's note refused to concede Dixon's claim, and defiantly gave his reasons for leaving the original passage unaltered. It appeared in the 1858 edition of *HE*, and in *CW*, vol. 1, pp. 510–12.

Tuesday – October 21

Stocken has sent me a vicarious carriage – To the British Museum – looked at a good many things – Read much old forgotten poetry. Then to Nutt's[1] and bought a copy of the Anabasis for T. To Brookes's – saw old Ld Strafford[2] there and shook hands with him – To G.C. Very pleasant talk with H and B and A. But to think that they had very nearly gone to hear Spurgeon[3] on Sunday. It is too horrible to think of – I should have died or killed myself. C. Buxton and A. Stanley to dinner – not disagreeable. The carriage came for me soon after nine; and I went home.

1. David Nutt, foreign bookseller, 270 Strand.

2. George Stevens Byng (1806–86), Lord Strafford (1853), had been a Whig MP.
3. Charles Hadden Spurgeon (1834–92), the popular Baptist preacher, had taken a lease of a music hall in Surrey Gardens. At a packed first meeting, a false fire-alarm led to a stampede in which seven people were killed and twenty-eight injured.

Wednesday – October 22

Beautiful day. Dixon is come – Trash – I wrote on the Taunton affair till one. Well satisfied. Walked on the turf and read Dred. It has merit, but is disfigured by very great blemishes. I do not know however, that it is much inferior to Uncle Tom's Cabin. Turned over Wraxall's history of the coalition[1] – The two lives of Romney[2] – Two quarto lives of a fourth rate painter – both very poor. Sayings and Doings – Cousin William.[3]

1. In vol. 3 of the *Historical Memoirs*.
2. Perhaps William Hayley, *The Life of George Romney* (1809); and John Romney, *Memoirs of the Life and Works of George Romney* (1830). Both are preserved at Wallington.
3. In Theodore Hook's *Sayings and Doings*, 3rd ser. (1824–8).

Thursday – October 23

To G.C. – They were out – To the Statistical Society[1] for the 1st time. Did not much admire the library – Ill provided with parliamentary papers. Back to G.C. – Found them at home – Chat – home – wrote Penn – Read Wraxall. At dinner Cousin William. Mrs Stowe has sent me a copy of Dred – Where to direct to her and what to say to her I do not know. Dr Renton called.

1. The London Statistical Society was founded in 1834. It met at 12 St James's Square. Its Hon. Secretary was Joseph Fletcher.

Friday – October 24

Staid at home all day. Wind NE – walked a little – finished the note on the Taunton affair. Well satisfied. Read Fielding's plays[1] – Generally poor – with excellent flashes of pleasantry – particularly in the Temple – Beau and the Comic part of Pasquin – The two burlesque pieces are excellent – especially the Covent Garden Tragedy. Pity that his indecency keeps him out of family libraries. At dinner Gervase Skinner.[2]

1. Perhaps in the *Works* (ed. Arthur Murphy) of 1762.
2. *Gervase Skinner*, in Theodore Hook's *Sayings and Doings*, 3rd ser. (1824–8).

Saturday – October 25

Today I am fifty six. Well – I have little cause to complain – Fame, opulence, most kind relations and friends. My health is the drawback; and my maladies are supportable, though disagreeable. I went to the Museum to verify a passage in Gerard Croese[1] and to try to learn something about Pere Mansuete.[2] Then to Covent Garden, and bought some fine grapes for the T's who are to dine here today. Home – annotated and corrected. Finished Fielding's plays. Walked in the garden – Wind S.E. – H, B, A, G and T to dinner. Very happy evening with them. Read them my long note on the Taunton business. They were quite of my mind.

1. Gerard Croese (1642–1710), also known as Gerardus Croese, *The General History of the Quakers ... by which is Added a Letter by G. Keith to the Author* (1696). TBM used this in his note on the Maids of Taunton in the 1857 edition of ch. 5 in *CW*, vol. 1, pp. 510–12.
2. A Franciscan friar, he was Confessor to James II.

Sunday – October 26

Very foggy. I did not stir out till the afternoon when it cleared up, and became bright and mild. Then I walked a little. T and G in the afternoon. I corrected Vol 1, read a good deal of Fielding, Cicero's speeches for Plancius and Flaccus,[1] at dinner G.S.

1. *Pro Plancio* (54 BC); *Pro Flacco* (59 BC).

Monday – October 27

Fine morning – Walked in the garden and read Cicero's speeches for Sextius and Coelius and the invective against Vatinius.[1] The egotism is perfectly intolerable. I know nothing like it in literature. The man's self importance amounted to a monomania. To me the speeches, tried by the standard of English forensic eloquence seem very bad. They have no tendency to gain a verdict. They are fine lectures – fine declamations – excellent for Exeter Hall or the Music room at Edinburgh, but not to be named with Scarlet's or Erskine's speeches, considered as speeches meant to convince and persuade juries. We ought to know however what the temper of those Roman tribunals was. Perhaps a mere political harangue may have had an effect in the forum which it would not have in the Court of King's Bench. We ought also to know how far, in some of those cases, Hortensius[2] and others had disposed of questions of evidence before Cicero's turn came. The peroration seems to have been reserved for him. But imagine a barrister now, defending a man accused of heading a riot at an election, telling the jury that he thought this an excellent opportunity of instructing the younger part of the audience in the galleries touching the distinction between Whigs and Tories, and then proceeding to give a historical dissertation of an hour on the Civil War – the Exclusion Bill – the Revolution – the Peace of Utrecht and heaven knows what. Yet this is strictly analogous to what Cicero did in his defence of Sextius. Wrote a sheet on Standing Armies – finished correcting Vol I. To G.C. to dinner – Cold evening – Sir H. Holland dined with us, fresh from America. Much amusing talk. Home – fire in my bedroom today for the first time since the spring.

1. *Pro Sestio* and *Pro Caelio* (56 BC). Vatinius was a tribune. *In Vatinium Interrogatio* was part of the former speech.
2. Quintus Hortensius Hortalus, 114–50 BC.

Tuesday – October 28

Read some of the old Evangelical Magazines of 1806 while dressing by the fire – News from America. The South has carried Pennsylvania.[1] What does it matter to me? Yet I felt a little vexed for the credit of human nature. Read wrote and corrected. G.S. Heard from E.

1. TBM seems to mean by this the Democratic Party, whose candidate James Buchanan (1791–1868) carried every southern state and five northern ones, including Pennsylvania. Fremont and the Republicans carried eleven northern states.

Wednesday – October 29

There was a tremendous fog. I staid at home, but sent the carriage to the U Club for Ellis, with some doubt whether he would chuse to come. He came however, and we had a pleasant evening. I have written several notes, and corrected a good deal of Vol II.

Thursday – October 30

The weather better – Took E into town. The Strand stopped up. We got out, and walked on to the Temple. I to the City – Bank. All right – Going home I bought a pamphlet which one faction of Congregationalists has published against another – Precious blackguards all. The Rivulet Controversy[1] – They seem to think that all the world is thinking of the Rivulet Controversy. Wrote and read – At 6 to the U.C. – brought E out – Another agreeable evening – Fesc H.

1. A dispute over Thomas Toke Lynch's *Hymns for Heart and Voice: The Rivulet* (1855). See O. Chadwick, *The Victorian Church* (1966), Part 1 (1829–59), p. 406.

Friday – October 31

Took E back into the Strand – To G.C. – chat – Home – Read wrote and corrected – Rummaging long to find the authority for one thing which I had said about Penn. At dinner finished G.S. Looked at Prior's Life of Burke[1].

1. James Prior, *Memoir of ... Edmund Burke* (1824).

Saturday – November 1

To the Museum – walking away [Greek characters deliberately obscured]

To Brooks's – To G C – dinner very pleasant – Dear children – The carriage came for me at ½ past 9.

Sunday – November 2

Fine morning – To Church – Guy Faux Sermon – The afternoon overclouded – Read, wrote and corrected – I found the passage which I wanted, after a long search, in Avaux – Wagenaar guided me to it – ιω μεγαλαυχ.[1]

1. (Greek): 'O great triumph!' Hereafter abbreviated to ιω μεγ.

Monday – November 3

All day working at home, except when James Stephen called – In the afternoon to the U.C. Brought E out. Dinner as usual.

Tuesday – November 4

Took E to W. Hall – then to G C – It was early – for we had breakfasted at 9 – Then into the City – the Bank – thence to Paternoster Row by appointment – made arrangements with Longman. Since Midsummer the four vols of my History have been steadily selling at the rate of about 200 a month – The revised edition will begin to appear, I think, about a year from this time. Walked to Piccadilly – thence by omnibus to Campden Hill. Walked a little – Read Prior, Sir C[harles] G[randiso]n, ιω μεγ.

Wednesday – November 5

Staid at home. Lovely day. Walked three hours in the garden – read Jowett's book about St Paul[1] – Hume's Dialogue on Natural Religion and a good many of his Essays – read over what I had written of Vol 5 and added a little – ιω μεγ.

1. Benjamin Jowett, *The Epistles of St Paul ... with Critical Notes and Dissertations* (1855).

Thursday – November 6

After breakfast to G C. Miss Laura Montague[1] there – H delivered to me a noble present from poor Sarah Anne[2] – the Etruscan publication of Egyptian Antiquities[3] – took it home with me. Beautiful day, though cold. I am much better, I think, than I was last year. By the bye this day year it was that, after an interval of some months, I began to keep my journal again. The air of Campden Hill is, I really believe, doing me good. Walked in the garden reading Hume's Essays. Wrote a little more of Chap XXIII. To the U C for E. Pleasant dinner and evening. Looked at some of the splendid Egyptian drawings.

1. Laura Caroline Montagu (*c.* 1826–1900), daughter of Henry Seymour Montagu (d. 1859), a Suffolk landowner. She married in 1861 Sir Frederick Montagu-Pollock (1815–74), second Bart.
2. Perhaps Sarah Anne Babington (daughter of John Pearson), whose husband, George Gisborne Babington, died 1 January 1856.
3. Ippolito Rosellini, *Monumenti dell'Egitto e della Nubia*, 12 vols (1832–44). The work was published in Pisa, hence TBM's word 'Etruscan'. Rosellini (1800–43) was a companion of Jean-François Champollion (1790–1832), who travelled down the Nile in 1828, recording inscriptions.

Friday – November 7

Chat about Sir C.G. – Took E to U C – Vile November day – but no tightness of breath or coughing. I really begin to hope that the Campden Hill air is doing me good – I am certainly better now than I was last May. Wrote – Standing Army – Egyptian Antiquities – Hume – ιω μεγ; three little French works sent me by Lord Holland.

Saturday – November 8

Wrote on – Standing Army – Wrote to Ld Holland. There is little in his French books worth remembering. But they are pleasant enough to lounge over – Coleridge Biog. Lit. – Dull miserable day. Forced however to go to G C. Dined at G C – very pleasant – CZM.

Sunday – November 9

Fine morning – To Church – poor sermon from a stranger – To G.C. H with a bad cold. Home – Coleridge's Biog. Lit. At dinner Gil[bert] Gur[ney].[1] Wrote a little.

1. By Theodore Hook (1836).

Monday – November 10

Went to Rowsell's in King William Street and bought Borrow's Bible in Spain,[1] Life of Dean Milner,[2] Correspondence of Knox and Jebb,[3] Life of Hume by Burton.[4] Called in G.C. H still poorly with cold. Home – wrote – Cottle – compared the two editions. In the afternoon to U.C. Brought out E. Pleasant dinner and evening.

1. Joel Rowsell was a bookseller at 9 King William Street. *The Bible in Spain*, by George Borrow (1843).
2. Mary Milner, *The Life of Isaac Milner, Dean of Carlisle ...* (1842).
3. *Thirty Years' Correspondence between Bishop Jebb and Alexander Knox*, ed. Charles Forster (1834).
4. J. H. Burton, *The Life and Correspondence of David Hume: from the Papers Bequeathed by his Nephew to the Royal Society of Edinburgh*, 2 vols (Edinburgh, 1846).

Tuesday – November 11

Took E to W H early – to G.C. H still not well – Home – read Coleridge's Table Talk – What trash! Wrote something – Still Standing Army – read or rather turned over the Correspondence of Knox and Jebb – at dinner Gil[bert] Gur[ney] – Burton's Life of Hume. It does not raise Hume in my opinion. The calmness and coldness which were attributed to him by others and claimed for him by himself seem to have been entirely wanting where his vanity was galled. He was as sore in that quarter as Pope or Voltaire. His paper on Ossian in the Appendix[1] is certainly excellent – quite decisive – and deeper poetical criticism than I should have expected from him.

1. Burton, *Life and Correspondence of David Hume*, vol. 1, appx. C, pp. 471–80.

Wednesday – November 12

After breakfast to the Royal Institution to look at the Statutes of Wm's Reign – No Mutiny Act in 1698. Home – wrote a little. Read Milner's Life. In the afternoon to the U C. E to dinner.

Thursday – November 13

Took E to the U C. Then to G C – took B to Marlborough House to see the Turners which have just been placed there.[1] The crowd was so great and the light so bad that we could see nothing, and came away without having been able to form any judgment or to get any pleasure. Left B in G.C. Home – finished Milner's Life. Read his Strictures on Marsh[2] – excessively prolix, and clumsy, and egotistical, with some passages indicating great force of mind. But a volume of 419 pages on such a subject! The personality too gives a notion of malevolence. Life of Fletcher[3] – heavy – Life of Paley[4] – better – At dinner G[ilbert] G[urney].

1. Turner died in 1851. His will was proved in September 1852, but because of legal difficulties it was not until March 1856 that the pictures he bequeathed to the nation could be exhibited at Marlborough House.
2. Isaac Milner, *Strictures on Some of the Publications of the Reverend Herbert Marsh* (1813). Marsh (1757–1839) was Bishop of Peterborough.
3. Perhaps *The Life and Death of John Fletcher* (Leeds, 1798). Fletcher (1729–85) was Vicar of Madeley, Shropshire.
4. There are lives of Paley by E. Paley (prefixed to his edition of the *Works* (1825)), by G. W. Meadley (1809) and others.

Friday – November 14

Into the City – Got a 10£ note for H. Home – read Gilman's Life of Coleridge.[1] Stuff. I do not know why the second vol never appeared – Read about Sunderland's resignation – G[ilbert] G[urney] – Colman's Memoirs.[2]

1. James Gillman, *The Life of Samuel Taylor Coleridge* (1838), vol. 1.
2. George Colman the Younger, *Random Records*, 2 vols (1830).

Saturday – November 15

Cold day. Read various things. No heart to write – In the afternoon to G C – pleasant dinner and evening, but coughed much.

Sunday – November 16

Did not venture to Church. Wrote a little – Bentinck's Mission to France[1] – Gilb[ert] Mar[ried][2] – finished Colman's Memoirs. I ought to have the Comedies of both the Colmans.[3]

1. January – June 1698. See *HE*, ch. 23, *CW*, vol. 4, pp. 388–410. Bentinck was by this time Earl of Portland.
2. Theodore Hook, *Gurney Married* (1838).
3. Both George Colman the Elder (1732–94) and his son (1762–1836) wrote plays. The latter was manager of the Haymarket theatre from 1789 to 1813. TBM's interest suggests some first-hand acquaintance with theatres, of which his father would have disapproved.

Monday – November 17

Another disagreeable day. Wrote a little more about Portland's Embassy – looked at old Journals. Read Ward's Memoirs.[1] Alsop's trash about Coleridge.[2] The

Archdeacon called – While we were talking H and B came; and he went away. Short but pleasant chat with them – E to dinner.

1. Robert Plumer Ward.
2. Thomas Allsop (ed.), *Letters, Correspondence, and Recollections of S. T. Coleridge* (1836).

Tuesday – November 18

Sent E to Westminster at ½ after 9 – Staid at home myself. Most unpromising morning. But it cleared up, and became a lovely mild sunny day. I walked on my terrace and read Ward's Diary – wrote something. At dinner G.M.[1] In the evening Ld Malmesbury. A letter from Ld Lansdowne – He is poorly, I am sorry to find at Lne House. A letter from a Mr Bell whom James Mills has importuned into asking to have an interview with me, in order to bring about a perfect friendship between us. I excused myself civilly.

1. Theodore Hook, *Gurney Married* (1838).

Wednesday – November 19

Mild day. To Lne House soon after breakfast. Ld L suffering from gout, but kind and cheerful. We talked till Sir H. Holland came – I sent Ld L Astley Cooper's Memoirs[1] which he had never seen. Home – wrote – and read Ld Malmesbury. Not well – nervous headache for a few minutes – a well known feeling. B to dinner. A very pleasant dinner and evening with her. A most amiable and intelligent companion she is. I made myself cough by talking, and she read some of Gisborne's clever dialogue between a Clergyman and a Country gentleman.[2] Sent her home.

1. Bransby Blake Cooper, *The Life of Sir Astley Cooper, Bart Interspersed with sketches from his notebooks of distinguished contemporary characters*, 2 vols (1843).
2. There is no such dialogue in the *Works* (9 vols, 1813) of Thomas Gisborne, Senior (1758–1846), but I have not traced one in the writings of Thomas Gisbourne the son (1794–1852) either.

Thursday – November 20

Dull damp day – Staid at home. Wrote a little – read Malmesbury – some of Fox's speeches – E to dinner.

Friday – November 21

Took E into town – to G C – H still not quite well. Pleasant chat. But B not there. Home – wrote a little, and read a good deal – Malmesbury with parliamentary debates – Gilb[ert] Gurn[ey] Mar[ried].

Saturday – November 22

Wrote a little – to the Museum – Dundas, Milman, D of Somerset, Hamilton, Murchison. Poor Ld Dalhousie dying[1] – a miserable object. That cursed malady. We looked into the question between us and the Treasury, or rather between us and that vulgar and impertinent fellow Wilson about the Bernal Collection.[2] We are clearly in the right. I walked away with the Dean. To G.C. Nobody at home – Sate half an hour reading Mure on Homer.[3] Learned and not without ingenuity but not much in it. Soon H and B came – then T – pleasant dinner. Very merry after dinner with A and her young friend Miss Merivale,[4] who, it seems had won two shillings at a gaming table at Baden in the summer. I made all sorts of extemporaneous couplets – which kept the party laughing during an hour. In the evening Mrs Stanley[5] – Home at ½ past 9.

1. James Andrew Broun Ramsay (1812–60), tenth Earl and first Marquis of Dalhousie, and Governor General of India; he retired ill in May. He is said to have died of kidney failure.
2. The Treasury made a grant of £4,000 to the Trustees to buy items in the sale of Ralph Bernal's collection in 1855 (*DNB*). Wilson is presumably James Wilson (1805–60), Financial Secretary to the Treasury, 1853–58.
3. William Mure, *A Critical History of the Language and Literature of Ancient Greece* (1850–57).
4. Probably Frances Isabella Merivale (1844–1911). She eventually married the diplomat William Peere Williams-Freeman (1834–84).
5. Catherine Stanley, née Leycester (1792–1862) was the widow of Edward Stanley, Bishop of Norwich. She lived at 6 Grosvenor Crescent, and was therefore neighbour to both the Trevelyans and the Hollands.

Sunday – November 23

Fine day but I did not venture to Church. I must take great care of myself this winter. I begin to feel the good effect of my change of residence. Wrote – P[ortland]'s embassy to France. Finished Ld Malmesbury. Gilb[ert] Gur[ney] married. Fox's Correspondence and Speeches.[1] Ld Campbell and Lady Stratheden called. Very obliging and friendly.

1. Perhaps Lord John Russell's *Memorials and Correspondence of Charles James Fox* (1853).

Monday – November 24

Not so fine a day. Yet pretty well. Wrote – Portland's Embassy. To R I to look at the Declaration against Transsubstantiation.[1] It evidently contradicts the notion of a real presence in all shapes. Home – Fox. Dunton's Mordecai.[2]

1. In the Test Act of 1673.

2. John Dunton (1659–1733), *Mordecai's Memorial ...* (1716). Dunton (1659–1733) is described in *HE*, ch. 21, *CW*, vol. 4, p. 171, as a 'crazy bookseller'.

Tuesday – November 25

Dundas, Milman and Panizzi to breakfast – pleasant talk – I walked an hour or two in the xystus. The wind north but the sun warm – Mordecai – and other old tracts – Wrote – A letter from Mrs Crinean again begging of me. I can do no more for her – G[renvil]le papers – Gurn[ey] Ma[rrie]d.

Wednesday – November 26

Staid at home – snow on the ground. But it thawed fast – Prior – Grenville Correspondence etc – H and T to dinner – Very pleasant evening.

Thursday – November 27

Again at home – G[renvil]le Correspondence – Gil[bert] Gurn[ey] M[arrie]d.

Friday – November 28

At home still. Fine but cold – Twiss's Life of Eldon.[1] Ryan called – then Derwent Coleridge – Read a good deal of Pliny – Nat Hist[2] – E to dinner.

1. Horace Twiss, *The Public and Private Llife of Lord Chancellor Eldon ...* (1844).
2. Pliny the Elder (AD 23/4–79), *Naturalis Historia.*

Saturday – November 29

Took E to U C – Then to G.C. – H and B out – Kissed Alice and home. Macleod called. L Hunt sent his daughter to borrow 10£ more. I am beginning to be a little weary of his applications. Ryan has sent me T's and Lefevre's papers about the Crimean affair. There is a want of neatness and clearness about the redaction, which I feel strongly, and yet do not well know how to remedy, except by re-writing the whole – And I doubt whether that be tacite – In substance the defence is complete. Twiss's Ld Eldon – περκ κηνσς.[1]

1. *Percival Keene* (1842), by F. Marryat.

Sunday – November 30

Fine, but very frosty – Staid at home – Finished Twiss. Ld C's Eldon[1] – Pliny. Crimean papers. Grote on the Δικαστ[2] – at dinner περκ – wrote about St Germains and the Embassy.[3] In the afternoon Ld Lne called. Talked about a plan of his for setting up a statue in our Ante-chapel at Trinity. He proposed Milton. Whewell with warm expressions of respect and gratitude, mentioned the obvious objection – that Milton was not a Trinity man. Ld L, though not convinced, yields very amicably and in a way like himself. The question then is who? I strongly pressed the claims of Bentley.[4] Ld L wished me to write and tell W what I thought. He took away Monk's Life of Bentley to read. I am afraid that B's Life will not much recommend him to favour.

1. In Campbell's *Lives of the Lord Chancellors*.
2. George Grote, *History of Greece* (1850), vol. 7, ch. 46, pp. 530–43. A dikast was a juror.
3. In *HE*, ch. 20, *CW*, vol. 4, pp. 1–4, TBM gave the last account of the Court of St Germains, and this was published in vol. 4. If he wrote a further description, he did not use it in the remaining chapters.
4. See Winstanley, *Early Victorian Cambridge*, appx D, pp. 436–9, for an account of the discussion on this subject, including TBM's letter to Whewell; *LM*, vol. 6, pp. 67–9.

Monday – December 1

Very cold – colder than any day yet this year. But I am pretty well – much better than last year. I kept within doors – wrote, with much labour, a letter to Whewell[1] – wrote a very little about the Embassy – read Campbell's Eldon. E to dinner. He agrees with me about Bentley. H and B called – B will dine here on Wednesday.

1. *LM*, vol. 6, pp. 67–9.

Tuesday – December 2

Very cold – Staid at home again, and sent E to the Temple. I read him part of Chap XXIII. He seemed to be amused, and indeed it was amusing. I read and wrote – read much – wrote very little – In the evening E again – Chat about Pliny etc. Ram Mag.[1]

1. The *Rambler* was published from 1848 to 1862 and was aimed at Protestant converts to Catholicism. It started as a journal covering literature, science and the fine arts. It became the *Home and Foreign Review*.

Wednesday – December 3

Very cold thaw – Disagreeable day. But I am strangely well – better than I have been in such weather these three or four years. Sent E back to town – Read all day – Lord Cochrane's trial[1] – Pliny. Dear B to dinner. Very pleasant – A little of W. Huntington's Bank of Faith.[2] Frost in the evening.

1. Presumably the trial of Lord Cochrane in 1814, when he was falsely accused in connection with a stock exchange fraud.
2. Perhaps William Huntington, *Bank of Charity at Providence Chapel* (1790).

Thursday – December 4

Still cold – but a little brighter. Staid at home. Wonderfully well – Will Huntington – Morris Moore's pamphlet against Stirling.[1] A most malignant stupid blackguard that Morris Moore is. My Peninsular and Orientals flourishing. I am a most prosperous man. Τωρ βαρ.[2]

1. Morris Moore, *The Debate of April 7 [1856]. Mr. Stirling MP and Raphael's 'Apollo and Marsyas ...'* (1856).
2. Unidentified.

Friday – December 5

Fog – Lefevre and Ryan to breakfast. Talked over T's business – agreed perfectly – pleasant chat – When they went, I walked and read – Τωρ βαρ.

Saturday – December 6

I meant to have gone to B M. But I did not like the look of the day and staid at home writing and reading – Τωρ βαρ.

Sunday – December 7

Staid at home almost the whole day – read Huntington to Miss Morton[1] – Pasquin's Lord Barrymore[2] – Brighton etc – T called – read to him about Whitehall[3] Τωρ βαρ.

1. W. Huntington, *Epistles of Faith, Addressed to Miss E. Morton, a rigid Papist ...* (1851).
2. Anthony Pasquin (pseud. John Williams), *Life of the Late Earl of Barrymore* (1793); *The New Brighton Guide ...*, 4th edn (1796).
3. Perhaps the account of the fire in *HE*, ch. 23, *CW*, vol. 4, pp. 379–81.

Monday – December 8

Mild day – but windy – walked a good deal. Wrote out Whitehall – read Hodgson's Life of Porteus[1] – Pliny – very curious – Hibbert called – Went to U Club for E – pleasant evening.

1. Robert Hodgson, *The Life of Beilby Porteus ... Bishop of London* (1811).

Tuesday – December 9

Took E into town – to a shop in King Street – Lord Hardwicke's Memoirs[1] – Toplady's works.[2] Home – wrote – finished Whitehall. Twisleton called. In the evening to G C – G there. He has done excellently, to our general joy. Happy evening. Wrote to Charles Wood today about Heaviside.[3]

1. George Harris, *The Life of Lord Chancellor Hardwicke, with Selections from his Correspondence ...*, 3 vols (1847).
2. Augustus Montague Toplady (1740–78). His *Works*, with memoir by W. Rowe, were published in 1794.
3. Perhaps James William Lucas Heaviside (1808–97); Professor of Mathematics at Haileybury, 1838–57; Canon of Norwich, 1860–97.

Wednesday – December 10

Wrote – Russia – walked – day windy, but not cold – read a good deal of Toplady yesterday and today. Very able, I must say. Seneca the Rhetorician.[1] Much interested. E to dinner.

1. Lucius Annaeus Seneca (*c.* 50 BC–*c.* AD 40).

Thursday – December 11

E into town. To the City. Found that only 10,000 of my 30,000 dollars of U S Stock are to be paid off at present. Made arrangements for investing what I am to receive. Home – Wrote – Czar – then Huntington – M. Seneca – the Ts to dinner. Very pleasant indeed.

Friday – December 12

Still fine and mild – Walked – read the Life of Henry More[1] the Platonist. Hampden Controversy. I am glad that Charles Wood is willing to apply to Palmerston in favour of Heaviside. Read some of Seneca Rhet – A delightful story about Albutius and his unlucky schemata.[2] To the the U.C. brought out E. The reliquiae of yesterday.

1. Perhaps Richard Ward, *The Life of ... Henry More* (1710).
2. L. Albutius Silo was a teacher of rhetoric. The story occurs in *Oratorum et rhetorum sententiae divisiones colores* by the elder Seneca.

Saturday – December 13

With E into town – to the B M. Panizzi detained in Dublin on a trial. We therefore put off what we could put off. Walked more than I have lately done, so as to affect my respiration. Home – to dinner in G.C. Afraid of venturing out. But it turned out better than I had expected – Ld Monck,[1] The Lowes,[2] the Vaughans,[3] the Stanleys, Ryan, the Reeves.[4] I talked much and gaily, and the day went off pleasantly.

1. Charles Stanley Monck, fourth Viscount (1819–94), was Commissioner of Church temporalities in Ireland. He was later Governor General of Canada.
2. Mrs Lowe was Georgiana Orred (*c.* 1806–84), daughter of George Orred of Liverpool.

3. Mrs Vaughan was Catherine Maria Stanley (*c.* 1821–99), daughter of the Bishop of Norwich.
4. The second Mrs Reeve was Christina Georgina Jane Gollup (1821–1906). She was the author of *Cookery and Housekeeping for Large and Small Families* (1882).

Sunday – December 14

Cold – staid at home – Read Sir T. Lawrence's Life[1] – Challoner's Life[2] – Gill's Life.[3] Macleod called. Talk about the Oxford peerage. At dinner – Births, Deaths and Marriages – poor stuff when compared with Theodore's earlier performances. He had drunk his wits away.

1. Perhaps D. E. Williams, *The Life and Correspondence of Sir Thomas Lawrence* ... (1831).
2. Perhaps James Barnard, *The Life of ... Richard Challoner* ... (1784).
3. Perhaps J. Rippon, *A Brief Memoir ... of the late John Gill* ... (1838).

Monday – December 15

Cold – But I went to G C after breakfast – H out – saw B for a minute – She was going to a drawing school with Miss Laura Montague. To the Athenaeum – found a heap of books awaiting me there. The new vol of the Encyclopaedia with my article on Johnson. Home – read the paper on Johnson. H called. I fear that Lydia Price is in a bad way. Read State Trials – Francis – Layer[1] – At dinner Births Deaths etc – Sent 10£ to Atherstone, a poor devil of a poet.[2]

1. Alban Francis (d. 1715) was a Benedictine monk, whom James II sought to impose on Magdalene College, Cambridge, in February 1687. The College refused to give him an MA because he claimed royal dispensation from taking the oaths. In 1691 he was sent to Newgate for possessing Jacobite documents. His trial is in W. Cobbett, *State Trials* (London, 1809–28), vol. 11, pp. 1319–37. Christopher Layer (1683–1723) was a Jacobite lawyer implicated in the Atterbury Plot; executed 1723. His trial is in *State Trials*, vol. 16, pp. 94–303.
2. Possibly Edwin Atherstone (1788–1872), author of *The Fall of Nineveh* (1828), *The Lost Days of Herculaneum* (1821), etc.

Tuesday – December 16

Very cold again – Hoar frost on the ground all day. Staid at home. The workmen in my xystus are preparing to set creepers, which, I hope, will flourish. Wrote a little – but saw my way better – read a good deal – Layer – Atterbury[1] – By the bye Alexander Gowrie[2] at breakfast lately. Had a very grateful letter from Heaviside. I have really no claim to his gratitude. Seneca Rhet. E to dinner.

1. TBM may have been reading about his trial in *State Trials*, vol. 11, pp. 1319–37.
2. *Gowrie, or the King's Plot* (1848), by G.P.R. James.

Wednesday – December 17

After breakfast B and G. Sent E to town – Read Wl and Cz. P[1] to B and G. They seemed to be interested. When they were gone wrote –St[andin]g Army – I shall improve this part of my book greatly. Creepers settling – Read the trial of Ld Macclesfield,[2] of the man who shot at Ld Onslow. Lawrence's Life. A viler scribbler than the writer I never came across – At dinner B[irths] D[eaths] and M[arriages].

1. William III and Czar Peter; see *HE*, ch. 23, *CW*, vol. 4, pp. 381–7.
2. *Trial of Thomas, Earl of Macclesfield, Lord High Chancellor ... for High Crimes and Misdemeanours ...* (1725); *The Trial of Edward Arnold, for Felony in Maliciously and Wilfully Shooting at, and Wounding ... Lord Onslow ...* (1724); *State Trials*, vol. 16.

Thursday – December 18

New order from the Post Office about putting an Initial letter in addresses.[1] Chose places for Rhododendron beds. Wrote satisfactorily – Looked into the Crimean papers – finished the Life of Lawrence – Life of Fuseli.[2] Really very curious and interesting. His lectures gave me great pleasure – the more as I saw last summer several of the paintings on which he passes judgment, and as I have lately been reading Pliny's criticisms on the great artists of antiquity. E to dinner.

1. The form of the new address was sent to Selina and Fanny. See *LM*, vol. 6, p. 73.
2. J. Knowles, *The Life and Writings of H. Fuseli* (1831).

Friday – December 19

Breakfast party H, B, Hibbert and Mrs H, Reeve,[1] Ryan, Ellis, Dundas. Lord Carlisle joined us uninvited, and was most welcome. Not an unpleasant morning. But I had an unpleasant letter – a begging letter from Mrs Crinean – I am out of patience – however I sent her 20£. I will give her no more. Lovely day – In the afternoon to Holborn to buy books. Found all that I wanted sold, except a Life of Jebb[2] – got Boswell's Letters[3] from Cawthorn's, an incomparably absurd book, read it at a sitting – Home – Doddridge's Correspondence.[4] A most amorous gentleman, but as excellent person as ever lived. If I had been his descendants however I should not have published the volumes – Jebb – A curious book – ιακ πιστ.[5]

1. This occasion is mentioned in *Memoirs of Henry Reeve ...*, ed. J. K. Laughton (London, 1898), vol. 1, p. 377.
2. Perhaps Charles Forster, *Life of John Jebb, Bishop of Limerick ...* (1836).
3. *Letters of James Boswell, Addressed to the Rev. W. J. Temple*. See *LM*, vol. 6, p. 73n.
4. *The Correspondence and Diary of Philip Doddridge ...* ed. J. D. Humphreys (1829–31).

5. *Jacob Faithful*, by Marryat.

Saturday – December 20

Into the City. Thornton not at the Bank so I came away without settling anything. At the Exchange bought the Athenaeum – why I hardly know. Found an article on my *Johnson* which I had not at all expected[1] – Laudatory – Home – wrote a little – read – Doddridge - ιακ πιστ. Will H[untingto]n's Posthumous Letters.[2]

1. *Athenaeum*, 1521 (December 1856), pp. 1563–4, which calls TBM's article on Johnson 'a little work of Art, choice alike in matter and in style'.
2. William Huntington, *Posthumous Letters*, ed. Lady E. Sanderson and T. Bensley, 4 vols (1815–22).

Sunday – December 21

At home the whole day – Fawcett's Life.[1] The Fly Sheet controversy.[2] Wrote something – At dinner Pars's daughter[3] – feeble and poor – Parr's Sequel to a Printed Paper.[4]

1. *An Account of the Life, Ministry and Writings of the late Rev. John Fawcett, D.D ...* (1818).
2. The controversy over the authorship and content of the anonymous *Flysheets*, attacking the leadership and policy of the Methodist Conference. The *Flysheets* began to circulate in 1845; they were widely ascribed to James Everett (1784–1872). who refused to acknowledge them, but was nevertheless expelled from the Conference in 1849. He thereupon became the leader of the attack on the Conference which led to the secession of many members and to the setting up in 1857 of the United Methodist Free Church with Everett as president at its first assembly in Rochdale in July 1857. See O. Chadwick, *The Victorian Church*, 379–86.
3. *The Parson's Daughter* (1833), by Theodore Hook.
4. S. Parr, *A Sequel to the Printed Paper ... by the Rev. Chas Curtis ...* (1792).

Monday – December 22

Parr's Sequel. To G.C. – Met Mary Parker[1] there – poor accounts of Lydia Price – Home – wrote something. Coleridge called, then my old schoolfellow Walker,[2] then the Dean and Mrs Milman. Very kind – Glad to hear that a new edition of his History of Latin Christianity is called for. It is creditable to the age. I began to read it again. It is very good in spite of the style. I will go through it. At dinner – Russell – and after.

1. Widow of James Parker, daughter of Thomas Babington of Rothley Temple.
2. A contemporary of TBM at Aspenden?

Tuesday – December 23

Into town to buy Nichols's Anecdotes[1] – eleven guineas – I hope for much amusement and instruction from them – Looked at Leaves of Grass[2] again – What madness! Wrote something – Read Nichols – E to dinner.

1. John Nichols, *Literary Anecdotes of the Eighteenth Century* (1812–15).
2. By Walt Whitman (1855).

Wednesday – December 24

Took E into town. To the Athenaeum – Looked at newspapers and magazines – Home by cab, looking in at G C by the way – Read. Wrote nothing – Nichols. At dinner Love Match[1] – Stuff. Found a blunder in the binding of my Nichols.

1. By Henry Cockton (1845).

Thursday – December 25

Christmas again – a happy Christmas. My health perceptibly improved by better air, though requiring care, my fortune easy, my family most affectionate, my fame, in spite of detraction, great, my mind cheerful and serene. I read – chiefly my own book for the purpose of making corrections. Reeve called. At three to G.C. – Passed a most happy afternoon and evening there. What a good happy family. True understandings, sweet tempers, warm affections, high principles. R. Hamilton[1] dined with us. A promising young fellow. I shall be glad if I am able to serve him. We had the old dinner – sent in by me. The cod, oysters, turkey, pudding were excellent – Then the Snapdragon and the salt and the laugh. Home – before ten. A very cold day. But I am not much the worse for it.

1. Robert George Crookshank Hamilton (1836–95), son of TBM's cousin Zachary Macaulay Hamilton, then in the Office of Works; knighted 1884; Governor of Tasmania.

Friday – December 26

Bright and frosty. I must stay at home. I read a great deal, particularly of Nichols – There is much that is highly curious, and interesting in these volumes, together with much trash and innumerable blunders of the grossest kind. E to dinner.

Saturday – December 27

Took E into town – Home – wrote a little – read a good deal – C called – Love M[atch] – then Nichols Warburton[1] – sometimes very clever.

1. In John Nichols, *Literary Anecdotes of the Eighteenth Century*, 9 vols (London, 1812–15), vol. 5, pp. 529–658.

Sunday – December 28

Intensely cold; but bright and cheerful looking. The sun shining full on the lawn and really warm, yet unable to melt the hoar frost on the grass. Wrote something – Correspondence with St Germains[1] – Read Nichols and Love M[atch] – T and G called.

1. *HE*, ch. 18, *CW*, vol. 3, pp. 494–8.

Monday – December 29

Cold – Staid at home – Read a great deal of Nichols – Wrote a very little. At dinner L M.

Tuesday – December 30

Very mild and moist. After breakfast to the Athenaeum – looked at papers and new books. Then home – read a good deal about the Darien affair – It will be impossible to tell the truth as to that matter without putting the Scotch into a rage. But n'importe. The truth shall be told – I forgot to mention that I lately read in the mornings while dressing Haldane's reply to Drummond on the question of the sinfulness of Christ's human nature.[1] Haldane has the better of the argument from authority. As to general reasoning both the combatants are in an equally pitiable situation. Drummond is, I must say, grossly disingenuous. Haldane, on the other hand, is, as he always is, quarrelsome, and takes a pleasure in finding fault. I forgot also to mention that my neighbour Vincent[2] who is confined with gout wrote to me yesterday to ask whether my paper on Johnson was to be had separately. I sent him the new Volume of the Encyclopaedia. I hope that it may entertain him. H and T to dinner – Very pleasant evening.

1. James Alexander Haldane, *Answer to Mr. Henry Drummond's Defence of the heretical doctrine promulgated by Mr. Irving* ... (1830).
2. Henry William Vincent (1796–1865) of Thornwood Lodge.

Wednesday – December 31

Mild day – Walked a little in the garden – Read – chiefly Nichols. A very good defence of Lord Cockburn against Ld Brougham reprinted from the Scotsman.[1] I have seldom seen anything of the sort better done. Letter from the Duke of Argyle. I must come down with my third part of the 500£ of blackmail which the builders are levying upon us.[2] At dinner L M. A venison pasty left by H was the chief part of my meal.

---

1. *Exposure of the Attack on Lord Cockburn's 'Memorials' etc*, signed A. R. (1856). This was Alexander Russell, for whom see above, entry for 11 October 1853, n. 2.
2. James Jordan (1833–77), a Paddington builder, was building eleven houses on the west side of Camden Hill Road. The 'blackmail' may have been a demand for money to save this enterprise. Jordan's business failed in 1857 and again in 1859.